The Voice in Violence

and other contemporary issues in professional voice and speech training

presented by the Voice and Speech Review

The official Journal of the Voice and Speech Trainers Association

Edited by Rocco Dal Vera

Cover photo of Tanya Dougherty in *The Bacchae*, courtesy of DEC Photography, University of Southern Queensland, Australia

Citation Information

Title: The Voice in Violence and other contemporary issues in professional voice and speech training presented by the Voice and Speech Review

Editor: Dal Vera, Rocco

Date: 2001

ISBN: 1-55783-497-0

Publisher: Voice and Speech Trainers Association, Incorporated, Cincinnati, OH

Distributor: Applause Books/Hal Leonard Corporation

Description: The official journal of the Voice and Speech Trainers Association containing 61 articles on a wide variety of issues in professional voice and speech use and training, many centered on the topic of vocal use in staged violence. 338 pages, 8.5" x 11", paperback.

Correspondence
U.S. Mail:
Rocco Dal Vera, editor
University of Cincinnati—CCM
P.O. Box 210003
Cincinnati, OH 45221

FedEx and UPS:
Rocco Dal Vera, editor
OMDA-Drama
Room 3713, Corbett Drive
College-Conservatory of Music
University of Cincinnati
Cincinnati, OH 45221-0003

Telephone:
(513) 556-1981, ms
(513) 556-3399, fax

Email:
Rocco.DalVera@uc.edu

Voice and Speech Review Editorial Staff

Rocco Dal Vera, Editor-in-Chief
University of Cincinnati

Ethics, Standards and Practices
Marian Hampton, Associate Editor
Illinois State University

Heightened Speech, Verse and Scansion
Neil Freeman, Associate Editor
University of British Columbia
Rena Cook, Assistant Editor
University of Oklahoma

Pedagogy and Coaching
Paul Meier, Associate Editor
University of Kansas

Private Studio Practice
Jack Horton, Associate Editor
Presenter's Studio

Pronunciation, Phonetics, Linguistics, Dialect/Accent Studies
Louis Colaianni, Associate Editor
University of Missouri-Kansas City

Reviews and Sources
Mandy Rees, Associate Editor
California State University, Bakersfield

Singing
Dorothy Runk Mennen, Associate Editor
Purdue University
Linda Carroll, Assistant Editor
New York University

Vocal Production, Voice Related Movement Studies
Marth Munro, Associate Editor
University of Pretoria
Ursula Meyer, Assistant Editor
University of California, San Diego
Marié-Heleen Coetzee, Assistant Editor
University of Pretoria

Voice and Speech Science, Vocal Health
Ronald C. Scherer, Associate Editor
Bowling Green State University

Jan Fairbairn, Design and Compositing

PN
2071
.S65
V65
2001

The Voice and Speech Review is an official publication of the Voice and Speech Trainers Association (VASTA), Inc.

VASTA is a non-profit organization and also a focus group of the Association for Theatre in Higher Education (ATHE).

4847761
12/30

Teaching Violence

One of my favorite undergraduate professors, Ron Arden, used to say, "Actors are the emotional warriors of our time"—and I loved him for it. I felt deeply honored by the acknowledgement. He meant that actors have the courage to visit emotional places that the rest of the population prefers to avoid addressing in their own lives. They pay us to do it for them.

Just as real warriors perform an essential though anguishing service for society, actors also serve as courageous soldiers of the psyche. When we dig deep into the dark underbelly of the human ego and express our shadow selves truthfully in performance, we are helping the audience process that side of their natures, too.

Society needs its stories in order to understand itself, and since drama is centered around conflict, violence lies at the heart of many great plays. One of the darkest and most difficult things to confront about us is our propensity for violence. Human beings kill. We make war. We rape, pillage, torture, and terrify. We can be brutal and animalistic. We even have the capacity to take joy in and revel in these horrors. One doesn't have to look much farther than the evening news to see the evidence in full color.

We as a society, and as individuals, have a need to confront our violent natures and come to terms with this aspect of ourselves. That which we suppress is the thing that will sub-consciously rule us. We won't get where we want to go socially or spiritually by denying or refusing to look at the ugly truths about ourselves.

People know this instinctively. One of the reasons that people go to the theatre is to be taken on a journey into their own souls. The audience begs to be led into and through the places they couldn't go alone. This journey requires a brave and well-trained leader, one who has learned the way, and in whose authority the audience can confidently place their trust. The actor is the modern day warrior-priest who has carefully trained to take the audience on this journey into the self.

And who trains these modern knights?

We do.

And who trains the trainers?

We teach each other. This publication is one of the ways we can do that. Through it, we share the best of ourselves with our colleagues. I hope you will find this collection of articles inspiring and useful as you set about your important mission.

The Voice in Violence

contents

Editorial by *Kate Burke*

Associate Professor Kate Burke heads the voice program and teaches acting at the University of Virginia. AEA member; acting credits: American Conservatory Theater, American Repertory Theatre, and others. Headed theatre voice programs at Universities of Michigan, Iowa, Nebraska, and Washington. Publications: essay in The Vocal Vision, article in the Iowa State Journal of Research; essay in Reflections on Teaching (University of Virginia Teaching Resource Center). Co-recipient of a $10,000 grant from National Institutes of Health. University of Virginia Sesquicentennial Associateship, she spent working with Andrew Wade, Head of Voice, Royal Shakespeare Company. B.A. from St. Mary's College, M.F.A. from Ohio University Professional Actor Training Program.

The second issue of VASTA's very own and very welcome brainchild! What a satisfying achievement. The first edition of this journal was a long time a-borning. The VASTA board of directors thought long, thought hard, thought some more, planned, gulped, deferred the decision a time or two, then committed funds and appointed an editor. I'd like to commend former board member Claudia Anderson whose insistent, firm words echoed and re-echoed throughout our deliberations: "I want this journal to HAPPEN."

If many hands make light work, the many hands that have turned to produce the journal should have made the work feather light. (Rocco will laugh as he reads this.) During the vasta 2000 conference banquet celebration Rocco asked that those involved in the creation of the journal stand to be acknowledged. Practically the entire assembly rose to its feet, and I felt proud of our ability to organize, to work together and to create.

The flip side of such communal spirit is the sobering theme of this compilation: Violence. Voice is inextricably linked to violence: the grunts of exertion, the moans of pain, and the epithets of scorn. Fight choreographers maintain that many combatants are loathe to vocalize reactions as they fight. Perhaps a young actor's discomfort with non-verbal self-expression accounts for this, although I believe the reluctance comes from a deeply rooted fear of violence, even the safe, choreographed kind. A fear that even going through the motions might awake the quiescent beast within.

The Climb Theatre Company in St. Paul has created 2 powerful theatrical antidotes to domestic and public violence, touring productions called *Ouch* and *Owie*. Scenes in these plays address the three most common and relevant behaviors exhibited by and toward children: physical violence, verbal violence and bullying. (Climb's mission statement and production photos of *Ouch* and *Owie* may be found on Climb's website *www.climb.org*.)

In a paper delivered at the 1998 ATHE Theatre Symposium on Theatre and Violence, Climb's Performance Company Director Leigh Anne Adams observed that by the age of 18 most Americans will have seen 200,000 violent acts on television alone—a fact which surely leads to desensitization and lack of empathy with victims. In *Ouch* a video clip is shown which depicts Lisa Simpson being put down by her brother Bart. Children in the audience typically cheer Bart on, until Cool Dude Mister Mind says

Violence hurts you or another.
It hurts our things, our bodies or each other.
Violence hurts our feelings too.
Violence hurts if it happens to you.

Young audience members typically fall silent and still as they realize the violence of their earlier reactions.

The writer Michael Ondaatje said in a recent NPR interview that "there is more danger in the violence you don't face." May the violence we "face" in this publication contribute to a greater awareness of the consequences of violence and promote peaceful alternatives. *Ouch* also features the Uh-huh Girls who, along with Cool Dude Mister Mind, exhort the audience.

When you feel yourself get tense—
Stop 2, 3
Breathe 2, 3
Think your way to sense.
❧

VASTA Mission Statement

VASTA is poised to become an exciting international organization and is actively planting seeds for global networking, other cultural involvement and resource-sharing. Our mission is to:

Practice and encourage the highest standards of voice and speech use and artistry in all professional arenas.

Serve the needs of voice and speech teachers and students in training and practice.

Promote the concept that the art of the voice and speech specialist is integral to the successful teaching of acting and to the development of all professional voice users.

Encourage and facilitate opportunities for ongoing education and the exchanging of knowledge and information among professionals in the field.

VASTA is all about:

Vision
Artistry
Standards of conduct
Training enhancement and
Advocacy for our profession.

vasta.org - The VASTA Website

Visit *www.vasta.org*, the **VASTA** website. The site includes: News & Updates, Resources, Communication and Publications, Professional Index, and Website Details. Any **VASTA** member may list contact information, resume, and teaching philosophy in the Professional Index. The site also includes information on conferences and workshops, links to voice and speech related websites, the Mentoring Program, the Newsletter Archive, and organization Bylaws. Questions regarding this site may be addressed to Eric Armstrong at *erarmstrong@earthlink.net*

VASTA Publications

VASTA Advocacy Information
Advocacy Information is FREE.
Available Online at *www.vasta.org*:
Guidelines for the Preparation of Voice and Speech Teachers
Available via US Mail
Guidelines for the Preparation of Voice and Speech Teachers
Evaluation Guidelines
Guidelines for Promotion and Tenure
Members: FREE
Non-Members $5.00

To Order Write:
Micha Espinosa, Membership Chair
Southwest Texas State University
Department of Theatre
601 University Drive
San Marcos, TX 78666-4616

The Combined VASTA Bibliography
is made up of 3 segments. All segments are available together.
Member price $10.00
Non-Member price $15.00
For those who have part but not all of the bibliography:
    1993 version only
Members: $6.00
Non-Members: $8.00
    1995 supplement only
Members: $2.00
Non-Members: $4.00
    1998 supplement only
Members: $4.00
Non-Members: $7.00

VASTA Newsletter,
published semi-annually.
Members — free
Individual Subscription $10.00
Institutional Subscription $20.00

Voice and Speech Review,
published annually
Members — free
Individual Subscription $35.00
Institutional Subscription $35.00

To Order Write:
Lisa Wilson, **VASTA** treasurer
1535 South Florence Avenue
Tulsa OK 74104

We are grateful to the following experts for their close careful reviews of material submitted to the Journal:
Barbara Acker
Michael Barnes
Kate Burke
Kathleen Campbell
Linda Carroll
Marié-Heleen Coetzee
Louis Colaianni
Carolyn Combs
Rena Cook
Kate DeVore
Alice Faber
Catherine Fitzmaurice
Neil Freeman
Emily Groenewald
Marian Hampton
Pamela Harvey
Jack Horton
Nancy Houfek
Dudley Knight
Barry Kur
Anna-Maria Laukkanen
Jacqueline Martin
Paul Meier
Joan Melton
Chan E. Park
Dorothy Runk Mennen
Kathy Maes
Ursula Meyer
Alan Munro
Marth Munro
Elbie Oosthuizen
Bonnie Raphael
Mandy Rees
Janet Rodgers
Ruth Rootberg
Karen Ryker
Ronald C. Scherer
Phil Thompson
William Weiss

The *Voice and Speech Review* accepts several types of submissions. While one of our primary missions is to publish peer-reviewed scholarship, we are also interested in presenting letters to the editor, opinion pieces, essays, interviews, reviews, poetry and other forms of writing. Material may be submitted to:

Rocco Dal Vera, editor
University of Cincinnati
CCM, OMDA
PO Box 210003
Cincinnati, OH 45221-0003
Rocco.DalVera@uc.edu

Letters to the Editor

1. Australasian Drama Studies Association, Australian Council University Art Departments, Council of Heads Australian Theatre Studies Institutes, National Australian Council of Heads of Music.

Qualitative vs. Quantitative Research—Problems in Publication

"The issue of research in the visual and performing arts has in Australia at least formed the basis for strong debate between scholars and funding bodies during the last 10 years or so. The debate has led to lobbying by national creative arts stakeholder groups like ADSA, ACUADS, CHAUTSI AND NACHTMUS.[1] To the frustration of scholar-artists engaged in performance based research, and despite continual lobbying, traditional attitudes to research kept them out of contention for recognition and funding throughout the 1990s.

Until as recently as February 2001 the principal national research funding organisation the Australian Research Council (ARC) would not allocate a category for the Visual and Performing Arts. As a result, the research status of the disciplines was not afforded recognition. The creative arts fitted uncomfortably for many into the broad areas of Humanities or Social Sciences. Many also saw inequities in a funding system that allocated 1% of the total of research funding to the creative arts, in itself representative of 5% of the sector. With the acceptance this year by the ARC of a discrete category (and thus an elevation in research status) the tide has turned at last to favour the creative arts.

The Visual and the Performing Arts were also problem children when it came to considerations of the nature and reporting of research. This was in all probability a result of the (acknowledged) difficulty of devising appropriate criteria for assessing the validity or 'worth' of research outcomes. In addition there was the often politically-charged challenge of allocating an appropriate research quantum to these outcomes. When it came to the way research was conducted, there could seem at times to be something of a stand-off between the qualitative methodologists and the empiricists—the round hole, square peg dilemma.

It is not perhaps difficult to understand the initial resistance by funding bodies to these 'come-lately' disciplines. The ARC's attitude was based on the empirical notion that, in order to test the validity of hypotheses, all research must be capable of replicability. This is the sine qua non of traditional research after all. However performance cannot by virtue of its nature be replicated; there are simply too many variables. Indeed the very essence of performance—its ephemerality—appeared to knock it out of contention as a valid research area.

There was an additional problem—that of reporting the outcomes of research. There is no doubt that the report of research is extremely significant when it comes to evaluation, recognition and reward. However it is the rule of *logos* (the word) and the written word that dominates when it comes to publication. For some engaged in the area of the spoken word i.e., in performance, the apparent domination of this form of research reporting (print-based publication) can be an irritant. The article neither validates nor stands instead of the research; it is the value-added component if you like. At times however it could seem as though the article had almost replaced the research itself when funding allocations based on output were doled out. There are a sufficient number of scholar-artists who see the performance act—the artwork—as a valid research outcome in itself. They keep on the boil the issue of what constitutes the issue of 'publication' in the creative arts.

It comes down finally to consideration of the constitution of the reporting mechanism, the evaluation mechanisms, and the availability of suitable arenas for publication in its broadest sense. A significant breakthrough has occurred with the new ARC guidelines which recognise that collaborative and individual creative works such as an exhibition, a concert, a piece of creative writing and a performance can all be recognised as publications—and appropriate publications in their own right.

There are of course many other researchers in the field who have no problem with the traditional reporting mechanism of the written word—with publication of qualitative or empirical research via the journal article, the book or another audio-visual medium capable of being recorded and recalled. They see it rightly as a way to disseminate research outcomes and indeed to stimulate and give credence to the work being done by themselves and others in the field.

Finding a place to publish and referees can also pose problems for the creative arts researcher who needs the authority of peer-review for their publications to be 'legitimated'. The traditional areas are the peer-reviewed articles in print publications. However these inevitably suffer the problem of time-lag and specialist journals in the field of the performing arts are hardly thick on the ground. As a side note, the wonders of the WWW don't seem to have made much of an impact in the field of performing arts publishing. E-journals with the benefit of cost-effectiveness, multi-media capability and quicker turn-around times for reviewing would be ideal. However if they are in existence, they are next to invisible. Perhaps developing such an outlet for publication is a next step for organisations like VASTA and ADSA.

As far as the performance act itself as a site for legitimate publication, ADSA has been pre-eminent since the early 1990s in developing an acceptable position towards the nurturing of research in the theatre. As far back as 1992 ADSA premised that theatre performance can be (i) an object of traditional written research and scholarship and (ii) an actively generative and processual mode of research in itself. ADSA also set itself the task of defining an evaluative process that would make a performance component of research accessible to evaluation i.e., to peer-review.[2]

2. ADSA Working Party, 1992.

When it comes to finding a publication focussed on (say) voice in performance, scholars and researchers had to wait till the birth of journals like the multi-faceted Voice and Speech Review VASTA's own journal.[3] In this annual niche publication there are peer-reviewed articles from both sides of the performance-based research arena. These have undergone extensive collegial interrogation and development to ensure reliability and quality-control. Last year's issue contained a diversity of articles from letters and reviews, short special-interest articles through to the peer-reviews. Some were founded on solid, empirical evidence whilst others clearly nailed their colours to the qualitative approach. Most were 'reports from the field' based on the authority of experience. It is a very welcome publication for voice practitioners, teachers and researchers.

3. Of course there are other journals, dedicated to the publication of voice and speech but not many. In Australia there are special interest 'newsletter' format publications, but no outlet for peer-reviewing of articles.

It may perhaps matter little what approach is taken or where and what kind of publication arenas are developed. Despite the newly defined category for creative arts research funding in Australia, there is undoubtedly increasing competition here and elsewhere for a part of the shrinking grants 'cake'. The ARC has to some extent reinvented itself through its self-proclaimed role as advisor to and broker between the arts and industry. In Australia we have high hopes that theatre researchers will eventually get their fair share of a bigger cake when it comes to serving up the slices.

Kate Foy

Rhoticity in the Accents of American Film Actors: A Sociolinguistic Study
I wanted to let you know I enjoyed reading Nancy Elliott's article.... It was exciting to see someone take such an interest in the evolution of rhoticity in the speech of film actors over five historically eventful decades. I am, however, intrigued to know why Elliott excluded African American female actresses from her study. In her first endnote she wrote:

> Choice of female subjects was controlled for race; however, in the subsequent examination of the speech of male co-stars, subjects in the male sample were not controlled for race. The desire to limit the number of nonlinguistic variables, coupled with the paucity of female African-Americans in film until quite recently, led to the decision to restrict the female sample to one race…

If this is her reason for excluding African-American females from her study I have two questions. First, what is her definition of nonlinguistic variables? Second, when she uses American Film in her title does she mean all American films or just "Hollywood" films?

I feel race is a linguistic variable. If you exclude race as a variable why not exclude actors/actresses born in Texas, Maine, Brooklyn etc. It seems she narrowed her study to some sort of "standard" yet she did not clearly define that "standard."

Secondly, unless Hollywood films are the only films included in American Films, there is an abundance of African-American Films from the 1930s and 40s. African-Americans in Hollywood films that fit the criteria set forth didn't start to appear until the 1960s. In the 30s and 40s there are many female African-Americans in films that played leads and supporting romantic and ingenue roles. These films starred all black casts and were the only outlet for African-American females to play romantic and ingenue leads and supporting roles. (Lena Horne, Francine Everett, Sheila Guyse, Edna Mae Harris, Savannah Churchill, Myra Hemmings and Una Mae Carlisle) The only dark period for African-Americans in film was the 1950s. Even in the 50s there might be one African-American female actress that fits the criteria, Dorothy Dandridge.[1,2]

Given the issues raised above I wonder if it would be worthwhile for Elliott to expand the parameters of her research. Or is there perhaps a reason which justifies studying African-American females separately?

Amy Sue Fall

1. Bogle, Donald. *Brown Sugar: fifty years of America's black female superstars.* New York: Harmony Books, 1980.

2. Richards, Larry. *African American Films Through 1959: a comprehensive, illustrated filmography.* Jefferson North Carolina: McFarland, 1998.

Nancy Elliott responds:

In the field of sociolinguistics, race is defined as a nonlinguistic variable. Other nonlinguistic variables are age, socioeconomic class, sex, etc. Examples of linguistic variables would be such things as voiced vs. voiceless (wh) in which, front or back realization of the (a) of aunt, a flapped vs. released (t) in writing, and pronunciation of the first vowel of either/neither as [i] vs. [aĭ]. Linguistic variables are language features that vary, be they phonological, lexical, or syntactic.

I restricted my subjects to white females between the ages of 18-42 who are native speakers of American English varieties, in order to limit the amount of data to that which would be manageable for one dissertation. Each additional nonlinguistic variable that is added to a study doubles the number of 'informants' (or subjects) and the amount of data. Race is a very important variable in American English; it would be very interesting and fruitful research to add the dimension of Black vs. White to my data, and I hope that I will be able to do that. In order to do justice to the subject, however, I would have needed 20 female subjects and 20 male subjects of each race for each of the decades studied, and 200 extra subjects is a lot to add. Interestingly, when I first designed my research, my plan was to study only (young, white) female subjects; how many times have you heard a professor advise a student, " Limit your project so that it is doable"? Fortunately, I soon added men into the mix, and it turns out that the gender differences are the most fascinating and revealing aspect of my findings.

I bent my rules a bit when I included Sydney Poitier and Bill Cosby (and Irishman Stephen Boyd, and Bristol native Cary Grant) in my male sample. My rationale was that I was studying the men in order to contrast them with the women starring with them, and whatever the men were saying might be important in relation to what their female co-stars were saying. I'd like to do much more with African-American actors. It will necessarily be a large undertaking. The films and the artists that you have listed are a useful starting point.

The variable of race is an important one in American sociological studies. Moreover, from purely a linguistic point of view, Black-White speech differences are highly marked in American speech, and rhoticity is one of the major markers of African American speech. Today, even though non-rhotic regional varieties are becoming more and more rhotic (less r-less), AAVE is still highly non-rhotic–more non-rhotic than white Southern speech and other non-rhotic regional varieties in America (see *African-American English: Structure, history and use*, ed. Mufwene, Rickford, Bailey & Baugh, pp. 90-91 for some interesting data on rhoticity). If you listened to the political speeches at the 2000 Democratic National Convention, you may have noticed that there was a big difference between the pronunciation of Ted Kennedy and Jesse Jackson, though both are from non-rhotic backgrounds and are in the same age range (born in 1932 and 1941 respectively). In their convention speeches, Jackson was much, much more r-less than Kennedy. The Boston-born senator's r-less rate was 11%, and the South Carolinian minister's r-less rate was 79%.

Jackson's r-lessness was comparable to that of another African-American convention speaker, New York Rep. Charles Rangel (70%), who was born in Harlem in 1930. Jackson's and Rangel's high rates of r-lessness are very similar to that exhibited by Dr. Martin Luther King, Jr. (born in Atlanta in 1929) nearly four decades earlier in his famous "I Have a Dream" speech in Washington, D.C. in 1963 (85%) Perhaps non-rhotic pronunciation is being preserved only in AAVE, useful as an important marker of African-American identity. The Black-White dimension of rhoticity is probably the biggest determining factor for rhoticity in American English today. Incidentally, the data I've just provided come from preliminary work I've started on the rhoticity of politicians and other public speakers...another fruitful avenue of sociolinguistic research awaiting me!

    Nancy Elliott

Iambic Pentameter

Oliver Gray is a man I would like to know. I'm pretty sure I would love to discuss Shakespeare with anyone who likens himself to Christopher Robin and makes his greatest discoveries while lying in a bath. Now, that's the way to live. Besides that, anyone who sees the music inherent in everything is someone to be reckoned with.

    Shawnie Morning Mulcock

Standard Speech

I was touched by Sanford Robbins' simple expression of love and respect for Edith Skinner. I thought that an important point Robbins made was that once he stopped resisting and opened himself up to the possibility that *hey, maybe there is something to this speech thing after all,* a whole new world was opened up for him. Edith Skinner taught him (and many others) to recognize and appreciate the relevance of speech in acting.

    Kirsten Hopkins

Despite my mild frustration at the cycle Knight has chosen to get himself into ever so dramatically in this tennis match of opinions, I rather enjoy the controversy. The back and forth between Knight and Hammond allows for some consideration of the ideas being posed. For instance, I tend to read historical information like that involved in Hammond's sidebar *Good Speech in Classic Plays: The Historical Perspective* and take for granted that it is accurate. Knight opens his [response], "Overall, David Hammond isn't far off history..." This statement caused me to rethink Hammond's historical accuracy—not because I doubted any of it—but simply because one should always further question the validity of a reading and continue to explore the issues at hand. I think this inspiration to question authority—so to speak—is perhaps the only aspect of Dudley Knight's writings I find useful. He certainly questions other's credibility constantly, not for the sake of curiosity, but more "ill naturedly" as Hammond points out. As for Hammond's response to Knight's comments, Hammond is full of clarity and specificity. He restates his *opinions* (as he stresses) regarding the use of substandard dialects in classic texts, alliterative patterns in actor dialects, and how speech, and Skinner in particular, relates to actors and classical texts in historical perspective.

    Maya Lawson

Style vs. Truth—Are they in opposition? Interviews with directors Steven Wadsworth and Seth Barrish

People who have the ability to talk about their art with candor and intelligence are inspiring. Also hearing how they apply the voice to theatre is interesting. I especially liked Steven Wadsworth['s] attitude and approach about combining theatre, music and other interests. His comment about shaping a rush of words against a stillness is interesting.

William Burke

Structure and Substance in Shakespeare's Verse

In his essay, Paul Meier offers an excellent argument of the significance of the tensions present in Shakespeare's writing between verse and thought. What excited me [about] the contrasts of these two existing forces in Shakespeare's writing is how much the tensions between them can inform the actor about the [character's] state and the conflict or comfort that they feel with what they are saying. Something that is present in almost everything we do: the balance between spontaneity and conformity, chaos and order.

Emily White

Your Presence is Requested

It is sad that today our language has been reduced to only a few words said as we are flying past each other in pursuit of our daily necessities. "Hey," "What's up," or "Call me," is often all we can get out. There is such beauty in the language of heightened text, and we struggle to dissect it in order to fully understand the true meaning. We relish in the complexities of the phrasing, rhythm and grammar that is lost to us today, I am so grateful that the professionals of voice and speech are concerned enough to do something to help each other and their students. Now, as individuals we can take al this information and make it our own. We are not limited by one idea or the "right" way. For me, a student who has little knowledge about heightened text or how to go about [speaking] it, I can find comfort in this section of the Journal where teachers and actors alike express their success and difficulties with this thing we call language.

Jennifer Downs

The Voice and Speech Review *welcomes comment from our readers. Letters may be edited for clarity or space considerations. Please send your responses to:*
Rocco Dal Vera, editor
University of Cincinnati – CCM
PO Box 210003
Cincinnati, OH 45221-0003
<Rocco.DalVera@uc.edu>

Marth Munro (Associate editor) has a Masters in theatre voice projection, is a CMA (LIMS/New York) and a Certified Lessac Teacher. Currently she is in the advanced stages towards completion of a Ph.D. investigating Lessac's Tonal NRG and Lino's Actor's formant in female voices. She teaches at the Drama Department, Pretoria University and the Opera Department, Pretoria Technikon, South Africa. She is involved in an inter-disciplinary research project about computer aided voice training. Munro works with actors, singers and musicians on optimal body and body/voice integration. She is the Chair of SAPVAME (South African Performers Voice and Movement Educators), she directs for musical theatre and does voice and movement coaching.

1. Please see Ursula Meyer's overview of Raphael's previous articles, below.

The Voice in Violence

It may be one of those obvious things to say about theatre, but it is still true: the very nature of theatre is wrapped around the concept of conflict. All plays have more than a fair share of conflict in them. Conflict regularly leads to violence, whether it is organised violence like sword fights (which is very often the case in period plays) or contemporary/domestic violence that can be found in modern plays. Whatever the case may be, these forms of physical conflict are the manifestation of the emotional conflict, which in turn necessitates the heightened use of body and voice integration. Even in plays that are what I like to call "fight free", the performer may be confronted with use of vocal violence. This section of the journal is less concerned with the concept of "verbal jousting" as it is with the challenges of voice and violence.

Raphael has stated that stage fighting could only be believable to the audience if the audible aspects of conflict support and enhance the visual and the kinaesthetic.[1] I want to underline this by saying that within the extra-daily activity of the performance, the audience will only experience empathy with the performance, if the audible aspects of the performance reflect and mirror the sign system that they are accustomed to in reality. This has a direct bearing on the performer's chosen mode of communication and the embodiment of subtext. The task of the performers is to create a moment of palpable conflict or a "believable fight", and it is in this striving towards "honesty" and "authenticity" that voice usage is often neglected or abused. Fundamentally, the fight must look like real life, but it may not be real life.

The old saying of "it is not what you say, but how you say it" puts the finger on the problem for the performer. Regularly, performers get carried away in "doing the real thing" instead of "creating the illusion of the real thing". In real-life conflict situations, highly emotional moments (and definitely in situations where violence is taking place) the voice is involuntarily "in service of" the unmediated emotion. Consequently, intense emotions like aggression or sadness usually lead to constriction in the laryngeal area, as the emotion "overcomes" the whole body. In reality, I may be hoarse after a good screaming session with my partner—but hopefully this does not happen more than once a month!

On stage though, the performer will find herself in a situation of vocal and physical violence during the one scene, while in the next scene she might have to embody and portray a completely opposite emotion without having any sign of vocal fatigue. Furthermore, this has to happen night after night in performance, or hour after hour in rehearsal. And the performer cannot afford any impediment of vocal range, quality or flexibility. From these demands certain questions arise: is there a "safe way" to create vocal sounds which appear to approximate "the real thing," and yet at the same time acknowledges the requirements of vocal health? Can a performer be trained to produce the "real thing" without damaging the voice? Can the vocal choreography be done in such a way that it reflects the "real-life" auditory signifier of the conflict situation so that the audience will be led to the experience of empathy?

This section provides the reader with different strands of thinking and practice within the sub-discipline "Voice for Violence," and through that provides different and differing answers to the questions above. These strands reflect off each other, focussing on one goal: guiding and assisting the performers to portray the "theatrical truth" performance after performance. The goal is ultimately to blend the craft and the art of "Voice for Violence" until they function as one.

The first part of the section highlights the work of the doyenne of "Voice for Violence:" Bonnie Raphael. Ursula Meyer weighs in with an overview of Bonnie's work, as well as an interview with her. Bonnie herself then leads the way, providing the reader with a game plan where the end product is bigger than the sum of its parts. Lise Olson takes over and shares some personal discoveries regarding the use of voice in stage combat. She specifically introduces the concept of "effort" as being used in the Estill system, in relation to vocal usage in stage combat. Liz Wiley follows as she shares with the Munros' a practical framework for orchestrating the music of the fight.

Michelle Ladd leads the second part of this section when she explains the deep and ominous emotions of domestic violence. Rocco Dal Vera links up with this and discusses the influence of human emotion on the voice. He proceeds to some helpful suggestions for the performance team. Karen Ryker reports on a recent research project in which she and her colleagues investigated and analysed the use of voice for violence. Kate Ufema and Douglas Montequin add their voices to Karen's when they specifically report back on research about the performance scream.

The third part of this section reflects the viewpoints and visions of "partners in crime"—so to speak! Matt Harding shares with the readers his survey on the perception of voice work amongst stage fight combatants, choreographers and fight masters. Marié-Heleen Coetzee follows up with an in-depth interview with two well-known fight directors: Erik Frederickson and k. Jenny Jones. Husband-and-wife team Marya Lowry and Robert Walsh give us a peek behind the scenes with a conversation between a voice coach and a fight director. Another husband-and-wife team James Newcomb and Ursula Meyer provide us with four golden rules when working with opera singers and stage combat. And with this slant towards another genre, Rocco Dal Vera introduces us to yet another angle of the use of voice in violence, when he specifically focuses on looping in film.

Lastly the readers are introduced to a colleague who may not be known to all of us, but who is doing equally important work in "body/voice integration" as well as in "Voice for Violence": Kevin Crawford from Dublin, Ireland.

A very full, very diverse section, clustered around a very important theme. I thank all who contributed: authors, peer reviewers, assistants, advisors, friends. May this section proceed to grow, like the rest of the Journal, as these questions affect all in the Voice and Speech Community across the world. ❦

Ursula Meyer (Associate Editor)(MFA, University of Washington) has been teaching Voice for 19 years at numerous institutions including four years at the Yale School of Drama. As a professional voice/text/ accent coach, she has worked extensively in regional theatres such as The Guthrie, Yale Repertory Theatre, the Oregon Shakespeare Festival, South Coast Rep., and, the La Jolla Playhouse. She trained with Cicely Berry, Patsy Rodenburg, Andrew Wade, Arthur Lessac and is a designated Linklater teacher. She graduated with distinction from the Advanced Voice Studies Program at the Central School of Speech and Drama in London. Also a professional actress, she has worked at Seattle Rep., Milwaukee Rep., La Jolla Playhouse, and fourteen seasons with Shakespeare Festivals throughout the country. She is currently on leave from the University of California, San Diego while working at the Oregon Shakespeare Festival.

"I met Bonnie in 1980 when I was an apprentice at Missouri Repertory Theatre and she was the resident vocal coach. I was immediately captured by her positive spirit, generosity, and knowledge of her craft. Bonnie embraced everyone, from the beginning undergrad to the experienced professional. Now, 20 years later, I am very pleased to have renewed my connection with her. She has fully accepted me as a colleague, for which I am honored. Bonnie is the same now as she was 20 years ago—positive, generous, and very skilled in her abilities. I take that back—she is even better."

Bruce Lecure, Associate Professor, Movement Specialist
University of Miami

Bonnie Raphael has been dealing particularly with the subject of Voice and Violence for quite some time now. She has written several articles on the subject, including "Staged Violence: Greater than the Sum of the Parts" found in this journal.

Bonnie's earlier articles are "Screaming Without Suffering" which was written for *Voice Talk* (Canadian Voice Care Foundation, Vol. 1, Issue 3, Fall 1995, p.9) and a series of articles called "The Sounds of Violence" which appear in *The Fight Master*, Volume XII, numbers 1,2, and 3, 1989.

"Screaming Without Suffering" is a short, succinct, treatise on *healthy* screaming for the theatre or opera. It is a clear, nuts and bolts, set of guide- lines to achieve a believable, repeatable scream. Bonnie focuses on the scream as "the perfect combination of tone and noise," and then goes on to explain how to approach the tone and the noise in a healthy manner.

Bonnie refers to the tone as based on a vocalized yawn, proper alignment hard-palate focus, inaudible inhalations, adequate hydration, breath support, and a relaxed jaw and tongue. Once this *tone* is achieved, the *noise* element is added to make the scream more convincing. The *noise* is "a relatively minor degree of throat constriction produced somewhere above the larynx and super-imposed on a free, yawned sound."

Finally, the article stresses general health in and around the scream, including the kind of exercises needed for both warming up and warming down ("to restore balance to the vocal mechanism") and how to preserve the voice when working the scream in an actual rehearsal.

"The Sounds of Violence" is a series of three articles that came out of several workshops that Bonnie taught on combat-related vocal techniques for the National Workshop of the Society of American Fight Directors.

The first article, or "Part 1 — 'The Real Thing'" defines what questions must be asked and what aspects of a fight must be explored in order to make the sounds of the violence believable. Bonnie emphasizes, particularly, that the sound impulse must originate from the center of the body with deep, low breathing behind it. She also discusses the effectiveness of changes in rhythm— "in the breathing, in the movement, in the use of sounds, in the delivery of lines" —as ways to keep the fight from sounding *staged*. Bonnie provides an extensive set of specific questions for the actors to ask themselves, such as, "Where is the particular blow received?, How much of a surprise was the blow just received?" How enraged is the aggressor?, etc." to help make the sounds more specific to the scene that is being played out. Bonnie also gives advice on how to prevent telegraphing the next move of a fight through breath techniques. She encourages performers to find the differences between the voluntary, more controlled sounds of the attacker and the reactive, more spontaneous sounds of the person being attacked. Finally, she gives advice to fight directors on what to keep in mind in order to preserve the actor's ability to deliver a speech during or after a fight.

Part 2 of "The Sounds of Violence" focuses on "Vocal Safety and Techniques" and is a comprehensive list of vocal health advice for any kind of voice work. She outlines a basic warm-up and warm-down and gives advice on proper grunting and screaming. She also includes several courses of action to follow if and when a performer encounters vocal strain or minor injury.

Part 3 is called "Topping the Competition" and addresses the visual and aural elements of a production that often seem to compete with the lines of the text for the audience's attention.

She examines "The Nature of the Competition"—visually compelling staging, background music, and various lighting effects including smoke, that often make the actor difficult to hear or understand. She encourages director awareness in order to assure the "actor's communicative effectiveness at these challenging times."

Bonnie Raphael

Bonnie then goes on to talk about the "Requisite Vocal Skills" needed to compete with these *outside forces,* She advises creating a sound with optimum breath flow, focusing on the hard palate, shifting the balance of tone and noise so that the voice that needs to be heard is more focused on clarity and intelligibility, and finding a color to the voice that is in a different "pitch neighborhood" from the competing noise. She also mentions the theory that often problems of inadequate projection are really about intelligibility rather than volume. She then gives three bits of advice on how to work on that clarity: the need to find the more projectable parts of the pitch range, the value of keeping the consonants from being under-emphasized and the vowels from being choked, and the importance of "functional and communicative phrasing." She also puts forth the usefulness of vocal variety between actors in a fight so that the two voices are never confused, even if actors are hidden from view.

The last section of the third article deals with crowd voices. The two most important factors here seem to be variety of sound (pitch, speed, rhythm and vocal color) and specificity of sound by making sure that each crowd member remains a specific individual. One suggestion to give variety of sound is to divide the crowd into smaller sub-groups with one actor talking in a low range, another in a high range, another in a mid-range, another perhaps listening, etc. To foster specificity, she includes examples of questions for each performer—"Whose side are you on?,

What do you have at stake should he win or lose the fight?", etc. Bonnie also stresses the importance of each performer's relationship to the world of the play and to the needs of the story that is being told.

The conclusion of the three articles talks about the importance of thorough grounding in "acting techniques as well as voice and speech and stage combat" and creating an environment where the actor can embrace the possibilities of a scene of violence rather than fearing for his or her vocal or physical safety, being able to engage in scenes that make the difference between "a run-of-the-mill encounter and truly magical on-stage event."

UM: When and how did you get started working with 'Voice and Violence"?

BR: Because my training is in both theatre and voice pathology, I have always been sort of wearing both hats at the same time. Therapists and physicians were telling actors not to cough or to scream or to sob or laugh because these behaviors are all ways of abusing the voice. Meanwhile, playwrights continued to write situation after situation after situation where these were called for. There had to be a way to solve this. Arthur Lessac discusses doing the wrong things the right way in his text. I started experimenting with taking easy, clean calls and "scuzzing" them up in order to produce a relatively safe scream. And one thing sort of led to another.

UM: When and how did you start working with actual fight choreographers on this subject matter?

BR: David Leong came to do the fight choreography for Michael Kahn's production of 'Tis Pity She's a Whore. I knew him by reputation and thought very highly of his work and his ability to be a team player. We got to talking and decided to see what would happen if we team-coached the combat scenes in this show. It was fabulous! We had a great time and were very satisfied with both the process and the product. David Leong then invited me to come down to Memphis, to teach a series of workshops for the Society of American Fight Directors' summer training program. I accepted and got a tremendous response to the work. David then suggested that I write up the workshops for publication in Fight Master, a periodical produced by SAFD. I wrote a three-part article which appeared in Fight Master. Another show biz story about how one thing leads to another if you're in the right place at the right time.

UM: In your opinion, what are the biggest mistakes that vocal coaches make when they work with texts/actors/productions that involve violence?

BR: As I say in my article ("Staged Violence; Greater than the Sum of Its Parts") which appears elsewhere in this publication, I think the biggest problems arise when vocal coaches are tunnel-visioned, when they concentrate exclusively on text and dialects and articulation and lose sight of the bigger picture. If and when a collegial relationship can be established with the sound designer, the lighting designer, the costume designer, the set designer, the fight choreographer *and* the director, then lots of little glitches never grow into big problems and the exchange of ideas, strategies and solutions is ongoing rather than motivated by crisis. More specifically, I would say that the biggest mistakes include not coming into the fight rehearsal process until late if at all, and/or being too protective and precious about the actors' voices, and/or not involving enough physical activity in vocal coaching sessions.

UM: What do you feel are the biggest mistakes that fight choreographers make when they work with sound/voice in scenes of Violence?

BR: Things are changing and moving very much in the right direction regarding collaboration. However, sometimes a fight choreographer fails to see the bigger picture and creates a fight sequence that is too long for the production and/or very taxing for the combatants. If the actors have important text to render around the fight, then that text is likely to suffer as a result. Or a fight choreographer may rehearse crowd scenes and big battle scenes without telling the actor-combatants to mark or save their voices or to sip water when they can. The less hierarchical and the more collaborative relationships are among specialists working on a show, the fewer breakdowns in communication occur.

UM: Who was influential in some of the discoveries that you made?

BR: Several different people have been influential in discoveries I've made, and continue to be so. By the time I started my Lessac training, I had "lost" my scream. I didn't have nodes, but had screamed myself hoarse in enough shows in which I'd acted to have just a croak where my scream once was. The concept of focusing the tone on the hard palate via *Call* and then doing that in head voice to *anchor* a scream was a revelation to me, and a life saver. Once I acquired this technique, not only did I recover my scream, but I was able to develop it in lots of different directions! When I was at the Denver Center, I had a dual appointment—half with the theatre company and half at the voice lab. My interactions with physicians and scientists, especially with Ron Scherer and Ingo Titze, were invaluable. One time, after I had been scoped for a research project, they let me keep the laryngoscope in a little longer while I watched my throat on a television monitor—fabulous! I was able to teach myself to scream by using my false vocal folds to create the noise element while using the true vocal folds to create a pure, clean sound. I was able to teach myself so much by watching what was happening to the physical mechanism and giving it instructions. Dr. Wilbur James Gould and Dr. Robert Sataloff invited me to present my workshops on "doing the wrong thing the right way" at several different Voice Foundation meetings. It's not a done deal, to be sure, but I think many more physicians and therapists are now willing to teach actors how to use their voices instead of simply saying, "You must never do that under any circumstances!" And Dr. Robert Bastian, on two separate occasions separated by many years, examined me and questioned me after I had demonstrated screaming at workshops to document the fact that my vocal folds were in good shape after what sounded like abuse.

UM: What is the most important thing for an actor to consider when working with scenes of violence?

BR: I think actors need to develop skills relating to physical violence before they go into rehearsal for a production in which those skills will be needed. In the same way that some actors take singing lessons or dancing lessons or learn to juggle or whistle or to use different stage dialects, it's a great idea for them to learn the basics of both unarmed combat and doing the wrong (vocal) things the right way. The best time to refine and habituate skills relating to grunting, groaning, coughing, choking, sobbing, screaming, etc. is not while you're in rehearsal for a show. It's far more productive to bring these special skills into the rehearsal process with you. And if there are new or different skills that need to be acquired, the actor must be sure that he or she is in good vocal and physical shape before rehearsals begin and must work on the acquisition of skills right from the beginning of the rehearsal period. One of the biggest mistakes actors make is to start working on these too late in the rehearsal period. Another big mistake is not marking. Even if your technique is strong, fatigue and overuse can compromise the voice greatly. Actors must develop enough assertiveness to be able to say to a director, "I'm going to be marking this sequence vocally until the last time we run it—just to preserve my voice." This is far preferable to showing up the next day hoarse.

UM: Can you review your basic warm-up for these kinds of scenes? What would have to be included?

BR: I think the four most important things are:

A) *Start with the breath and return to the breath throughout the rehearsal,* keeping it full and deep and unencumbered as much as possible.
B) *Be sure that the warm-up is physical,* that the shoulders and neck and jaw and rib-cage are limber and that grounding work is included.
C) *Do not overdo the warm-up;* if you know you're in for a physically and vocally demanding rehearsal, then just get the breath and the body connected to the voice, and vocalize both in the speaking part of the range and the screaming part of the range, if that's to be used as well.
D) *Be sure to warm down as soon after a strenuous rehearsal as possible.* Put your toys back where they belong after you're finished playing with them. The best time to restore balance and ease in the vocal mechanism is right after you've used it strenuously. Some sips of tepid water, some yawns and gentle head and shoulder rolls, some gentle humming in the middle of the pitch range, some breathing in a full bend-over position to bring circulation into the laryngeal area, some easy deep breathing—these are the ingredients for a brief but effective restorative warm-down.

UM: What is left to be done on this issue other than simply making people aware that there are ways to scream without suffering, etc.?

BR: I think that educating directors about what they can expect from actors and what they need to watch and listen for to prevent voice loss is essential. I think that educating physicians and therapists about techniques we've developed is equally important. I think that educating vocal coaches about serving as an advocate for sensible rehearsal and performance demands is important. But most important is teaching actors to be assertive. They so want to please! In fear of being labeled as uncooperative or difficult, they fear speaking assertively when it comes to their own safety and health. It is perfectly okay to mark vocally at a rehearsal. It's perfectly okay to ask whether another piece of business could be substituted for the cigarette the playwright wrote in.

UM: Do you think that there are a lot of research possibilities in this field—can science and art meet—or is it only a creative process?

BR: I think there is a myriad of research possibilities in this field! I think studies of how to teach a safer and/or more effective scream or howl or sob or coughing fit or laughing sequence would be very, very well received by the performing sector. Unfortunately, solid scientific experiments with human subjects are not easy—there are so many variables to consider. But they can be done. Ron Scherer has solicited questions from the VASTA membership for what he hopes will be an ongoing column in future issues of the *Voice and Speech Review*. This would be an excellent starting point for collaborations and research across disciplines to enrich our knowledge and skills. Karen Ryker and several others have already begun research in this area. I look forward to the continued growth and development is this particular cross-discipline sub-specialty.

Staged Violence: Greater Than the Sum of Its Parts

Bonnie N. Raphael has taught and coached professional voice users for over thirty years — at the University of North Carolina, the American Repertory Theatre and its Institute for Advanced Theatre Training at Harvard, the National Theatre Conservatory, Northwestern University, and the University of Virginia, etc. Bonnie has coached hundreds of productions, at PlayMakers Repertory Company, American Repertory Theatre, Missouri Repertory Theatre, Dallas Theater Center, Denver Center Theatre, Repertory Theatre of St. Louis, Colorado Shakespeare Festival and elsewhere, working with Garland Wright, Andrei Serban, Jerry Zaks, Robert Brustein, Michael Kahn, Anne Bogart, Robert Wilson, Ron Daniels, and others. Actors she has coached include Annette Bening, Christopher Lloyd, Cherry Jones, Christopher Walken, Kathleen Widdoes and Claire Bloom.

1. Although I am well aware of the fact that fight directors prefer to be called just that and that many voice coaches prefer to be called vocal directors, I am using these labels to insure the greatest clarity in distinguishing among the director, the person who stages the fights and the one who coaches the actors in matters of voice, speech and text.

2. In the fight between Viola (disguised as Cesario) and Sir Andrew Aguecheek in Shakespeare's TWELFTH NIGHT, for example, ineptitude and fear on both parts can create a delightful comedic exchange and provide additional information about both characters.

3. i.e. stage management, fight choreographer, voice coach; set, costume and props designers; actors.

Since physical violence is by its very nature dramatic, it is only a matter of time before directors, fight choreographers[1] and voice coaches encounter the challenges inherent in staging, rehearsing and presenting scenes involving combat. In the most memorable productions I've seen or coached, the stage combat sequences make an enormous contribution to the story being told. There is an appropriateness about their conceptualization and execution that keeps them integral to both the script and the particular production. The length, the components and the very nature of the most effective fights are compatible not only with the given circumstances but also with the characters participating and the style of the production as well.[2] Furthermore, the most impressive fights are executed in a manner that enables audience members to be totally immersed in the seeming reality of the danger faced by the characters while not having to worry about the actual safety of the actors.

A seamless transition between a well-designed moment of combat and the dialogue or circumstances surrounding it is best created through collaboration among the director, the actors, the fight choreographer, the designers and the vocal coach and reflects the axiom that the whole is greater than the sum of its parts. When such collaborations are not taken into consideration as the production is being conceived, there is often a price to pay that is both aesthetic and practical. Aesthetically, a fight sequence might have a "pasted on", arbitrary or generic feel to it. Practically, the spoken lines might be muffled or unintelligible, or the actors might appear to be uncomfortable or in danger while performing the fight sequence itself. This can throw off the rhythm or the integrity of the whole, because such a fight sequence might be perceived (consciously or unconsciously) as "off," taking audience members out of the play momentarily.

Similarly, one can observe the cost of non-collaboration during the rehearsal process itself: the actors are quite likely to get caught in the middle, if only because requests made by the director, the fight choreographer, the designers and the vocal coach may well conflict with one another. Even worse, the actors might suffer the consequences of trying to comply with conflicting requests. Such consequences might include physical injury, vocal strain or loss, lack of confidence, inconsistency in characterization, and growing frustration. When the actors suffer, not only is there the possibility of personal loss for them but the production will inevitably suffer as well if only because they are unable to do their best work. Experienced directors and coaches know that lack of adequate preparation and rehearsal can preclude the possibility of an otherwise exciting and unique encounter between adversaries.

On the other hand, a game plan can be created that will benefit all concerned[3] especially when the director knows basically what he or she wants even before rehearsals begin. As someone who has worked in the theatre for more than 30 years, I am well aware of just how precious and scarce the director's time is during a given rehearsal period. If, during the pre-production phase, the voice coach can either meet with or at least make contact with the director, then there is a greater likelihood that the director will be thinking about these matters and that the coach's time will be used more efficiently. When a director consults with the fight choreographer and the voice coach in advance of rehearsals and is willing to be present for at least portions of the fight rehearsals, then time will not be wasted in rethinking, re-staging and re-rehearsing sequences because of lack of communication. In my experience, fight choreographers and voice coaches can be both highly creative and greatly collaborative people, but we are not as successful as mind readers. A director is likely to be far more satisfied with the final product if, early on, he or she has communicated specific ideas about the intention of a fight sequence, its approximate length, the relative importance of the surrounding or embedded dialogue, the capabilities of the actor-combatants and the set, lighting and costumes.

Victorious "War Stories"

Experienced fight directors and vocal coaches can recall numerous examples of potentially competing demands on the actor-combatant. Examples include:

- the final act of *Hamlet*, in which a formal duel, commencing under specific rules of engagement, quickly escalates into a rout involving exchanged weapons, poisonings, and the death of duelists and spectators;
- the comic beating of Arnolphe in *School for Wives*, in which the humor is derived basically from the inflicting of physical pain on the master by his two servants;
- the comic duel between the victimized Viola (disguised as Cesario) and the ill-equipped and cowardly Sir Andrew Aguecheek, followed closely by a skillful and far more dangerous encounter between Sir Toby and Antonio in *Twelfth Night*.

I would like to offer a few examples from my own experience that I hope will illustrate how several members of the production team were able to collaborate regarding:

- devoting time to the development of the actors' skills and stamina (enabling them to successfully meet the demands of complex violent interactions);
- scheduling and running of fight rehearsals;
- design modifications that enabled a more skillful execution of the fights as staged.

At the American Repertory Theatre, I was privileged to serve as vocal coach for Michael Kahn's excellent and exciting production of *'Tis Pity She's a Whore*, with the very talented and collaborative David Leong as fight choreographer. Often when both a voice coach and a fight choreographer are included on a production team, their sessions with the actors are separate from one another. However, David and I scheduled joint rehearsals for all scenes in which both fights and dialogue occurred—and there are several such scenes in this play. Often, Michael Kahn came in for the last 10-15 minutes of these rehearsals, giving both actors and coaches a combination of positive feedback and excellent suggestions for further development or modification of what we had rehearsed.

All of us made sure that the actors were collaborators in this process rather than puppets to be manipulated to suit any arbitrary conceptual decisions. For example, the physical violence between Soranzo and Annabella was modified to accommodate the fact that the actress would be wearing her long hair loose as she was dragged around the floor. Another wonderful collaborative sequence occurred in the scene in which Bergetto is murdered. What started as an actor's suggestion to use an umbrella rather than a sword as his weapon grew into a lovely piece of staging for which the lighting and sound designers provided rain effects. The fight choreographer created a sequence that was unique: character-driven, touching and even humorous in places.

With the help of stage management, the actors were given time to rest after strenuous sessions rather than immediately going back into rehearsal. This integrated scheduling requires flexibility, creativity and continued attention on the part of stage management but is definitely worth the effort.

To avoid unexpected injuries or the need to limit possibilities, time was allotted throughout the rehearsal period for the actors to become both physically and vocally conditioned.[4] Such conditioning included learning correct techniques for screaming, for carrying (resistance on the part of the victim to being carried was postponed until later on in the rehearsal period), for marking and for performing difficult sequences at half speed without undue tension. Each of the actors involved grew in strength, coordination and stamina. By the time the show opened, all were up to the tasks demanded of them— or the tasks were simplified just enough to give primacy to the most effective telling of the story. For example, for purposes of clearer communication, we discovered through trial and error that one of the more demanding pieces of text was far more effective when spoken by the actress playing Annabella before rather than after being thrown to the ground. If director and coaches are in the fortunate position to be working with actors who are well trained both physically and vocally, then process is greatly facilitated and far more enjoyable.[5]

Ongoing consultations with both the costume designer and the set designer made it possible for us to adjust both blocking and stage business in such a way that by the time technical rehearsals came around, other potential stumbling blocks were avoided as well. For example, the long scarf worn with Annabella's nightgown was removed, at no detriment to the costume design, shortly before Soranzo's entrance in order to facilitate a very physically active sequence.

At the American Repertory Theatre, I was vocal coach for Adrian Hall's compelling production of *King Lear* as well. Near the end of the play, there was a compelling broadsword sequence between Edgar and Edmund, beautifully staged by Bill Finlay. That duel to the death occurs at the same time that each of the brothers is required to speak lines important to the ultimate resolution of the play. By collaborating on the "music of the fight"[6] and by paying attention to intervening dialogue as an intrinsic ingredient of that music, we were able to create a sequence that featured character, language, and combat without sacrificing any of those in the process. In addition, by starting early in the rehearsal period and working collaboratively, we were able to pace the actors in their development so that they were prepared to stage the best possible fight for this particular production.

Unfortunately, late in the rehearsal period, one of the actors was replaced, so that a great deal of rehearsal time and preparation were ultimately for naught. Communication among the specialists involved had been consistent up to that point however, so we did not have to go back to "square one" in order to

4. There are several ways in which this can be done. I generally provide stage management with both a wish list and a list of available times on Sundays for the following week. By increasing the length of session requested for a particular actor, or by requesting two actors for coaching simultaneously, I can build in time for the actors to acquire necessary skills.

5. With actors who are either untrained or out of shape, all concerned must resolve to apply the wisdom of "Less is More". If a sequence can be designed and rehearsed that will serve the purposes of the play without sacrificing either the credibility or the safety of the actors, then that choice is preferable.

6. i.e. the artistic design of the dynamic interplay between the class of the weapons, the sounds of both armor and footsteps, the beating of the ceremonial drums, the spoken dialogue, the non-verbal vocalizations on the part of both the combatants and the spectators, etc.

integrate the new actor. Fight choreography was simplified somewhat so that the actors would be both safe and confident in what they were doing. Bill Finlay was understandably disappointed that the original fight sequence could not be executed by the new actor with only the small amount of rehearsal time remaining, but the fight was impressive nonetheless—simply another case where, given these particular circumstances, Less proved to be More. The lighting designer contributed by providing more illumination for this tricky fight. The result was not quite as atmospheric as it might have been, but the design adjustment contributed significantly to the actors' confidence.

These methodological descriptions and admonitions may sound like simple common sense but good sense does not always prevail. A director may not think it important to see the fight sequences until a late run-through or even technical rehearsals. When this is the case, it is far more difficult to make conceptual changes that can be rehearsed well enough for the actors to feel comfortable. Sometimes the fight choreographer creates a sequence that is too long or too demanding, failing to take into consideration the capabilities and experience of the actors or the other demands being placed on them by the production. These actors may get through the sequence as staged, but perhaps at the cost of their acting effectiveness, their ability to phrase effectively, or the play's momentum. On the other hand, an over-protective voice coach can make the actors nervous enough about the possibility of incurring damage to their vocal mechanisms that the length, the choreography or the music of the fight is seriously compromised. The best defense against such occurrences is a good offense, and a good offense begins with a game plan that emphasizes forethought rather than crisis management, a plan that includes ongoing communication among all members of the production team throughout the rehearsal process.

Pre-Rehearsal Text-Centered Considerations for the Vocal Coach

Just as a production's success can be attributable to the director's game plan, the success of the voice, dialect and text work can depend on the voice coach's ability to prepare and to collaborate. When preparing the play, the vocal coach can usually ascertain where the fight sequences occur and how each of these sequences relates to the dialogue. Some of the questions that might be asked include:

- How much important text either interrupts or immediately follows the fight itself? Are the surrounding or intervening lines all vital to the forward thrust of the play? If so, then coaches must consider how quickly "injured" or how winded the actors can afford to get during the fight. An alternative is for the director or fight choreographer to create some rest or interruption in the combat sequence so that the audience might more easily hear an important line or passage. Or it might do no harm for the actor combatants to "throw away" some of the lines or even for the director to cut them in order to better feature what's most important.
- Is this a formal combat, held before an onstage audience, perhaps part of some ritual or rite of passage and following a prescribed set of rules of engagement (e.g. the beginning of the duel between Hamlet and Laertes in Act V of *Hamlet*)? Or does the fight erupt spontaneously as a consequence of a failure in earlier communication (e.g. as happens in Sam Shepard's *Fool for Love*)?

- What sounds might be competing with the lines as the fight and/or the dialogue takes place (e.g. heavy footsteps, sound effects, music, clash of weapons, etc.)?
- The voice coach will read as well for clues to plot and characterization:
  —If a character receives a hurt, how bad is it and where is it located? What are the effects of this particular hurt on the breathing and/or the voice?
  —Does this character want to, dare to reveal the injury or its severity?
  —Are this character's non-verbal sounds likely to be aggressive, threatening, or are they defensive, protective, evasive? (This consideration has a direct relationship to vocal rhythm at any given point during the fight.)

Some of these considerations will depend on the actual design of the fight, of course, but this preparatory work is quite useful nonetheless.

Separate Rehearsals/ Integrated Strategies

There are certainly times during the early rehearsals (before the actors are off book, before the fight has been choreographed) where it might be appropriate for the fight choreographer and the vocal coach to work separately with the actors. However, even then, these coaches can do their work in such a way as to keep one another in mind.

For example, during the preliminary blocking, the fight choreographer can make sure that the actors are warmed up not only physically but vocally as well, so that the actors are not in danger of injuring the vocal mechanism by grunting, groaning, coughing, and other activities related to fighting. He or she will be sure that the effort of learning the fight techniques and sequences does not move the breathing location up from a relaxed and engaged center, essential to effective and safe vocal production. The fight choreographer can be monitoring stridor as well (i.e. audible inhalations due to generalized tension, poor habit, or to swelling or constriction in the throat muscles), and can remind the actors to keep the jaw loose, the tongue relaxed and the throat in a half-yawn configuration as much as possible. The fight choreographer might even get to a point where he or she is asking the actors to release a free sound (initiated with /h/ to protect the vocal folds from hard glottal initiation, of course) in order to prepare them for the actual sounds and words that will be spoken during or after the fight. If, during the staging rehearsals, the actors do get fatigued or experience any vocal strain, then the vocal coach can make sure that the actors warm down[7] as soon as possible after that strain has occurred.

This is not to say that the fight choreographer can or should be doubling as the vocal coach, of course, unless he or she has the requisite training and experience. It is certainly quite useful for both these specialists to use the same or compatible vocabulary. However, responsibility for monitoring vocal production, range, stamina, articulation, and the effective communication of text--even during or around the occurrence of a combat episode—remains the task of the vocal coach.[8]

When the vocal coach works with the actors, he or she can, in the same way the fight choreographer does, make sure that the exercises chosen are serving the eventual combining of text and physical movement. Such exercises are

7. As soon as an actor feels throat discomfort, he or she should take time to reestablish balance and ease in the vocal mechanism: by sipping tepid water; by loosening the shoulders, the neck, the jaw, the tongue and the lips; by humming gently into the mask using pitches from the middle of the range; by hanging over in a full bendover position to encourage blood circulation into the throat area; by yawning and swallowing.

8. An analogous example: if the actor were to develop hoarseness in the voice or an upper respiratory infection that lasted for more than just a few days, then he or she should be referred to an appropriate medical specialist for treatment.

not confined to the table; energetic physical involvement can be incorporated long before combining the text and the fight in order to get the actors into condition. The actor can swing the arms, keep a ball in the air, move around the room, and eventually begin to approximate the fight's blocking without either a partner or a weapon.

If there is important dialogue occurring at the same time as demanding physicality, then a three-step vocal release sequence that I learned from Kristin Linklater might be useful. In this sequence, the actor deals with the words of each beat[9] of his speech on at least three levels:

1) The first time through, while thinking the beat itself, the actor simply drops the breath into center and releases full sound on *huhhhhhhhhh*. If the throat is tight enough that there is stridor as the breath is dropped in or if there is significant restriction of the outgoing sound, then the actor repeats this preliminary step until he or she is able to release the unstructured sound on a free voice and in a manner springing directly from emotional connection.

2) Only when this is achieved, the actor releases sound on an "inflected babble". The melody of the babble resembles the inflection of the line to be spoken, as determined by both the particular demands of the text and the actor's intentions. However, instead of articulating specific words, the actor is substituting *huh-muh-muh-muh-muh-MUHHH* or some variation thereof in order to make sure that the vocal channel is both open and responsive to intention. Again, if there is difficulty in releasing this inflected sound, then the actor stays with this part of the sequence until a free release is effected.

3) Only then does the actor move on to speaking the actual text. If the text is constricted or unintelligible because of tension in the diaphragm (which will compromise the breath support), in the throat (which will compromise the actual sound), in the jaw, the tongue or the lips (which will compromise the articulation), or in the phrasing (which will compromise the audience's comprehension), then the actor repeats and develops that step of the exercise until the text can be fully released, even under duress.

The actor then does the same sequence of three levels on the next beat, until the end of the speech is reached. If he or she happens to get to a place where the speech begins to tumble out freely, then the actor can continue speaking it out—but only until such time as he or she gets "stuck" on another given beat, at which time the actor once again reverts to the three-step sequence until that particular beat is released.

This exercise should be done only after a solid vocal warm-up and should not be done for more than 20-30 minutes time in any one coaching session or rehearsal. This will lessen or eliminate the possibility of vocal fatigue or strain and will allow the actor to return to and to fully participate in other rehearsals scheduled on the same day. The exercise should be followed by a warm-down[10] as well in order to reestablish balance and ease in the vocal mechanism itself. If, in these early individual rehearsals, the basic groundwork is laid, then when the time comes to combine the parts into the combat sequence, the desired behavior will be nothing more than the next step in the process.

9. Beats may be defined as important or discrete sections of the script between which a character's intentions or objectives alter. Such beats may be anywhere from a single syllable to a number of sentences in length.

10. See Footnote 7.

Seeing the Bigger Picture

Most audiences today, especially in America, seem to suffer from a rapidly shrinking attention span. Furthermore, many audience members seem to be far more aware of what they see than of what they hear. If given something compelling enough to look at, they may fail to listen at the same time. Many directors understand this competition for audiences' primary interest and have figured out how to provide actors with visual focus at times when important dialogue occurs. However, some directors are more visual than aural in their strengths, preferences or training. As a result, they may create staging that actually interferes with an audience's ability to listen. Other directors may be so taken with a particular piece of music or a series of sound effects or even atmospheric lighting that they do not notice that the dialogue may have gotten somewhat lost in the process.

Failure to achieve an optimum balance is sometimes attributable to other members of the production team. For example, there are some fight choreographers who insist on realizing a particular idea about the clash of weapons or the sounds of effort during combat and can wind up paying insufficient attention to the script and to the importance of telling the story. Some voice coaches get protective enough about the language to seek an artificially quiet environment in which to place a particular speech or exchange during a violent encounter. Both of these scenarios can ultimately compromise the integrity of the production as a whole. However, when the fight choreographer and the voice coach are both focussing their attention on the overall production rather than confining their contributions to their respective specialties, then they can work more collaboratively with one another and with the director in order to achieve a more effective final product. Keeping the bigger picture in mind throughout will make imbalances apparent, will make adjustments easy and efficient, and will certainly help to avoid or abort any battles for dominance. In this way, the fights will occur onstage between characters, not offstage among members of the production team.

Of course, this discussion presupposes a given director's willingness to accept input from members of a production team. This is not always achievable despite the very best efforts of the fight choreographer and/or the vocal coach. In my experience, I have found that there are many directors who welcome and appreciate suggestions about the production as a whole, while others prefer each specialist to stay on his own turf and to contribute only there. And (much as I would prefer to think otherwise) a production can be successful whether or not the director chooses to collaborate by welcoming suggestions about the production as a whole from his or her entire team.

Only if and when any team member is able to take a step back and make choices (and sometimes edits) for the overall good of the production is the final product the best it can be. A fight sequence evolved through such generosity and open-mindedness provides security and challenge to its actor/combatants, artistic satisfaction to its director and coaches, and wonderfully exciting entertainment for its audiences. When the collaborative process is successful, the whole is indeed far greater than the sum of the parts.

Selected Bibliography

Lessac, Arthur. *The Use and Training of the Human Voice*. (3rd ed., rev.) Mt. View, California: Mayfield Publishing Company, 1997.

Linklater, Kristin. *Freeing the Natural Voice*. New York: DBS Publications, 1976.

Raphael, Bonnie. "Dancing on Shifting Ground: Voice Coaching in Professional Theatre" *Voice and Speech Review* (Voice and Speech Trainers Association, 2000), pp. 165-170.

Raphael, Bonnie. "Screaming without Suffering". *Voice Talk*, (Canadian Voice Care Foundation) Volume I, Issue 3, (Fall, 1995), p. 9.

Raphael, Bonnie. "The Sounds of Violence: Vocal Training in Stage Combat", *Theatre Topics*, Volume I, Number 1 (March, 1991), pp. 73-86.

Voice in Violence—a series of articles published in connection with the International Paddy Crean Stage Combat Workshop. Edinburgh, Scotland: Queen Margaret College, August 15-22, 1999. Articles of particular interest:
   Dal Vera, Rocco. "Cry Havoc! The Voice in Heightened Affective States", pp. 26-41.
   Olson, Lise. "Blinded by Science", pp. 53-59.
   Ryker, Karen S. "To Train and Test the Voice in Violence", pp. 42-52.
   Wiley, Elizabeth. "Orchestrating the Music of the Fight", pp. 16-23.

Peer Reviewed Article by *Lise Olson*

Some Personal Discoveries Regarding Vocal Use in Stage Combat

Lise Olson is an ex-pat American who has lived in the UK for a decade. Currently at the Liverpool Institute for Performing Arts and Cameron Mackintosh's *The Witches Of Eastwick* in the West End.UK Credits include Head of Voice at Welsh College of Music and Drama, Central School, Rose Bruford, East 15, The Drama Centre, Bristol Old Vic, Birmingham Rep, various regional theatres and the West End. Previously, Lise was Head of Voice at Purdue and has taught at Duke University, NCSA, U. of WA and other schools. Member of VASTA, British Voice Association and British Academy of Dramatic Combat. Also, she's a BBC *Masterchef*.

1. Ludlum, Charles, *50 Observations on Acting*

2. Raphael, Bonnie, "The Sounds of Violence", *The Fight Master*, Journal of the SAFD, 1988.

3. *Voice in Violence*, published proceedings from The International Paddy Crean Stage Combat Workshop, Queen Margaret College, Edinburgh, Scotland, 1999.

4. Roget, Peter Mark, *Roget's Thesaurus*, Tophi Books, London, 1988.

5. Kayes, Gillyanne, *Singing and the Actor*, A.C. Black, London, 2000

6. Effort can be quantified by a system of Magnitude Estimation and Magnitude Production developed by S.S.Stevens (Harvard University) to measure sensory perception.

Charles Ludlum, a gifted actor noted for his great theatricality once said,
…at the heart of the dramatic event lies the spirit of masochism. In the boxing ring or at a tragedy it is the delight in conflict and the illusion of opposition that enthrals. The primary desire of the audience is to witness suffering. The actor willingly undergoes the ordeal of passing through various states of physical and mental torture."[1]

The actor is purveyor of illusion. One of the many ways that the actor appears to pass through that torture is through the use of onstage violence. Practitioners of stage violence require certain physical skills—the safe use of the voice in moments of violence is merely one of the requisite skills required of an actor-combatant in today's employment market. Stage fighters have specific needs due to the physical work they are likely to be engaged in whilst speaking. A number of voice practitioners have published groundbreaking work in the field of vocal violence—most notably Dr. Bonnie Raphael,[2] Karen Ryker, Rocco Dal Vera and Elizabeth Wiley have all recently written on this subject.[3] My studies in the area of vocal violence are based on the fact that I am that very odd dichotomy—a voice teacher who fights. As a result of my 'vested interest', my quest is more personal than professional, more anecdotal than strictly scientific.

The Concept of Effort in Stage Fighting
Effort has been described in many ways:
"Exertion, strain, tug, pull, stress, force, struggle, work, toil, take pains, show one's best, set one's shoulder to the wheel, labour, go through fire and water, by the sweat of ones brow…".

My colleague, Gillyanne Kayes, has said that effort is "having an awareness of what you are doing when working with your voice. You need to
1. know how hard you are working
2. isolate the muscles used in tasks
3. monitor the spread of effort and decide whether it is appropriate to the task."[5]

Gillyanne writes primarily for the actor who sings, but the concept of effort rings true for the actor who fights as well. The actor may want to consider the following: How much effort do you use to sit in your chair? To walk to your room? To hold a broadsword? Can we quantify effort? If we consider the active use of energy in producing a result, how do we measure it so there is parity in our measurements? Although science can help us,[6] if we view the quantifying of effort as personal, we can use it to our advantage.

If we are able to define our personal effort in pursuing tasks, we are more likely to achieve consistency through rehearsal and performance. At the most basic, we grasp a particular weapon at a specific effort level, attack at one effort level and parry at another. This constantly changes throughout the fight. If we recognize what effort levels we use and begin to use effort as part of our vocabulary, we save time. If we choose to rehearse a fight in slow motion, at effort level 3 (on a scale of perception from one to ten), it doesn't mean that proper technique or focus is lacking, only the effort use is different. Effort can be used to define pace, rhythm, and phrasing of the fight. One area in which I have found the definition of effort useful is vocal work with actors.

When fighters lose breath, when the throat constricts and everyone hears vocal strain, many applaud the realism—however, this actor may be damaging one of his most valuable assets. Using the effort model, the actor can quantify the effort—deduce how much work is taking place and where, specifically, in the body, that work is placed and then make adjustments to rid himself of constriction.

To make these deductions, and others related to healthy voice usage, it can be handy for the stage combatant to revisit basic anatomy (the actual skeletal and muscular systems in the body) and vocal physiology (the working of those systems responsible for sound and speech). The actor will realise that good breath support and sustained speech use several connecting systems that rely on plenty of air and flexible respiratory muscles as well as healthy and flexible vocal folds and unencumbered use of the resonators.[7] The use of the effort model combined with knowledge of vocal physiology can assist the actor/combatant in extended vocal use.

7. Jo Estill, *Primer of Compulsory Figures*, California

Extended Vocal Use

Extended vocal use is often referred to as "extraordinary" use of the voice. This includes, but is not strictly limited to, vocal use during stage fighting, howling, screaming, shouting or using the voice in a large theatre or outside venue. Use of the extended voice, like stage fighting, is a physical skill—it involves the entire body, and proficiency can only be gained through training and repetition. Training "is a process of self-definition…a process of self-discipline which manifests itself…through physical reactions."[8]

8. Barba, Eugenio, "Words or Presence", *The Drama Review*, Volume 16, No.1, New York, 1972.

In a set piece of stage fighting, vocal sounds can be rehearsed as the fight is rehearsed. The muscle memory of correct voice usage is congruent with the correct technique in execution of thrusts, footwork and parries. The rehearsal of vocal sound need not be mechanical—if the voice is the organic growth of what happens in the fight (as it should be), the vocals need rehearsal for the same reasons that a fight needs to be rehearsed—for reasons of safety. Practise the vocal sequence that includes the extended voice use away from the physical action of the fight to make sure the technique is solid before adding it, at volume, to the fight rehearsal.

When coaching extreme vocal use, I insist upon three things. The first is a vocal limber, or warm-up, that includes sirens, glides, and goes above the vocal peak desired in the performance. The reasoning behind this is the same for having a fight call prior to performance—to make sure that the particular muscles are working .A revisit of this vocal limber may be done in absolute silence offstage before the fight itself. As long as the same amount of effort is being used, the muscles are still working, even without sound.

The second is solid and dynamic support. In extreme uses of the voice the sound must be well supported to avoid damage. There are many different way to do this, the most familiar is sound supported by breath using the intercostals and the diaphragm. As most stage fights are linked to high

9. Rodenberg, Patsy, *The Right to Speak*, Methuen, London, 1992, p.225-6

emotional stakes, I turn to Patsy Rodenburg, Director of Voice for the National Theatre of Great Britain. In her excellent book *The Right to Speak*, she addresses volume in regard to emotional content, "The higher our emotional tension, the louder our voices become…the bigger the context the more clamorous the voice."[9] She also specifies two precepts that control extended voice usage, and one comment on why it is often not successful:

1. Always work from support. The louder the sound, the more support you need.
2. The vowels in any word are the main body of the voice…we have to allow the vowels room to escape…vowels must have their full capacity so that the jaw opens wide to let them through.
3. …the fear of being too loud or too emotionally committed creates a common habit of pulling the vowel back…the greater support needed for the emotion wants to release through the word, but the speaker's denial suppresses it midway…the energy stays bottled in the throat.[10]

10. Ibid.

One way to support extended voice use involves the term "postural anchoring", as described in the Estill model. In reporting this, Kayes tells us that by anchoring the body we make a firm scaffolding for the vibrating mechanism of the voice and a solid resonating case for the instrument. She offers two rules to remember when anchoring:

1. The greater the vocal task, the harder you must work to support the vibrating mechanism. (see Rodenberg, above)
2. Isolation is essential to anchoring.[11]

11. Kayes, Gillyanne, op.cit. p.69.

Let us think about effort once again. In extreme vocal use, effort spreads to even the small area of the vocal folds. In anchoring, we move the effort to the torso, which enables us to create a powerful tone with less vocal fatigue. It is possible to use postural anchoring on an object—a weapon (sword, buckler), a piece of furniture (that table that is placed for your forward roll), even another person (think unarmed combat or a domestic quarrel). What is required is increasing the level of effort in your grasp of the object, putting the greatest effort in the areas of the latissimus dorsi, the biceps, triceps, deltoids and pectoralis minor. Regardless of the amount of effort used in the anchoring, the effort needs to be isolated to the target areas. You must ALWAYS be able to breathe in and out. Owing to the great amount of effort used in postural anchoring, it is possible to physically lock if you sustain this state for too long and continuously. This will hamper the physical movements required by your fight. Monitor your effort levels. If you rehearse well, your muscle memory will take over and anchoring will become part of the physical sequence of your fight. Always remember that it is best if the need for the scream or shout comes organically and you use technique to safeguard your voice as part of the rehearsal, and later, performance process.

Different methods of support continue to be taught not only by voice practitioners, but also in many martial arts disciplines and are usually connected to the breath.

The third essential is a well-lubricated instrument. For extreme vocal use it is essential for the mucous membranes that surround your vocal folds to be kept moist—you can do this by using water, gum, or throat sweets. When all else fails, bite your cheeks or tongue and saliva will usually appear. One of the best treats you can give your voice is a good steam.

Finally, a reminder that the impulse for the sound/line/scream should be organic—if the impulse for sound is supported by the same breath that is also the impulse for movement, the chances improve that you will have a free, unconstricted sound.

As much as you may enjoy using your voice during your fight, the weapons themselves create sound and much of the dramatic element of the fight comes from the sound (or silence) of the weapons to create tension.

Although a striking degree of vocal athleticism and flair both contribute to believable vocal violence on stage, rehearsal of technique makes it secure and safe.

Remember, your voice is also a weapon. Fight well.

Acknowledgements
Jo Estill, Karen Ryker, Elizabeth Wiley, Rocco Dal Vera and Steve Wilsher, the Welsh Dragon.

Essay by *Elizabeth Wiley, Marth Munro and Allan Munro*

Orchestrating the Music of a Fight

Elizabeth Wiley is the Head of Acting at the College of William & Mary in Williamsburg, Virginia where she teaches acting and voice. Liz has worked professionally for fifteen years as an actor, voice specialist, and director, often in collaboration with her husband, director/ fight choreographer David "Pops" Doersch. Liz has taught Voice in Violence at stage combat workshops in the U.S., Canada, the U.K., Sweden and Estonia. She is the Voice Liaison for the International Order of the Sword and Pen, and serves on its Artistic Advisory Committee. She has also taught Voice and Speech in the MFA and BFA programs at the University of Mississippi.

Marth Munro (Associate editor) has a Masters in theatre voice projection, is a CMA (LIMS/New York) and a Certified Lessac Teacher. Currently she is in the advanced stages towards completion of a Ph.D. investigating Lessac's Tonal NRG and Lino's Actor's formant in female voices. She teaches at the Drama Department, Pretoria University and the Opera Department, Pretoria Technikon, South Africa. She is involved in an interdisciplinary research project about computer aided voice training. Munro works with actors, singers and musicians on optimal body and body/voice integration. She is the Chair of SAPVAME (South African Performers Voice and Movement Educators), she directs for musical theatre and does voice and movement coaching.

Allan Munro has an Honours Degree and a Post-Graduate teaching diploma from Natal University, Pietermaritzburg, and an MA and Ph.D. from The Ohio State University. The thrust of his doctoral work was on ambiguity and deception in resistance theatre. Allan has also presented numerous papers at national and international conferences, and has written a number of plays that have been produced. He has also won a number of teaching awards. Allan is currently Chair of the Drama Department at Pretoria University, South Africa.

(Liz Wiley is a well-known voice coach in the United States specializing in working as a voice coach alongside fight directors. Speaking directly from this practical framework Liz shares with the Munros very important guidelines to succeed in "orchestrating the music of the fight.")

Much of the believability of a fight sequence revolves around the auditory elements of the fight. The very sound of weapons clashing, knaps, footfalls, the breath and the voices of the people involved in the action guide the audience to follow and enhance the visual story, to understand the "impact of a blow," to accept the fight as real and believable. Through the use of these auditory elements, the audience is lead to accept the "illusion of reality." The auditory elements thus have to be planned and orchestrated in a way that will support and enhance the "believability" of the performance. Focussing on the vocal orchestration, the process should be a collaborative effort amongst director, actor, fight choreographer and vocal coach. For the actor-combatant this will mean that the character's inner life must be fully embodied vocally. For the director and/or voice coach, this means, "composing a piece of music," so to speak, using the possible sounds of violence for each specific fight sequence designed and created by the fight director. For the fight director this will entail choreographing fights that will allow theatrical vocal embodiment as an enhancement of the believability.

From an acting point of view, the fight sequencing is always considered something that must be rehearsed technically. This is so, but for the purposes of authenticity, and the development of the psychophysical whole of the character, it is imperative that the planning of all three elements (voice, character, and choreography) occurs simultaneously. Sequentially, as Stanislavski suggests, the actor moves from preparing his/her own body for the task of acting, then moves into the realms of honing skills for character development, and finally into the specifics of a particular role, in a particular cast, with a particular artistic crew. It is in this spirit that the following is offered:

It is the responsibility of each actor-combatant to realise that voice for violence can only happen when there is optimal body/voice integration and where the voice (and the body) usage is healthy, flexible and free. Inevitably this should occur during the actor's work on him/herself as an actor, during the training years. The interrelationship between the body and voice as an integrated communication tool cannot be overstressed.

Whilst learning a fight, it is advisable to consider and rehearse the fighting, the acting and vocal requirements simultaneously. Because the actor draws on inner intentions, motivations, cause and effect analyzes, and the like to develop a logical and then theatrical chain of events, and then presents this chain physically, vocally and dynamically, it is imperative that the body-voice-mind holistic approach be considered. Furthermore, the "imposition" of one aspect of the triad onto the others, undermines the organic nature of the process, and disturbs the theatrical and communicative whole that the actor wishes to present. Finally, this imposition also leads to changes in focus during preparation, which may lead to safety concerns being compromised. (The actor who has learned the fight sequence, and then is allowed to go at it "hammer and tongues" because the breath dynamics have been added or "summoned up" is a case in point in this regard.)

It may seem redundant or feel inauthentic to the actors to use vocalization when rehearsing a fight in slow motion, but the slow motion effect allows for the development of the logical sequencing of the fight, the motivations, the action and the accompanying vocalization.

The cornerstone of acting is action and reaction. Fundamentally, the orchestration of the vocal sounds therefore must be drawn from the two clusters of sounds that would be associated with action: attacking, advancing, intimidating and the like, on the one hand, and reacting, on the other. This latter would include sounds that are associated with preparation, defense, retreating, wounding, pain, dying, and the like. Two important points need to be made here. In the first place, any action has a stimulus, and a sequence, and this should be understood and prepared (in general, and in the specifics of the moment). Coupled with this is the determining of the intensity of the action. Secondly, these sequences (and this intensity) have physiological manifestations, which have to be understood so that they can be theatricalised. By this is meant that the actor needs to find the balance/harmony between inner experience, and safety of the physical (and emotional) apparatus, namely the body and the voice.

It is important to realise that the vocalization of the fight will consist inevitably of words and sounds, or, alternatively, but not directly, voluntary and involuntary sounds. Actors in their training regularly learn to accommodate voluntary sounds (i.e. words). The difficulty and danger lie primarily in the involuntary sounds that might accompany the fight—grunts, groans, screams, sounds of effort, surprise, fear, and so on. It is these potentially harmful moments that need careful attention by the actor and the vocal coach, to determine the optimal way that these types of sounds/effects can be produced. The sequence of preparation should run from identifying the sound required, to analyzing the process "in nature" of making the sound, to finding the theatrical and safe alternative.

Inevitably the purpose of a fight is to subdue or to inflict pain. This implies that fighting will lead to injury. The nature of such an injury must be theatricalised. The effect on the vocalization of the moment of injury and its aftermath must therefore be carefully considered and planned. Two key points need to be made here. In the first place the nature of the injury manifested in the body will have a direct impact on the vocal quality and this needs to be determined. A blow to the solar plexus might prevent the character from launching into an opera aria, for example! Alternatively, an arm slashed by a sword might not. What is important is that the effect that the physiological impact that the injury will have to the body, in all its manifestations, need to be considered and then theatricalised. Secondly, the vocalising of the recovery (should there be any) from the injury needs to be sequenced physiologically and theatricalised. This will impact directly on the vocal selections made. The organic centre for the explorations around this issue should be the breath and the breathing mechanism. It is important to consider in this work the urgency of pain, and in doing so, to examine and carefully balance verisimilitude against theatrical clarity and the dramatic arc. One must be clear without allowing the violence to become cavalierly devoid of consequence, and conversely, the vocal coach must help the actor to embrace the "virtuality" of the injury without losing the necessary textual content given by the playwright.

One of the cornerstones of good acting is the attention to detail. This is even more so in fight sequences that demand accuracy, safety, and high elements of theatricality. Concomitant to this, inevitably, is the detail that goes into the preparation for the vocal orchestration. The stress here is upon the logical/organic development of the fight and vocal sequence both in terms of the real and the theatrical. The inner life of the play determines the rhythms of the production, and these rhythms are to be reflected in the rhythms and orchestration of the vocal qualities that lead into the fight and the consequences of the fight and the sequences that follow. It is useful, therefore, to "listen to" the sound sequences as they are produced, without necessarily watching the action and the sounds that go with it. This "distancing mechanism" allows for the perceptions of the orchestral effect to be gauged.

It is useful to think in musical terms implied by the use of the word "orchestration" when defining elements involved in arranging the music of the fight. Developing a rhythmic element, a melody and counter-melody, rests, fermatas, crescendos and sforzandos, sustained chords and the like, assist in developing a vocabulary for the voice coach to parallel the fight choreographer. Furthermore, these terms allow the actor to develop an understanding and appreciation of the rhythm and duration of sounds, variety in pitch, volume, and tonal quality. Thus one has three interwoven strands in place: the logical sequencing and inner intention of the action, the theatricality of the fight sequence, and the orchestral dimension of the sound sequences.

Period style and attendant weapon style have a direct bearing on the vocal orchestration. An actor needs to be vocally prepared for the demands of the weapons he/she will have to wield, simply because the weapon will throw the body/voice integration out of kilter. The two-handed broadsword, for example, will "close" the chest and thus hamper the breathing apparatus. Couple this with the weight of the sword, and the necessity for exertion and recuperation needs to be built into the vocalization (and fight) decisions. This consideration becomes more complex as one encounters various period movement (and costume) styles. These considerations of effort, weight, physical and costume inhibitions and restraints, and the vocal demands that text style differences demand, makes it imperative that early planning for the fight sequences takes place.

Aural considerations need also to be extended into other dimensions. Vocal similarities (in terms of pitch, range, timbre and rhythm) between two or more combatants needs to be attended to and orchestrated to resonate with the inner life of the play and the director's vision. Furthermore, sounds other than vocalised sounds need to be considered, such as: recorded and live sound effects, moments of silence and pivotal action or plot moments that need to be enhanced by sound or undergirded by signifying mechanisms.

Coaching massive battle sequences is a huge challenge for the vocal coach, given the recommendations made above. Without vocal orchestration, whatever clarity there may be in the choreographic composition of the battle will be lost in the resulting cacophonic jumble as each character responds to his or her own circumstances in the battle. The vocal coach has to make vital choices in this regard. Options open to the coach include stylizing the sound, producing symbolic sound structures to represent sides in the battle, unifying sounds, or orchestrating tempo, pitch or volume intensities with the ebb and flow of the battle. The key deciding factors should cluster around clarity, the inner intent of the play, the style of the period and production, the flow of the battle, and the vision of the director. It is fundamentally important in all of this for each actor to be aware of the physical and vocal environment, as well as the theatrical focus at the various moments in which he or she is operating in the battle sequence.

Ultimately, it is the infinite variations of animate and inanimate sounds, the finely-tuned interplay of thump, grunt and pause, the harmonies of triumph and despair, the majestic ebb and flow of human vocal patterning, textual interaction and physical presence of actors, caught in the moment of conflict and tension, that makes theatrical violence the vibrant art that it is. In searching for "honesty" in stage violence, ultimately, the actor must remember that his or her entire being is the instrument that must be played. As the actor carefully constructs his/her movements through the choreography, and meticulously develops motivations and inspirations through the acting process, attention must also be paid to effective vocal communication. With mindful and detailed vocal orchestration, a combat sequence can transcend the technical, in which it is so often mired, and carefully play upon the emotional chords of the audience, while protecting the vocal instrument of the actor.

Peer Reviewed Article by *Michelle Ladd*

"Neglected and "Abused": Domestic Violence

Michelle Ladd: performer and choreographer of acting, dance, and stage combat for over 10 years, performed and taught stage combat and movement in North America, Britain, Scandinavia, Europe and Asia; stunt performer for TV and film, guest artist for dance companies like Demetrius Klein Dance Co.; recently featured in Korea's *Theatre* magazine; Certified Teacher—Society of American Fight Directors, stunt performer—United Stuntmen's Association and Dueling Arts International, and Secretary for International Order of the Sword and Pen; MFA—Acting, University of Alabama; maintains a commitment to higher education by teaching stage combat and dance to colleges, universities, and conservatories.

Although typically treated as extreme physical violence in most theatrical productions, domestic violence (hereafter DV) has a much darker, ominous emotional aspect. The perpetrator's ability to manipulate and control a victim's mind often causes more stress and pain than physical abuse. Tapping into this mental energy can be more horrifying to an audience than is visible abuse. Contemporary theatre tends to present the stereotype of an animalistic man delivering heavy-handed gratuitous physical violence against a defenseless, naive, hysterical woman. This tendency to play primarily the physical drama may have two effects: it strays from the reality of DV situations, which involves more emotional control rather than control by sheer force; and it gives the violence a staged look which often borders on a sexy, sado-masochistic physical experience. Shakespeare wrote that the purpose of acting is "to hold, as 'twere, the mirror up to nature" (*Hamlet* III, II). If this is the case, as a mirror of society it is irresponsible for the theatre community to neglect the complicated and disturbing psychology of batterers and victims when representing DV on stage and screen.

The U.S. legal system recognizes domestic violence as a pattern of behavior(s) that is psychologically damaging, and includes any kind of physical, psychological, emotional, and/or sexual abuse within a family or dating relationship (King Co. 1). It is blind to race, nationality, religion, age, and socioeconomic status. Although female battering is the most common type of reported DV, it also includes spouse, child, sibling, and elderly abuse. Batterers do not insult, threaten, or attack people they love because of wrong-doing by the victim or because of drug or alcohol abuse—two common misconceptions. Battering is a socially learned behavior which is used to establish and maintain control over others (King Co. 16).

Domestic violence statistics in the United States are terrible, especially towards women. The American Medical Association reported in 1979 that a woman is beaten every nine seconds by an intimate partner in the U.S. (DVIP 3). Those statistics have not changed much. FBI reports from 1998 indicate that 2,000-4,000 women are killed each year in the U.S. as a result of DV (King Co. 8). Nashville, Tennessee's Channel 2 News reported in December, 1999, that one of four women suffer from domestic abuse, and data collected by the National Crime Survey shows that women are the victims of violent crime committed by family members at a rate three times that of men (Claus, 1984). In fact, violence will occur at least once in two-thirds of all marriages (Roy, 1982), and approximately 95% of those victims will be women (Bureau of Justice Statistics, Oct. 1983). Unfortunately, few statistics reflect incidences of male battering, which does occur but is rarely reported, primarily due to this country's sex-role stereotypes and the lack of male victims' sustained DV injuries requiring medical treatment. Regardless of victim gender, domestic violence is a growing problem in society and must be responsibly addressed through theatre.[1]

Generally, when a script calls for violence, a fight director is called to choreograph those scenes to effectively create the illusion of violence while ensuring actor safety. At this point, the fight director is not concerned with the psychological factors that create a batterer, although numerous studies have identified those characteristics. By the time the violent scene reaches the fight director, his/her immediate concern is how the characters have moved

1. Due to the high statistics presented for female battering and for clarity's sake, although male battering is recognized and taken seriously, batterers will be addressed in the masculine gender and victims in the feminine for the remainder of this paper.

Poetry by *Jan Gist*

Jan Gist studied with Jerry Blunt at L.A.C.C.,
Edith Skinner and Bob Parks at Carnegie
Mellon U. (BFA '74), and received her MFA from
Wayne State's Hilberry Rep. Co., ('76). She's
been the Resident Voice, Speech, and Dialect
Coach at Alabama Shakespeare Festival for 9
years and 130 plays. She's also coached
numerous productions at Utah and Oregon
Shakespeare Festivals, The Shakespeare
Theatre of DC, Arena Stage, Milwaukee Rep.,
among others. She taught at CSULB for 9 years
prior to joining ASF and its MFA faculty. She
also consults with businesses and other theatres. She was an originating member of
VASTA and is delighted to be a part of its journal.

I contribute these poems as a "first
person's" account of the "inside" of
the experience of violence in true life.
I hope they serve as "primary source
material". I encourage all stage fight
directors, vocal coaches and actors to
consider their job to be two-fold.
First: Research the real/surreal experience of real people in the hyper-reality
of violence. Real life violence includes
shock, trauma, betrayal, shame, over-
whelm, secret-keeping, and terror.
Real life violence is a hell of not
knowing how much damage you will
receive, fend off, or inflict. Real life
violence is a ripping apart of civility
and you do not know if you will live
through it or if you can live with
yourself afterwards. Second: Depict
the play's story, style, era, and rhythm,
using reality with respect, to move the
audience into sensitivity and not just
sensation, enlightenment and not just
entertainment, question and not just
acceptance, and catharsis and not just
applause.

Thank you.

BATTERED.   SOUNDS.

I remember clearly
the WHACK sound
as my skull hit and bounced off
the wooden door
he had punched me up against,
and the muffled SNAP sound
as my rib broke when he threw me
into the edged corner of the bar,
then the CLINK of bottles
rattling their response to my fall,
and the sound of THUD inside my ears
as the shot glass he threw
landed BANG on my cheek bone,
and the sound of THUMP
as his fist bruised my thigh
or his kick shaped my back,
and the sound of the CRACK
of my nose being broken
(not like an egg shell's CLICK,
more like the SMASH of glass inside the cloth
the bridegroom steps on at the wedding).
I remember the sound of my voice,
of my whimpering and pleading and silence,
loud loud silence
as my heart pounded blood noises
through my nerve endings
in expectation of the next punch.

Noise is muffled when being beaten up.
Flesh covers it over,
cooperating in the keeping of secrets.

into this volatile situation and how their bodies handle this physical and emotional stress. Usually the director has already worked with the cast and has blocked out any action prior to the DV scene. The technical limitations of the playing space have been considered, and the director has indicated to the fight director and vocal coach what sort of image should be represented during the staged violence. Voice and movement personnel should work together, when possible, to create a dramatically effective violent scenario that does not actually harm the actors' voices or bodies. At this point in the process it is valuable for them to consider the three recognizable phases of DV often referred to as the Cycle Theory which was originally recognized and named in 1979 by Lenore Walker (Walker 95).

Phase I - **Tension Building**: This generally involves name calling, verbal abuse, cruel intentional behaviors, and/or minor physical abuse. The victim attempts to placate the batterer, but victim withdrawal tends to be misinterpreted by the batterer who becomes more controlling and possessive.

Phase II - **Battering Incident**; A barrage of verbal and physical aggression is released on the victim. This is an explosive, acute, and unpredictable phase. When the abuse stops, after a duration of anywhere from a few minutes to several hours, the desired reduction in tension (by both parties) is created. The lesson learned is that violence has worked to ease tension.

Phase III - **Calming and Reconciliation**; The batterer is contrite and apologetic. He shows remorse, tries to help the victim, and showers the victim with gifts and promises. Both believe the batterer's sincere apologies, which provides positive reinforcement for the couple to stay together and excuse the violent act.

As the cycle repeats itself, Phase I occurs much more, and Phase III begins to occur much less. The violence increases and, unless stopped, generally leads to abuse with "weapons." Recognizing and playing these phases within a script can build tension, heighten both the drama and the tragedy of the characters' situation, and aid through-line and cohesive plot development. Playwrights naturally build in at least some elements of the Cycle Theory in their scripts. For example, rarely does a character simply erupt into violence. There is usually a build up of frustration or tension for at least a page or two of dialogue (Phase I) and perhaps an "apology" scene after the violent incident (Phase III). It is the responsibility of the director to build those moments of tension into the scenes prior to the physical "violence" and pay attention to whether or not Phase III behavior is implied afterward. A vocal coach can be of tremendous help during the rehearsal process by providing actors with vocal choices that express the plot's building tension without damaging the actors' vocal folds. It is the responsibility of the fight director to choreograph the plot's escalating tension and violence, yet maintain absolute physical safety for the actors. Again, the vocal coach may offer insight into how to portray the hysteria experienced by victim and batterer while maintaining good breath support and minimizing damage to the larynx by proper use of the diaphragm and relaxing the throat and neck.

To create more thorough character development the director and performer can use recognized tactics employed by batterers. These tactics by nature are controlling, like using coercion and threats, intimidation and blame, children as exploitation, and traditional sex-role privilege (i.e., male as despot);

BATTERED.   LOOKING BACK.

I almost died
I nearly almost died
in his hands
in his rage.

One more twist of my spine in his hands
and I'd be gone
and he would have twisted
if he felt me struggle
so I melted into his twist
and I dropped the life out of me
dropped the fight out of me
and so I won my life back
by default
because he lost interest
when the struggle stopped.

I almost died
I nearly almost died
of shame, of terror,
of shame that I was terrified
by him,
this man who swore he was protecting me
during the very moment his sharp elbow
cut off my breath
in a swift butt to my gut.

I almost died
I nearly almost died
trying to keep up with him,
his smokes his drinks his pills his highs his demands his threats
and I lost myself so far lost
I couldn't tell if I had or had only almost died.

And now in dreams
still twenty years past then
I continue to almost die
continue to fight and drop and fear and run away and never quite
get away.

I didn't die, I don't die.
But still in dreams I almost nearly die
almost every night.

breaking or striking objects; and employing force during arguments. More subtle tactics are also used to get a desired response: unrealistic expectations, isolation of victim from family and friends, "joking" verbal abuse, "playful" use of force during sex, and exertion of financial control (King Co., pg. 3). Victims often state that the batterer has a dual personality: that no one would ever believe he could be so abusive and violent some moments after being so tender and loving at other times (Walker, pg. 23). The batterer has a different idea of himself. He feels he has a right to control his partner's actions, and can even feel as if he is the victim (Walker, 1999 "DV in the New Millennium" Seminar). Any good actor will use this mindset and find a way to empathize with his character despite his through line of actions (much like the victim tends to rationalize and justify her attacker's behavior). An actor's body and voice should express this dichotomy between periods of calm (regular breathing, normal speech patterns, and a relaxed physical state) and periods of tension (irregular breathing, broken speech patterns, changes in volume and pitch, and a tense physical state).

Because battering is a *pattern* of behavior, it is ongoing and tends to get worse and more frequent with time. Victims develop coping and survival strategies to avoid more harm and injuries. They repress, minimize, and deny violence or rationalize it by concentrating on why it occurred. When they do seek help, they make self-blaming statements (as if their behavior caused the abusive incident) and make excuses for the violence they have been through. Interestingly enough, many battered women are intelligent, well-educated, competent people who hold responsible jobs; and they demonstrate great resiliency and inner strength. These women find other ways to control their lives to make up for the lack of control in their home life (Walker 10). Unfortunately, the violence often escalates and gets much worse when the victim finally decides to leave her partner. When a victim chooses to defend herself, it is almost always in self-defense with *defensive* actions during the most violent incidents (phase I) or with more *offensive* actions during the calm periods (phase III). The small percentage of women who resort to homicide do so after suffering frequent and brutal abuse (Maury Co., 1991 "Fact Sheet").

Once recognized as the aforesaid pattern of behavior, a decision must be made based on the given circumstances of the play regarding whether or not the violence has previously occurred or is an initial incident. If violence is used for the first time between the characters, it tends to be less brutal and the characters react (both batterer and victim) with more shock and apology after the fact. For example, initial incidents tend to involve more pushing, shoving, slapping, hitting, spanking, wrestling, and/or twisting arms. If the physical extends into sexual abuse it is marked by jealous behavior, crude sex talk, unwanted touching, and/or forced intercourse and pornography. Hence, there is often increasing shame and guilt regarding sex with batterers as the cycle repeats itself. With time, as the batterer feels less and less in control, he exerts more force. The use of physical control escalates to punching and throwing the victim bodily or hitting her with an object. More serious instances include attempts to burn the partner, drown her, or hurt her with a knife or a gun. As the cycle escalates to this kind of extreme force, the characters may display more anxiety over when and how the impending violence may manifest itself and less shock or "making up" as the incidences become

Poetry by *Jan Gist*

HOPE AND DREAD

Hope and Dread, twin sisters of us wounded ones,
wind their snaky reptilian slithers
through my ribs and lungs and
that ever pumping engine heart pulsing
their rhythms of our all time favorite tango
woulda-coulda-shoulda-mighta-couldn'ta-won't,
a lacy snaky braided motion
tracing slime and echoing the almost silent
barely perceived flickering flutter
of their reptilian black forked tongues.

Samba on, girls,
your duet of never ceasing always teasing
maybe-mights   if-onlys
sure keep us awake, us wounded ones,
sure keep us busy flinching
cowering begging hiding
(and our all time favorite) waiting
and waiting and waiting and

WITNESS

They thought they were alone
in the alley
in the dark
only moonlight and my apartment window
lighting up their talk.

I thought I was alone
in my room
in the dark
only lamplight and my thoughts
lighting up my brains.

He yelled and threw things till she cried
in the alley
in the dark
and then he leaned in and sweet-talked her
selling her on how she'd been wrong
again.
If she'd only stop.
If she'd only, then he wouldn't have to.
Don't you see babe...
All you have to...
God I love you...
If you'd just...

more frequent. To accurately tell the story, the director, fight director, and vocal coach should pay careful attention to where the violence falls within the time line of aggressive acts in the history of these characters.

Despite the physical trauma, psychological degradation and humiliation are reportedly the most painful abuse sustained (Seattle Forensic Institute, 1999). This fact is key to create a successful DV scene on the stage. Physically and vocally this sustained assault on the psyche can be expressed by withdrawn behavior and communication, increased tension and strain in the body and voice, and an inability to relax and open up to other people. Physical pain, once experienced, can be dealt with and its cost can be measured; but emotional abuse (especially insults, assaults on self-esteem, isolation, stalking, and threats to hurt loved ones) delves into "what might happen," triggering fear of the unknown. One has only to examine the effect of Hitchcock's films to see what an effective tool an audience's imagination can be for a director.

Some fight directors strive for "even-handed" domestic-combat scenarios where both partners get in their fair share of slaps, punches, hair pulls, and chokes. But mutual combat occurs *very* rarely and usually occurs when the victim strikes back in self-defense. It is important to consider this major difference between retaliatory violence against an unknown assailant and violence against someone familiar to the victim. When a stranger attacks, the victim is likely to respond loudly to attract attention and solicit help. However, a DV victim rarely wants to call outside attention to the situation. Usually, rather than cry or scream for assistance, the victim becomes mute, only uttering small non-verbals in reaction to specific attacks. They do not want their familiar assailant to be maimed or killed; they have an emotional commitment to the batterer's well-being and simply want him to stop the abuse (Walker 30, 41). Physical defense against further DV crimes typically involves biting, kicking, scratching, shoving, or pushing back. These are reciprocal pain control techniques. These physicalities would most likely be supported vocally by effort sounds: grunts, strong breath exhalations, and guttural noises as the reciprocal pain techniques are delivered. Vocals for the batterer tend to be more aggressive. They are louder, more potent, and verbally commanding than the victim, as they try to establish and maintain their control over the situation. Domestic violence is NOT mutual combat. It is one person dominating and controlling the other, therefore the vocal qualities should match the intentions of both victim and batterer.

With this information, directors and performers have more tools to effectively represent DV situations to an audience. Of course, drama has the all-important element of "willing suspension of disbelief," but that should not be an excuse to exaggerate the action or to treat this issue as something that only happens to characters in a play or movie. The reality is that it does happen and has happened to many people. Playwrights writing about family violence, such as Eugene O'Neill and Tennessee Williams, more likely than not, speak from personal experience. If the tenor of the playwright's writing and production style is realistic, and if these incidents were important enough for the playwright to expose them publicly in furthering his tragic plots, then the emotional violence should be treated with the seriousness and integrity with which it was intended when written. This is not to say that all scenes of DV should be portrayed with absolute realism, but I believe that fight directors

HOWLING

How many almost empty houses
are filled with the howling of women?

Surrounded in the safety of silence
embraced by the carefully chosen colors
and simmering boiling smells
and watered plants
and curtained light,
how many women howl
the losses of the world
the mysteries of the soul
the memory of chaos
the passing by of promise?

How many almost empty houses
house in with echoing walls
the howling women?

And is it then the penetrating emanating
howling
that then shimmers the outside air
vibrating to the skies
that turns the earth
and causes to circle
the sun and moon and stars
so life goes on
and on and on and on?

and vocal coaches do themselves a great service by investigating and respecting the intentions of the playwright. To what degree and in what manner does the author want these scenes of emotional and physical abuse portrayed—comic, stereotypical, or tragically honest? The director makes the ultimate choice of staying true to those intentions or not, but they should be reviewed.

William Mastrosimone's play *Extremities* and the typical aggressive physical treatment of its violent material tends to fit the aforementioned stereotype of Neanderthal vs. Pearl White. Despite Raul's very violent control tactics and attempted rape, our heroine, Marjorie, is able to fight back against this "crime of passion" by outsmarting her assailant and using her own brand of violent maneuvers to save herself, including spraying him in the face with wasp spray. This play has a great deal of action, excitement, and entertainment value. But a more honest example of domestic violence that has true potential to strike a chord with audience members on a more intimate level is Tennessee Williams' *A Streetcar Named Desire*. An analysis of the characters in this play shows an obvious DV situation: emotionally, psychologically, physically, and sexually. Without the emotional and psychological abuse and control Stanley heaps upon Stella and Blanche, the play ceases to be a tragedy and is reduced to a soap opera about passion and personal disagreements. The question of whether Stella will leave Stanley in the final moments of the play, and her clear decision to stay with him, has no impact unless Stanley's isolation tactics, emotional and physical control, and subsequent remorse and apologies are also present (Williams, Act I, Scene III). These are classic batterer patterns of behavior. Stella, as the immediate victim, exhibits learned helplessness and other coping mechanisms including denial, self-blame, and justification of Stanley's behavior (Williams, Act I, Scene IV). Although Stella is a more pure example of "DV victim" than her sister, Blanche's downfall should not be viewed as a problem she entirely brings upon herself. Her slide into insanity as a result of Mitch's rejection and Stanley's rape in Act III makes more sense psychologically when her already fragile and abused psyche is seen as being further victimized by Mitch and Stanley's needs to exert emotional and/or physical control over her for their personal ego needs. Blanche's loss of control is evident in the written language in the latter acts of the play. Her lines contain punctuation that indicates pauses and uncertainty in speech, and she expresses herself by alternating between vagueness and rushed statements seeking escape from her current situation. Contrast this frailty and confused mental state with the calm, comforting language she slips into when escorted out of her sister's house by the doctor as she is taken to the mental hospital. In light of the recent research on DV, there is no excuse for not using the available scientific knowledge and the clues presented by the playwright regarding the effect of abuse on the characters to create intense realism in this and other domestic violence plays.

Unfortunately, actors, along with directors, have been unwittingly trained to neglect the psychological reality and intricacies of DV and instead think in terms of the stereotype. This is no fault of their training, but is more likely due to a lack (until recently) of thorough, accessible data based on facts rather than myths regarding DV. Therefore, if a director makes a choice to produce a DV scene "realistically" without understanding the underlying control issues, the above-mentioned inadvertent stereotyping makes the violence seem gratuitous as opposed to furthering the plot. Once the control issues

Poetry by *Jan Gist*

MY WEAVING

My weaving of words
of sounds of words
my weaving and stringing
of bead bauble words
on lines and threads and strings,
is a singing of soul
of ache of change
of past of prayer
of battered hope
despair of hope
of wordless terror
that smashes hope
but my weaving and singing go on,
and my weaving of words
the weaving itself
of words and sounds
of bright bauble beads
of words on strings
of sounds of words
on lines and threads
is a singing of hope reborn.

And Their smashing and Their terror
and Their stealing of my soul
is Their failure of Their evil
for They never got control

of my weaving of words and sounds.

are understood by a director, he/she can more easily identify the elements of the Cycle Theory as they are woven within the circumstances of the play. The physical violence must be tied to intricate, honest emotional build-up and it must look messy and not choreographed to appear natural. Many schools of acting training emphasize realism, private moments, emotional honesty, and research of period styles. Yet, it is my opinion that DV is still allowed to be played melodramatically. Is delving into the honesty of the situation too close to home? It is so prevalent in today's world that it should be…. True, DV can be difficult material to explore mentally and commit to vocally and physically as a performer. But, when DV is misrepresented to an audience, the public's misconception of this social problem could remain. However, once the more subtle characteristics of DV are displayed to the public, they are better able to identify DV "next door" and this common social problem can be dealt with more openly. Many of those subtleties can be indicated by the vocal coach and expressed by the performer through small vocal changes: uncomfortable non-verbal expressions, un-nerving changes in breath patterns, small vocal expressions of surprise and suppressed fear, brief commanding vocals by the aggressor, and moments of breath-holding silence.

As an artistic entity, theatre professionals by trade hold a mirror to society by recreating on stage what they witness in life. In the case of combat professionals, violence inspired by real-life is promoted in their work. Therefore, I feel they have an unwritten social obligation to educate society to recognize violence in daily life so that action may be taken to help others in emotionally and physically detrimental situations. The work of the vocal coach alongside the director and fight director is very important in recreating emotionally compromising scenes to the public. National studies show that the most common reason given for not reporting the violence is the belief that DV crimes are a private or personal matter. But, once DV is recognized by public citizens (and victims), and reported to law enforcement, action can be taken which significantly reduces the number and degree of violent incidents. Through the choices the fight director and vocal coach help actors make during representation of DV, theatre can show a very sincere reflection of this social problem to an audience. One role of theatre, therefore, is to address the issue of DV and aid the community in early recognition and intervention before domestic violence lives up to its potential and becomes a lethal problem. 🐞

Works Cited

Claus, P.A., and Rand, M.R. *Family Violence.* U.S. Department of Justice Bureau of Justice Statistics Special Report. Office of Justice Programs, April 1984.

Domestic Violence Intervention Program. *Peacing It Together... General Education Packet: Domestic Violence.* Iowa City, NY: Doubleday, 1982.

Mastrosimone, William. *Extremities.* Garden City, NY: Doubleday, 1982.

Maury County Mental Health Center. *Domestic Violence Fact Sheets.* Columbia, TN, 1991.

Metropolitan King County Council. *Domestic and Dating Violence.* Washington, July 1998.

National Training Project. *Duluth Domestic Abuse Intervention Project.* Duluth, MN.

"News 2." WKRN. Nashville, TN. December 1999.

Roberts, Albert R. *Battered Women and Their Families.* NY: Springer Publishing Co., 1984. Vol. 1 of *Series on Social Work.*

Roy, M., ed. *The Abusive Partner.* NY: Van Nostrand Reinhold Co., 1982.

Seattle Forensic Institute. *Domestic Violence in the New Millennium.* Seattle, WA, September 1999.

Shakespeare, William. *The Riverside Shakespeare.* Ed. G. Blakemore Evans. Boston: Houghton Mifflin Co., 1974.

U.S. Department of Justice. Bureau of Justice Statistics, Office of Justice Programs. *Report to the Nation on Crime and Justice: The Data.* Washington, D.C., October 1983.

Walker, Lenore E. *The Battered Woman Syndrome.* NY: Springer Publishing Co., 1984. Vol. 6 of Springer Series: Focus on Women.

Williams, Tennessee. *A Streetcar Named Desire.* NY: Dramatists Play Service, 1981.

The Voice in Heightened Affective States

Rocco Dal Vera, (editor) co-author with Robert Barton of *Voice: Onstage and Off*; professor, University of Cincinnati; founding editor of *Voice and Speech Review* for Voice and Speech Trainers Association; resident vocal coach, Associate Artist, Cincinnati Shakespeare Festival; former head, BFA Professional Actor and Musical Theatre Training Programs, Wright State University; taught at National Theatre Conservatory, Willamette University, United States International University and former chair of Voice and Speech Department at The American Academy of Dramatic Arts; voice and speech coach at numerous theatres including Oregon Shakespeare Festival, Denver Center for the Performing Arts, Dorothy Chandler Pavilion, Indiana Repertory Theatre, and Los Angeles Theatre Center.

What psychological diagnostic techniques and research on the vocal expression of human emotion can teach us about vocal behavior under emotional stress, and how that information can be applied to actor training and performance.

Not too long ago I got a call from a well-known director who needed some assistance.

"We're doing ____, and the actress playing ____ just isn't able to deliver during the rape scene."

"What is it you're looking for?"

"Well, I want her to scream throughout the whole thing. She's a good actress, but she's just not coming up with the stuff. She's being really tentative. Can you help?"

Yes, I thought they did indeed need some help.

My first reaction when I hear a director say he wants an actress to scream all the way through a long scene is that he must be generalizing. No one really wants to put an audience through that. When I arrive I'll surely get a more detailed and layered set of instructions. As it turned out, I only got a two-minute meeting with the director, who assured me that I was wonderful and would certainly work miracles, then I was left in a room with the actress while he ran off to solve larger problems.

He obviously trusted me. Privately, I was surprised that he trusted me so completely. "Oh well," I thought, "a little insecurity at the start of a new job is normal." After my flash of self doubt passed, I adopted my customary mask of sagacity and got down to work.

The actress was wonderful. And smart. As we set about crafting the beats in the scene and finding emotional cues in the text, she peppered me with some quite insightful questions about how people actually behave in situations of extreme emotional stress. She was interested in really probing to the center of the character's experience, and realizing as truthful and realistic a scene as she could.

I thoroughly enjoyed the process, and felt that the outcome was just what the director wanted (what he really wanted, not just what he asked for). But, on the way home I began to have second thoughts about the quality of my work. I reviewed the questions the actress had asked me. If I were completely honest with myself, I would have to admit that I made up answers to her questions. I told her that a person in her character's circumstances was likely to breathe this way, and vocalize that way. She followed my suggestions, and put her faith in me because she thought that I knew what I was talking about.

In one sense, I did. I have a good theatrical instinct, and am experienced at coaching scenes like this. I know how to give the director and the audience their money's worth. I know how to protect the actor's voice, and to inject variety, discovery, and intensity into these scenes.

But I didn't really know how people behave vocally in situations of extreme emotional distress. As I drove home, I wondered if I was just an impostor.

Even later, after getting a lovely thank you note from the actress, and the director, and reading the good reviews (that praised this scene in particular), I still was troubled. I had a degree in acting, and another in voice and speech coaching for the theatre. In our classes we had studied extensively about the mechanics of the voice, and how to train actors for the stresses of performance, but there had been no coursework in how people behave vocally in states of extreme emotion. I had only my personal opinions and guesses about the subject.

So, I decided that it wasn't too late to correct my ignorance. I would do a little investigating, and see what I could learn from the field of psychotherapy, and from those who had done research into the vocal expression of human emotions.

I had some preconceptions and questions going into this investigation. I surmised that emotional feelings resulted in certain specific physiological reactions, which in turn would lead to certain vocal behaviors. If that were true, then the questions I was interested in were:
   1. What do behavioral researchers consider to be the categories, types or primary states of emotion?
   2. What is the physiological behavior associated with each of the primary emotions?
   3. What happens to the voice when these physiological reactions occur?
   4. Can I find an inventory of vocal behaviors that are congruent to certain emotional states? Would such an inventory be useful in making character choices?
   5. Do performances sometimes fail to reflect a real inner state that compares accurately with actual experiences?
   6. What do actors do (as a result of the process of acting, and because of the theatrical event) that is different from a person in an actual state of intense emotion?
   7. Is it possible to take this information, and make some general recommendations for actor training and vocal coaching?

In order to put some limits on this paper, I decided to investigate research on the vocal characteristics of people in states of extreme emotion, and to draw from diagnostic techniques used in the discipline of psychotherapy.[1] Without pretending to be an expert in those fields,[2] I would like to share what I found with you.

Emotion from a Clinical Perspective
When one leaves the boundaries of one's profession and goes sniffing around another discipline, one of the first things that changes is the vocabulary. My use of the word *emotion* was inexact. *Affect* is the term used by those in the mental health professions to identify "behavior that expresses[3] a subjectively experienced feeling state (DSM-IV[4]).

The layperson might assume *affect* to be synonymous with *emotion*, but clinicians use this term to make an important distinction: "*affect* is responsive

1. The fields of anthropology, sociology and linguistics also have important contributions to make to these questions.

2. Credit here for setting me off in the right direction should go to Linda Brennan, who has the rare distinction of being a voice and speech specialist with an MFA in acting from Brandeis University and a degree in counseling from Antioch University. She is the head of the Voice and Speech Department at the American Academy of Dramatic Arts/West and has a clinical psychotherapy practice in the Los Angeles area.

3. The word "expresses" here relates to a key concept. Clinicians observe the expression or the affect of a patient to identify that person's inner state. In the literature, affect seems to be used to describe both the state itself and the observed expression of that state.

4. *Diagnostic Statistical Manual*, fourth edition. This is a searchable electronic database used by the mental health professions to standardize the terminology used in diagnosis and for references in billing and patient charts. Since a database was used, no page references are listed for citations from this source.

6. Also *aetiology*: the assigning of a cause.

7. Also *symptomotology*: the study of the symptoms of a disease, collectively.

8. Much of the research that is being done to codify and analyze the component parts of human emotion and the voice appears to have been conducted by scientists trying to find a way to make computer-simulated speech have a more human quality. Programmers could make the artificial voice intelligible, but it would sound non-human unless it had an emotional attribute as well. Developers of voice stress analysis machines have also contributed to the studies in this area (Murray and Arnott p. 1097). In time, actors may be able to learn a great deal about emotional vocal expression from research just now underway in this field.

to changing emotional states, whereas *mood* refers to a pervasive and sustained emotion [emphasis added]" (Ibid.). In this conceptualization, emotion is a broad term, which can be divided into two separate kinds of experience: long-lasting emotional states, termed moods, and short-lived or transitory emotional events, called affects.

This paper will focus on the voice in heightened affective states, rather than in moods. The rationale for this is that with few exceptions,[5] moods don't usually present the same degree of vocal challenge for the actor.

Typical affective states include happiness, anger, and sadness. *Heightened* affective states occur when a changing emotional condition has an unusual intensity. Examples of this might be when anger extends into rage, happiness into euphoria or hysteria, and sadness into lamentation or weeping (Ibid.).

It can be difficult to express an abstract concept like emotion in rigorous concrete terms, and much of the research literature reflects a frustration with that problem (Murray and Arnott, p. 1098). One of the guiding sources of this paper is the Diagnostic Statistical Manual, fourth edition (DSM-IV). This manual is used by psychotherapists to standardize the language and classification of mental health conditions.

The Emotional Content of Affective States

Even with the DSM-IV manual as a guide, it becomes clear that classification of emotions themselves is a different activity (and much more difficult) than identifying mental states and behaviors that contain many emotional components. For example, a psychotherapist may diagnose a person as having an "Impulse Control Disorder" (an objective diagnosis) with drives and/or temptations manifesting in aggressive bouts of anger, frustration and rage (a subjective description). The subjective nature of the descriptions of emotion is evident in "contradiction[s]… in the literature" (Murray and Arnott, p. 1103). One person's *hostility* is another's *irritation*.

Until recently, research seems to have been organized around understanding the cause of psychopathological affect for the purposes of treating specific disorders rather than investigating the elements constituting the particular emotional components of Affective Disorders. It was, for example, more important for a therapist to know that a patient was suffering from Post-Traumatic Stress Disorder, and the reasons for that condition, than to codify the specific tone of fear that the patient was experiencing in a panic state. Therapists focus on etiology[6] and symptomology[7] because the goal is to cure psychopathology. Codifying distinct emotional nuances is the focus of different professions—acting (and interestingly, computerized voice synthesis[8]).

It should be noted that in their reviews of the literature related to research on how human emotion is expressed vocally, both Brennan (p. 2), and Murray and Arnott (p. 1097) commented that the current research is fragmented and incomplete.

Nevertheless, it is possible to organize the existing research into workable categories for study. In their survey of the literature, Murray and Arnott, admitting that semantic difficulties created some apparent contradictions, resolved the discrepancies by creating a rough table of equivalencies (1103-6). In a broad sense, affective states may be arranged into the categories of Primary and Secondary emotions (see Table 1[9]). Secondary emotions are placed as divisions of the Primary emotion.[10] Though limiting, this categorization makes it easier to discuss emotional states with some context.

9. This table is derived primarily from Murray and Arnott (p. 1103-6) and reconciled with Bloch, et al. (p. 200-3).

10. These are the emotions most discussed in the research literature. One might observe an arbitrariness to the terms. A trip to the thesaurus could provide many more emotional terms, each with a subtle distinction, but these terms seem to be in the widest use by researchers in the field (Murray and Arnott, p. 1103-6).

	A.	B.	C.	D.	E.
PRIMARY EMOTIONS	anger	happiness joy humor euphoria	sadness	fear anxiety	disgust hatred contempt scorn
SECONDARY EMOTIONS	rage frustration boredom impatience	affection satisfaction tenderness eroticism[11] coquetry	grief sorrow	surprise astonishment fright	sarcasm irony complaint

Table 1. Organization of emotional states into Primary and Secondary classifications, derived from Murray and Arnott (p. 1103-6) and Bloch, et al. (p. 200-3)

I now had an answer to my first question: What do behavioral researchers consider to be the primary states of emotion? My next question was: What is the physiological behavior associated with each of the primary emotions?

11. Susanna Bloch, et al. (significant researchers in the area of acting and emotion) place eroticism and tenderness separately and in the category of primary emotions (p. 200-3).

Heightened Affective States and Psychophysiological Behavior

In the subject area of heightened affect, the research on *physiological* behavior is much more developed than the information available on *vocal* behavior. There are even a number of excellent acting methods that have a firm rooting in the research on human behavior under extreme emotional stress. One example of a specific method that employs behavioral science in a psychophysiological way is Alba Emoting (also called BOS method, or Effector Pattern Training). It was developed through research in neuroscience and psychology. Its fundamental premise (supported by considerable research) is that if a person adopts certain detailed patterns of breathing, posture, facial expression, and (sometimes) vocalization, then that person can enter into an emotional state easily and deeply. In the training, actors develop the skill to quickly enter and step out of strong primary emotions, and later to mix emotional states in complex ways.

In reading the material on Alba Emoting I realized that one of my first assumptions when beginning this journey was limiting as a model. Earlier, I had surmised that "emotional states resulted in certain specific physiological reactions, which in turn would lead to certain vocal behaviors." That ideation makes the equation:

affect → physiological reaction → vocal behavior.

An alternative model can be extrapolated from the Alba Emoting research. It is: states of heightened affect *are* physiological states, and vocal quality is an aspect of the affective state, not merely an output of the state. So, now the equation reads:

affect ↔ physiological reaction (vocal behavior).

Essentially, this model suggests that we know that we are feeling an emotion because we feel it in a specific way in our bodies, and hear it in our voices (Bloch, et al, p. 199). My earlier model might have described anger, for example as a feeling that made me tense certain muscles, and yell. The second model (described simplistically) suggests that the equation can operate in either direction, so tensing my muscles in a specific manner (and perhaps yelling) will make me feel angry.

The effector pattern approach to entering heightened affective states has several advantages for the actor. It is based on scientific observation, and so is likely to come closer to an individual's natural behavior than some other methods. Since actors learn to isolate, and tense or relax very specific groups of muscles in order to perform the effector pattern, they are more likely to respond to instruction about the need to keep the muscles related to voice and speech relaxed, and thus can be trained to have fewer tension related vocal problems. The training emphasizes the ability to remain objective while in a strong affective state, and to step cleanly and fully out of that emotion on command, so actors are less likely to have an "emotional hangover" or to form a neurotic attachment to the affective state. It also helps the actor to "eliminate undesirable 'cliches' by allowing the actor to present physiological parameters which are close to the genuine emotion" (Bloch, et al. P. 218).

One of the other useful elements of the Alba Emoting approach, from the perspective of a vocal coach, is that the use of specific breathing patterns is a key component of each emotional state. Information on respiration seems to be absent from many of the other analyzes[12], so that makes this method especially valuable. On the other hand, almost no information is included on the subject of vocalization.[13] Bloch, et al., seem to have not regarded vocalization as a useful establishing factor of an affective state. (I could find no evidence that they have investigated the question, so it is not possible for me to speculate on the reasons for this apparent omission.)

The following table (2) is a collation of the primary elements of the effector patterns used in the Alba Emoting training to generate the emotions of happiness/laughter, sadness/crying, fear/anxiety, anger/aggression, sex/eroticism, and tenderness.

12. One exception is the notation on hyperventilation as an aspect of some panic disorders (DSM-IV). Moses also notes some respiratory behaviors, though not in a systematic way.

13. The two small references made to vocalization are: under Fear-Anxiety, a sigh-like vocalization on both inspiration and expiration, and under Tenderness, a humming vocalization.

Table 2. Collation of the elements of the Effector Patterns of Basic Emotions (Bloch, et al., p. 202-3).

EMOTION	RESPIRATION PATTERN	POSTURAL ATTITUDE	FACIAL EXPRESSION
Happiness Laughter	Deep and abrupt inspiratory movement followed by a series of short saccadic (jerky) expirations which may even invade the expiratory pause.	Relaxed. Distribution of the phasic muscular tonus has a tendency to diminish in the extensor muscles, esp. in the antigravitational groups. (subjects may tend to sit or fall).	Mouth open, contraction of the musculus caninus, and m. zygomaticus results in exposure of the upper teeth. Eyelids relaxed, eyes are semi-closed.
Sadness-Crying	Rapid saccadic movements modulate the inspiratory phase, and may be prolonged into the expiratory phase, and into the respiratory pause.	Relaxed, and antigravitational muscles are relaxed, esp. during the sharp expiratory movements, leading the body to a posture in which flexion predominates (the body "hangs").	Relaxation of m. masseter, m. perilabialis, and the palpebral muscles. Eyes are semi-closed, or tensely closed, brow contracted by a frown.
Fear-Anxiety	A period of inspiratory hypopneic (slow, shallow) movements followed by passive incomplete exhalations, and sometime by an expiratory-inspiratory 'sigh-like' phase. This can alternate with normal breathing cycles making the pattern irregular. 'Sigh-like' vocalizations on both inspiration, and expiration.	Withdrawal posture; massive increase in muscular tonus mainly affecting the antigravitational groups, esp. those involved in extending the head.	Increase in the overall tonus of facial muscles, with large opening of the mouth and eyes (which may protrude with strong mydriasis (dilation of the pupil).
Anger Aggression	High frequency, and high amplitude with breath channeled mostly through the nose.	Muscular tonus increased in all the antigravitational extensor muscles, esp. those related to a posture of attack.	Tense facial muscles, lips pressed together, eyes are semi-closed owing to the contraction of the superior palpebral muscles.
Sex-Eroticism	Even breathing pattern which increases in frequency and amplitude. Inspiration occurs through a relaxed open mouth.	Posture of relaxed approach, with m. quadriceps femoris, and m. rectus abdominis increase tonic activity tending to give phasic synchronized discharges. Rhythmic pelvic movements are added which increase with frequency.	Facial muscles relaxed, eyes closed or semi-closed. In female version, head is tilted backwards, and neck exposed.
Tenderness	Low frequency breathing with even and regular rhythm. Vocalization includes a humming type lullaby sound.	Postural attitude is one of approach, with antigravitational muscles very relaxed.	Mouth is semi-closed, relaxed lips forming a slight smile. Facial muscles relaxed. Eyes open and relaxed. Head slightly tilted to one side.

Now that I had better information on the *physiological* states associated with each of the primary emotions I wanted to move on to my third question, and get more detailed information on the *vocal behavior* associated with those physiological states.

Vocal Behaviors of the Primary Emotions
Psychotherapists recognize that vocal expression is a key factor in diagnosis. The voice is an important component in nearly every diagnostic model of a heightened affective state (DSM-IV). That makes sense when one considers that a therapist is asked to make a diagnosis when presented with only the patient's behavioral and emotional history, and the evidence of that individual's current physical and vocal behavior. Often clinicians use observation of vocal behaviors as a diagnostic tool (Moses, p. 1). The voice holds important clues to understanding the inner life of the person.

In the DSM-IV, observations about the patient's vocal characteristics appear to be divided into two large areas: the manner of expression and content. Since, in the theatre, the playwright usually supplies content, the focus here is on the expressive elements of voice and speech. Questions of content are left for literary analysis.

In an effort to identify the component parts of human vocal emotion, researchers examined the following vocal characteristics: speech rate, pitch average, pitch range, pitch changes, intensity (loudness), quality,[14] and articulation. The following table (3) is a summary created by Murray and Arnott (p.1106) from their survey of the research literature.

14. Quality is, perhaps, the vaguest of these terms. Rate, pitch, intensity, and articulation can all be objectively measured. Quality, as interpreted by researchers in different fields, was related to concepts like placement, resonance, timbre, tonal focus, etc. With the exception of pitch overtone as a measure of resonance, it is a more subjective and undefined area (Murray and Arnott, p. 1103).

	ANGER	HAPPINESS	SADNESS	FEAR	DISGUST
SPEECH RATE	Slightly faster	Faster or slower	Slightly slower	Much faster	Very much slower
PITCH AVERAGE	Very much higher	Much higher	Slightly lower	Very much higher	Very much lower
PITCH RANGE	Much wider	Much wider	Slightly narrower	Much wider	Slightly wider
PITCH CHANGES	Abrupt, on stressed syllables	Smooth, upward inflections	Downward inflections	Normal	Wide, downward terminal inflections
INTENSITY	Higher	Higher	Lower	Normal	Lower
VOICE QUALITY	Breathy, chest tone	Breathy blaring	Resonant	Irregular voicing	Grumbled chest tone
ARTICULATION	Tense	Normal	Slurring	Precise	Normal

Table 3. Summary of human vocal emotion effects. The effects described are the most commonly associated with the emotions indicated, and are relative to neutral speech (Murray and Arnott, p. 1106).

The terms used in the table are quite general. This is because data used to form the table was from multiple sources. Murray and Arnott collated and generalized the data to give a comparative summary of vocal behaviors.

I found some benefit in seeing the elements of the vocal expressions of heightened affects gathered for comparison. This collation confirmed many of my personal observations and instincts. (Maybe I wasn't that grievous an impostor after all.) It also added some details that I had not considered. For example, I didn't realize that people in a state of fear tended toward "irregular voicing," and it surprised me to see that happiness resulted in a "breathy blaring" quality.

It struck me that the most useful way to employ this information was to merge it, and the table of Bloch's effector patterns (Table 2). Together they would form a fairly complete description of the physiological/vocal behaviors of someone in each of the primary states of heightened affect.

I was also able to construct inventories of vocal behaviors used to diagnose affective disorders by culling the DSM-IV, and other sources (since that list is extensive, it has been placed in an Appendix). These inventories contained quite a few vocal behaviors that I had failed to consider when coaching actors. I was obviously working from a limited palette. (That impostor question came back again.)

I thought back on some of my recent experiences as a voice coach, and considered how I could do a better job. My biggest limitation was a result of incomplete information. Now that I knew a little more, it seemed important to ask what challenges actors face in playing scenes demanding extremes of emotion. A better understanding of the problems faced by actors could make me a more effective coach.

Problems in Playing Heightened Affect
Scenes of intense emotion are the moments in a play that ask the most of an actor's talent, concentration and commitment. They are often the climax of the play as well, and so a great deal of significance rests on them. Actors, generally, want to bring truth and power to these scenes but may not know enough about actual behavior in these circumstances, and will have to contend with some personal inhibitions as well.

Here are some of the most significant issues I identified:
   Lack of direct objective knowledge — Most people have notions about what happens to someone in an extreme emotional state. Those ideas of what happens to someone in that kind of state may be at odds with what really tends to occur, however. One experiences these states subjectively, not objectively, and tends to reinvent the details or suppress the memory of these events. Thus, the actor's personal experiences are not a clear guide (Brennan).

   Poor models — Unless one is in a profession like psychotherapy, where objectively observing heightened affective states is a trained skill, and a routine occurrence, contact with someone in a state of extreme emotion is upsetting. One either becomes involved in trying to comfort or assist the person or looks to find a quick exit. Neither the actor's direct experience, nor our observations of others, provides the opportunity for impersonal observation. Because the actor lacks a clear, direct and objective under standing of the nature of a heightened emotional state, she may unconsciously turn to the most accessible objective models available—performances by other actors. It is likely that, for many actors, the most objective contact with what they think of as states of high emotion has been while watching a play or a film. The problem here is that those performers are not necessarily any more informed. Thus, acting based on their acting becomes more stylized, self-referential and derivative, rather than more truthful. If my concern is accurate, then misrepresentations can be easily recapitulated from performance to performance in the name of authenticity.[15]

As a result of poor modeling, and lack of direct knowledge, when asked to portray a person in a state of extreme emotion, an actor can encounter creative, emotional, and vocal problems when an objective understanding of heightened emotion is missing, and assumptions about those states are incorrect (Brennan).

> **Personal fear of entering into a powerful emotional state** — Actors often worry, "Will I be pulled into the undertow of this emotion, and not be able to emerge, or be psychologically harmed by this experience?" Indeed, "actors very often become identified with the emotions of the roles they play, frequently with neurotic after-effects" (Bloch, et al., p. 214). Actors can also unconsciously defend against a difficult personal emotion, and deny the reality of the character. For example, an actor who has personal difficulty with rage could find that he cannot meet the vocal demands of the scene because his own voice softens when experiencing extreme anger. He may overcompensate vocally, and create strain (Brennan).

> **Embarrassment** — Heightened states of emotion aren't usually pretty. They can, in fact, be quite grotesque. One has to be uninhibited, well trained and acclimated to what Stanislavski called "public solitude" (Moore, p. 33) in order to risk a display of naked emotion (Bloch et al, p. 205).

What do actors do, as a result of these challenges, that is different from a person in an actual state of heightened affect? There are many ways an actor can fail to realize a truthful connection to a character in a state of heightened affect. Aside from questions of "bad acting" there are some important issues that even skilled professional actors will sometimes tend to overlook.

> **States of heightened affect are brief and transitory. Actors can hold onto an emotion for too long.** In emotionally demanding scenes, actors tend to stay in one strong affective tone, rather than allow the character's emotional life to be fluid, changeable, and irrational. In many affective states the person's emotions will swing wildly without an externally observable logic, and without warning (DSM-IV, Moses p. 44). In contrast, actors will often play a reasonable emotional arc, with smooth transitions, and

15. This is not to assert that everything that happens on stage must be "authentic." There is a wide range of effective stylistic choices to be made in a scene or a particular production that have no connection to actual behavior whatsoever. My assumption here is that it is useful to know the difference between stylized and actual behavior.

rational, observable motivations, or they might find a deep emotional experience, and remain in that state for an extended time. An actor can also unconsciously extend his or her expression of emotion as a way to "work through" or resolve her own feelings. This is problematic due to the fact that an actor's extended emotion may not be analogous to the character's emotional state or the playwright's intent (Brennan). When sustaining one emotional tone, an actor will also extend one set of vocal postures. That can lead to increased chances of vocal strain.

Actors tend to scream, and rely on volume as a primary means of expression. While people in intense emotional states will sometimes tend to raise their voices, that is by no means the sole or even a primary characteristic. Vocal intensity will tend to rise in states of anger and happiness, but will drop in sadness or disgust, and remain normal in states of fear[16] (Murray and Arnott, p. 1103-6). It is not unusual to assume that a normal response to a sudden fright might be a scream. Interestingly, the research seems to indicate that total aphonia (a complete inability to make any sound) is a much more likely result (DSM-IV), (Moses p. 107)[17]. Justification for shouting or screaming on stage is rare, and even then the actor should bear in mind that it is an unattractive sound, and the audience is alienated by it — no matter how much the character is deserving of sympathy.[18] Vocal strain from shouting or screaming is a common complaint from actors. Screaming, and shouting are the blunt instruments of expression in scenes of heightened affect. Though there are a range of more subtle, complex, and interesting choices an actor can make, many will find themselves shouting or screaming any way. Rodenburg called screaming "the Ph.D. of voice work" (p. 266). Many actors simply don't possess the level of technique or control to perform that activity without causing damage to their voices.

Actors tend to investigate a role from the perspective of their own limited experiences. There is often a tendency for an actor to assume that a character would behave "just the way I would." It can be difficult to project oneself imaginatively into the full life of another person — a problem in any acting situation, and one that is intensified by the special circumstances of playing heightened affect.

Careful rehearsal processes are often employed to mitigate many of these problems. Sometimes, however, there are special problems that arise specifically in rehearsal. The imperatives of producing an impressive theatrical event by opening night create unusual pressures on actors.

Directors (and the actors, themselves) may push the actor beyond the performer's current skill level. Operating from insecurity or from an anxiety to please, many actors can be persuaded to push themselves to perform at a degree of intensity that their present level of technical or physical development cannot sustain. In searching for a particular theatrical effect or result, a director can, unintentionally, ask too much of an actor (Barton and Dal Vera, p. 54). Actors are particularly vulnerable to this form of pressure. They want to satisfy. They want to grow with each role. They may not be experienced enough to know their vocal limitations until they have lost their voices. Then it is too late.

16. See Table 3.

17. It is interesting to note that in all of Moses' behavioral descriptions (see Appendix), only once does he note unusual intensity (loudness) in the voice, and he suggests that it alternates with extreme softness. Not once does he cite screaming or shrieking as notable behaviors in heightened affect.

18. There will be times when a director or playwright wants that alienation. In that case the concern shifts from one of aesthetics to a consideration of vocal hygiene—will the actor be able to sustain the requested level of vocal stress without harm?

Directors may not structure a safe or careful approach to scenes of heightened affect. Although directors will carefully stage scenes of *physical* combat, they will often overlook the *vocal* component of those scenes (and scenes of purely verbal combat) with the expectation that when the actor organically "finds it" the voice will automatically release into a natural, free and realistic expression. There is almost a prejudice against a technical approach to a highly emotional scene. Directors some times fear that a structured and technical analysis will lead to a stilted or "canned" outcome. A director with this concern may encourage the actor to do a thorough emotional preparation, and then to jump into the scene to discover what spontaneously erupts. This is an invitation to the very problems listed above.

Because there is really no other safe way to do it, physically violent scenes are usually blocked from a technical perspective — not an organic one. (One would never hand actors weapons and say, "Go at it! Use your anger to 'find' the fight!") This keeps the players safe. Organic and aesthetic considerations are usually mitigated by a watchful integrity on the part of all the artists involved. Directors should consider employing a similar technical approach to scenes of purely vocal violence, in adding voice to choreographed fight scenes, and in scenes of extreme emotion.

There are probably a number of additional problems that I have overlooked, though, from my experience, these are the most common. What, then, should we do to help actors?

Solutions and Suggestions

Here are some ideas to help actors, directors, coaches, and trainers to find a safer, and more effective way to play scenes of heightened affect.

Encourage more research — In examining this topic, I was surprised to find how little investigating had been done on vocal behavior in states of heightened affect. Of the studies that were available, many used actors to provide the data. If actor performances tend to be as distant from actuality as I suspect they are, then those studies are unreliable. In our modern world, there may be better ways to study human behavior in action. The increasing popularity of "reality television," the ubiquity of security cameras, and even taped emergency 911 telephone calls all give us access to recordings of people in real states of heightened affect.

Employ the information we currently have on the physiological and vocal behaviors of people in extreme emotional states — Actors and directors might do well to examine what researchers have identified as common physical and vocal traits among people in states of heightened affect. A study of the tables here, and the following collations of vocal behaviors (see Appendix) might offer up a wider range of possible behavioral choices to an actor, and may point out some false assumptions.

Train the voice and the body for the demands of extreme emotion — While it isn't the function of this paper to propose a detailed syllabus for vocal study, there are a couple of particular issues which need to be addressed:

It is important to remember that the vocal system (including the vocal folds themselves) is, like the body overall, made up of muscles, cartilage, bone and tissue, etc. As such, it can be trained to be stronger, more flexible, and to have a quicker response to stimuli. In this sense, voice training for the actor needs to be approached in the same manner as physical training for an athlete.

In addition to fundamental training in strength and flexibility, specific instruction should be given in the more unusual behaviors such as inspiratory phonation (Smolover, 11-38), and methods of generating measured amounts of vocal tension, hyper-adduction or turbulence to create the theatrical illusions of distress without actually harming the actor. An emphasis should be placed on the actor maintaining "voluntary control of the body or part of the body involved in the emotional and verbal behavior to be presented" (Bloch et al, p. 198-9).

Actors should also be trained into good vocal habits and discipline. Structured time in rehearsal for a thorough physical and vocal warm-up, and after a session, a period of cool-down activities, are useful components of this discipline.

Training in a psychophysical approach to emotions should be integrated alongside other methods such as sense-memory. Through effector pattern training, and other methods like it, actors can have a safe and specific method of exploring states of heightened affect without many of the psychological and physiological/vocal risks created by some approaches.

Coaches and trainers should also consider becoming well versed in psychophysical methods of accessing emotional states. The Alba Emoting literature contains repeated warnings about the need to study only with a fully certified teacher (Rix, p. 1). This is probably sound advice, since a deep understanding of the method is unlikely to be achieved without dedicated study. Given the apparent absence of attention to vocalization in that method, it would be especially useful for voice coaches to master that discipline. The integration of skills would be quite beneficial to all parties.

Finally, directors should treat scenes of vocal violence in the same careful manner they would any scene containing physical violence.

As for me, I'll try to be a little less of an impostor, and do more careful research before I claim to know exactly how someone would behave in a state of heightened affect.

Epilogue
I recently got another request (from the same actress I mentioned at the start) to help in a scene where the character is in a state of extreme grief. She felt that she was doing an effective preparation for the scene, that she understood the character, and could project herself into the character's circumstances, but at the crucial moment just couldn't release into the emotion.

This time I felt a bit more prepared.

As I watched the scene I noticed that she was stiffening her upper back, lifting her shoulders, widening her eyes, and extending her head forward. From my reading, I recognized that this was a lot more like the pattern for fear than grief. When I side-coached her to relax those muscles, let her focus soften, and "hang over" a bit more, she released into the emotion, and really wept.

Later, we were able to develop some postural and breathing cues to place in the scene so she would stay on the right track, and not let her anxiety over the scene short-circuit her performance by leading her from grief into fear. Since this was a scene of really extreme grief, I showed her how to build the emotion by adding elements such as vocalized inspiration, and progressively stronger saccadic respiratory patterns. I noticed that parts of the script were written in a way that was congruent to qualities such as derailment, and pressured speech. We explored disconnecting content, and literal meaning in places, and adding sudden inappropriate changes in pitch and loudness. We found that these elements could be crafted in highly specific ways, and that the act of doing them, technical as the decision process was, still pulled her further into the emotion. It was a very productive session.

On the drive home I thought about the last time I had coached that actress, and the personal journey that session had initiated. This time I should write her the thank you note.

❧

Works Cited

Barton, Robert and Rocco Dal Vera *Voice: Onstage and Off*. Fort Worth: Harcourt Brace College Publishers, Inc., 1995.

Bloch, Suzanna, Pedro Orthus and Guy Santibanez-H. "Effector Pattern of Basic Emotions: A Psychophysiological Method for Training Actors." *Acting (Re)Considered*, Phillip B. Zarrilli, ed., London: Routledge, 1995, p. 197-218

Brennan, Linda *The Relationship of Voice to Emotion and Psychotherapy*. Antioch University, Research Methodology, 1994.

Brennan, Linda, telephone conversations, and written communications with the author.

Diagnostic Statistical Manual, fourth edition. Electronic DSM-IV plus [computer file][19] Washington, D.C.: American Psychiatric Publishing Group, 1994-1998.

Moore, Sonia *The Stanislavski System*. New York: The Viking Press, Inc., 1974.

Moses, Paul *The Voice of Neurosis*. New York: Grune and Stratton, Inc., 1954.

Murray, Iain R. and John L. Arnott. "Toward the Simulation of Emotion in Synthetic Speech: A Review of the Literature on Human Vocal Emotion." *Journal of the Acoustical Society of America* 2 (1993): 1097-1108.
Rodenburg, Patsy *The Right to Speak*. London: Methuen Drama, 1992.

Rix, Roxane. "Learning Alba Emoting", *Theatre Topics* 8:1, 1998.

Smolover, Raymond "Vocal Behavior Analysis and Modification Under Conditions of Expiratory and Inspiratory Phonation." *Journal of Research in Singing* December, v. 7, n. 1, (1983): 11-37.

19. Because the author used an electronic search able file for citations from this reference, no page numbers are available for this source.

Appendix
This is an inventory of vocal behaviors mentioned as symptoms of heightened affective states.
The material is derived primarily from two sources: the *Diagnostic Statistical Manual*, fourth edi-
tion ('98) and *The Voice of Neurosis*, by Paul Moses ('54).

Moses, in his detailed study *The Voice of Neurosis*, gives some excellent examples of the vocal
behaviors of people in heightened affective states. Some gleanings follow:

—The general irritability and shifting of moods and the mixture of shyness, frustration and
resentment which characterize anxiety neurosis are more evident from the voice than from any
other behavior expression (p. 107).

—One of the known symptoms of hysteria is illogical emotional impact in speaking or emotions
expressed by the voice that are contrary to content. The patient will say something quite trivial
in an elated or aggressive voice. Content and voice are therefore disconnected (p. 44).

—An inebriated person may lose his inhibitions and his range will become wider and wider until
it literally gets out of control and he utters merely low mumblings or high, whining sounds (p. 44).

—Enthusiasm and joy break through the limitations of conventional speech and will play on
a wide range (p. 44).

—Acute fear, extreme anxiety or depression may inhibit or paralyze all or some motor functions.
This is as archaic a reaction as aimless panic. Aphonia and mutism are vocal expressions of such
emotional states (p. 107).

—Normally, phonation occurs only on expiration. [In states of high affect where the individual's
thoughts race faster, the sequencing of breath and the adduction/abduction of the vocal folds can
become confused. In this state voiced and articulated inspiration is not uncommon.] It is easy to
demonstrate what happens when one phonates on inspiration. The harder one tries, the worse
the sound becomes in terms of normality. Eventually, total aphonia results (p. 106).

—Under emotional stress the voice will fall apart much sooner than speech will. In other words,
articulation of words is less affected than phonation (p. 107).

—The voice can be changed by both hypo (breathy) and hyper (pressed) function, and can even
alternate between those states becoming spastic under certain conditions (p. 107).

—In states of panic or tantrums the speaker tends to raise the last syllable of his sentences (and
frequently individual words) so that statements are twisted into questions (p. 107).

—The mucous membranes of the mouth often become dry when the speaker is hysterical, and
resonance and articulation is modified. The speaker may compulsively swallow (p.108).

—When the hysterical person is aggressive, sudden bursts of dynamics are common; words are
delivered with a hard attack, last syllables are given uncommon emphasis, and too many words
are crammed into one breath(p. 108).

—In strong emotional states a person may become indecisive, confused or overcome with
a vague sense of unreality. This may result in a voice that is alternately (and inappropriately)
too soft and too loud (p. 107).

—It is interesting to note that in all these descriptions, only once does Moses note unusual
intensity (loudness) in the voice, and he suggests that it alternates with extreme softness. Not
once does he cite screaming or shrieking as notable behaviors in heightened affect.

The *Diagnostic Statistical Manual* adds the following vocal behaviors related to heightened affect
to Moses' inventory. A person in a state of heightened affect may display:

Aggression: Forceful physical, verbal, or symbolic action. May be appropriate and self-protective,
including healthy self-assertiveness, or inappropriate as in hostile or destructive behavior. May
also be directed toward the environment, toward another person or personality, or toward the
self, as in depression.

Aphonia: An inability to produce speech sounds that require the use of the larynx that is not due to a lesion in the central nervous system.

Blocking: A sudden obstruction or interruption in spontaneous flow of thinking or speaking, perceived as an absence or deprivation of thought.

Blunted speech: Severe reduction in the intensity of affective expression.

Clanging: A type of thinking in which the sound of a word, rather than its meaning, gives the direction to subsequent associations. Punning and rhyming may substitute for logic, and language may become increasingly a senseless compulsion to associate and decreasingly a vehicle for communication. For example, in response to the statement "That will probably remain a mystery," a patient said, "History is one of my strong points."

Derailment: ("loosening of associations") A pattern of speech in which a person's ideas slip off one track onto another that is completely unrelated or only obliquely related. In moving from one sentence or clause to another, the person shifts the topic idiosyncratically from one frame of reference to another and things may be said in juxtaposition that lack a meaningful relationship. This disturbance occurs between clauses, in contrast to incoherence, in which the disturbance is within clauses.

Flat Speech: Absence or near absence of any signs of affective expression such as a monotonous voice and an immobile face.

Flight of Ideas: A nearly continuous flow of accelerated speech with abrupt changes from one topic to another, usually based on understandable associations, distracting stimuli, or playing on words. When severe, however, this may lead to disorganized and incoherent speech. Flight of ideas is characteristic of manic episodes,... and, rarely, acute reactions to stress.

Hypomanical Speech: [Hypomania is a] psychopathological state and abnormality of mood falling somewhere between normal euphoria and mania. It is characterized by unrealistic optimism, pressure of speech and activity....

Inappropriate Speech: Discordance of voice and movements with the content of the person's speech or ideation.

Incoherence: Speech or thinking that is essentially incomprehensible to others because words or phrases are joined together without a logical or meaningful connection. This disturbance occurs within clauses, in contrast to derailment, in which the disturbance is between clauses. This has sometimes been referred to as "word salad" to convey the degree of linguistic disorganization.

Labile Speech: Abnormal variability, with repeated, rapid, and abrupt shifts in affective expression.

Logorrhea: Uncontrollable, excessive talking.

Loosening of Associations: A disturbance of thinking shown by speech in which ideas shift from one subject to another that is unrelated or minimally related to the first. Statements that lack a meaningful relationship may be juxtaposed, or speech may shift suddenly from one frame of reference to another. The speaker gives no indication of being aware of the disconnectedness, contradictions, or illogicality of speech.

Major Depressive Episode: ... [is characterized by] slowed speech, thinking, and body movements; increased pauses before answering; speech that is decreased in volume, inflection, amount, or variety of content, or muteness.

Manic Speech: is typically pressured, loud, rapid, and difficult to interrupt. Individuals may talk nonstop, sometimes for hours on end, and without regard for others' wishes to communicate. Speech is sometimes characterized by joking, punning, and amusing irrelevancies. The individual may become theatrical, with dramatic mannerisms and singing. Sounds rather than meaningful conceptual relationships may govern word choice (i.e., clanging). If the person's mood is more irritable than expansive, speech may be marked by complaints, hostile comments, or angry tirades. The individual's thoughts may race, often at a rate faster than can be articulated. Some individuals with Manic Episodes report that this experience resembles watching two or three television programs simultaneously. Frequently there is flight of ideas evidenced by a nearly continuous flow of accelerated speech, with abrupt changes from one topic to another. For example, while talking about a potential business deal to sell computers, a salesperson may shift to discussing in minute detail the history of the computer chip, the industrial revolution, or applied mathematics. When flight of ideas is severe, speech may become disorganized and incoherent.

Perseveration: Tendency to emit the same verbal or motor response again and again to varied stimuli.

Poverty of Speech: Restriction in the amount of speech; spontaneous speech and replies to questions range from brief and unelaborated to monosyllabic or no response at all. When the amount of speech is adequate, there may be a poverty of content if the answer is vague or if there is a substitution of stereotyped or obscure phrases for meaningful responses.

Pressured Speech: Rapid, accelerated, frenzied speech. Sometimes it exceeds the ability of the vocal musculature to articulate, leading to jumbled and cluttered speech; at other times it exceeds the ability of the listener to comprehend as the speech expresses a flight of ideas (as in mania) or unintelligible jargon.

Restricted or Constricted Speech: Reduction in the expressive range and intensity of vocal affects.

Tic: An involuntary, sudden, rapid, recurrent, nonrhythmic stereotyped motor movement or vocalization. A tic may be an expression of an emotional conflict....

Peer Reviewed Article by *Karen S. Ryker*

To Train and Test the Voice in Violence

Karen Ryker is currently Director of the MFA in Acting program, Associate Professor, Head of Voice and Speech at University of Wisconsin, Madison. MFA from Brandeis University, MA from University of Michigan, trained with Shakespeare & Company, Grotowski's, Polish Lab Theatre, and in a variety of voice training methodologies. Performance or voice coaching credits include American Players Theatre, Madison Repertory Theatre, Shakespeare and Co., The Huntington Theatre Company, Lyric Stage, and La Mama E.T.C. Areas of specialization include Shakespearean performance, training actors to make full use of the voice, and producing vocal violence in a manner that protects the voice from excessive damage.

1. " ....actors usually strain themselves in the exciting moments. Therefore, at times of great stress it is especially necessary to achieve a complete freeing of the muscles. In fact, in the high moments of a part the tendency to relax should become more normal than the tendency to contraction." P. 94

During my tenure as a professor of Voice and Acting in the Department of Theatre and Drama at the University of Wisconsin-Madison, I have the continuing privilege of collaborating with respected Speech/Language Pathologist colleagues in UW's Department of Communicative Disorders. We exchange guest lectures; we share technical expertise and make referrals for our students and clients; we facilitate the occasional cross-registration of our students; our graduate students share techniques and experiences to mutual benefit. And we conduct research of mutual interest. A recent study which we conducted jointly and which involved the effects of voice training on the actor's production of vocally violent sounds (see Appendix C), led to my thoughts about the benefits of using science to enhance actor voice training techniques, the importance of conducting scientific research on vocal technique, and the problems which must be solved when the rigorous discipline of science encounters the no less rigorous, but quite different discipline of art. I offer the following discussion in the hope that more voice trainers will join forces with speech scientists to pursue investigations of mutual benefit to both disciplines.

> "Yes, I have tricks in my pocket, I have things up my sleeve. But I am the opposite of a stage magician. He gives you illusion that has the appearance of truth. I give you truth in the pleasant disguise of illusion." (Williams, *The Glass Menagerie*)

The actor's work is a mixture of image and fact. To paraphrase Tennessee Williams, we create illusion that has the appearance of reality. An impassioned fight to the death between two mighty camps of warriors brandishing lethal weapons is represented by a small number of actors repeating practiced choreography with blunt-edged stage weapons and dying even two or three times in the space of five minutes. The cacophonic battle cries, clash of weapons, and groans of pain of real person-to-person combat are recreated by actors producing the carefully orchestrated sounds of violence which accompany the choreographed battle. Often these are communicated to an artificially large group of people (an audience) by means of the unadorned human voice and body as instrument.

It may seem paradoxical to the uninitiated, but in order to create the illusion of often chaotic and emotionally charged response, it is important that the actor work from a relaxed body and focused intellect. Constantin Stanislavski, the father of acting technique in the western world, stressed that the more intense the emotion, the more relaxed the actor need be (Stanislavski, p.94).[1] This balance between "real" relaxation and "illusory" tension is vital to the actor, but is not easy to achieve. Indeed it constitutes a primary focus in vocal and physical training for the actor, and science may be called into service in the training process.

My experience with training actors in effective voice production has been that some actors respond to image, and some to fact. For instance one actor would rather think of the channel for sound as a long hose with a spigot at one end which controls the pressure and a nozzle at the other end which focuses the spray of sound. Another actor would rather know about the actual organs which control respiration, phonation, resonation and articulation and the interaction of ribs, lungs, abdomen with the vocal folds, the pharyngeal, oral, nasal cavities and the jaw, tongue, velum in order to produce efficient sound. In actuality it matters not which language one uses, so long as the end result is effective. As voice trainer, I find myself jumping between factual, scientific explanations and fanciful imagery in order to assist actors in effective use of the voice.

I have found it useful to teach from a knowledge of physiology but through the medium of inspiring imagery. When the trainer works only from imagery, a breakdown can occur as people begin to believe their imagery, and to substitute fiction for fact. Speech-Language Pathologist Tom Hixon suggests that an example of this breakdown is the classic dictum offered by voice teachers to "support from the diaphragm." (Hixon) Hixon cites studies which indicate that one doesn't sing from the diaphragm—the diaphragm doesn't work like that—the singer is really supporting the sound from the abdomen. Without an understanding of kinesiology and physiology, the bag of clever tricks which aid and enhance the actor's and voice trainer's skill remains limited.

But why the need for this training in voice accompanying fight work? When the novice actor argues against the need for special training, argues to simply support her/his combat moves with the real bloodcurdling battle cries, grunts of exertion and groans of pain which accompany to-the-death fights, the answer is obvious. Unlike the musician who can purchase—and even upgrade—a new instrument at will, the actor (like the singer) has but one instrument to serve a lifetime of artistry. It should be tuned, played and cared for in a safe and hygienic manner in order to prolong its effective life. And this instrument, which must be flexible and responsive to the demands of theatrical communication, is tested to the extreme when played in scenes which require the extremity of human passion as do the typical fight scenes. How much better it is to draw from scientific fact as well—particularly when dealing with vocal extremes where abuse and long term permanent damage can easily occur. Science can support the voice trainer. And in these days of excessive litigation, the voice trainer who teaches without benefit of scientific support—solely from image—could be at risk.

Although to date there has been little scientific research on the actor's voice in theatrical extremes, voice science has already determined that "abusive" sound can contribute to vocal dysfunction, and that there are effective methods for preserving the instrument from vocal abuse and misuse. As example, Dr. Alex Johnson (p.155) lists a variety of behaviors thought to contribute to voice disturbance. Not surprisingly, nearly all of the factors he enumerates are regularly engaged in by the actor during performance: loud talking, yelling, screaming, hard glottal attacks, sound outside acceptable physiologic range, speaking in noisy environments, excessive coughing and throat clearing, grunting, excessive talking, loud, hard abusive laughing. These characteristics of onstage speech are compounded by special circumstances that make the offstage work and lifestyle of actors particularly conducive to vocal difficulties. Some of these circumstances, as described by noted voice trainer Bonnie Raphael (p.87) are long working days, travel, varying performance spaces and personalities, extreme vocal production. Add to these circumstances the extreme physical demands of the typical stage fight, and the requirement to train a hygienic—vocal as well as physical—athlete is evident.

The challenge of balancing the trained (and relaxed) voice and body with focused intellect for stage fight is further explained by Nan Withers-Wilson (p.99) who uses the example of Shakespeare's Richard III's famous speech "A horse! A horse! My kingdom for a horse!" She summarizes,

> "As craftsman, the actor must simultaneously be saying to himself, 'Keep your throat relaxed. Call the words in your middle range. Use vowel extension. Take a breath before "A horse!" Take another breath before the next "a horse!" This mental 'juggling' act can be made less awkward if the actor pinpoints such moments of technical difficulty early in the rehearsal period and, through the process of repetition, makes the means of execution an integral part of the character's behavior. The actor allows the character's thoughts, feelings, manner of movement and voicing to be "housed" in his mind, heart, and body. But in performing the role, a part of the actor's consciousness must always be monitoring the execution of his character's physical and vocal expression so that he does not inflict injury upon himself or others."

Over decades, voice trainers such as Withers-Wilson have developed techniques which aim to produce potentially vocally violent behaviors in a more hygienic, less abusive manner, and thus limit damage and extend longevity of the actor's voice. While approaches vary, the techniques appear to have principles in common, which I shall endeavor to describe in Appendix A.[2] Theatre voice specialists would argue that these common principles have proven effective because, in their experience, the actors' trained voices have been preserved and strengthened. However, hard scientific assessment of their effectiveness is in its early stages and more studies are needed to support the experiential evidence. Although today there may be voice trainers who would avoid scientific investigation of the theatrical art fearing that the artistry might evaporate under scientific scrutiny, many recognize that much is to be gained by interfacing with speech-language pathologists for more than remedial measures (Verdolini, p.225-229) and in this most recent decade, have begun to benefit from the more frequent exchange of information.

My recent study in collaboration with colleagues at University of Wisconsin-Madison[3] involved an investigation of the consequences of vocally violent behavior (grunting, groaning, shouting, sobbing), and whether prescribed voice training does indeed render the performance of that vocally violent behavior more efficient and safe (Roy, Ryker, Bless, pp.215-230). During the testing period we measured the sound production of twenty-seven actors, using audio recordings and videostroboscopic recordings. The sound production was measured before, during, and after producing vocally violent sounds. Then the actors were trained in hygienic release technique, and re-tested using the same protocol. The first phase of analysis involved acoustic data, and the results of this phase, reported in the *Journal of Voice* (Appendix B), indicated that vocal training does indeed protect the laryngeal system. But interesting questions were raised regarding which aspect of training is primarily responsible for the effects, and further study is suggested. The second phase of study, an analysis of the physiological correlates, is in process at this time (Papangelou, et al.).

In response to a casual description of this study, an eminent voice trainer colleague exclaimed, "But Karen, we know that! We've been doing these things for years!" Yes, we voice trainers may "know" it, and can testify anecdotally to the results of safe, efficient use of the instrument, but these

2. This list of common principles could serve as a starting point for additional research projects, as suggested in Appendix A.

3. Primary author, Nelson Roy, completed his tenure at UW-Madison, and is currently in the Department of Communication Disorders and Otolaryngology-Head and Neck Surgery at the University of Utah-Salt Lake City.

techniques have not been adequately and scientifically measured to see if what we *think* we are doing is different from what we're actually doing. When we investigate a process in a scientific manner, we may gather evidence to support our current practice, or we may find that what we thought was true is, in actuality, very different from what we expected (note Hixon's example "support from the diaphragm" cited previously.) The result of scientific inquiry may be that even though something seems perfectly reasonable, in fact, the opposite might be proven true. This is the risk and responsibility of putting vocal technique under the microscope (or in this case, "stroboscope") of scientific scrutiny. But it is a risk which, when taken, can lead to more effective voice training whether the results support our experiential evidence or lead to new insights and more sound methods.

In investigating the history of recent collaborations between the speech-language pathologists and the theatre voice and speech trainers, I was surprised to find that there is not an overabundance of published studies (the hard evidence of meaningful interaction). In 1999, I uncovered a mere handful of published studies through traditional library searches, and several more through a call to colleagues in the Voice and Speech Trainers Association (VASTA) via internet. (Appendix C) Under inspiration of Robert Sataloff of The Voice Foundation and other eminent speech language pathologists connected with the National Center for Voice and Speech and other internationally recognized centers of Communication Disorders and Speech-Language Pathology, there has been more research involving the singer (and sometimes the actor) in recent years, but even here, much is yet to be accomplished.

In order for science and theatre to merge and benefit from one another there are important aspects that must be considered and problems to be solved. In my own collaboration with speech language pathologists (SLP) and in discussion with other authorities engaged in these questions, I have already encountered several interesting challenges. There are the obvious challenges of exposing one's ignorance of the other's discipline, learning different terminology and thought processes, or testing methods which may seem utterly counterproductive. There are the limitations of equipment. For example, in the case of the vocal violence study, we initially intended to investigate the extremely violent vocal behavior "screaming". But during several pilot studies in which I endured flexible nasal endoscopy while screaming repeatedly, the SLP was unable to visualize the vocal folds because during each scream, some of the supra glottic structures made contact with the tip of the endoscope and obstructed the camera's view. So the most vocally violent behavior "screaming" had to be eliminated from this particular study.

A major challenge is that scientific investigation usually demands that the scope of the study be sufficiently narrow as to make the study feasible, and this almost always means restriction in some aspects of a holistic discipline such as acting. For instance, the restrictions under which actors were measured in the vocal violence study (in small studio with instruments attached and inserted, with limited mobility, without benefit of the stage environment which helps to generate the authenticity of the violent moment) made it difficult to effectively recreate the staged violence.

Each actor-subject was recorded and measured in a small office-sized lab. S/he listened to a scenario describing the stage situation and was asked to produce four different sounds (grunt, groan, sob, shout) similar to what s/he would have produced on stage in the actual four staged violent episodes. In addition to the confining space of the lab, the actor was standing not quite upright against a "leaning board" with a video camera pointed from approximately six feet away, with an electroglottography (EGG) band attached at the throat, with flexible laryngovideostroboscope inserted through the nasal passage which was held and maneuvered by a SLP standing approximately one foot in front of the actor-subject. The violent sounds could only be produced on the vowel "eee" (the vowel most readily visualized by the camera) and were to be repeated until the SLP recorded four adequately visualized tokens of the behavior. Apart from the obvious restrictions to authentic performance behavior, in this situation we were already two steps removed from the *real* violent situation, from which was reenacted the staged violent situation, from which was reenacted the *laboratory's* violent situation. Thus the measurements were taken from the thrice-removed situation.

In attempting to scientifically measure the states in which real vs. staged violence is produced, one could hypothesize an additional challenge: that the *performed* violence in studio doesn't reflect the real inner state of the actor on stage, which may not reflect the real situation of the violent person engaged in life or death action. Although each might be emotionally charged, one would assume the actor to be relaxed and focused on performing the task safely but with the illusion of danger. One would assume the violent person to be agitated and focused on inflicting real damage. Therefore there may be more (or less, or different) manufacturing, more (or less, or different) physical and emotional stress.

The restrictions described in previous paragraphs may indicate to the reader the extreme measures one must take to isolate factors enough to record and measure behavior in order to ultimately aid the actor in safe and more effective use of voiced violence on stage. The task is difficult but not impossible, and could be well worth the effort. In order to preserve the artistry and to render the scientific inquiry effective, we need to determine what non-invasive measures can be made of the actor so that the actor is not changed or distracted in significant ways. Our mission should be to protect the actor's artistry and, at the same time, improve the actor's instrument and increase its longevity. In this there is a delicate balance between measure and performance, between fact and fiction, between reality and illusion. We can certainly benefit from the use of science and fact to enhance art and illusion.

Such collaborations may be the heart of the future. The convergence of speech-language pathology with theatrical voice and singing voice training can work to our mutual advancement. We can clarify and share information—especially along the lines of technique—and while avoiding excessive possessiveness, can still retain the necessary "walls" between the two disciplines. Since science may be generalized for many different applications, the results of studies engaging the two aforementioned disciplines can be of use not only to those in the theatrical and singing professions, but to the general population as well.

Works Cited

Williams, Tennessee. *The Glass Menagerie* opened in New York in 1944.

Stanislavski, Constantin. *An Actor Prepares*. New York, Theatre Arts Books, 1977:94.

Hixon T. "Respiratory Function and Classical Singers" and "To Breathe or Not to Breathe" both articles collected in his book *Respiratory Function in Speech and Song*. San Diego, CA: Singular Pub. Group, 1991.

Johnson A. Disorders of Speaking in the Professional Voice User. In: Benninger M, Jacobson B, Johnson A eds. *Vocal Arts Medicine: The care and prevention of professional voice disorders*. New York: Thieme, 1994.

Raphael B. Special Considerations Relating to Members of the Acting Profession. In: Sataloff R, ed. *Professional Voice: The science and art of clinical care*. New York: Raven, 1991.

Withers-Wilson N. *Vocal Direction for the Theatre*. New York, Drama Book Specialists, 1993.

Verdolini K. Interface: Theatre Trainers and Speech Pathologists. In: Hampton M and Acker B, ed. *The Vocal Vision*. New York: Applause, 1997.

Roy N, Ryker K, Bless D. Vocal Violence in Actors: An Investigation into its Acoustic Consequences and the Effects of Hygienic Laryngeal Release Training. *Journal of Voice*, Vol. 14, No. 2, pp. 215-230.

Papangelou M, Roy N, Ryker K, Bless D. Vocal Violence in Actors: A Study of Physiological Correlates. Study in process, anticipated submission to The Voice Foundation for presentation at its annual symposium, summer 2001.

I wish to thank the following people for their assistance through telephone conversations and email communications:

Rocco Dal Vera, Associate Professor of Voice, University of Cincinnati, College-Conservatory of Music; Tom Hixon, Speech-Language Pathologist and Professor of Communicative Disorders, University of Arizona at Tucson; Lise Olson, Lecturer in Acting and Voice, Liverpool Institute for Performing Arts, England; Ron Scherer, Voice Scientist, Professor in the Department of Communication Disorders, Bowling Green State University; Elizabeth Wiley, Associate Professor, Head of Acting, College of William & Mary.

Additional Information gathered via email from:

Susan Abbott, Ph.D. candidate, Dept. of Communication Disorders, Florida State University; Katherine Behenna, Speech and Language Therapist, London; Linda Cartwright, School of Performing & Screen Arts - Acting Major, UNITEC Institute of Technology, Auckland, New Zealand; Hilary Jones, Lecturer in Voice, The Royal Scottish Academy of Music and Drama, Glasgow, Scotland; Marya Lowry. Head of Voice Training, Brandeis University; Doug Montequin, Ph.D. candidate at University of Iowa; Bonnie Raphael, Professor of Voice, North Carolina School of the Arts; Kate Reid, Speech Pathologist, Ph.D. candidate at University of Sydney; Brad Story, W J Gould Voice Research Center

Appendix A

Common Principles Involved in Producing the Voice at Vocal Extremity for Stage
In my judgment, these principles appear in most voice training methodologies. They have been gleaned from my own research and experience and compiled from print resources, lectures, conversations, collegial exchanges on the topic in Vasta.vox. This list could serve as a starting point for further research projects. With the help of Speech Language Pathologist colleagues, research projects could be developed to test each of these principles.

Torso Alignment and Muscular Release. The torso and limbs should be aligned, loose and ready to respond, with the three major "joints" of the body: neck, shoulders and pelvis loose and responsive. The center of gravity should be low in the torso with the knees loose and legs balanced over released feet. Back and back ribs should be well exercised for better flexibility and power.

Throat and Facial Posture. There should be no unnecessary throat, tongue or false fold tension. Throat should be open and relaxed, jaw and its surrounding musculature loose and responsive, the tongue should be relaxed and not bunched up in the mouth, flexible and responsive.

Breath Production (respiration). Breath full and supported with released inbreath focused to ribs and belly, outbreath focused from the back ribs and abdomen to the lips. There should be no holding of breath at the throat level.

Sound Production (phonation and resonation). Efficient engagement of the vocal folds with minimal glottic attack. The tone should be focused from the abdomen to the facial mask. This adds "ring" and carrying power. A useful image here is to bypass the throat. Any vocal "noise" which can add realism to the sound (i.e. the sound of roughness or scratchiness for a threatening shout, the "broken" quality sound for a scream) should be minimal and moved away from vocal folds.

Speech Production and Intelligibility (articulation). The flexible organs of articulation—the tongue, lips and jaw—should be loose and responsive to the clarity and specificity of thought. The impassioned quality of content can be played effectively by extending the vowels (which adds carrying power) and playing the consonant qualities with commitment and duration (which increases intelligibility).

Transfer of Effort. The impulse for sound comes from the same place as the impulse for the physical effort (low center). Initiate the effort in the belly and buttocks or feet for support and power. Transfer any effort from the throat to the articulators for carrying power and intelligibility. Transfer any "noise" away from vocal folds to other throat tissue (again, the image of bypassing the throat).

Variables. Pitch, loudness, tone, quality adjustments, rhythm, intelligibility should be varied to suit the intent and to add the noise and erratic qualities that lend authenticity to the sound. Build in "breathers" in which to rest, realign, release tense muscle masses, and refocus the object of attention. Develop the sound with a sense of flow and follow through. Balance or top the aural "competition" (i.e. other voices shouting or crying; environmental noise such as thunder, trumpets, the hiss of fog machines or recorded music or voices; noise of clanging weaponry, running feet, thudding bodies) with contrasting pitch, tone or loudness.

Vocal Hygiene. To keep the voice instrument operating at peak efficiency, exercise it at extremes in short practice sessions. Drink adequate fluids to combat dryness (external environmental dryness due to inadequate moisture in the air, as well as internal physical dryness due to water loss and lack of optimal hydration). Warm up the voice to encourage efficient operation of the vocal folds and muscles, and warm down the voice to realign the vocal folds and soothe overworked muscles.

Awareness of Environmental Hazards. Combat backstage and onstage dust, sawdust, dirt, dryness with adequate moistening of the air and space. Investigate the chemical content of theatrical clouds of smoke and fog to ensure actor safety. Balance the extra weight and stress of armor, weapons, facial masks, prosthetic devices which demand excessive force or impede loudness and intelligibility.

Appendix B

Abstract for "Vocal Violence in Actors: an Investigation into its Acoustic Consequences and the Effects of Hygienic Laryngeal Release Training" authored by Nelson Roy, Karen S. Ryker, Diane M. Bless. Published in Journal of Voice Vol. 14, No. 2, pp. 215-230

Acoustic analysis techniques were used to investigate the short-term consequences of vocally violent behavior, and to compare voice production before and after training in "hygienic laryngeal release" (HLR) techniques. Twenty-seven actors ranging in age from 17 to 48 years were audiorecorded before and after multiple productions of four vocally violent behaviors: grunting, groaning, sobbing, and shouting. After training in HLR techniques, the experimental protocol was repeated. Audiorecordings of vowels (produced at three pitch levels: model Fo, minimum Fo, maximum F_0) before and after vocal violence, and before and after HLR training, were analyzed using the Multidimensional Voice Program (4305, Kay Elemetrics Corp., Lincoln Park, NJ). After vocal violence, no consistent acoustic changes were detected for voice generated at modal and minimum F_0; however, significant increases in both fundamental frequency range and maximum F_0 were observed. After training in HLR techniques, acoustic measures sensitive to pitch and amplitude perturbation, and non-harmonic noise, improved across pitch levels. The results also indicated that vocal training does defend the laryngeal system from undesirable changes related to vocally violent maneuvers that might surface at the extremes of an actor's pitch range. Because the HLR technique used in this investigation was multimodal, interesting questions are raised regarding which aspect of training is primarily responsible for the observed effects. Further study is required to identify such factors.

Key Words: Actors, Vocal violence, Vocal abuse, Voice training, Hygienic laryngeal release techniques, Acoustic analysis

Appendix C

In addition to works cited previously, the following is a listing of research investigations involving the performer's voice in extended vocal technique.

Some recent studies point to how vocal abuse disturbs voice production (1996 Cobet et al) and (Masuda et al 1993); how vocal hygiene education can improve the voice signal (Chan, 1994) and (Wang et al 1994); the external laryngeal frame function in voice production (Vilkman at al 1996); a review of 25 years of voice research and the importance of utilizing voice research to confirm traditional management techniques (Stemple 1993); how persistent "muscle misuse"— phonation with abnormal laryngeal posture can lead to organic changes (pathologies) (Morrison et al 1993)

Gelfer MP, Andrews ML, Schmidt CP. Effects of prolonged loud reading on selected measures of vocal function in trained and untrained singers. *J Voice.* 1991;5:158-167.

Hixon, T. & Watson, P. *Respiratory Function in Speech and Song* approx. 1989, College Hill, Little Brown.

Jones, H. (1999). Vocal Problems Encountered by actors when involved in theatre forms outside of the usual work on language and text. Presented at National Voice Centre conference "Voice and the Physical Performer" at Sydney University 1999.

Kitch, J.A., & Oates, J. (1994). The perceptual features of vocal fatigue as self-reported by a group of actors and singers. *Journal of Voice*, 8(3), 207-214.

Montequin, Doug. Ph.D. studies investigation into the safe scream University of Iowa.

Novak, A., Dlouha, O., Capkova, B., & Vohradnik, M. (1991) Voice fatigue after theater performance in actors. *Folia Phoniatrica*, 143, 74-78.

Pikes, Noah, (1999) "Giving Voice to Hell: a visually and vocally illustrated presentation of the pioneering multidisciplinary work of Alfred Wolfsohn (1896-1962) and Roy Hart (1925-1974) on the expressive potential of the human voice, including film." (Included some early research in 1940's, 50's, 60's concerned Alfred Wolfson's singing students, Jenny Jones and Roy Hart (founder of the Roy Hart Theatre which involves extended vocal techniques)

presented at the 1999 "Giving Voice" Festival, Centre for Performance Research, Aberystwyth, Wales.

Raphael, B.N., & Scherer, R.C. (1985) Repertory actors' perceptions of the voice in relation to various professional conditions. In V. Lawrence (Ed.), *Transcripts of the Fourteenth Symposium: Care of the Professional Voice* (pp. 102-113). New York: The Voice Foundation.

Scherer RC, Titze IR, Raphael BN, Wood RP, Ramig LA, Blager RF, Vocal fatigue in a trained and an untrained voice user. In: Baer T, Sasaki C, Harris K, eds. *Laryngeal Function in Phonation and Respiration.* San Diego, CA: Singular; 1991.

Sherman D, Jensen PJ. Harshness and oral-reading time. *J Speech Hear Dis.* 1962:27:172-177.

Stemple JC, Stanley J, Lee L. Objective measures of voice production in normal subjects following prolonged voice use. *J. Voice.* 1995;2:127-133.

Stone RE, Sharf DJ. Vocal change associated with the use of atypical pitch and intensity levels. *Folia Phoniatr.* 1973;25:91-103.

Sander EK, Ripich DN. Vocal consequences of loud talking. Paper presented at the American Speech-Language-Hearing Association Convention; November 1981; Washington DC.

Reimers Neils L, Yairi E. Effects of speaking in noise on vocal fatigue and recovery. Asha. 1984;24:182 (A).

Peer Reviewed Article by *Kate Ufema and Douglas W. Montequin*

The Performance Scream: vocal use or abuse?

Kate Ufema, Voice and Speech Specialist— Professional Actor Training Program, Department of Theatre, University of Minnesota Duluth; an Equity actress, singer, professional director, musical director, vocal/dialect/text coach, and professional voice consultant and trainer. Trains and coaches voices in all performance media; contracts with CNN, CBS, NBC, ABC, National Public Radio and American Public Radio. Acted, directed, and coached in theatres across the country, presented workshops and adjudicated theatre competitions and festivals from Colorado to the East Coast. Charter member of VASTA, and currently its President-Elect. BA, MA, and MFA degrees from Penn State University.

Douglas Montequin received a B.A. in Theatre from the University of Maryland, College Park in 1995. In an effort to understand the physiology and teaching of voice production, he continued his training at the graduate level. He received his M.A. in Speech Pathology and Audiology with special certification in vocology from the University of Iowa, Iowa City in 1998. Currently, in a continuance of his graduate work at Iowa, he is completing his dissertation for his Ph.D. in Speech and Hearing Sciences.

Voice Science Background

Adjustments of the vocal tract play an important role in determining voice quality and vocal intensity. Often vocal performers will modify vowels for easier voice production. For example, a singer may modify a closed vowel like /i/, as in 'beat', towards a more open vowel like /ɛ/, as in 'bet', for a more effortless sound, especially when in a performer's higher-frequency range. Ultimately, vowel modification facilitates increased vocal projection. Additionally, singers often adjust their lower vocal tract to increase vocal projection by producing vocal ring, which provides additional acoustic energy around 3000 Hz (Bartholomew, 1934; Sundberg, 1974). Physiologically, vocal ring can be created by a narrowing of the airway in the supraglottal region (just above the vocal folds) as shown by videolaryngoscopy (Yanagisawa, Estill, Kmucha, & Leder, 1989) and by electron-beam computed tomography (EBCT) (Story, Titze, & Hoffman, 1996).

But how is vocal projection increased? Is it simply due to the open mouth allowing more acoustic radiation? Or are the vowel shape changes (vocal tract changes) altering the vibration at the source (the vocal folds)? Titze and Story (1997) discussed acoustic interactions of the source with the lower vocal tract and suggested that strong interactions can exist between the vocal folds and the vocal tract due to the small diameter of the supraglottal narrowing. Thus, it is possible that singers can enhance vocal projection by using this supraglottal narrowing to produce greater ring.

Professional voice users are often required to perform vocal extremes, some of which are believed to be unhealthy to produce. Vocal extremes, as defined throughout this essay, are vocal productions including: screaming, shouting, coughing, laughing, crying, and any additional vocal sound that employs considerably more air flow/pressure/intensity or pitch variation than average conversational speech. One such feared, yet necessary, vocal extreme is the scream. A scream, by definition, is a loud, sharp, piercing cry (Neufeldt & Guralnik, 1996). It is often confused with shouting. The scream is different from a shout due to its sharp, piercing noise quality. This loud noise is the predominant feature which causes most voice professionals to assume that the vocal folds are being abused during a scream. For years, some vocal coaches have trained actors to scream without creating voice pathologies. They follow specific techniques which have not yet been documented in writing. The purpose of this essay is to provide a description of the training technique, anatomy, and physiology of one particular approach to screaming. What follows is shared as an attempt to de-mystify the process, and to set forth preliminary evidence which suggests that trained screaming and shouting need not be injurious to the performer.

A Brief Walk-Through of an Approach to the Vocal Extreme of Screaming

Step #1—The Breath
Since all phonation begins with an appropriate breath (be it conscious or unconscious), breath awareness and breath isolations are the first elements to be introduced at the threshold of vocal extreme training. The first anatomical demand is to breathe low into the system, as with diaphragmatic breathing, where front, sides, and back expansion in the midriff and abdominal areas is in coordination with the air intake. In this first isolation, all chest expansion is consciously eliminated, encouraging all coordinated contractions to occur below the sternum. Allowing contractions to occur above the sternum will usually cause inappropriate laryngeal tension and strain during scream production. Therefore, securing both the awareness and the practice of this isolation is crucial before continuing.

Once the low breath and the 'dead chest' are under control, additional air is 'invited' into the system. This additional air is accommodated by added expansion under the armpits as the external intercostal muscles located at the sides of the chest cavity begin to contract in further coordination with the additional air intake. All the while, the chest is still 'dead', with minimal rise of the anterior chest, and no rising of the collarbone or the shoulders. This type of breathing is necessary for the high pressure/flow requirements of the eventual scream. Again, if high, shallow, chest breathing is used, the scream will feel tense and pushed, and there will be inadequate breath support. Thus, the chest should remain 'dead', allowing the side external intercostal and the abdominal muscles to become the eventual bellows for the extreme phonation. Once these combined breath isolations are under the participant's control, phonation can begin.

Step #2—The Warm-Up
Hydration
Before any type of phonation begins, the participant should be reminded that research has shown hydration to be an important factor regarding phonation (Verdolini-Marston, Titze, & Druker, 1990; Verdolini, Titze, & Fennell, 1994; Verdolini-Marston, Sandage, & Titze, 2000). Thus, water bottles should always be at hand in a voice class, and increased water intake hours previous to any vocal session or performance is extremely important. Systemic hydration takes time. Therefore, drinking 'on the spot' may soothe the mouth and throat but will have no immediate effect on the vocal folds.

The Arc of Vocal Extreme Projection
At this stage, phonation begins with focusing on pitch control. There are three predominant pitch control types of a vocal projection. These three pitch control types are (1) scooping—raising the pitch at the end of a production, (2) straight tone—maintaining pitch, and (3) arcing—'giving pitch loft' as demonstrated by the imaginary arcing path of a thrown ball. These types are explained, demonstrated, and experienced within an exercise format using the word 'hey', and then moving onto one-word commands such as: stop, come, cry, go, now, and fight. It is during this time that ear-training and physio-

vocal sensitivity are initiated, as the arced sound projection is isolated as being the chosen pitch control type for vocal extremes. Other uses for scooping and the straight tone are acknowledged, while emphasizing their unsuitability when creating a vocal extreme.

Extended Pitch Range
The main objective now becomes having the participant phonate comfortably into the high, head/falsetto pitch range (women and men respectively), approaching, but not as high as a squeak. At this point, the men should be producing the same actual pitches as the women, though the quality of sound will be different. Short, puppy-dog, whine-like sounds are often a good start. Specifically, these sound productions are sustained nasal sounds which are: (1) short in duration, (2) low in intensity, (3) descending pitch glides, and (4) starting in the mid- to upper- pitch range. The goal of this exercise is to end with full pitch-range sirens incorporating the appropriate breath coordination discussed in Step #1. These siren productions are vocal imitations of the sirens used for emergency vehicles. Specifically, the participant's full-pitch range is exercised by performing open-vowel-sound glissandos of varying duration, from low in pitch to high in pitch and back to low in pitch.

'Pure' tone Glissandos
After several successful full-range siren productions, the participant is asked to sustain the head/falsetto portion of ascending and descending 'pure' tone glissandos. The participant needs to become highly familiar and comfortable with the upper-pitch range. There need not be fear or concern about the quality of the sound, or the 'breaks' which lead to that part of the range. As long as the pitches are open, free, and supported by the breath, the quality really does not matter. But the phonation should not sound or look forced. The participant is not singing, but rather simply working the range.

Often with men, using their upper range takes courage and additional time to habituate. In these instances, a trusted female partner or an experienced male can be of great help to the male initiate to encourage him to match their pitches, though not necessarily their quality. Beyond a doubt, once a male is trained to scream effectively, there are few phonations that are more chilling or more frightening.

Again, having the head/falsetto pitch range under control is a necessity for vocal extreme production. Vocal extremes, for the purpose of safety, cannot occur in the speaking range of the instrument. Extremes occur in the extreme range. As a result, an ease and familiarity with the upper-pitch range must be cultivated before continuing.

Step #3—Anatomical Awareness
The participant is now asked to sustain a hum on a comfortably low pitch— a pitch well within the speaking range. He/she is then instructed to place two adjacent fingertips on the throat where the most vibration is externally felt as a result of the hum. With fingertips remaining stationary, the participant is asked to produce a full pitch-range siren on an open-vowel sound, and to perceive what the fingertips feel, or do not feel, with reference to the change in pitch. Inevitably, it will be discovered that the larynx rises when the pitch rises and lowers when the pitch lowers. If asked to depress the larynx,

the initiate will feel this also, as well as all the constricted musculature, a constriction which should be noted as dangerously undesirable with regard to vocal extremes.

Before discussing or explaining any further, the participant should be asked to once again place fingertips on the throat, and commit to shouting the word 'help' in order to save a best friend's life. But just as the vocal folds are ready to oscillate, he/she should be instructed not to produce any sound, but rather to freeze/hold the anatomy in place and observe what is felt. Again, it will be noted that the larynx has risen, and has remained elevated in the throat.

As a visual demonstration of this anatomical 'elevator', find a male participant with a highly visible protruding Adam's apple. Have him stand in profile to the other participants and execute a full-range, open-vowel siren going high into his falsetto. As the pitch rises, the laryngeal elevation will become visibly evident.

The fact that the anatomy naturally rises when the pitch rises, and also when we are about to negotiate an arced shout or scream, is the focus at this point. Thus, beginners need not learn to initiate this naturally occurring laryngeal elevation, but rather to simply trust it, and to refrain from creating inappropriate neck/shoulder tension which may inhibit the laryngeal 'elevator'.

Step #4—The 'Noise' Element

Human vocal productions can be basically separated into two types of voiced sounds: quasi-periodic and aperiodic. Quasi-periodic sounds have a repeatability or 'somewhat' periodic element to them. Quasi-periodic sounds are often considered to be 'pure' tones because of the steady nature of these productions. 'Pure' tone, as defined here, is a clear, resonant voice production which uses diaphragmatic breath support. Conversely, aperiodic, or 'noisy', sounds do not have a quasi-periodic nature to them. Vocal noise, as defined here, is a rattling, grating, unpleasant sounding voice production.

Regarding vocal extremes, specifically shouting and screaming, one can shout in 'pure' tone or with the addition of noise. Both 'pure' tone shouts and shouts with added noise are effective, and each is desirable depending upon the purpose. Screaming, on the other hand, usually, if not always, includes the noise element (that blood curdling sound), unless one is creating a farcical scream that is only 'pure' tone and not the least bit convincing in realistically conceived settings.

How to produce this noise element is next in the sequence, and the historical bone of contention, fear, and ultimate rejection because of anticipated injury. Hopefully, 30-years of successful experience without incident, along with the endoscopic views to follow, will help support the technique discussed.

Clearly, if noise is produced by the vocal folds under the kind of air pressure that a scream demands, the phonation would be abusive. This means that the noise of a safe scream must be created elsewhere. The physiological goal is, while the vocal folds are producing the 'pure' tone pitch of the scream, other supraglottal (above the glottis) structures/tissues are producing the noise

simultaneously. This is prepared for and approached in the following manner.
Production of Vocal Noise

The vocal warm-up continues including: gargling with and without water, making vicious velar cat sounds (velar/uvular hissing sounds of sorts), and speaking words like the Yiddish chutzpah (hutzpah) which uses the velar /x/ as opposed to the glottal /h/. Both /h/ sounds are voiceless, but only the velar /h/ incorporates the desired noise, which is created by constricting the back of the mouth, just as are the cat and the gargling sounds. Again, these sound isolations are critical for developing 'muscle memory patterns' in the mouth. Since these productions are voiceless, and by definition not engaging the vocal folds, injury to the folds as a result of these productions seems unlikely. However, the mouth may get dry, while the throat produces more mucus in response to the vibrating tissue.

After about ten minutes of constant engagement, the supraglottal tissue will seem to 'burn' a bit upon swallowing, as is also common with song 'belted' phonation. This 'burning' sensation, in the back of the mouth, is a result of tissue use/friction under high demand. This engaged tissue is suggested to have been used, but not abused. Numerous foreign languages employ similar sounds and may suggest evidence that these supraglottal tissues can withstand the engagement. However, the vocal folds should feel nothing because they are not involved in the noise production.

The aforementioned 'burn' should dissipate within 10-20 minutes after the noise production ceases, if the noise element is properly produced. Once the participant clearly feels the above described tissue engagement, can sustain it, and recognizes that in order to sustain it the larynx is high in the system, he/she is then ready to begin to work into a scream.

Step #5—Screaming
All effective blood-curdling screams are a combination of 'pure' tone and noise. The 'pure' tone is very high in pitch and is produced by the vocal folds as in resonant voice, while the noise introduces even higher pitches, but is produced supraglottally. As a result of little sensory feedback from the supra-glottal elements involved in creating the noise, it is impossible to sense what these structures/tissues are specifically doing to create the noise. However, experience suggests that the previously-mentioned voiceless sounds are due to shaping the back of the mouth and lower vocal tract in a manner as needed for the scream's noise to occur.

At this point, even though the larynx is held high in the system, the vocal folds and the supraglottal tissue are independently controllable. One can be manipulated without perceptually affecting the other as has already been accomplished previously in the warm-up isolations. Putting the two together is when experienced hands-on training is likely to be needed.

The best way to proceed is for an experienced, previously trained screamer to lead the initiate in the following manner. A single command word is chosen. A good choice is the word 'now', as it contains a long, open diphthong sound with a nasal consonant which engages the 'higher resonators'. Another good word is 'fight', with its initial, voiceless, air-producing 'f' and the final forward 't'. The trainer and the participant will alternate phonating the word, as the trainer initiates and the participant closely mimics the sound, the pitch, and the inflection. If the ear-training in the warm-ups has been emphasized, there should be no problem mimicking the trainer with relative ease and accuracy.

The trainer will begin easily, although committed to the intent/chosen subtext of the word, and gradually work sequentially through the following phonations: (1) arcing the word in a 'pure' tone manner at a conversational sound level, (2) arcing the word in a 'pure' tone manner at a shouting level, (3) very high-pitched, 'pure' tone shouting, and (4) very high-pitched, shouting with added noise – the scream.

This added noise is achieved by posturing the velar/uvular anatomy as if to re-create the velar cat warm-up sounds, while simultaneously eliciting a 'pure' tone production from the vocal folds. By watching, listening, and mimicking, the participant will follow both the intent and the body language of the trainer, as well as mimicking the sounds. If the trainer perceives that the novice needs to further physicalize, or needs a pitch change, or even the slightest additional manipulation to better succeed, the trainer will produce it and the participant should follow. Clearly, the abilities of the trainer are very important, as the trainer must serve as both exemplary leader and observant monitor, simultaneously.

After each screaming encounter, the instructor should ask the participant exactly where the friction (the 'burn') is felt in the system. As long as the screamer points to the back of the mouth, top of the throat, back of the head, between the ears—all is well. Often, because the feeling is so high, the sensation is confusing. So the screamer may even indicate somewhere at the back of the neck. All is fine as long as the screamer is not touching or pointing to the larynx, or experiencing a painful cough during or immediately after the production.

If the participant should indicate the larynx, or exhibit signs/symptoms of a painful cough, the sensation will not be a burn, but is rather like sandpaper. This feeling is not good. In this instance, the larynx most likely lowered during the process, suggesting possible vocal fold involvement, as in episodes of clearing the throat. In this instance, give the screamer a few minutes of vocal rest and instruct him/her to drink some water to soothe the mouth and throat. If discomfort still persists after 20 minutes or so, using a steam inhaler may further soothe the system.

After resting and hydrating, revisit the 'sandpaper' issue by encouraging the participant to follow the leader again, only higher in pitch this time. And make sure the novice can sustain the high, head/falsetto, 'pure' tone pitches before re-adding the noise. Move slowly and confidently with commitment to the chosen word to maximize success.

After the novice has successfully mimicked productions on several separate occasions, he/she is asked to lead the trainer. Again, the trainer closely monitors the new, eager, but inexperienced leader, and remains as a safeguard to make adjustments if and when necessary. With careful monitoring, the anatomically aware and experienced trainer should catch and adjust anatomical-approach problems before phonation even begins. Again, the trainer's abilities are paramount.

Once the trainer becomes confident with a participant's progress, the novice screamer should be asked, under supervision, to lead another novice. And thus the learning progresses from initiate to initiate until repeated success, with ease, is achieved upon command.

Step #6—The Time Element

The length of time that one screams is really not a step in the approach, but rather an on-going gauging process. Initial sessions, when all is explained and experienced from correct breath usage to 'pure' tone shouting, can last as long as 90 minutes or be as short as 30 minutes. A well-trained individual who already has breath isolations and pitch variance under control can be taught to scream in 30 to 40 minutes. In contrast, someone who is a high/shallow chest breather, and/or a habitual laryngeal depressor, may take the full 90 minutes, or additional sessions, before being ready for vocal extreme production.

Physically, vocal extreme productions should be considered to be as taxing as any other respiratory/musculatory exercise involving such high intensity. Those who practice this screaming technique can be considered vocal 'athletes' who get a physical workout. Thus, some vocal fatigue and body soreness can be expected. To work the body as hard as needed for vocal extremes for long periods can, and usually does, result in intercostal muscle soreness the following day. Initial sessions lasting longer than 90 minutes are usually physically exhausting. As with athletes, the concepts of pacing and rest should be respected. Therefore, 90-minute sessions are a wise limit.

Once the initiate understands the technique, and as 'muscle memory patterns' become more habitual, stamina increases. Experience has shown that skill and stamina are achieved only through practice. Thus, sessions will include more continuous extreme phonation and fewer breaks for explanation and/or slow experimentation. Then, 45-60 minutes of continuous vocal extreme activity is usually possible, and can easily be followed immediately by a dance class or a singing lesson. Longer than 60 minutes may tire the system to excess.

Finally, once the performer is solidly grounded in the vocal extreme technique, the state of being can be slowly added, much the same way that fight choreography is learned and executed. In other words, all the anatomical 'motor patterns' must be clearly established and well rehearsed before any real emotional commitment is made by the performer. This does not mean that purpose, subtext, or focus is removed from the training to this point—quite the contrary—but rather just the emotion is removed, initially. For, as in stage combat, emotion can never be added too soon or allowed to overpower technique, as injury may result.

Step #7—The Warm-Down

Short, puppy-dog sounds are used both during warm-ups and warm-downs. Humming successive ascending/descending five-note scales is good also. Swallowing silently to check for the 'burn' is informative. The 'burn' should be felt if the individual has been screaming for longer than five minutes continuously. A voiced swallow is also informative. If laryngeal pain is evident after phonation, something is wrong. The 'burn' should be in the mouth, not at the laryngeal level.

Drinking water prior to, during, and following a screaming session is a must. Paradoxically, the mouth will be dry, while the lower vocal tract produces excessive amounts of mucus to accommodate the vocal extreme, often causing the screamer to want to clear his/her throat. Both the 'burn' and the excessive mucus production will exist, and usually dissipates within 10-20 minutes following the screaming session. There are clearly side effects to any vocal extreme as with any intense exercise. But if the extreme is produced with care, experience suggests that these side effects should disappear quickly and completely.

Description of the Mechanism for Theatrical Scream Production

Laryngeal Endoscopy
In order to investigate and describe the mechanism for theatrical scream production, a laryngeal endoscopic investigation was conducted using the Kay Elemetrics Rhino-Laryngeal Stroboscope (RLS) Model 9100. A brief description of the theory and equipment is supplied (see Appendix A). Evaluation protocol is fairly standard for laryngeal endoscopy, where several laryngeal measures of interest are possible for interpretation (Bless, Hirano, & Feder, 1987; Morrison & Rammage, 1994).

Important Anatomy and Physiology
The stroboscopic images obtained will now be discussed relative to basic anatomy and physiology (see Figure 1). The image obtained is as if one peeked over the back of the tongue and down into the throat of the subject. The top of the image would be the back of the throat, while the bottom of the image would be the front of the throat. Thus, the left side of the image is the subject's right side and the right side of the image is the subject's left side.

Figure 1. Endoscopic orientation

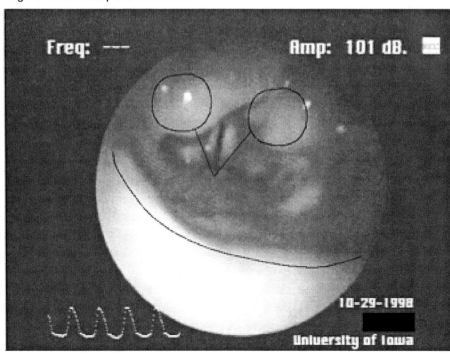

The vocal folds are the two white bands inside the V-shape in the center of the image. The glottis is seen as a black strip between the folds. The point of the V-shape is where the folds attach in a fixed location called the anterior commissure. The circles at the top tips of the V-shape encircle the location of the cuneiform cartilages within the aryepiglottic folds (marked with circles). This marked region is superior to (above) the arytenoid cartilages, which are the cartilages that attach to the posterior (rear) end of the vocal folds. The arytenoid cartilages provide mobility for the folds as needed for opening and closing the glottis, as well as posturing the folds for voicing. The third marker is a curved line near the bottom of the image. This marker outlines the superior (upper) portion of the epiglottis.

Three other displays are provided by the Kay Elemetrics system. The electroglottographic (EEG) waveform is at the bottom left of the image, the fundamental frequency (Fo) at the top left, and acoustic intensity at the top right. The EEG waveform describes how laryngeal structures, usually the vocal folds, cycle in and out of contact and is collected using two non-invasive paddle electrodes placed on the neck. The F_0 describes the frequency at which the folds vibrate and is measured by making fundamental time-period calculations from the EEG waveform. The acoustic intensity would correspond to the loudness of the sound and is collected using a small camera-mount microphone.

Image Collection and Analysis
Unsafe screaming may relate to trauma to the vocal folds. Impact stress has been considered a primary variable in creating traumatic lesions in the larynx (Verdolini, Chan, Titze, Hess, & Bierhals, 1998). The most common trauma result, vocal nodules, is found at the mid-membranous point on the vocal folds (Verdolini, Hess, Titze, Bierhals, & Gross, 1999). This mid-membranous portion was found to have the greatest impact stress (Jiang & Titze, 1994). In short, relatively high impact stress is usually assumed in the production of high pitch, high intensity screams. The difficulty has been measuring impact stress safely and reliably in human subjects. Finding a comparable measure seemed necessary.

For this purpose, flexible-scope endoscopy was employed making use of mid-membranous peak amplitude of vibration as a measurement (Hirano, Kakita, Kawasaki, Gould, & Lambiase, 1980). This measurement describes how much amplitude of vibration exists for the vocal folds at the position where the greatest movement is known to occur. It is assumed that for similar fundamental frequency, mid-membranous impact stress increases as mid-membranous amplitude decreases. This assumption is based on Newtonian theory that force is equal to the product of a mass and its acceleration.

The difficulty in using any image for detailed calculations is defining common distances between structures. In short, the camera provides fixed images, but the imaged structures move. As a result, difficulty exists in comparing separate images that have no common magnification or fixed-distanced landmark. To help estimate laryngeal measures, an amplitude-of-vibration versus length-of-the-vibrating-fold ratio is used. This ratio removes the need for a fixed distance calibration. To use this measure, it is important not to vary the length of the vocal folds much, otherwise actual length does become an issue. In addition, optical limitations exist when using a flexible scope versus a rigid scope. The flexible scope lens has a 'fish-bowl' effect, which distorts the images more than a rigid scope lens. This distortion was considered, but image collection with the rigid scope was unsuccessful. Since the same analysis technique was applied to all visual measures, this distortion was not considered great enough to invalidate the measurement for comparative purposes.

Since screaming is traditionally believed to be abusive, the examination consisted of comparing a vocal fold variable in both the scream production versus a resonant voice production of similar pitch. The subject was a 25 year-old male with over three years of shouting/screaming experience using the above-described approach. The video samples were collected while the subject executed the ascending/descending 'pure' tone glissando exercise, eventually adding noise at the top of the ascending trials.

Figure 2. Resonant voice image

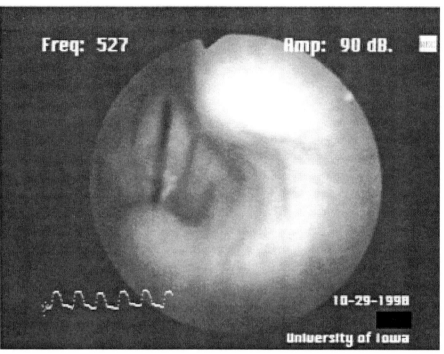

The endoscopic evidence was analyzed using paired-still images. The first image consisted of the top of the pitch range using resonant voice, milliseconds prior to the scream. This resonant event was supported by perceptual judgement, the high Fo, high acoustic intensity, and the quasi-periodic EEG waveform (see Figure 2). The second image consisted of the top of the pitch range immediately following the addition of the noise for the scream. This event was also supported through perceptual judgement, the even higher Fo, higher acoustic intensity, and the low amplitude, spiked quasi-periodic EEG waveform (see Figure 3). From these images, the amplitude-to-length ratio of the mid-membranous vocal folds was obtained.

Figure 3. Scream voice image

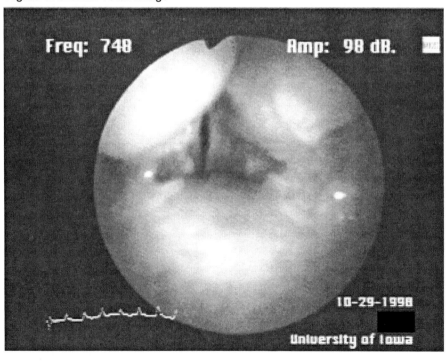

Overall, a total of six sets of paired images were analyzed using Matlab, a commercial engineering software package. The analysis technique for collecting the amplitude and length measures was designed and tested for the purpose of this study. The techniques involved tracing the glottal perimeter using approximately fifty points to define the 'region of interest'. After which, glottal width and membranous vocal fold length were estimated as minor and major axes of the 'region of interest', which was basically elliptical in shape. Glottal width was divided in half to provide amplitude of vibration. When collecting known distances and areas, the designed software yielded measurements with less than 2% error from repeated trials. This error was assumed to be due to human error in defining the region of interest.

Endoscopic Findings
The endoscopic still-image analysis revealed no significant differences between amplitude/length ratio measurements of resonant and scream

productions (see Figure 4). As evident, no clear trend is seen regarding Figure 4. The increased F_0 and increased acoustic intensity for the scream may suggest greater impact force. However, the lack of significant amplitude of vibration differences may suggest that the impact stress for the scream production is not significantly more than for resonant voice when well trained. The vibratory differences seen do not seem responsible for creating the perceptual acoustic differences of resonant voice versus scream productions.

Figure 4. Amplitude versus length ratio

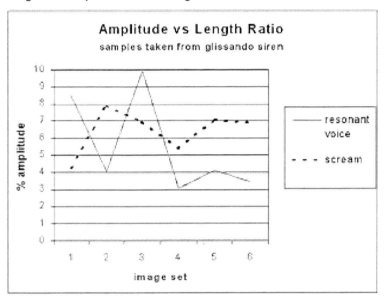

Video analysis revealed several key supraglottal differences. The first most noticeable difference is the supraglottal narrowing evident at the scream onset (see Figure 5). This series of still images shows that in part (a), the resonant voice production had an open supraglottal configuration and a skewed sinusoidal-like EEG waveform. In part (b), some supraglottal constriction was noted, although the EEG waveform had not registered any changes at the vocal fold level. By part (c), the supraglottal constriction was completed and the EEG registered a low, spiked waveform, which was still quasi-periodic. Since the EEG waveform was still quasi-periodic during the scream, the vocal folds could not have been the source of the added noise. The lack of normal shaping of the EEG waveform is most likely due to the repositioning of the larynx for the scream, relative to the location of the EEG electrodes on the neck.

Further video evidence supported that the vocal folds were not the source of the added noise. As the flexible endoscope was retracted during scream production, the aryepiglottic folds were observed vibrating erratically. The epiglottis was also noted as vibrating at a different rate than the vocal folds, but was difficult to view in combination with the true vocal folds. Vibration of the epiglottis was evident, but was not as apparent as the aryepiglottic fold vibration, when using stroboscopy. It should be noted that the false folds did not appear to be involved in the scream production. It is the aryepiglottic folds in combination with the epiglottis that are believed to provide the noise, while the vibration of the vocal folds remains quasi-periodic.

Conclusions

The endoscopic evidence collected suggests that the scream's characteristic noise is produced using secondary sources, the aryepiglottic folds in combination with the epiglottis, not the vocal folds. Overall, the scream appeared to involve high air pressure and flow, but these conditions are not necessarily abusive. Since the larynx and vocal tract give little bio-feedback to the user, it is no surprise that guided learning is needed for correct, safe production.

Currently in practice there are hundreds of students, singers, and actors who will attest to the above technique, and will produce a blood-curdling scream on command that will give one chills. Until the findings included herein, to the knowledge of the authors, no scientific evidence existed concerning trained screamers. These findings strongly suggest the need for further study, especially more investigation into the biomechanics behind pathology-free screaming.

Finally, and foremost, it should be emphasized that the conditions for creating the noise source for the scream are controlled by the voice user. These conditions are easily repeated once the trained behavior becomes habitual. However, when a performance scream is required, emotional motivation is also expected. Therefore, the performer must create the illusion of being completely present in the emotional moment while still remaining conscious of the vocal technique. It is maintaining this delicate balance between human physiology and emotion that we recognize as craft. This delicate balance separates reality from theatrically-created illusion, keeps us healthy to perform another day, and ultimately allows us to call ourselves … artists.

References
Bartholomew, W.T. (1934). A physical definition of good 'voice-quality' in the male voice. *Journal of the Acoustical Society of America*, 1, 24-33.

Bless, D., Hirano, M., & Feder, R. (1987). Videostroboscopic evaluation of the larynx. *Ear, Nose and Throat Journal*, 66(7), 289-96.

Hirano, M., Kakita, Y., Kawasaki, H., Gould, W.J., & Lambiase, A. (1981). Data from high-speed motion picture studies. *Proceeding of the Vocal Fold Physiology Conference* (pp. 85-93). Tokyo: University of Tokyo Press.

Morrison, M., & Rammage, L. (1994). *The Management of Voice Disorders*. San Diego: Singular Publishing Group.

Neufeldt, V., & Guralnik, D. (Eds.). (1996). *Webster's New World College Dictionary*. New York: Simon & Schuster, Inc.

Story, B., Titze, I., & Hoffman, E. (1996). Vocal tract area functions from magnetic resonance imaging. *Journal of the Acoustical Society of America*, 100, 537-554.

Sundberg, J. (1974). Articulatory interpretation of the singing formants. *Journal of the Acoustical Society of America*, 55, 838-844.

Titze, I.R., & Story, B.H. (1997). Acoustic interactions of the voice source with the lower vocal tract. *Journal of the Acoustical Society of America*, 101(4) 2234-2243.

Verdolini, K., Chan, R., Titze, I., Hess, M., & Bierhals W. (1998). Correspondence of electroglottographic closed quotient to vocal fold impact stress in excised canine larynges. *Journal of Voice*, 12(4), 415-423.

Verdolini, K., Titze, I., & Fennell, A. (1994). Dependence of phonatory effort on hydration level. *Journal of Speech and Hearing Research*, 31(10), 1001-1007.

Figure 5. Scream Progression

a
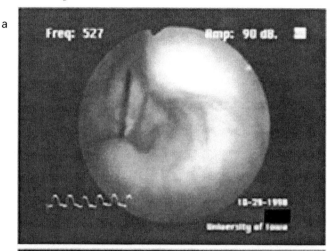

b
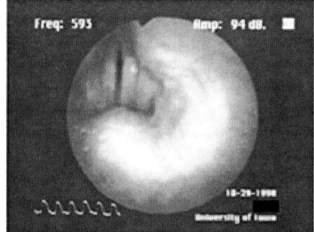

c
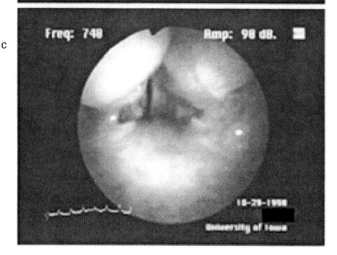

Appendix A.
Endoscopy uses a two-bundle fiberoptic cable system, where one bundle provides illumination using a cold-light source while a second bundle relays the image to an eye piece/camera providing a visual display. Either steady or strobe light sources can be used for either static or dynamic viewing. The strobe light source can be auto timed or user controlled. In either more, the vibrating structures are viewed for only a short part of successive cycles—when there is illumination. If timed exactly to the fundamental frequency (F0), no significant vibration is noticed even though the structures are vibrating. If timed slightly greater than the F0, vibration is seen and is significantly slower than the true vibration.

Laryngeal endoscopic systems vary slightly depending on the manufacturer. The Kay Elemetrics Rhino-Laryngeal Stroboscope (RLS) Model 9100 is a popular endoscopic system for voice and speech application, and stores data sessions on S-VHS tape.

Verdolini, K., Hess, M., Titze, I., Bierhals W., & Gross, M. (1999). Investigation of vocal fold impact stress in human subjects. *Journal of Voice*, 13(2), 184-202.

Verdolini-Marston, K., Sandage, M., & Titze, I. (2000). Effect of hydration treatments on laryngeal nodules and polyps and related voice measures. *Journal of Voice*, 8(1), 30-47.
Verdolini-Marston, K., Titze, I, & Druker, D. (1990). Changes in phonation threshold pressure with induced conditions of hydration. *Journal of Voice*, 4(2), 142-151.

Yanagisawa, E., Estill, J., Kmucha, T., & Leder, S.B. (1989). The contribution of aryepiglottic constriction to 'ringing' voice quality – A videolaryngoscopic study with acoustic analysis. *Journal of Voice*, 3, 342-350.

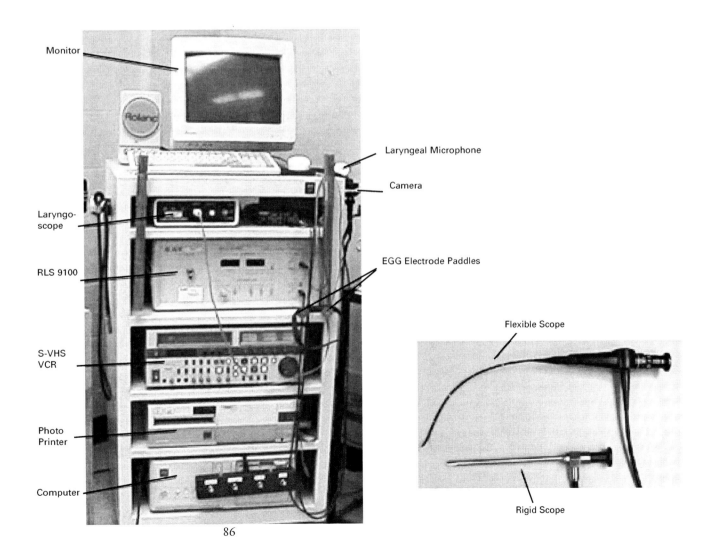

Essay by *Matt Harding*

Voice and the Choreography of Staged Violence: a survey

Matt Harding is a member of VASTA and the SAFD. He holds the rank of actor-combatant, having studied unarmed, rapier and dagger, quarterstaff, smallsword, broadsword, and sword and shield. He has had several opportunities to perform and choreograph staged violence personally. Mr. Harding holds a BFA in Acting from Wright State University, an Advanced Certificate in Voice Studies from the Central School of Speech and Drama, and an MA in Theatre with an emphasis in Voice and Speech from Northwestern University. He coaches voice, speech and dialects for productions and private students in Chicago under the auspices of Vocal Enhancement Instruction (VEI).

In order to explore the use of voice training as it applies to the choreography and teaching of staged violence an e-mail survey was submitted to Certified Teachers, Fight Directors and The College of Fight Masters of the Society of American Fight Directors (SAFD). The contact list was taken from the Directory of the Fall/Winter 99 edition of *The Fight Master: Journal of the Society of American Fight Directors*. Out of the nearly 80 members polled, eighteen responses were received. These responses were used as the source material for this essay.

The SAFD is an organization dedicated to "training and improving the quality of stage combat," with a commitment "to the highest standards of safety in the theatrical, film and television industries" (*Fight Master*, 44). This national organization attracts educators in "violent" movement from all walks of the entertainment industry and martial arts disciplines. Thus the range of voice use and the understanding of the vocal mechanism is widely varied.

The questions posed to the SAFD members covered the following points about voice work accomplished by participants in the teaching and choreography of staged violence:

- Perception of importance
- Frequency of usage
- Common vocal issues encountered
- Methods employed

Following is a sampling of answers given by the SAFD members who responded, and while much of what is stated is not surprising, it is encouraging to see our brothers and sisters in arms are as concerned about the performer's voice as one would hope them to be.

Perception of Importance
The most heartening aspect of doing any type of study involving professionals with similar interests is the fact that many of the same goals are present despite the possibly apparent diversity of the fields. The SAFD and VASTA are both concerned with not only preserving the well-being of performers' instruments, but also in finding ways to improve them. In fact, John Robert Beardsley plainly states that "Voice work within choreography is as important to me as the physical actions themselves."

This sentiment is completely illustrated by the use of the words: *very, important, essential, imperative, vital, integral* and *crucial* in response to questions about the importance of voice work in the teaching and choreography of staged violence. This is the one item that respondents agreed on unanimously. "In the performance of staged violence, vocal reactions—both by combatants and on-stage observers—make a fight come alive" (Ravitts). "The sound is part of the experience" (Beardsley), and without it the "violence doesn't work" (Woolley).

Many choreographers discuss the concept of using the voice as part of the orchestration when *scoring* a fight. "In choreography, I punctuate the action with a variety of sounds—knaps, objects hitting the floor and vocalizations" (Burt). "The voice is the musical and aural underscore to the physical action" (Byrnes).

In addition, many teachers and choreographers agreed that it is the coupling of the voice with the movement that creates the visceral reaction that will draw an audience into a fight. Otherwise, from the back of a theatre, actors will look like *toys* fighting. It is the "vocal yelps, howls and grunts" of the human voice that "travel undiminished and grab the audience" (Cheatham).

On the other hand, one subject of the survey, Bill Lengfelder, admitted to having trouble vocalizing in a fight himself having originally trained as a boxer and a mime. Still he attempts to shield his students from learning "this nasty habit of silence by osmosis" with constant reminders to *act* the fight.

If the performers do not recall how important voice work is in the end product—the showing of a fight scene—they suffer. "I have literally graded down my finest theatrical 'jocks' because of lack of acting...and graded up safe, but not so exciting physical actors because they used acting intent to extrapolate their meager physical skills" (Lengfelder).

In the previous example, students are being rated on vocal technique amidst a sea of complicated physical techniques. "Unfortunately, given the framework of the usual fight class (and...much of modern theatrical training) 'technique' is an ugly word, whether that technique be to control a sword point or the lower ribs" (Sandys). This lack of technique is nowhere more prevalent than in a fight without sound. "There is nothing as dull as silent combat," except perhaps a scuffle in which "the combatants constantly roar at each other like WWF contestants" (Sandys).

But as important as believability is the safety of the performer. Not only must the combatant be capable of performing the same physical motions day in and day out during rehearsal and performance, but "they must be able to survive with their voice intact" (Burt). In fact, most teachers and choreographers mourn the fact that they are unable to pursue more vocal work in their teaching and choreography, primarily due to time constraints.

Often even in theatre training programs, there is a lack of time in a ten-week class. Plus, there is an expectation by many fight teachers and choreographers that students are being taught proper technique in their voice classes. Some teachers and choreographers were quick to point out that though they find voice work to be of the utmost importance, they are not voice teachers themselves and feel voice work should be left to specialists in that field, just as combat concerns should be left to specialists in their own.

"I am not a voice professional, and [I] always defer to the vocal coach when there is one on staff in rehearsal" (Suddeth). "As a combat teacher...I have no time to act as a vocal coach—nor do I feel I should. I can only incorporate into my work principles that I hope students are learning in their vocal training" (Sandys).

Along with voice and movement professionals who keep their ears and eyes open for dangerous practices and solutions to them, Bruce Lecure suggests, "Actors must be responsible for their own instruments. No one can feel what they feel." Even so, the counter-argument has been made by more than one individual that "many actor-combatants lack...vital breathing and vocal techniques, just as they lack other acting skills" (Sandys). Lecure concurs citing a disturbing trend of actors' "inability to self-monitor."

The question is then begged as to whose responsibility it is to make sure the performer finds the necessary training and/or treatment. Many teachers and choreographers of staged violence feel their best course of action is to listen for potentially harmful vocal behavior and remind students and clients to remember their vocal training. Finally if necessary, Drew Fracher's practice is to "sic the voice coach on them" if one is available.

Frequency of Usage

Three answers, or combinations thereof, tend to surface regarding questions about the regularity of voice work being used in the teaching and choreo-graphing of staged violence. Either "daily" or "all the time," "infrequently" or "not as much as I wish" or "the majority of voice work happens toward the end of the class or choreography process," once movements have been learned and other safety issues have been addressed.

Often the teachers and choreographers who are using daily vocal work are focusing on warm-ups, breath and the release of unnecessary tension. The use of voiced exhalation can be indicative of proper technique, as with vocalizing through a roll or fall. This proves that a student is indeed breathing.

John McFarland incorporates voice work "ALL THE TIME [sic]," by telling students that he will "work the body as a whole. The body, the mind and the voice." He goes on to state that "the first day of combat on the beginning level is spent on Impulse work; listening to the body's involuntary reactions. Breath and voice work is included in this."

Work done "early on in the process in connection with full, relaxed breathing" assists actors in getting appropriate easy vocalization and respiration into their "muscle-memory as a fight moves" (Cromer). Free, optimally functioning breath and vocalization attached to a specific movement promotes "safety and efficacy of the movement" (Suddeth).

Attuning students of combat to the breath necessary for staged violence at an early period allows them to "incorporate the illusion of muscular effort and the effort to control breath under stress;" due to the fact that, "exertion and contact" produce "both bodily and vocal noise…the more attention paid to the sounds of violence and to shaping the story through sound as well as action" will engender a higher degree of comfort and mastery for a performer in both the breath and vocalization. This also aids in the believability of a fight, "but if [a student or performer] hasn't been used to breathing and mak-ing noise earlier, they find it very difficult to relax into the fight, physically and vocally" (Sandys)

Happily the group that reports to daily concentration on vocal issues is the largest, though those who don't often cite support from voice colleagues. J. Allen Suddeth assures that there is always a voice professional he will defer to in a LORT theatre, "at least in A, B, and C levels," but this is not always the case in film, television or for private coaches who may work with a client for no more than a few weeks at a time.

For those teachers feeling the crush of a grueling schedule, "If time permits…" is a common opening clause. This trepidation grows larger with the feeling that "the fight work itself is very time consuming" (Lecure). "There is never enough time to do everything—acting/fight/voicework/etc." (Ravitts), especially in situations where teachers and choreographers are working without a specified professional vocal support network. *Tempus fugit*. Time again becomes the enemy.

After initial time has been spent and other elements have fallen into place, some choreographers feel there is more time to breathe and focus on vocal issues. In fact, James Cheatham notes that "during the final week of rehearsal, 85 – 95 percent of my notes are generally vocal notes." And he is not alone. Once the movements, costumes and other external concerns are in place, actors must recommit to not only the physicality of combat, but also to acting which is, of course, intrinsically tied to vocal impulse and production.

Common Vocal Issues and Methods Employed
Many vocal issues were identified by the choreographers and teachers surveyed. These include:

- Faulty Production
  — Constricted Throat
  — Inappropriate Breathing and Support
  — Vocal Damage
- Silent Fights
- Tension
- Added Intensity
- Inappropriate Reactions
  — Overlap
  — Overkill
  — Over and Over
- Vocal Apathy

Most of the issues identified revolve around faulty vocal production by stage combatants. And the most common issue of faulty production is a "clenched throat" brought about by the natural tendency of the body to tense for action in stressful situations such as those being represented by staged violence.

Participants in the survey identified this constriction of the vocal tract and supralaryngeal structures as tightening in the tongue and throat muscles constriction around the throat or neck, and a tendency to "clench" vocally. Directly tied to this is what J. Allen Suddeth terms a tendency to "lock up" during "displays of aggression." This practice leads to inappropriate breathing technique and sometimes a lack of support all together that may result in a silent fight or vocal damage. Certainly the realism of the combat will suffer.

Of greater concern than an unbelievable fight is the likelihood of vocal damage in performers and students who grunt and grind their vocal folds. Bruce Cromer identifies this more colorfully as a tendency to "rake" the vocal folds with harsh, raspy screams and yells. It is understandable that the human body is confused by the psychosomatic processes that occur within a performer's body as he or she attempts to replicate fight or flight instincts and yet remain free and rid of tension in the interest of longevity of performance. The subglottic pressure needed to hurl a boulder is fake, but the body is tricked and often the performer's body is as well. This can lead to far more tension than necessary in the vocal tract during sound production.

As mentioned before, another very common tendency in the performance of staged violence is the "silent fight," which has already been flagged as detrimental to realism. More importantly, a silent fight is often indicative of poor breathing. The breath is either inappropriate, unsupported or nonexistent. Some combatants hold their breath through an entire phrase and then gulp for air!

There are various methods used by stage combat teachers and choreographers to address the aforementioned issues. Foremost is the search for a good, deep centered and consistent breath. Tina Robinson has begun the practice of singing through phrases to cause students to feel a good diaphragmatic breath. James Cheatham suggests that students produce what he terms "roller coaster" noises throughout a phrase once they have achieved three-quarter speed. Ricki Ravitts slows down fights as an exercise and adds "huge" vocal reactions on every move.

These are some examples of exercises used by respondents to combat held breath and tension, and many others follow the same pattern. In general, it is work done after a series of movements is mastered and often is exercised at slower than normal speed, attaching deep breath to kinesthetic posture. This allows muscle memory to recall an optimal breath when entering into said position at performance speed.

In addition to specific exercises, many teachers and choreographers include as much breathing and relaxation work as possible from the beginning of work, especially in warm-ups working up to more intense vocalization during the choreographing process. John McFarland, who has done extensive work in the field of voice and violence, including work with Bonnie Raphael and Marya Lowry, states:

> Most of the voice work relating to combat is touching vibration on the breath to allow freedom of the sound production mechanisms, and to focus on the constant release of air. One thing I stress in the beginning is exhalation on every action. The body will inhale [naturally] and the student does not need to focus on inhalation.

Bill Lengfelder uses "voiced sighs" on each action to inform vocal production and free combatants of unnecessary tension. Bruce Cromer believes in "actors who consciously choreograph their breathing in fights, who pay attention to skillful, healthy and consistent reactions." J. Allen Suddeth recommends "constant gentle reminders" and "specific breathing beats" within the choreography and is willing to adjust choreography so a combatant has "longer breaks within a fight."

Many stage violence practitioners cite Bonnie Raphael's articles "Sounds of Violence" and "Screaming Without Suffering" as the basis for work they do to enable performers to effectively and consistently perform otherwise damaging sounds. Coupled with work on breathing, this is an effective method for safeguarding against vocal trauma.

Another common problem associated with a lack of breath and inherent in the previous discussion is that of "locking tension." Physically, performers not only lock their vocal mechanisms, but also cause their bodies to become stiff. Nicholas Sandys calls breath and relaxation the "central issue" to voice work and inherent problems in its relation to staged violence. "If the actor does not breathe, then tension builds, the body loses flexibility, the techniques become stiffer and contact too hard—and there is, of course, no noise!"

Fortunately, coming back to breath seems to be the answer to alleviating sympathetic physical tension, presupposing a performer's effective training and comfort with vocal technique. Good breath use is seen as "very important for the relaxation and centering of the performer, and the complete integration of character into movement" (Suddeth). "Relaxation is the key" (Sandys).

Payson Burt concurs stating, "When teaching, I spend a lot of time working on breathing, maintaining the breath through an action and not clenching muscles unnecessarily." Brian Byrnes reminds, "What is important to learn, is that by working with ease, precision and physical focus—a performer can still achieve 'intensity' without 'clenching' physically and vocally."

Other issues mentioned by those polled are potentially less damaging, but can be dangerous nonetheless, whether physically, or to a combatant's credibility. The added intensity of vocal response to a phrase or fight can often rev up the performers in such a way that fighting technique is all but forgotten.

"Vocal energy is energy" (Cheatham). This energy added to the physical dynamism a combatant is attempting to keep reined in can be too much and send a powerful adrenaline rush. The basic method of combating this malfunction is to slow back down and either specifically place vocal responses within the choreography or to examine a fight phrase by phrase until the vocal energy becomes a natural part of a piece of staged violence, (Ravitts).

Compounded with a tendency to speed up, performers have a myriad of inappropriate vocal reactions that crop up when sound is added to staged violence. Most of these problems are easily overcome with a little attention, much like that used to temper the effects of vocal energy racing a fight. Overlapping responses are easily corrected by deciding which sound is more important to the story of the violence at the particular moment being examined, especially when there is text involved.

Also not uncommon is the tendency for performers to overdo the sounds of their vocal reactions. As mentioned earlier, Nicholas Sandys likens this to an action-movie or WWF match in which an actor "produces the same sound no matter where the victim is hit." This practice is neither believable nor exciting. Furthermore, if the sound is incongruent with the action presented, an otherwise serious fight can become unintentionally comical. Not to mention that overdone vocal reaction can hurt the voices of performers" (Cromer).

By far the most common complaint of the violence specialists polled is the use of repetitive vocal response during fights, often identified as "grunts."

Continuing with the example of an "action-movie soundtrack," Sandys reminds that the practice of repetitive grunting "is equally stylized and unconvincing, yet it is just as common a trait in much stage combat in the professional and non-professional theatre."

Sandys' solution to his own lamentation is to "ask the actors to employ their own experiences and imaginations" while "focusing their breathing and vocal energy on the place of impact." He believes this helps to "isolate resonators by shutting down other areas or shutting down the area itself...with these focuses, the victim produces more specific and varied vocal responses."

And there are many other methods for correcting the irritating habit of grunting the same sound over and over. Bruce Cromer's students are similarly exhorted to find appropriate sounds to fit the injury. John McFarland explores what he terms "the chambers of the voice" and then relates them "to the part of the body that is being struck or affected." He goes on to state:

> I use four basic chambers of the voice and within those chambers use rhythms and patterns that parallel the action or response of the body. Most of this work is to make realistic connections with the action. I then explore an opposite or inappropriate sound for a given movement. This helps the student understand appropriate corresponding sounds. It also lends itself to the development of comedy.

Ricki Ravitts suggests that her charges try a different reaction on every move and eventually either she or the combatants edit or score the soundtrack. James Cheatham reminds students of grunting when pushing a large object, and then points out the sounds made with the release of subglottic pressure once the object budges. The result is generally a more open sound. He also ties this into someone getting punched and "taking it" versus someone who is punched hard enough that he or she cannot "take it," or hold in the air, thus creating the result of a much more powerful and often more interesting blow. Breath release is inevitable.

The final area of concern, and quite possibly the most dangerous, is pointed out by David Leong. Often actors don't believe the area of vocal work "is important when fighting." It is the job of all theatre practitioners, whether voice, movement, or acting specialists to disabuse them of that notion.

Final Thoughts

This survey has merely scratched the surface of a dialogue that obviously needs to take place between not only VASTA and the SAFD, but with other movement and voice specialists who may not belong to either organization. "Teaching stage combat is a 'full instrument' challenge" (Suddeth). And it is my belief that teaching voice is as well. Who knows what could be accomplished with continued conversation between voice and movement specialists? My hope is that the well-being of performers at large will be preserved and enhanced both physically and vocally.

Fortunately the work of many professionals in both fields has begun the discussion—most notably Bonnie Raphael's work. Many SAFD professionals stand by "The Sounds of Violence" and her screaming technique in particular, and many additional notes in survey responses contained the sentiment that voice is "one of the most important issues and the most overlooked in stage fighting and stunts" (Robinson). In essence then, it is the duty of both voice specialists and violence specialists to seek each other out and bring mutual work to a higher level.

"Sound is the music of the dance of stage combat," (Beardsley), and with our brothers and sisters in arms, voice specialists can move forward in striving for a more exciting, believable and safe environment for performers to work *ad infinitum.*

Bibliography

Beardsley, John Robert, Fight Master, SAFD. e-mail response to survey, 10/13/00.

Burt, Payson, Fight Director, Certified Teacher, SAFD, President - Los Angeles Fight Academy. e-mail response to survey, 10/23/00.

Byrnes, Brian, Fight Master and Chair of the SAFD Health and Safety Committee. e-mail response to survey, 10/18/00.

Cheatham, James, Fight Director, SAFD. e-mail response to survey, 10/16/00.

Cromer, Bruce, Certified Teacher, SAFD. e-mail response to survey, 10/12/00.

Doersch, David "Pops," Certified Teacher, SAFD. e-mail response to survey, 10/12/00.

Fight Master, The, Fall/Winter 1999, Volume XXII, Number 2, Pp. 42 - 4.

Fracher, Drew, Fight Master, SAFD. e-mail response to survey, 10/12/00.

Hayes, Andrew M., SAFD. e-mail response to survey, 11/15/00.

Kelly, Colleen, Fight Director, SAFD, Alabama Shakespeare Festival. e-mail response to survey, 10/12/00.

Lengfelder, Bill, Certified Teacher, SAFD. e-mail response to survey, 11/8/00.

Lecure, Bruce, Certified Teacher, SAFD. e-mail response to survey, 10/12/00.

Leong, David, Fight Master, SAFD. e-mail response to survey, 10/12/00.

McFarland, John, Fight Director, Certified Teacher, SAFD, VASTA. e-mail response to survey, 10/12/00.

Ravitts, Ricki, Fight Director, SAFD. e-mail response to survey, 10/13/00.

Robinson, Tina, Certified Teacher, SAFD, Fight For It International. e-mail response to survey, 10/16/00.

Sandys, Nicholas, Fight Director, SAFD. e-mail response to survey, 10/23/00.

Suddeth, J. Allen, Fight Master, SAFD. e-mail response to survey, 10/11/00.

Woolley, David, Fight Master, SAFD. e-mail response to survey, 10/12/00.

www.safd.org, website, visited 11/28/00, 9:50p.m.

N.B. All information in the bibliography was taken from the listed printing of the Directory in *The Fight Master,* the SAFD website or specifics provided in the e-mails themselves. Apologies are extended for any omitted qualifications or upgrades in SAFD status since that time.

Interview by *Marié-Heleen Coetzee*

Voicing the Visceral: an Interview with Erik Fredericksen and k. Jenny Jones

Introductory notes by Fight Masters David Bouchey and J. Allen Suddeth

Erik Fredericksen have advanced the combat arena in North America with his business savvy and his technical abilities as teacher and practitioner. His individual ability to organize via his work as former president in the Society of American Fight Directors has moved the industry forward. He should be appreciated for his efforts and contributions in this small corner of the theatre. He has learned from me and I from him, which is the way it is supposed to be and hopefully will continue to be, with those who follow in our footsteps however large or small. He has been a great friend and colleague, as well as a wonderful practitioner of his art and the fight community owes him a great deal of gratitude.

David Bouchey

k. Jenny Jones is one of the hardest working S.A.F.D. Fight Directors in the United States. More than simply a Certified Teacher of stage combat techniques, she is a well versed acting teacher as well, who is able to blend the two disciplines into an unmatchable training regime for her students. Ms. Jones works in, Ohio at the University of Cincinnati's College-Conservatory of Music, Drama Department with the students enrolled in the theater programs. There, she trains young performers in the details of staged violence from various periods in history. She also works with the department staging whatever violence is necessary in the shows produced each season. She also is a hard working professional fight director, at home in Regional Theater situations such as the Cincinnati Playhouse in the Park, as well as outdoor drama, such as the famous production of *Blue Jacket*. The latter is a historical tale involving up to 50 performers each summer on a stage of about 5 acres. Additionally, she is on faculty at the Celebration Barn Theater, where she teaching acting techniques each summer in an exclusive workshop for emerging fight directors and actors.

J. Allen Suddeth

Marié-Heleen Coetzee: Drama Department , University of Pretoria, formerly University of Zululand. Lectures: stage movement , educational drama/theatre, drama/film theory. Researching the physical and cultural-anthropological dynamics of Zulu stick fighting and its application to theatre. Received Masters degree with distinction, currently writing her doctorate. Presented at national and international conferences and workshops, and has published academically. Choreographed, performed in, and directed various productions. Organised, and taught at, the inaugural Rendezvous South Africa! international stage combat workshop, co-organiser for SAPVAME conferences, an executive member of SAPVAME, involved in previous Paddy Crean workshops, serves on the Artistic Advisory Council of the IOSP.

Contextualisation:
The interest in, and attention given to, stage fighting is assumed to be an age-old institution. However, it is seemingly only in the last part of the twentieth century that stage combat started to develop as distinctive *performance skill*. Fight directing, fight choreography and fight performance have become a specialist enterprise that is tailor-made to suit the environment of a theatrical performance. Stage combat as performance skill mediates between fiction and reality; actuality and theatricality; the daily and extra-daily. In contemporary theatrical performances where violent interactions abound, stage combat has become a vital and compelling dynamic of performance, complementing dramatic action whilst *safely* creating the illusion of physical violence.

Stage combat techniques alone are not enough to ensure the effectiveness of a stage fight. The ineffective use of other elements of performance can render the illusion of physical conflict contrived or unbelievable. The use of the voice is one of these elements. It has been argued that the most compelling stage fights are exciting to audiences visually, kinaesthetically, *and aurally*. The heightened physicality demanded by a fight scene necessitates sound vocal practise in order to use the voice optimally for expression and communication. Working from the assumption that the safe and effective use of both the voice

k. Jenny Jones is an actress, teacher, and fight director currently residing in Cincinnati, where she is on faculty at the College-Conservatory of Music, teaching acting and stage combat. A Certified Fight Director and Teacher with the Society of American Fight Directors, k. Jenny has served as a master teacher through out the US and currently heads the Actor's Ensemble Workshop at the Celebration Barn/SAFD Actor's Ensemble & Fight Director Training Workshops. Having choreographed over 100 productions, her credits include: Cincinnati Playhouse in the Park, Portland Opera, Cincinnati Shakespeare Festival, Ensemble Theater of Cincinnati, Kentucky Opera, Pennsylvania Renaissance Faire, Dayton Opera and numerous Colleges and Universities through out the Midwest. She has studied the acting techniques of Michael Chekhov with Mala Powers, Andre Malaev-Babel, Joanna Merlin, and Russian Laureate Viacheslav (Slava) Kokorin and is in demand as a Chekhov teacher and coach through her Bard Alley Studio.

and stage combat can assist in producing a visceral impression of physical violence and intensify the believability of a fight, SAFD Certified Fight Director k.Jenny Jones and SAFD Fight Master Erik Fredericksen share their thoughts on vocal integration in training and performing stage combat.

M-HC: *Stage combat and voice specialists (such as Dale Girard and Bonnie Raphael, to name a few) have addressed the importance of the integration of voice in stage combat; arguing that the effective use of the voice enhanced the believability/authenticity of the fight and offers the performer a wider range of creative choices in the portrayal of physical violence. What are your thoughts on the subject?*

kJJ: It has taken me a while to actually believe I have thoughts on the subject. My own opinions and any conclusions I reach, are still in a process of development. I too, believe the effective use of the voice enhances believability. Dale Girard adds two points to the theories that Bonnie Raphael introduced back in 1988 [published in the SAFD journal, *The Fight Master*]. The first point being how "forced sound has the same effect on the body as suppressed sound, creating physical tension and restricting bodily movement;" and the second wonderful snippet of advice reminds the actor how

they "are creating the illusion of effect, and not trying to survive its reality." Both Dale and Bonnie talk of concepts such as voluntary and involuntary sounds, preventive voice care, healthy vocal technique, and competitive sounds, etc. For me, most of what I am currently exploring is less voice work and more breathing. One of the issues that neither Bonnie nor Dale address, is how the performing of stage fights directly contributes to its own unbelievability: tension, stress, even anxiety. All these elements interfere with the free flow of the breath, hence the voice.

Those who fight well are few. What is the formula for an extraordinary actor combatant? Hence a believable fight? The best fighters I know are those who are naturally blessed with a physical countenance and ability to move with ease. The Michael Jordan's, of stage combat, such as Fight Master Brian Byrnes, Certified Teachers J.P. Schielder and Richard Ryan. Just as all of those who desire to be actors, few are born with the actual ability. Talent can only be trained, not taught. My average student is the *average* fighter. In his book, *Actors on Guard*, Dale makes a comment about how the beginning fighter usually holds their breath and is too tense. I disagree. This is not the beginning fighter, this is the average fighter. The mere act of focusing with purpose and determination upon an intended target creates small amounts of stress and tension upon the body; the sense of setting or fixing oneself into a course of violent action while attempting to "be safe" naturally contributes to the desire to control the gesture. And I would argue that it takes an equal amount of focus and determination to move an average, even an 'unblessed' body with ease as it does without it, especially while fighting. In other words, outside of 'neutral movement', meaning combat without emotion, one can achieve what is asked of them. Add the visceral emotion, and ease is the first element to get booted out the window.

In other words, it honestly takes tremendous purpose to want to kill or avoid being killed, and the focus needed to do it safely naturally creates tension. The question is how to remove it and keep the fight believable. I am not certain if it can be, or should be. Yes, the actor should be at ease while the character is tense, but in reality a small amount of tension will exist. It has to; it is what keeps me from loosing my sword during a head swipe. So lets focus on how to work through it, in spite of it, rather than do what is impossible for the average fighter. It is about creating good habits, the Alexander or Feldenkrais of violence. On a practical note, the question is what kind of training this demands? How many hours, or even years? One of my fears is how easily we get caught up in our ideologies of what 'ought to be', while allowing ourselves less time for being practical. As my mom used to say, "Jenny, be a practical idealist. You will get more done." So we can talk and discuss about breathing from a grounded center, Meanwhile, our students and actors are turning blue from the cardiovascular, aerobic and emotional demands of the choreography.

Both Dale and Bonnie talk about adding the voice early on in the fight in order to learn the fight with accompanying sounds, as the longer one waits to add the voice, the more difficult it will be to find the connection. This is vital. My concern is related to the performance. How can an actor consistently breathe and generate sound from their center under such extraordinary circumstances and feelings? What I observe in the average fighter, even those who are considered 'advanced' in skill, is how the breath begins, but gets caught, trapped, clutched in the throat or chest right as a move is about to be released. Tell them to breathe, and they control the exhale: pushing, focusing, or sustaining the exhale in such a way that disallows freedom. The theory that if the foundation is laid early then it should hold later is right, but even still I observe, that the foundation we stage combat teachers and choreographers use is not sufficient for the average fighter. Not once full emotional commitment under performance conditions is added. What I am discovering is how when one makes a choice for a sound, that it is the quality of breath that should be choreographed, not just the timing of it. Meaning is embedded in the artistic use of breath. Not just breath from a grounded center, but breath that is painted with qualities.

EF: I absolutely believe that the effective use of the voice can further the believability of the fight and extends the actor's creative choices in staged violence. My experience is that, essentially, most actors, *young* actors of *today*, have very little appreciation or interest in the value and complex possibilities of the voice. Their experience (film primarily) show them that voice—what

Erik Fredericksen:
Currently Professor of Theatre (acting and theatrical combat) and Department Chair at University of Michigan, Eric has been a master teacher at institutions including Juilliard, Carnegie Mellon, and Dartmouth College. He also served as Interim Head of Acting and as Associate Dean at California Institute of the Arts. Fredericksen began his career as an actor and stage combat choreographer at the prestigious Guthrie Theatre in 1971. He has worked as an actor and choreographer at many major regional theatres and in New York and Los Angeles, including the Guthrie, Cincinnati Playhouse in the Park, Bucks County Playhouse, Indiana Repertory Theatre, The Long Wharf, Seattle ACT, The Folger, The Seattle Rep, and The Manitoba Theatre Centre of Canada. He has worked with the New York Shakespeare Festival, Colorado Shakespeare Festival, Dallas Shakespeare Festival, and the Stratford Festivals (Canada and Connecticut). He's worked directly with some of the leading directors in the country, a few of which include Joseph Papp, Michael Langham, Des McAnuff, John Hirsch, Jean Gascon, Arvin Brown, Libby Appel, and Stein Weinga of the National Theatre of Oslo. Fredericksen has choreographed numerous luminaries, including Christopher Plummer, Morgan Freeman, Holly Hunter, Denzel Washington, John Lithgow, Frank Langella, and Don Cheadle.

little text there is—is usually supported by dubbed music and they have no need for variety, subtlety, or, even, volume. Thus, in working with young actor combatants, their voices are simply at the level they have been lead to (if they are lucky) through the vocal training present in a particular curriculum. Effective and creative use of the voice is essential to the concept of acting any "high stakes" psycho-physically invested scene. "High stakes" to me, as an acting coach, means finding those objectives that come closer to life and death, discovery and loss, etc, than "behavioural mimicry". The voice, in a scene requiring the investment of a body engaged in a life and death struggle must also resonate those "stakes". In films, frequently, we will see *a la* Clint Eastwood a behavioural style that dictates that even though one is facing death and perhaps doing "high stakes" physically invested movement is a service of those stakes, the voice remains 'cool' and disconnected to the physical event. Young people, weaned on film, are of course prone to think that this is 'real' behaviour. It is of course, not. It is simply reflective of a style of acting that distances the voice (and frequently the body) from a consideration of fully involved, "high stakes".

M-HC: *Stage combat, as a discipline, accentuates the safety of the performer. This concern about safety seems to be mainly related to the use of stage combat techniques, weaponry, and the staging of violence. I am curious as to why, seemingly, it is only fairly recently (in the last decade) that emphasis has been placed on the safety of the performer's vocal instrument as well. Could you propose an answer to this issue?*

kJJ: In the early seventies, stage combat was just coming onto the scene (here in the USA), and although voice training had an earlier birth, it was not the mixture of specific methodologies it is today. The explosion of interest in and knowledge of both disciplines in recent years has also shifted view points and provoked a re-evaluation of methods and pedagogy. The integration of these two disciplines in actor training is a natural continuum.

EF: I think the primary reason why this is now being considered is that many more actors (trained as such) and directors are becoming involved in the "fight game". Where stage combat is still considered primarily for its "stunt" affiliation, that is less, indeed seldom, an interest or a part of the experience of those individuals who come to it that way. We know that the voice can be misused in any situation that requires extraordinary physicalization. In a recent "non-combat" production of *Lysistrata* we noted stressed and damaged voices from improper vocal production. Certainly stage combat could be one such occasion. The incorporation of stage combat into training curricula is a good thing and partly responsible for this heightened awareness. In my own training as an actor, there was, of course, extensive training in voice. However, there was not a class or workshop that addresses the voice in staged conflict. Combat training started in the MFA program I was in, in 1970.

M-HC: *From a pedagogical point of view, how could voice be integrated effectively into stage combat programmes (university and stage combat workshops)?*

kJJ: I believe that the average teacher of stage combat (myself included), is unprepared and unskilled to handle issues concerning the voice alone (give me a sprained ankle, not a sore throat). When we trained as actor combatants what was not spent on the actual physical discipline, was on history and style. Voice is simply taken for granted. It is taken for granted that a professional actor will know how and when to use their voice as easily as making a choice about an acting issue. I am not certain if I can answer the question. I know the voice is not effectively integrated, and I do not know of anyone who has practical solutions. I feel comfortable teaching a punch; a thrust; a kick, but not a primal scream (even though I have been trained and am familiar with the practice). Teachers of stage combat have varied backgrounds, they are mostly actors or movement specialists. I cannot think of any who have significant vocal training. Paul Denhardt, in Wisconsin, however, is seeking his teacher's certificate from Kristen Linklater.

We need more Voice teachers who are interested in Stage Combat. We need to invite them to the regional and national workshops and provide significant results for students to witness. Quite honestly, people come from places where they do not have opportunities for swordplay, and they go to workshops and classes to fight, not vocalize. I do not intend to demean, but call it as I see it. A product needs to be made available to stir the interest of the combat teachers and their students. Part of me hates that idea, but in our American culture, people will not buy into an idea unless they know beforehand it will serve them, that they need it. Currently, people feel they have been getting by, and so why the change? Why is it that Bonnie's articles appeared twelve years ago, and almost nothing since?

Voice teachers need to be invited into the classroom for master classes, at least. Teachers of both disciplines need to find the time to get together and develop a series of exercises that directly contribute to the use of voice and breath during physical and emotional exertion. Ideologies need to be workshopped, and the results distributed. It is not enough to read a review or conclusion of what went on in Chicago, or Banff. People need to witness it, be an audience to it. They need to be moved by it. Once it is taken to the teachers, then it will be taught. Once it is taken to the actors, it will be used upon the stage. What I am looking for, I suppose, is some sort of formula that I know will have effect not only in the rehearsal hall and classroom, but in performance as well. I am weary of seeing performance anxiety and the natural tension of fighting push aside a centered breath and an open free voice in the average fighter. Teachers demonstrate to their students bad vocal technique; trapped breath, forced sound, repetitive qualities, and so forth, but they do not have the tools to correct these problems. Suggestions as to what should *not* be done abound, but not enough practical exercise is offered on *how* to effectively use the voice.

EF: I would think a 'team taught' approach best. For example, at some time during the/a stage combat course, text should be introduced. Acting *and* emphasis on safe and effective vocal production should be addressed as part of the scene coaching focus. I could see the vocal coach being involved once the basics of the choreography (blocking) are learned enough to add the variable of vocal concentration. Indeed, I should think the vocal coach (most actors are not trained in dance, combat, martial arts, or athletics) having a role in assisting the actor to become aware of breath control that would help...even in the absence of text.

I am not a vocal coach, but years ago I did teach Lessac based voice work (I also studied with him), and find the physical metaphor of instruments as consonants as well as "Y-buzz" and mask placement very useful. Also, some of Bonnie Raphael's work, particularly 'new breath new image' useful for the broad, holistic 'vocal scoring' that could be useful in heightening choreographic 'beats' where there might be text.

I have had occasion as an actor (Hamlet, Cyrano, Richard III, Macbeth, to name a few) to act and fight. However, most of the time, there is little extended dialogue during fight scenes. Generally, my experience has taught me (i.e. incorporating the MacDuff/Macbeth text in the last fight) that frontal placement, strong stomach center that leaves the shoulders and neck free (relatively free...one is swinging a sword!), and frontal mask placement of tone help keep the text "out" and focussed while not over-working the neck, etc. in an incorrect fashion. i.e. as sound producer and primary resonator. That, by the way, is the major problem when actors attempt to produce intelligible sound while involved in major physical action.

M-HC: *In your fight choreography, to what extent do you consider the safety of the performer's vocal choices (characterisation, developing the fight, rhythm, communicating intent)?*

kJJ: I confess I tend to take small elements of the safety issue for granted. I know, and can feel when someone is not using their voice properly, but I do not have the tools to help them correct it. As a fight director, I am barely given enough rehearsal time to stage a fight, work out the acting intentions for the story, let alone be a vocal coach. If anyone tells you they take the time to work out the moves with equal devotion to the voice, they are speaking from their ideology, and not from reality, unless they also direct the production and give themselves as fight directors all the time needed. Even in University the time is scarce. Fight Directors are the last people to be brought into the production and the first to leave. Producers have only recently become aware that they need fight directors and vocal coaches. I am looking forward to the day when both individuals will grace the rehearsal hall at the same time.

When I choreograph, I score the breath and emotion with the action as much as possible. What usually happens is that by the time I return, it is gone. When the actors rehearse on their own, they tend to only invest in the gestures of the story. Once this aspect of the fight is neglected, whatever my intentions, there is no time to correct the problems. Just getting them to breathe is a struggle enough. Whenever possible, if I find an actor is actually abusing their voice, I will cut the acting intention behind the move, and substitute it with another. Changing the reason for the sound is more efficient than my trying to discuss how to improve it.

EF: Essentially, my experience has seldom included long passages (indeed, even short passages) of text necessitated during intense combat. Should, however, that occur, I would seek to approach it in a manner similar to any highly active emotional scene where vocal demands are made: properly funded breathing, placing the voice as much as possible in major resonators *other* than the throat, and, simply 'suiting the action to the word (voice)'.

M-HC: *Optimal body integration influences both the use of the voice and how stage combat techniques are learned, and performed, and as such, how the body/voice responds to a given performance situation. How much attention do you pay to optimal body integration in teaching and choreographing stage combat?*

kJJ: From the outset, almost completely. As I have alluded to before, the main element I find that is missing from the theories currently on the table is the emotional element: learning and rehearsing in neutral gesture. I hold that waiting to be emotional is as detrimental as waiting to include to voice. Mind, body and spirit. To me, emotions are the spirit of the actor, hence feelings and their expression are as much a part of the body as anything else. Yes, there is talk that the emotion must be psycho-physically connected, but mostly what I have read or heard is how emotion is the last element to be included. I strongly believe that qualities of breath stir and stimulate feelings that can be later acted upon more fully. How can a voice be connected unless the emotional support is within the breath that carries it? I tend to teach technique in neutral form, but never when I choreograph. However, when I do teach, I make strong efforts to propose qualities of breath for the students to explore while drilling. It is very difficult to teach students to commit emotionally to the fight when the demand for cognitive activity is so extraordinary. Knowing when to make the shift from drilling to emoting without loosing parts of the foundation is something I am still searching for.

EF: This is a major focus of mine, and I seek constantly to emphasise the following: to have the actor identify where he or she must live; to have the actor adopt (put on) the 'postural/character garment' necessitated by the script; and to understand that they are performing a highly sophisticated dance with dangerous communicative cues that must integrate a total psycho-physical (martial) awareness. To explain the meaning of 'postural garments', I return to a concept Paddy Crean expressed in his line, "Well, Erik, it's all in the face, isn't it." That was valid for a close-up in film. On stage, the body must adopt not only the physical center (garment) of the character (M. Chekhov's work with Psychological Gesture is useful here), but also the 'psycho-physical condition' that the body would normally express *if* (Stanislavky's "Magic If") the character were in a fight. In other words, the 'cool' postural garment that says nothing is at stake, is very popular with the young thinking only soap acting, but is not the postural garment necessitated as an *acting choice* made by an artist portraying in character in extremis on stage and in a fight. Closely related to the concept of 'postural garments', is that of a psycho-physical (martial) awareness. A total (martial) awareness is a heightened state of connection to environment and partner. The 'cues' are the beginning of those actions and/or thoughts, and words that 'cue' the actor to continually blend and respond. Together, these focal areas may assist in integrating the body/voice effectively in stage combat.

M-HC: *By the time that the fight director and voice coach get a chance to work together on a scene (if at all) the fight is generally set; performers have started working on the fight choreography, on fighting in character, on integrating the acting baseline, and so forth. As such, vocal responses would necessarily have been emerging to support the action and dialogue. My concerns here are that, by this stage, the performer may already have made unsafe vocal choices or misused his/her voice producing organs, all of which may have gone unnoticed. Further, it is easier to learn bad usage of the body/voice that to unlearn it. How would you suggest addressing these concerns?*

kJJ: I feel the voice and breath are *part* of the action more than a support of the action. Your question partly lies within the difference between a fight director and a fight choreographer. If a fight director waits to direct until after they have choreographed, then what you see as concerns do arise, however, if a fight director directs as they choreograph, the emerging emotional 'vocal responses' should (ideally) be connected and healthy. This is when I take it for granted that an actor knows how to use their training. However, if performers rely upon their human instincts, rather than their training, changing the quality of the action is more efficient than trying to 'unlearn bad habits". I fully agree with you on this issue. In addition, (and this relates to Dale's advice) as long as a Fight Director can prevent an actor from behaving 'instinctually', but rather guide actors to rely on creative behaviour, the chances for preventing vocal problems are greater. I also observe that stage combat fights are often over choreographed. As choreographers and teachers we are romanced by what we do. We love a fast *riposte* and *triple envelopments* on the retreat, when all the audience wants is to be thrilled and moved by conflict. I tend to believe we create vocal problems by over exerting our actors, causing difficulties in breathing and concentration.

EF: This concern can never be fully addressed unless there is a sensitive director who understands that the fight scene, and all that accompanies it, is not just an interruption of his/her 'directing concept', but an integral part of the progression of the play. This is why we must continue to affect/infect the training curricula of not only actors, but directors and stage managers.

M-HC: *In disciplines such as creative movement, physical theatre, dance and acting, breath and breathing techniques have been used to optimise sensitivity towards a partner, create a heightened sense of physicality and psycho-physical connectivity, intensify the communication of intent, and create a sense of rhythm. Do you think these concepts can be related to teaching, choreographing and performing stage combat?*

kJJ: Can the breath and breathing techniques be related? Yes, a fight is no good without it and is what I have been alluding to thus far. I have always tried to get my students and actors to breathe, but it has only been in the last two years that I have developed some techniques that consistently work through and into performance. Not only do I paint the breath with qualities, but I work a good deal with unvoiced "tremoring", while I even have looked for ways to delay inhales and exhales for story telling purposes. While a creative inhale can catch the audience off guard, it also gives them (the audience) permission to hear the feelings unexpressed solely through the voice. The actors are simply breathing through the story as if they were speaking. Focusing on the idea that the breath is equally important to the communication as the gesture, allows the fight partners to come together. It forces the actors to consider creating their work as wholly integrated artists, and not merely movers.

EF: These concepts must be related. However, that growth in importance will continue only as long as fight teachers/directors, etc. are regarded (by vitae and reputation) as bona-fide teachers of acting. Until only recently, they have been (in the old League of Professional Training Schools curricula) as "trick of the month" visitors who perhaps were sandwiched in between the clown lady and the tap dance teacher. This is changing, thank goodness. In my own work, I try to convince the young actor that they are first and foremost, *acting*. It is not a circus trick. The hardest thing, aside, from the physical demands, is the concept that they must 'receive' the attack (insult, hurt, outrage) and have a *reaction* just as they should in good acting (poor old Clint Eastwood aside). If you are scared, punched, stabbed, almost hit, etc, there should be reactions that lift the choreography above the level of a low stakes dance. I carry this same concept, of course, into non-combat acting and it is just as challenging. People don't wish to appear 'weak', and thus are afraid to receive. This makes for mediocre acting and unconvincing theatrical combat. In the thrust of this article, it should be clear that the voice, and let's please assume it is part of the actor, must also be receptive and thus specifically reflective.

M-HC: *How do you envision the ideal process of collaboration between the fight director and voice coach?*

kJJ: The ideal situation would leave both parties open to explore and accept the other's methodologies. Ideally, whether it be a performance or classroom setting, both individuals should seek ways to yield to the needs of the other. Whatever result, the work will be a union of thought rather than a mere combination. In the past, I have secured the help of voice teachers, but never outside a clinical situation. These circumstances were devoted to process, and mostly were devised of "testing" theories. I have kept some, but not all of what was discovered.

EF: I envision such a process of collaboration as involving two artists who understand and respect the interrelatedness of each discipline and consider the contributions of each as indispensable to the making of safe and effective theatre. Additionally, they may need to share a similar vision of the need for team taught approaches to the making of an actor and, of course, have a good chemical balance in their working relationship. It can't be an 'academic' exercise to fill a time slot. A practical example of a collaborative working process can be found in my work with Ms. Irene Connors at the California Institute of the Arts. When I was there, I was able to involve Irene in some of the Sport Fencing/Scene work. This segment of the work occurred when basic attacks and parries and some strategy has been acquired for foil fencing. The actors then memorized text, Shaw and Chekhov in particular, and 'fenced' the scenes with masks, speaking the text on the action. The actors 'debated' physically and vocally through the medium of fencing. It was quite productive.

M-HC: *Do you have any other thoughts related to the topic that you would like to share?*

kJJ: I feel that what the *Voice and Speech Review* aims to do is fabulous. I hope the door between our two worlds will continue to open. The booklet on the use of voice in stage combat that was prepared for the International Organisation of the Sword and the Pen's 1999 Paddy Crean Stage Combat Workshop in Edinburgh, was a great initiative.

EF: Only that this topic, and this investigation is very valuable and long over-due. Stage combat organizations/societies should play a role in promoting the integration of voice in staged combat. After all, we are becoming a valid "performance art" in our disciplines, and we should not willingly eschew the theatrical validity and contribution of the voice. It, along with heightened physicality, can make our discipline unique from Dance and Martial Arts.

❧

Essay by *Marya Lowry and Robert Walsh*

Voice/Combat Conversation

Marya Lowry and Robert Walsh are a husband and wife team. Lowry is a voice and speech specialist and Walsh is a fight director.—ed.

ML: How do you begin working on a fight?

RW: Preliminary discussions of stage combat for a production invite disclaimers like no other category of theatre! Fights get framed by any number of people who are ready to explain how quick and easy staging them will be before you've even conducted a conversation with the director! Notwithstanding, the critical information to gather is the point of view of the director about his or her particular production. We then discuss how the fight(s) will fit into the conceit for the show. Stylization or authenticity? What should the audience feel? Visceral responses, metaphors, etcetera. I also get a strong visual blueprint from my collaboration with the designers.

ML: Could you discuss your working process with actors?

RW: My first meeting with the actors is one part dramaturgy, one part first impressions, and one part piecing the story together on your feet using a very large brush. We sketch the fight built upon the character's goals and needs, and continue to contextualise it by the dialogue and the given circumstances. The more ownership actors have of the fights from the beginning, the better. It will promote each actor's individual investment, as well as encourage what I term "the collective energy". We then show this sketch to the director and dialogue about the clarity and direction of our storytelling. After the initial sessions, we layer in the details of the moment-to-moment fighting. At this point in the process, each actor is preoccupied (for good reason) with his or her individual movements, so their ability to interact and play off of each other is limited. I will introduce sound as a rehearsal technique to facilitate the music of the fight.

ML: What do you mean by the music of the fight?

RW: A fight is like a jazz score, there are rhythms and syncopation, dynamics and nuances. My goal is to incorporate these into the rehearsal process as early as possible and one of the techniques I use is to encourage the actors to vocalize some of these rhythms in connection with effort or reaction sounds. I do this for two reasons: One, it communicates to each partner the mutual music in which the actors are working, and two, it gets them to breathe. The disadvantage is that it can over simplify the true quality of sound that the character might legitimately make in the scene.

Marya Lowry: Artist-in-Residence in Brandeis University's MFA program, specializing in voice and acting Shakespeare. Professional voice/text coaching includes: Broadway, Off-Broadway, the NJ Shakespeare and Berkshire Theatre Festivals. Taught voice and acting at Purdue, Duke, and Virginia Commonwealth Universities and the School for the Riverside Shakespeare Co. in New York City. Recent performances include: American Repertory Theatre, Merrimack Repertory Theatre, Boston Center for the Arts, NJ Shakespeare Festival, Lyceum Theatre in San Diego and Roy Hart International Arts Centre in France. At Boston's Symphony Hall, Marya has been a featured performer with Boston Pops and Handel & Haydn Society.

Robert Walsh is the Artistic Director of the American Stage Festival, a LORT D theatre operating year-round in Nashua and Milford, New Hampshire; Artist-in-Residence at Brandeis University, teaching stage combat in the MFA program; on leave from Boston University, fulfilling the same role in the BFA program; fight director, certified teacher with the Society of American Fight Directors. Staged fights in New York and all over the country, most recently at American Repertory Theatre, Huntington Theatre Company and Hartford Stage Company; acting assignments include off-Broadway and regional theatre, soaps and feature films, the latest being *State and Main*, written and directed by David Mamet.

ML: When do you shift focus from the use of sound as a rehearsal technique for a fight scene to the use of sound for character work in the fight scene?

RW: Generally, much later. It typically takes the whole rehearsal period for the actors to gain comfort with the fight. Throughout the bulk of rehearsal, the natural tendency is to delay the use of the vocals due to the concentration on technique. There is also a place early on where authentic vocalization can take the tempos well beyond what is safe so, occasionally, I must actually restrain actors from using more emotionally charged vocals. As we move toward the technical rehearsals, there is greater ownership in all areas: acting, fighting, and vocalizing. Any vocal notes I have are typically given then. I must confess that I respond more to what isn't working, rather than embellishing on all the possibilities that may exist. This is principally due to the fact that there never seems to be enough time, particularly once you're in technical rehearsals. As such, if the fight rehearsals have been compromised, you can guess where the vocals are at that point. At what point do you come into the process? When do you start working on the sounds in a fight as a voice coach on a show?

ML: It depends whether it's a professional or student production. If it's professional, it's usually around technical rehearsals, I'm sorry to say, because the fight rehearsals are separate from the main rehearsal, where I'm spending most of my time. I often arrive at a technical rehearsal and discover that there is either very little vocal soundscape or it's a general cacophony of grunts and other sounds of violence. As you've pointed out, the actors have so much to focus on when preparing a fight scene, the voice work is not the priority. Because of that, I tend to wait until the fight has been developed and the actors are comfortable with it.

RW: Would you prefer to start your working process at an earlier stage? For example, during the initial sessions or sketch between the fight director and the director?

ML: That seems to me a good time to have the voice coach get the story of the fight, assess the vocal possibilities of the actors and get them to think about the story from a vocal point of view. It also solves the problem of the voice coach being an 'outsider', by introducing the voice coach early enough to allow her/him to provide more effective input. Bringing in a voice coach at such an early stage can also provide the necessary endorsement from the fight director.

RW: Definitely. Identifying the voice coach as a collaborator earlier on will help to make it a more fully realized fight scene. It would also open the door during technical rehearsals to share the limited rehearsal time. Toward this collaboration, the voice coach could be given a specified amount of time immediately following the sketch, or initial sessions, to make suggestions and give the actors some practical methodology.

ML: Regardless of what has been done earlier in the rehearsal process, technical rehearsals are the time when the vocal elements get refined. It's the time to strengthen vocal choices that will enhance the story of the fight, and attend to specific problems the actors may have with regard to the execution of those choices.

RW: What are you listening for vocally when you see the fight?

ML: As with the rest of the play, I'm listening to hear if the voice is telling the same story as the physical life of the character. The use of the voice should inform the fight, so I am listening for sounds that are connected physically and a true reflection of the degree of effort, danger, or pain that the character experiences. In humorous fights, I am listening for sounds that enhance the comic elements. Are there occasions where you are more actively involved in choreographing vocal responses?

RW: Beyond what I have worked out with the individual actors performing the fight, I spend the most time with characters on the periphery. This is especially true when no sound/music underscoring exists and the actors viewing the fight are obliged to fill the atmosphere with vocal reactions. It's difficult for the actors to avoid feeling self-conscious, particularly if the responses require a lot of emotion or improvised verbal communication. Nonetheless, the scene will die without that texture, so I tend to do some fun game playing to break the ice and get everyone comfortable with heightened vocal responses. The other central reason I require their flexibility and ease in supporting the sound envelope, is that it helps me to focus the fight, particularly if it is a large group. In my collaboration with the director and the sound designer, I do everything I can to make sure all of the aural elements are orchestrated effectively to produce a strong visceral response in the audience. One example would be the opening scene from *Romeo and Juliet*: multiple fights; people watching; people running; a variety of weapons; staggered entrances of characters we don't yet know: the sum total of these elements will be mayhem and chaos. I enjoy playing conductor, particularly as I add in live sounds like furniture falling over or props crashing around the actors. One aspect I must monitor is the energy of a fight being over-fueled by both the on-stage sound/music and by recorded sound/music, driving the performance tempos into potentially dangerous areas. *Hamlet* and *The Illusion* are both good examples of plays where this could occur. At certain points I build in rests which help to punctuate what is happening and retard any energies that may be spinning out of control.

ML: The notion of fighters feeding off sound energy is important. The combatants, the other characters in the scene, and the audience, are all fed by the power and energy of the human voice. Sadly, it has become one of the most under utilized design elements in the theatre. With greater frequency, directors and sound designers are relying upon musical or other recorded underscoring and I recognize its power when used judiciously. It is, however, often used to manipulate the emotions of the audience and eliminates the range of possibilities offered by the authentic use of the human voice. The human voice possesses an extraordinary ability to inform character, define story and draw both actor and audience alike into the truth of the moment. There are countless occasions in scenes of violence when the singular use of the sounds and silences of the human voice could be far more evocative. Take, for example, a common stage slap. Emphasis is usually placed on the physical response and sound of the knap alone. However, it can be doubly effective to focus attention onto the character's vocal response. A sharp inhalation of breath at the shock or surprise of a slap or a vocalized sound—a sob, a cry, a semi-voiced breathy exhalation—is both unexpected and highly dramatic. Conversely, in any kind of fight to the death, I want to hear the specific sounds of effort; exhaustion; pain; rage; and to hear the progression of the fight aurally right down to the agonizing sounds of death. Adding extravagant vocal color can help make the fight grittier thereby enhancing its effectiveness.

RW: Do you find similar issues in university theatre as you've addressed in professional theatre?

ML: Yes. The issues are basically the same, though the climate is very different. In the university setting my input is assumed, the actors know me and are eager for my ideas. In the professional situation, I have to earn the confidence of the actors with each new production. Within the training program, I can immediately work towards reaching my objectives. In school I have the advantage of access to the students (the graduate students) in class. Frequently I have them bring the fights into class where we begin to explore the vocal life of the scene. Some of the questions we examine are: Which character uses more exertion in delivering his/her fighting movements? Whose vocal response will give us the most information in a given moment? The person on the attack or the one on the defense? Is the character relishing the act of fighting or trying to disguise their effort? What is the physical cost to the character engaged in the fight? When does fatigue set in and how does that effect the sounds emitted? Again, I want to see the actor work with breath as a means of telling the story. Actors often behave as though it's embarrassing to breathe fully or audibly, to let us see that they are aerobically stressed. However, since many fights produce aerobic stress, audible breathing is an organic response, and can provide valuable insight into the character's journey.

RW: Much of what you're identifying here is also a part of my early discussions with the actors. How these two areas coalesce to form strong visual and aural storytelling is certainly obvious. It's a microcosm for actor training, really.

ML: You train actors every year for the SAFD Certification Test. How do you prepare student-actors for this test?

RW: Briefly, each student has three semesters of training that culminate in the Society of American Fight Directors weapons skills proficiency test. Formerly, they would certify after two semesters, which made it a real "crash course". I mainly focussed on technical proficiency in order to accomplish this goal. The ability to continue training in a third semester has been transformative. In my work as a fight director in the professional arena, I have been fascinated by the paradox of untrained actors who demonstrate more skill and flexibility than the trained actor. This has led me to a shift in emphasis. Increasingly, the focus of my work with the students has been to help them gain ownership of a methodology that resembles the way they think and work as actors and to continue to attach that point of view to their understanding of what drives the technique. My classes now are far more an acting class than a movement specialization course. Consequently, the certification test is much less the focus of what I want them to get in the long run, though the certification test's function as an opportunity for the students to integrate the different aspects of stage combat training is still quite wonderful.

ML: The certification test also serves my work as a voice trainer. Teaching combat voice in a program where the actors are engaged in combat training offers lots of advantages. The most obvious is that we already have a common ground for the work: Continual voice training; a working relationship; a common vocabulary; and time to lay the groundwork for specific vocal techniques. I know the actors' skills level and I can incorporate training in combat voice on a parallel track with their physical combat training. Teaching specific skills is easier when the student has an immediate need for their application and when they can envision the benefits.

RW: What's your process to prepare them for performing a fight scene?

ML: Before the student-actors connect voice to fight choreography, we will have worked in class with all those generalized sounds I referred to earlier that I would prefer not to hear in performance. They learn to keep the throat open, to free and deepen the source of the breath, and release all types of sounds using a wide variety of vowels. The actors will then connect these elements to released and integrated physical movements.

RW: Some of my biggest concerns are alignment, balance and foundation, all of which are necessary for the released and integrated physical movements you mentioned. These concerns seem to be a cornerstone of your work as well.

ML: Absolutely. Getting the actors to lower their center of gravity and find a deep connection to their feet and legs is an essential part of my approach to voice training. The physicality required for good fighting reinforces these concepts, it puts student-actors in a position to access and support the breath low in the body. They will also learn to scream, create choking-like sounds, and learn how to vocalize the sound of physical trauma without traumatizing their vocal folds. Then we take specific series of moves they have developed in fight class and add the voice. By using the same choreography and changing characterizations or altering the situations (making them humorous, danger-ous, murderous, etc.), I can teach vocal technique and at the same time, assist the actors to think specifically about how to make vocal choices that reveal character and situation and bring clarity to the story of the fight. In addition to learning a healthy, safe technique, I'm preparing them to contribute cre-atively and originally to the aural elements of fight choreography when they are working on a production.

RW: That's similar to what I do inasmuch as a safe technique has to be separated out and appropriated first, then other elements of the scene can be layered on top.

ML: Exactly. I'm trying to avoid the pitfall of introducing vocal elements when the actors are already emotionally connecting to a fight and fully com-mitting to their actions. This is a recipe for disaster. Incorporating voice into physical violence has to be done with a certain amount of emotional detachment and a lot of control. Ultimately, fine tuning vocal responses will involve the actor more deeply in the reality of the fight and help to "sell" the fight to the audience. When training actors, I talk a lot about the importance of the soundscape and how the human voice can enhance the physical choreography. However, another important element is silence. When consciously employed, silence can be devastatingly powerful and theatrical.

RW: Admittedly, aspects of a fight I enjoy the most are the moments leading up to it. Silence can begin to play an important part even before the first blow. If the onset of the fight is not effective, we tend not to have any interest in what follows.

ML: We are both referring to the kind of silence that is alive with anticipation. Silence because the actor is holding his/her breath is completely ineffective. One of my favorite stages of the fight rehearsal is when the actors perform the fight in slow motion; marking, but fully connected to the action of the fight scene. The combination of focus, physical ease, and accompanying silence, never fails to draw me in.

RW: It is certainly the foundation of the rehearsal process. Not only are the student-actors (or professional actors) obligated to see everything, but their bodies must "hear" everything, as well. They are required to make thousands of tiny adjustments that can only be accomplished by learning at a slower speed, but nonetheless played with intention: physically, emotionally and vocally.

ML: And, for me, that's the point: how to mine the vocal/physical life of the actor combatant to create the fullest total impact.

RW: It would be great to get a room full of fight directors and voice trainers together to share current best practices and brain storm ways to push the boundaries even further.

ML: Now that would be a gathering full of sound and fury signifying something truly exciting.

Essay by *James Newcomb and Ursula Meyer*

"I'm a Singer, Not a Fighter!" A few Brief Thoughts on Voice, Violence and the Opera

James Newcomb and Ursula Meyer are another husband/wife combat-voice team. James has been choreographing and teaching fights since 1979. He has worked with numerous Shakespeare Festivals and regional theatres on a wide variety of violence challenges. Five years ago, he was introduced to the world of opera and discovered some new challenges to satisfying the needs of the fight and the performer. "It's all about the singing", he said. "The fight must never compromise that in any way." The following observations served him well.

Keep It Simple
There are several reasons for this. The amount of rehearsal time is much shorter than that of a theatre production. A Shakespeare production has many hours/days/weeks dedicated to the fight sequences, e.g. the Tybalt-Mercutio encounter. In an Opera there are often only two weeks to rehearse the entire production. A fight director might get two hours to set the fight and then a half-hour here or there to review it.

The fighters/singers are understandably concerned that they will be able to learn the fight in such a short time. Most classical stage actors are trained in fight techniques. Many opera singers have to learn *how* to fight as well the actual moves of the fight in the same amount of time. They are also naturally anxious that complicated fight moves will not compromise breath for singing during or after the fight.

It is paramount that the singers be able to see the conductor. Moves which take the performers behind scenery or to any other position which blocks their view of the conductor have to be avoided at all costs. Even if there is no singing during the fight, the performers must be able to keep track of where they are in the score at every moment.

Be Flexible
Many singers have performed the opera and the role before. This is much more common than in the theatre. So there is often another version of the fight that the singer already has in his head. The director has also often directed the opera before and he or she will often want a fight that is similar to one that was used in other productions.

In addition, moves may often have to be changed at a moment's notice.
In *Lohengrin* there was a high note at the end of the climax of the fight. The move needed to be altered in order to provide the singer with the kind of physical posture he needed to be able to manage the note. A healthy knowledge of physical alignment methods (e.g., Alexander Technique) was invaluable during moments like these.

Ursula Meyer (Associate Editor) (MFA, University of Washington) has been teaching Voice for 19 years at numerous institutions including four years at the Yale School of Drama. As a professional voice/text/accent coach, she has worked extensively in regional theatres such as The Guthrie, Yale Repertory Theatre, the Oregon Shakespeare Festival, South Coast Rep., and, the La Jolla Playhouse. She trained with Cicely Berry, Patsy Rodenburg, Andrew Wade, Arthur Lessac and is a designated Linklater teacher. She graduated with distinction from the Advanced Voice Studies Program at the Central School of Speech and Drama in London. Also a professional actress, she has worked at Seattle Rep., Milwaukee Rep., La Jolla Playhouse, and fourteen seasons with Shakespeare Festivals throughout the country. She is currently on leave from the University of California, San Diego while working at the Oregon Shakespeare Festival.

James Newcomb began working with stage violence in the early 1980s with B.H. Barry.He has since worked as resident fight director for seven seasons at the Oregon Shakespeare Festival and directed fights for numerous theatres and universities including, among others, the La Jolla Playhouse, the Old Globe, the San Diego Opera, U.C.S.D., U.S.D. , and the Malashock Dance Company. James has also taught stage combat for both the UCSD and USD graduate programs as well as the National Theatre Conservatory in Denver and the Yale School of Drama. Also a professional actor, James has worked at numerous regional theatres, including seven seasons at the Denver Center Theatre Company, South Coast Repertory Theatre, Berkeley Repertory Theatre, Shakespeare Santa Cruz. He is currently in his eighth season at the Oregon Shakespeare Festival in Ashland.

Learn the Music
Jamie's background as a singer and performer was very useful. The fights in

opera are always scored by the composer. There are very specific rhythms and punctuated moments that are meant to be part of the fight choreography. The fight can only be as long as the music will allow. The moves of the fight need to be orchestrated for breathing like an aria. The structure of the fight must follow the dynamics of the music and, unlike in the theatre, the music is never thought of as underscoring.

Understanding the music also helps establish rapport with the performers. If the fight director needs the singers to understand his or her language, the fight person must speak the language of the singer. Also, it is extremely important for the fight director to have good communication with the conductor. When Jamie worked at the San Diego Opera, there was quite a commotion on the opening night of **Lohengrin**. One of the characters on stage hit a shield three times in order to signal the beginning of the fight sequence. That evening, the conductor came in with the music for the fight after two bangs on the shield. Singers who knew the ins and outs of extremely intricate pieces of music were completely flustered. Needless to say, it is a great advantage if the conductor is sensitive to the needs of the fight and the singers in relation to the fight.

Respect the Chorus and the Supers

The fight director is often asked to design military moves or battle sequences with members of the chorus and/or supernumeraries. As with the principles, the singers must be able to see the conductor, the fight experience of the performers is usually limited, and the time is short. In addition, the supers are often paid very little for long hours of standing around. On the other hand, the singing is still the priority, so careful language and respect for individuals and the circumstances of working in the chorus can make a huge difference in the appearance of the production. The choreographer cannot assume that the performer has any knowledge of fight technique. Some have never held a sword before. The breathing is all-important here as well. Keeping the chorus relaxed and focused on the score, coordinating moves with the music, and a knowledge of physical alignment are, once again, invaluable. Also, many of these performers will be working with the opera for a long time to come. And for future reference, whatever knowledge that the fight director can share can become a boon for movement and fight choreographers in other operas.

Finally

Because the high stakes in opera often parallel the high stakes of a well-orchestrated fight, performers who are confident and relaxed about the mechanics of the fight will make it as much a part of their performance as any high note. Then, perhaps someday, we might hear "I am a Singer, and a Fighter!!"

Essay by *Rocco Dal Vera*

Introduction

The room is dark, with a screen the size of the one at the local art cinema, only lower, just a couple of feet off the floor. There are no theatre seats in the room. The floor is covered with a green carpet that curves partway up the wall, and I always felt like I was on a pool table in the land of the giants waiting for someone to switch on the lights and start knocking me around with a big cue stick.

This was the Looping (or A. D. R.)[1] Stage on the backlot at Twentieth Century Fox, a dark place similar to many where I would spend hours staring into the light of that screen, and though giants ran the place, they were the giants of an international industry, and it wasn't a game room. It was all business. This was one of the stages where the post-production sound wizards would try to live up to the mantra of the filming units: "We'll fix it in post." Whenever something goes haywire on a shoot, and it's too complicated or expensive to rework it, you can hear someone mutter those magic words. Of course, that person doesn't really mean "*we* will fix it." He really means "*they* will"—the picture and sound editors and their teams. They will smooth over all the rough spots, add richness and color, create the subliminal emotional impact of a scene, and bring the whole project to a polished finish.

Many people think of filmmaking in terms of the camera. Interestingly, shooting the film is usually the shortest period of production and, barring the star's salaries, the least expensive. A film that shoots for ten weeks, may have had a year or two of pre-production (working out the scripts, locations, props, sets, costumes, logistics) and several months to a year of intense post-production (where the raw footage is shaped and crafted into a film).

Post-production editing requires a special kind of person. The work is often solitary, intensely focused, and full of technical issues and tiny details. It requires a group of almost fanatical artists and master craftspeople to take command of all the minute elements. This team must make the mosaic of disparate components look and sound so seamless that the audience forgets that they are seeing a movie and enters into a completely compelling cinematic experience.

Post-production is divided into two areas: picture and sound. The Picture editors handle everything from special-effects, to balancing color and contrast, as well as the selection of shots. They tell the story by controlling where the audience looks, what they will and will not see, and how long they will look at it.

Sound editors handle the musical underscoring, sound effects and dialogue. They will manipulate nearly every moment of the film before it is finished. That green carpet on the looping stage can be rolled up revealing a series of *foley pits*.[2] These are hollows with various surfaces like gravel, sand, concrete, linoleum, macadam, squeaky boards, metal stairs, water, etc. Foley artists (sometimes called *foley-walkers*) will work on these surfaces and with an array of props to replace or enhance footsteps, and other auditory elements of the physical action, like the creak of a leather jacket, or the sound of a martini being shaken and poured.

Rocco Dal Vera, (editor) now an associate professor in the University of Cincinnati's College-Conservatory of Music, spent a number of years in Los Angeles working in the film and television industry. During that time he looped a gazillion films and television shows, voiced scads of cartoons and gobs of commercials.

1. A. D. R.: Automated Dialogue Replacement. The modern version of looping. A process where the sound track and the picture are synchronized in a recording studio so that adjustments can be made to dialogue, and foley or other effects can be added.

2. Foley, Foley Stage: foley is the process in which sound effects are created specifically to match action on the screen; the stage is an A.D.R. studio made with traps in the floor covering a variety of surfaces: gravel pits, concrete, creaky boards, water tanks, etc. Specially trained foley artists, or *foley walkers* are hired for this work.

3. Loop Group: group of actors hired to do A.D.R. for a film or TV show, improvising and filling in the sound for crowd scenes, stunts, and replacing specific lines.

4. Looping: now A.D.R., but still in use, is an old film term from pre A.D.R. days when in order to replace a line of dialogue and synchronize it properly, a section of film would be cut containing the line to be replaced, and spliced into a continuous loop. It would be projected over and over until the actor got the timing and reading right.

5. These loop groups have names like Superloopers, Loop "D" Loop, LA Maddogs, Loop Therapy, Loopers Unlimited, etc. and though actors are members of Screen Actors Guild and work under standard day-player contracts, they do their work so late in the post-production process that they are rarely listed in the credits.

6. Looping is one of the least commonly known and most insular areas of voice acting. In the classic "it's who you know" sense, groups hire actors from those known to them. There are almost never open auditions, or calls to agents. New actors are usually found through referral by trusted members of the group. Even when special skills or unusual languages are required, the casting is usually through referral.

7. Walla: group looping term for non-specific crowd noise; related to the theatrical slang term *rhubarb*.

8. Lip-Synch: A.D.R. where an actor exactly (or nearly) matches the lip movements of the character on screen.

My small part in this large process, was to come in with a group of people and loop[3] the film. We would replace or augment the voices of the actors on screen.

Looping[4] work is done in the one of the last stages in post-production. Usually, I would receive a call from a coordinator for one of the groups I worked with regularly.[5] The owner of that company and I would go out to preview the black and white *work print* and discuss with the sound editor the details of their looping needs. We would settle on the number of actors, ratio of men and women, any special vocal qualities or skills such as languages, dialects, ages, vocal timbre, etc. (we would almost never be given a script). Then we would cast the actors[6] and arrange the details of the recording session. In special cases the director had a close hand in casting, but usually we had wide discretion. I was also responsible for researching any special terms, dialects/accents or languages, having that material ready for the actors when they arrived, and though there were no rehearsals, having the actors prepared to respond to the specific needs of the film.

Nearly every film and television show (except daytime dramas and sit-coms) requires some looping. The projects we would work on could vary widely. Most hour-long television shows could be completed in half a day using about six to eight actors. A film with a lot of action sequences could take a dozen actors a couple of long days, and a mini-series, three days to a week. Occasionally we would re-voice every word of a foreign film or of a really badly shot English language one. (An axiom in the industry is: the lower the budget the more looping a film will require.) Those projects could take considerably longer. During my time in Los Angeles I looped over five hundred films and television shows and provided the voices for a number of animated shows as well.

Throughout those years I worked with some astonishingly talented actors. And I watched a lot of them abuse their voices. This is a cautionary tale for actors working on this side of the industry.

Looping
Looping usually involves general *group walla*[7] and *lip-synch*.[8] Both can present vocal challenges.

Group Walla
In this situation the scene on film has two levels of action. Usually there are the principal players and their story, and then there is a crowd of people framing the action in some way. This can range from a quiet restaurant scene to a huge pitched battle. In both cases the production sound track often isn't useable because there is either no way to control the sound input with that large a group of people, or the crowd is miming speaking, so that there is no interference with the principal actors' lines being clearly recorded.

In post-production, the A. D. R. Editor will need to fill out the scene with all the sounds he wants to paint in. This could range from a murmur of conversation to massed battle cries and the shrieks of the wounded and dying. In the studio, the actors will watch a preview of the scene, pick out the people on camera to re-voice and then do a take. I might find myself saying to one actor, "Okay Jack, do the guy in blue getting the arrow in the throat then we cut to that group as the burning oil is poured on them—catch the guy on the ladder, then at frame 1190 it cuts back to arrow-neck falling off the parapet and crushing that guy with the spear. You do them both on subsequent passes and fill in with some general fight sounds as you see it." This discussion would continue with all of the actors pitching in, then, "Remember, this is England in 1066, and its for television, so no surfer-talk, and no swearing. Okay, let's make it real, everybody. "And they do.

A large battle scene might take several passes through each section to fill it out, with the actors skipping around and using multiple voices on each take. They make a point to reflect what is shown the way the camera sees it, cutting in and out as the camera cuts. On tracking shots the actors will *walk the donut*,[9] or walk past the microphone at the same speed as the camera appears to move so they will realistically pass into and out of range while improvising dialogue. Occasionally one actor will do a separate take to pick up some highly detailed feature.

Depending on the project, this sort of activity can go on for hours or days, and much of that time can be spent performing extreme vocal activities like screaming and shouting.

Lip-synch
In this situation, a looper is replacing either an entire performance (because the director didn't like the original, and so is looking for an improvement) or is matching the original actor's voice on sections of dialogue (because the actor isn't available, or using loopers is cheaper and more efficient). Usually this is needed when the production sound has a problem (there's an airplane in the background, the actor became unexpectedly loud and distorted the sound—a frequent occurrence on highly emotional scenes—or because of other sound problems). In order to do this work, a looper needs to have a keen sense of visual and auditory timing. The lines need to match the precise lip movement of the original speaker. The vocal quality needs to reflect that person's type, and current emotional and physical state.

There are a number of issues that also factor in to make this even more challenging. The original role may have been done by an actor and a stunt-person or other body double and maybe even a dummy—or a combination of all of them. Then, this performance was edited by the film editor. This can result in a performance rhythm that evolved for practical and aesthetic reasons having nothing to do with acting beats. The editors tend to choose the cuts and their timing from an artistic perspective that emphasizes the pace of images and is designed to control the emotional development of the scene. They don't always attend to the realistic physiological or emotional needs of the character. So, for example, in a scene which has been assembled from pieces of several different takes, the character's breathing may be irregular, unpredictable, or non-existent. The transitions and flow of thought and feeling are often different from those the actor might have originally chosen.

In addition to the challenges of timing the line to match an unusual rhythmic pattern and an anti-intuitive emotional build, the recording session will follow the standard dictates of filmmaking: the usual thinking is that once the

9. Walk the Donut: technique used by looping groups, actors walk in a circle past a mike while improvising dialogue, to reproduce the effect of a camera tracking past a changing crowd of people.

technical crew is set up, the actor should be ready to go. So, rehearsals are rare and the looper usually gets one preview of the scene before recording starts.

In order to lip-synch, the actor stands before the microphone with a headset over one ear and watches the screen. Below the screen are cue lights: green for playback, yellow for standby, and red for record. There is also a footage counter showing the reel number, feet and frames.[10] The actor can use these numbers to reference key action points in a scene. When the recording begins, the cue lights change to yellow, the film rolls and the actor hears three rhythmic beeps in the headphone. On the imaginary fourth beep, the system goes into record, the cue lights change to red,[11] and the actor speaks. While speaking, the actor hears the original sound track in the headphone. This provides an audio guide that the actor is expected to match—while at the same time making an improvement in the overall performance.

Actors who survive and thrive as loopers

Looping is an unusual and not often discussed niche in the acting profession. The work is only available in those world centers of film: mostly, Los Angeles, New York, London, Rome, Sydney and Paris. A number of actors specialize in this field and make excellent careers out of it, while a great many of their colleagues don't even realize there is work in that area.

The work does demand a set of highly developed skills. The actors in this occupation need to have an unusually strong and durable vocal mechanism, either from a natural talent or by acquiring exceptional vocal technique. They may be screaming for hours on end and for several days in a row. Many are trained singers as well as voice actors. Loopers who sing tend to be the most vocally healthy, having developed an ability to *sing* the scream and skillfully modulate their level of vocal stress.

The actors need to have speech that is free of idiosyncrasies like regionalisms or articulation lapses, yet they can't be overly articulate. They need to have a ready command of a wide range of dialects and accents, many read phonetics, and can speak one or two foreign languages (and invent gibberish in any language requested). They must have a ready library of believable character voices and the ability to match another actor's voice.[12]

These actors need to have an excellent sense of rhythm—good *eye-mouth* coordination—to lip-synch accurately.

Most will have years of experience doing improvisational theatre, and have the ability to be creative and facile in inventing dialogue that is fresh, but ordinary enough to be real, non-intrusive, and not overly clever—a surprisingly difficult combination.

Filmmaking is expensive. A looping session with a full union crew and actors can cost thousands of dollars an hour. There is a great deal of pressure to get it right on the first take. That is only occasionally possible, and that kind of obligation is antithetical to the relaxed creative state so necessary to good acting. Actors who thrive in this kind of work are those who have developed the ability to work in a relaxed manner under pressure.

10. In digital or video looping these numbers are replaced by *time code* reflecting hours, minutes, seconds, and fields.

11. Most of us are conditioned to think of a red light as a *stop* command. In recording it means go. This probably was originally designed as a warning light to signal all those on set (except the actors) to be quiet.

12. Matching another voice is different from impersonating. An impersonation is like a cartoon: some distinctive elements are magnified and presented in a broad, noticeable way—usually for comic effect. When matching, the actor tries to make a seamless and subtle reproduction of another's voice—usually while listening to a guide track with the original actors voice on it in one ear.

Looping is *instant acting*. It requires the ability to go from zero to full-speed in a second. There is no emotional lead-in for the acting moment, no continuity or emotional through-line. The emotions need to be believable and tuned to fit another actor's physical performance.

Conclusion

Looping is an unusual and interesting corner of the acting profession. It can also be among the most vocally demanding activities for an actor.

When hiring actors we looked for a number of qualities, but very high on the list was the ability to still be speaking by the end of the job. Those who couldn't last weren't hired again. That decision wasn't made out of concern for the actor's voice. It was driven by the practical reality that the final take of the day is as important as the first.

Voices from Around the World: Kevin Crawford

Marth Munro (Associate editor) has a Masters in theatre voice projection, is a CMA (LIMS/New York) and a Certified Lessac Teacher. Currently she is in the advanced stages towards completion of a Ph.D. investigating Lessac's Tonal NRG and Lino's Actor's formant in female voices. She teaches at the Drama Department, Pretoria University and the Opera Department, Pretoria Technikon, South Africa. She is involved in an inter-disciplinary research project about computer aided voice training. Munro works with actors, singers and musicians on optimal body and body/voice integration. She is the Chair of SAPVAME (South African Performers Voice and Movement Educators), she directs for musical theatre and does voice and movement coaching.

Last year I proclaimed that this column would put its ear close to the ground and listen to the distant sounds of disparate countries until we become friends across continents. It is with jubilation and exultation that I call out "Eureka". Although Body/Voice Integration is a relatively new sub-division in our field, I can report that it is an ever-growing core element of our discipline defining itself through the special people attending to it.

Kevin Crawford comes to us from Dublin, Ireland. Kevin is an actor, director and voice coach who currently has a full-time position at The School of Drama, Trinity College Dublin. It is perhaps fitting, therefore, that the kiss of the Blarney Stone should infect and affect his work, and our work, too!

Background and training

Kevin's work as a practitioner is rooted in his formative years of study and collaboration with Roy Hart in London in the late sixties and early seventies. Kevin is a founder member of the company Roy Hart Theatre and a director from 1986-1990. His extensive training in vocal use for the performer also included intensive study of many movement forms from modern and classical dance to Contact Improvisation, Feldenkrais work and the Alexander method through his father, a certified practitioner. Research and collaboration with Pantheatre and the Theatre of Movement were crucial to his development as a practitioner integrating Voice and Movement.

Approach

His work with students is designed to extend their vocal capacities within a pluri-disciplinary framework. Kevin's approach enables the student to find a fullness of connection between her/his vocal and verbal skills and their physical presence as performers, while developing their emotional and imaginative sensibilities. The focus is on the triad: skills, presence and sensibilities.

Because of the sometimes extreme vocal areas that are investigated in his classes the question of vocalising violence is a very pertinent one. One aspect of Kevin's research in the past few years has been centred on tragedy in both the classical Greek world and in Shakespeare.

In order to approach the intensity of key moments in these plays Kevin has devised strategies for accessing and expressing extreme areas of emotion including horror, violent lust and raw brutality. Gradually students make the transition to a fuller textual manifestation of that violence. Choreographic forms are often used to give a structure to the rawness of the vocal expression.

The aim here is to allow each student to access areas of emotion that may not be part of their everyday range of experience. (Kevin notes, for example, "As one student said to me only last week: 'Is this a way of contacting the unconscious in us?' My response was to say: 'Yes, but its also a way of reaching out to a cultural consciousness.'") There is a sense in which he believes that one

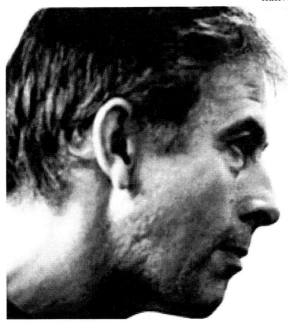

Kevin Crawford

can experience violence in its elemental forms of grief, rage and lust through a common collective memory. For him the key lies in an imagination embodied in vocal and physical action in a safe and controlled environment. The triad is ever-present: sensibility, skill and presence in environment.

Kevin believes that the deeper one goes into this area of human emotion, the more one needs to take genuine discipline with you. Then "we can stare in the face of such consuming emotional fires and not be crushed by them."

Workshops and availability
Recently Kevin has led workshops at Dartington College, Central School of Speech and Drama and The International Workshop Festival. He continues to direct seminars in France, and is a guest facilitator at The Abbey Theatre, Dublin. Kevin also notes that he is available to conduct workshops and seminars, should anyone out there want to know more about his methods and practices.

In so many ways Kevin's work resonates across the field. Bravo Kevin!

Kevin Crawford

Finally
Folks, please share with us your contacts with all the other special coaches and thinkers on voice from around the world that you feel should have the work introduced to our readership, and we shall make sure that the "spotlight" will fall onto them and their work.

Ethics, Standards and Practices

Marian Hampton: professional actor singer, director, voice coach, has performed and directed in San Francisco, New York, Chicago and Canada; MFA in Acting from Yale University School of Drama, BFA in Drama from Illinois Wesleyan University. Doctoral dissertation: *Teaching Actors to Sing*. Member of AEA, SAG, AFTRA; served as President of VASTA and on the Governing Council of ATHE. Published a number of articles, initiated and co-edited *The Vocal Vision*, associate editor and contributor to *Voice and Speech Review*. Taught: Allegheny College, San Francisco State, U. of Tennessee at Knoxville, U. of Texas at Austin. Currently teaches graduate and undergraduate voice and speech in the School of Theatre at Illinois State, and serves on the Academic Senate.

Credit Where Credit is Due

"Of all the words of tongue or pen, the saddest are these, 'You'll pay me when?'" This wry take on the old adage was a favorite joke of my grandfather. Yet, embodied in this statement is an age-old truth about the human experience which we teachers of voice can really take to heart, for don't we spend too much of our lives trying to get others to understand what we do, so that they will pay us what we're worth as compared with peers in comparable professional fields, or so that they will just give us credit for what we do, or so that they will just, please, pay attention. It never ceases to amaze me, about many of those colleagues with whom we work side by side, how little they appreciate what we do, even while they are enormously profiting from our work. Beverly Byers-Pevitts, a past president of the Association for Theatre in Higher Education, once commented in a seminar that, not only did she believe the voice person's work extremely valuable, she had seen productions saved by the voice coach. We know what she was talking about, don't we?

Recently, I was reminded of our benighted situation by a series of events in connection with a production on which I worked long and diligently. I was asked to serve as dialect coach on a production involving both Nigerian and British accents. After designing and overseeing the execution of a practice audiotape, made with a colleague who is Nigerian reading first a series of Nigerian words and phrases I'd typed out from the text, then a section of that text, and then talking about his childhood; after creating a chart of changes from the students' speech to that of the dialect, teaching the dialect to nine African-American students; and, subsequently, teaching a colonial British accent to the other students in the production; I then attended a first run-through and gave notes afterward. That evening, upon discovering that my name was not on the distributed contact sheet listing actors, director, designers, choreographer and technicians, I called this to the attention of the stage manager, gently asking if he would please include me when he redrafted the list, and he assured me he would. A week later, I was involved with individual sessions with actors who wanted more help with the dialect, and was working with some students in my classes on their text, with the director's agreement, and I found that, again, I was not included in the newly posted online contact list, supposedly a revised and corrected version.

Now I was angry. I wrote an e-mail message to the stage manager, suggesting that it might be necessary for actors who had arranged meetings with me to alter or cancel a meeting sometime and that they might need to have my phone number in order to do that. I also asked if I was to assume that, in his eyes, my work was somehow inconsequential as compared with the others working on the show, and then I spoke to his supervisor about the problem. As I came down the stairs that afternoon, the student stage manager sighted me, rushed in from outdoors to fall on his knees before me, his hands in an attitude of prayer, begging my forgiveness. Laughingly, I forgave him but told him he'd have to make it up to me by correcting the contact list, and by also promising me that my credit as dialect coach in the show's printed program would not be listed at the end of the student technicians' names, below the wig dresser, as had been done before. He promised to take care of it, and he did. I spent many more hours on the show, attending rehearsals when I could, taking notes, consulting with the director and working to achieve the delivery of text he wanted, which most often involved far more than dialect. The show was a critical success, and students and faculty alike praised the work (while reserving the right, as we faculty always seem to do, of criticizing the show for the ways in which it differed from how we would have done it!).

In the above instance, I had the satisfaction of a difficult job well-done. I knew that I had heard, noted and taken responsibility for every word which had come out of the students' mouths. Imagine my surprise when the head of my area revealed, in a later conversation, that he hadn't realized I had taught the students the dialects: he thought the Nigerian fellow, our departmental advisor, who had played a drum in the production, had taught them. Almost despairing of getting people to understand, I wrote a brief description of my work on the show and included it with copies of my dialect charts and phonetic transcriptions of the text with my annual report to the Department Faculty Status Committee, which decides annually on merit. Oddly, this prompted a card with a thank-you note from the director, who serves on the committee.

This lengthy and perhaps seemingly self-indulgent story serves to illustrate what almost all of our colleagues face, on a daily basis, in one form or another. As we think back to why VASTA was founded, we will remember that, less than two decades ago, many voice teachers felt that their work was not understood, that they were sometimes found to be threatening to directors, and that it was hard for them to be considered seriously for tenure. By and large, voice teachers tended to be overworked and underpaid, in addition to being misunderstood. As VASTA members, we believed we had an opportunity to share information and ideas, to disseminate information about what we do to administrators and professional peers in other disciplines, and to better the lot of voice teachers everywhere. In an almost miraculous way, these things have actually come to pass, by dint of hard work, good will and a lot of faith.

What has not quite come to pass for many of us is the acknowledgement of equality with other colleagues involved in the artistic direction of productions. It is an anomaly that the vocal director (to use a term urged by Nan Withers-Wilson in her fine book, *Vocal Direction For The Theatre*), who influences the major portion of every scripted work, should be seen as having only negligible affect over the final production, in contrast to the director and, curiously, often the choreographer. In another but somehow related instance, I note that whenever I ask graduate students to design a comprehensive warm-up for a voice class, they most often compose a regimen of mostly movement exercises, even though I have done a full voice and movement warm-up with them in every class. I find myself reminding them that we are, indeed, in a voice class. I take all of this to imply that: voice is still the more sensitive and fragile art, more mysterious than the visual arts of movement and staging, and thus, perhaps, stilt less validated professionally and more threatening personally. I'd be happy to hear that this is not true for my colleagues, but I fear it is all too true for too many of us.

Consequently, it seems to me that we have still a great deal to do in terms of teaching what we do to those with whom we work and who have administrative power over us. In this sense, I was drawn to a discussion on VASTAVOX during the autumn of 2000, in which a post regarding the possibility that a director might steal a voice teacher's expertise by attending private voice sessions unbidden elicited a brief but lively discussion on what actually constitutes intellectual property in our field, the importance of prior agreement and contractual arrangement in all work situations, and the value of sharing ideas between director and vocal coach. Finally the original post was clarified in such a way that the original situation did, indeed, seem like an egregious breach of "etiquette," but the question remained as to whether we need to be afraid of people "stealing our stuff," as the character in *For Colored Girls...* would say.

Yet, where would we all be if we couldn't "steal" great ideas and techniques from others sometimes? While some of our colleagues in voice have developed a complete and comprehensive system of training, unique to themselves, most of us tend toward eclecticism, using whatever we have found to work over the years, while adding our own exercises here and there. I still remember the liberating ring of Bonnie Raphael's pronouncement, "...but I steal from only the best!" Kristin Linklater, in sharing with us her wonderful "body mouths" exercise in Chicago a few years ago, urged us, if we used her ideas, to make them our own. I took that to mean that we should find those ways of adapting her ideas into our own practice and cosmology which would make them useful to us and our students, but I always remember to give Kristin the credit for the idea when I use it with my students.

Surely, our experience in VASTA would have been far different had our members chosen not to share their ideas and techniques, but rather to protect them. I think it is safe to say that another voice teacher—or a director, or whoever wants to utilize a voice teacher's work—owes a mention of credit to the person who dreamed up the idea; and, that even a very skillful and multi-talented individual would not be able to completely appropriate another person's work. After all, who can compensate for an individual's ear and spirit, creating the same magic as the voice teacher herself or himself? I believe, from what I have heard among our members, that attribution of credit is a duty and a skill which all of us have learned, as we have continued to learn precious gems of vision and technique from each other.

But we still have an obligation to demystify what we do for those with whom we work, so that it may be seen just as obviously necessary to the success of the whole artistic endeavor as what they do—and just as worthy of receiving credit. At the same time, we must have the confidence to know that what we do is very special to us individually—that none of us is entirely replaceable, and that each of us is of great value to our students and clients.

Back when I was an adjunct professor at San Francisco State University, I remember that a much younger and far less qualified person came into the department to teach voice and speech in a tenure track position that I coveted, and she asked me to let her have my books, having none of her own. I said no, that I was using them. While I'm sure I'd do the same today, still it seems to me that I have come over a long and hard road since then, but that I am separated from that experience by many difficulties overcome and by many accomplishments. At the least, I have exchanged the problems I had then for a higher order of problems. I believe that VASTA has also overcome so many of the obstacles to our success which we saw at our beginning, and that our collective vision has carried us far along the path of enlightenment and increased capability. That we still have some hurdles to cross in terms of validation for our art should really surprise no one. It's a worthwhile struggle, to educate those around us, and it's one we are uniquely suited to continue, for ours is the realm of the spoken word, still the currency of the theatre and of human communication.

We need to reveal certain things about the nature of our work to the people who matter: the types of research in which we've been involved for a certain project, the hours we've spent in preparation and actual creative work with students/actors/clients, specific tasks accomplished in regard to productions as well as to individual student/clients; and, where possible, we can provide audio and/or videotaped evidence of our work. Perhaps administrators need to become painfully aware of the breadth of artistic, scholarly and health issues which fall beneath our purview, and the countless hours we spend studying, designing programs, consulting, lending tapes, sharing ideas, keeping up with the most recent information in our profession, bolstering our professional colleagues, serving the larger professional and academic communities—I could go on and on.

We also need to become strong advocates, for our students and clients, for our professional standards, for our jobs, and, yes, even for ourselves, for to some extent, we are our jobs, at least as far as the welfare of our students is concerned. Thereby, we have an obligation to observe the highest possible standards in our practice, as well as to advocate for our position in the scheme of things. We need, of course, to advocate for each other, as we are often privileged to do when given the opportunity to review someone's tenure or promotion file or to recommend someone for a job. Maybe, we should even become agents for each other, helping to negotiate contracts, as we have the chance to do when we advise a friend and colleague on securing a viable contract for a new position. We must never lose sight of the need to honestly give credit where credit is due, and to demand the same for our profession and for ourselves.

❦

The Cultural Voice: An Interview with Danny Hoch

Stan Brown is an Associate professor of Theatre at the University of Nebraska, Lincoln. His voice work draws heavily from the Alexander technique, Berry, and Linklater. His related areas of research and specialization are in contemporary Shakespearean performance, psycho-linguistics, multicultural impacts on spoken English as it influences the actor in training and performance, and ritual and ceremonial language. (How the two exist and influence contemporary society). He's worked professionally for sixteen years as an actor, director and voice specialist both here and in the United Kingdom.

Contrary to what many purveyors of theatre would have us think, North America isn't just people who live near strip malls in two story houses somewhere in the suburbs. This nation is teeming with communities where rich and middle-class white people are not at the center; yet we see who is deemed deserving of our stage time.

Danny Hoch: from the introduction to *Jails, Hospitals and Hip Hop* and *Some People*

Who's Danny Hoch? A thirty-year-old, award winning actor, writer, performance artist, filmmaker, social activist, Hip Hop artist/historian, living-dialect-encyclopedia, and white Jewish kid from the Bronx are among the many identities he takes on, sometimes within the course of one day. That list lengthens on stage when he inhabits the dialect, language, or speech impediment of one of the twenty multi-ethic characters he creates in his two one-man shows. *Some People*, his first show, won a 1994 Obie Award at Performance Space 122 and the Joseph Papp Public Theatre. It went on to become an HBO special and was nominated for a Cable Ace Award. In 1998 his second one man show *Jails, Hospitals, and Hip Hop* was nominated for a Drama Desk Award. He is still touring that show, and also stars in the film. If you've never caught Danny live on stage you might have encountered his writing in film, television or periodicals like *Harper's*, *New Theatre Review* or *American Theatre*.

As undeniably impressive as his professional credits are, the Danny Hoch that really fascinated me was the Danny Hoch that existed prior to his current celebrity. Danny was born in 1970 in the borough of the Bronx, New York—one of the most culturally diverse communities in the world. His mother, a single parent, was a speech pathologist. According to Danny, on the floor of the apartment building where he and his mother lived, there were six languages spoken and different dialects among those six languages. This almost constant immersion into diverse languages and dialects was what Danny encountered every day of his life as a child and young adult. His tremendously rich experience of verbal communication coupled with the heightened sensitivity to speech he received through observing his mother's work, gave Danny a rare insight to spoken language. What I found most rare about this was the total absence of a minority or majority culture to dictate a standard speech. How did this uncommon inheritance of language ultimately fuel and direct Danny's perceptions of culture, race, dialect, mainstream theatre and conventional actor training? I had to know.

sb: Your Mother was a speech pathologist?

DH: Yes, A speech pathologist and speech therapist. Worked clinically in hospitals for 20 years and in high schools for 10.

sb: As a child and young adult you observed her, as you've described it,"...helping people regain language?"

DH: Yes, occasionally, she would allow me to watch and sometimes participate in some of her sessions with patients. Also, I got to perform for many of her patients.

sb: What kind of performances did you do?

DH: Magic shows, mime shows, Impressions. I was young.

sb: Your mom was a single parent? Was your initial exposure to and interest in her work because she had to take you to work with her to solve child care issues?

DH: Yes, absolutely. Although, she instilled in me the tremendous value on "listening" at home, I doubt I would have gained interest unless I saw it up close. Although she did (and still does) recount work stories to me that I still find fascinating.

sb: Do any of your mother's clients stand out in your memory as particularly good examples of what it means to reclaim language?

DH: They all stand out. There is not one. And I would rather not comment on it, because then I become a true anthropologist/ethnographer in the academic sense—like Anna Deavere Smith—and that's not my goal with my work. My goal is to commit the act of theatre.

sb: How do you think your exposure to your mother's work shaped your skill of observation and language acquisition—especially within the multicultural environment in which you grew up?

DH: Tremendously. My mother never taught me accents in any way, nor do I recall her ever mentioning accents, unless it related to a neurological disorder or cleft palate. In fact the only "speech work" she ever did with me was cure my lisp at a very young age. But growing up with someone who's perception of speech language was so heightened, combined with growing up in a place where there was no standard English dominating the cultural landscape, I somehow became a sponge to language and accents, tuning into every detail of everyone's speech totally naturally and never academically.

sb: In an article on your website you mention a guy named Garth Belcon who was, and still is a significant person in your life. Who is Garth and why, when you were a kid, did you believe you were blacker than he was?

DH: Yes. He's a best friend of mine from high school. *Within* our hip-hop dominated generation, color wasn't associated with culture, until high school age. Although Garth was Black, from the Bronx, somehow I had mastered the skills of rap and break dancing better than he (actually better than many Black classmates of mine. I was in a rap group with 5 other Black kids, and they made me the lead rapper cause I was the best rapper). In addition, Garth came from a strict West Indian household. So, his manners and mannerisms were almost British more than they were Bronx ghetto. Therefore, when we'd hang out, people used to say, "Damn Garth, Danny's Blacker than you are." As highschoolers, not understanding the connotations it had, that statement felt good to both of us at the time, as if it had fortified our individualities. Him not wanting to be associated with, or lumped into "Blackness", as it were; and me certainly not wanting to be associated with "Whiteness", since the only Whiteness I ever experienced at that time was on TV. To me, that whiteness seemed very foreign, bland and certainly not as "cool" as even stereotypical Blackness, let alone hip-hop. And it paled in comparison to all of the richness in language around me at home.

sb: Tell me about "the dime bag" incident with you and Garth and how that led you to conclude that hip hop was, in your own words, a "cultural unifier" but not a "social unifier." What's the difference between the two from your cultural and social viewpoint?

DH: I was a drug addict and drug dealer in High School. Garth was a straight A student, didn't even drink. One day, I needed my dime bag, and convinced him to come with me. This was not a big thing in the 80's—buying drugs. It was like buying gum. Well, we hadn't bought it, but the spot was being watched by undercovers. They stopped us, and weren't even interested in questioning me. Garth became the suspect immediately. Which at the time, was so funny to me, because he was a little nerdy, but it didn't matter. He was Black, and I was apparently White—even in my hip hop clothes. I wouldn't say that related to hip-hop in any way. This was about racial profiling and police stereotypes. According to them, even if I was in a drug spot, it must have been the Black guy that brought me there, that is the *criminal*. This was a clarifying moment in my life, because I never thought about my White skin as *privilege* before that incident. Back to the subject of hip-hop, I think that hip-hop was and still is a cultural and social unifier, because as culture, it crosses color, race, class and language lines all over the world, thus unifying in the sense that many very different people are bopping to the same shit. And sometimes, getting the same messages and feelings from hip-hop. Even hip-hop language has forced its way onto the tongues of many folks who even don't know who Biggie Smalls was, let alone participate in hip-hop in any way. But hip-hop has not erased skin privilege, class systems, color issues, and certainly ain't stopped no racial profiling.

sb: One of the things that is so remarkable to me about coming to one of your performances is the number of people from the under-twenty crowd that fill the theatre. Apart from commercial success, what do you think it is that that age group, as well as older people, are relating to in the language of hip-hop?

DH: Look at the Hippies and Rock & Roll. Although Rock is just music, there is a whole culture and many subcultures coming from it, that informed an entire generation if not two generations, Informed them on how to party, think, talk, make love even. To me, hip-hop was the last culture of resistance at the end of the millennium in the entire world. It's so powerful, so rebellious, so codified (yet absorbable), and at the same time, so just plain funky- all people gravitate towards it. In addition, now there is an entire generation (if not two) that grew up in the context of hip hop *culture* (not music). That context includes Reaganomics (very influential, and still), increased multiculturalism (in practice, not theory), proliferation of guns, crack, murder, incarceration. Someone said recently that the civil-rights struggle of this generation is going to be prisons. Period. I'm inclined to agree.

sb: Is your focus on the one man show format in anyway a response to difficulty you have as a performer in what might be more collaborative settings?

I include theatre in those collaborative settings but your experience as an actor on Seinfeld comes to mind. (Having seen Danny's HBO special, the producers of the sitcom Seinfeld hired him to do a guest appearance. The character was a "pool guy" named Ramon. Danny objected to playing a stereotypical Spanish speaking character and was fired.)

DH: No, I love collaborating with folks. The Seinfeld incident was not a collaborative issue, it was a racism issue. I chose not to collaborate in the trafficking of racist stereotypes by means of an international television program. But I swear I tried to collaborate artistically, in order to avoid that, looking for all sorts of solutions to the problem. But they were on another planet and not getting the point. I'm sure they thought the same of me.

sb: You attended the High School of the Performing Arts then North Carolina School of the Arts, and you trained in London as well; where?

DH: It was a post grad program (even though I never graduated undergrad) at BADA (the British American Drama Academy). All the teachers from RADA and Central School of Speech and Drama would moonlight there for some extra quid.

sb: You write in the introduction to *Jails, Hospitals, and Hip Hop*. "Although my teachers were wonderful and my training was intense, I was being trained to drop the languages I grew up with. In order to be a successful actor I was supposed to forget all the rich language that was my cultural foundation." I'm willing to bet that *no* voice or speech teacher would admit that they were actually requiring you to "drop the languages" you grew up with or to "forget the rich language" of your cultural foundation.

DH: Of course they weren't technically requiring us to forsake our cultural foundations. But the *only* emphasis was on the British and *accepted* American literary canon. As if that is the only framework for theatre and storytelling. Fuck that bee. The same could be said for the way American History is taught. If you're Black (which you are, sir), and you sit in class and all you hear is the Indians were savages, the Africans had no culture or religion and had to be civilized, etc. Then when you come across some Cheikh Anta Diop, or even some Frantz Fannon or Malcom X for that matter, it's not going to seem as valid to you because all you were taught was this one canon and perspective.

I was happy doing Moliere and Hamlet in high school. My dream was to do Hamlet one day on a British stage in an Elizabethan accent. Why? Because that's what we were supposed to aspire to. We were even kept away from the theatre happening in our own city that was *about* us. "Oh, that's community theatre...." "Real theatre is on Broadway, off-Broadway...." Well Broadway and off-Broadway theatre *also* ignored us New Yorkers, our language, accents, stories, and still does. These are supposed to be the theatres of the "people," yet millions of dollars are spent celebrating Tom Stoppard and that Irish motherfucker, I forgot his name. They are great playwrights, but there is an imbalance in the theatre world *greater* than the imbalances on television.

sb: What might appear to be your rejection of the classical and even modern canons raises the question of whether or not you believe they are irrelevant. If you believe this, do you think they can ever be made relevant?

DH: They are not irrelevant, and I have not rejected those canons as art. But I feel that they are the least effective means we have to make contemporary art. They are old; not powerless, but old. Language and cultural specifics have changed. Art loves to either be obsessed with the classical, or obsessed with the avant-garde/experimental. Seldom do either deal with what is actually happening *today* in our society. Hello, wake up—where is the language? Today's language? If you ignore today's language then you ignore today's people. That's criminal, and yes, there are criminal artists out there. I got you mutherfuckers on my list.

sb: What is your response to training tools and conventions like the IPA and standard speech for the stage? Do you think they have *any* place and function in contemporary actor training?

DH: Whoa, I don't know what IPA is. Iambic Pentameter Association maybe? Good guess? I think that standard speech is important to learn because it is neutral and from there you can go anywhere; but it's not the speech to aspire to attain. No one speaks like that culturally. It's just an accent that is universally understood by all English speakers. However, it is bereft of a cultural foundation, and therefore doesn't belong on stage in a play that is about reality (at least in any English speaking place I've been to) unless of course there is a character who speaks that way. What a character that would be.

Essay by *Kate DeVore*

Teachers and trainers of voice often face the question of whether to refer a student to a speech pathologist or otolaryngologist. A student's voice may have some persistent breathiness, for example, and the voice teacher might notice inconsistent improvement. Is there an underlying organic pathology, or is it simply a matter of optimal use? Or a teacher may know a student to have deleterious off-stage vocal behaviors (such as smoking, high alcohol and caffeine consumption, and lack of rest). Is this student's vocal gruffness simply a function of these behaviors, or is there the possibility of a vocal pathology? This paper addresses some of the issues involved in referring a student to an otolaryngologist or speech-language pathologist (SLP).

Referring to an otolaryngologist or speech pathologist

When in doubt, refer. It is better to err on the side of caution. If a student's voice is consistently or frequently hoarse or breathy, or if she has difficulties with high and/or quiet phonation, or if the voice just doesn't sound healthy to you, it is safest to refer the student to an otolaryngologist (ENT). The fact that a student sounds better when he uses his voice optimally in no way rules out a pathology; indeed, optimal voice use is the way many vocal pathologies are treated. A proper medical diagnosis is essential to ensure appropriate treatment, which may entail more than voice therapy.

Preferably the otolaryngologist to whom you refer the student is known to you and has expertise in voice. Some ENTs are specialized in voice while others might be specialized in sinuses, for example. Whenever possible, work with an otolaryngologist you know to be specialized in voice. The ENT will evaluate the student, and if the student has given permission, the physician will send you a report as the referring party. The otolaryngologist will make a diagnosis and prescribe any appropriate treatment, possibly including referral to a speech pathologist.

If a voice teacher has a relationship with a speech pathologist, a direct referral is appropriate. The SLP is likely to refer the student to an otolaryngologist before initiating therapy to rule out or confirm an underlying medical cause of the voice problem. Most speech pathologists are happy to talk to other voice trainers at the client's request, and to discuss ways to collaborate in the care of the student.

Speech pathology is a broad field with many sub-specialties. Whenever possible, it is important to refer a student to an SLP who is specialized in voice. Speech pathology training alone does not guarantee expertise in voice, or in any of its specialty areas. While an SLP who is not specialized in voice is likely to know the anatomy and physiology of voice production, she might not have been taught how to elicit healthy voice. An SLP with training and experience in treating patients with voice disorders, however, is familiar with all of the aspects of voice. In seeking a speech pathologist, ask if he is specialized in voice.

The language used when referring a student to an ENT or speech pathologist can be important. So as not to incite panic, it might be helpful to a) point out to the student what you hear that prompts the referral, b) show her examples of the behavior in question, c) explain that it is important for you to know the source of the issue in order to confidently continue with her

Kate DeVore, M.A., CCC-SLP, is a voice, speech and dialect trainer in Chicago. She teaches Voice for the Actor at Columbia College, works as a voice/speech pathologist at Gottfred Speech Associates, and runs a consulting business called Total Voice, as well as a private practice in healing and voice enhancement & rehabilitation. Before moving to Chicago, she spent four years in Boston as a voice/speech pathologist at the Voice, Speech and Swallowing Division of Beth Israel Deaconess Medical Center while also coaching and teaching in Boston area theatres and theatre training programs.

education, and d) suggest that she see your colleague to rule out any medical problems. "Rule out" is a calming term with a positive slant, as it implies that a medical issue is unlikely. In contrast, "nodes" is often a whispered word with a stigma of shame. The less fear surrounding the concept of voice disorders, the greater the chance a student will feel confident seeing an ENT in time to take advantage of the benefits of early intervention.

Referring to a voice and speech trainer

A speech pathologist would serve a client well to refer to a voice/speech trainer if the student's needs exceed the clinician's expertise. While some speech pathologists have extensive training in voice enhancement and training of the non-disordered voice, many do not. If a client seeks voice training beyond the education provided for injury healing, referral to a voice/speech teacher is appropriate.

Speech pathology treatment is often mandated by insurance, and duration of treatment is sometimes dictated by the number of visits an insurance company is willing to cover. Few speech pathologists have the time to cover extensive voice training in a medical setting. If the client enjoys voice work and wants to continue, or if it seems that the student would benefit from continued monitoring after treatment ends, the SLP may choose to refer to a knowledgeable voice trainer for ongoing work after therapy has been completed.

Who does what

An essential difference between theatre voice training and speech pathology intervention is duration. Most speech pathologists use a medical model, and a course of treatment is commonly six to ten sessions. Another important distinction is the differentiation of voice training and voice therapy. Voice training brings out the best qualities of a healthy vocal mechanism and directs them toward a desired goal; voice therapy is intended to heal a vocal injury or disorder.

The ultimate goal of mos SLPs is to retrain the client's voice use patterns to those that reduce or eliminate vocal pathology and prevent its recurrence. Many voice pathologists aim to train phonation with an optimal laryngeal configuration that not only facilitates healing and discourages recurrence, but also allows for increased resonance and vocal freedom. Vocal education, including care and maintenance of the voice (often referred to as vocal hygiene), are also important factors of most voice therapy protocols.

Most voice and speech teachers want to train students to have healthy, flexible, expressive voices. This surpasses the goal of most speech pathologists, who rarely have the time to consider flexibility, range and expression; their goal is focused around healthy voice production. Vocal flexibility and range sometimes improve along with vocal health, but they are usually not specifically addressed. In working within the guidelines of most managed care policies, once the pathology is gone, insurance-covered treatment by a speech pathologist must end. If managed care coverage is not an issue, treatment can continue for as long as the SLP and the client agree it is beneficial. If the SLP is adequately trained, the treatment can bridge into areas of vocal enhancement, public speaking, presentation skills and more.

The guidelines established for scope of practice by ASHA (American Speech-Language-Hearing Association) are quite vague. Legalities are generally established by individual states. ASHA's loosely worded stance is, essentially, that a student with a vocal pathology/disorder should be treated by a speech pathologist with training in enhancing voice quality. After initial therapy has been completed, their position becomes more vague. A representative put it this way: "Whatever you're doing, you need to be properly trained." ASHA seems to come down in favor of what is in the best interest of the patient, assuming all parties are providing services for which they are well-trained and experienced. In this case, however, ASHA governs not laws, but ethics. Knowledge of the state of residence's laws is advisable for those trainers who do not have legal certification from ASHA but are interested in working with students who have voice disorders.

How a speech pathologist may be helpful

Voice and speech training colleagues have referred students to me as a speech pathologist in a number of ways, and I will offer some examples. Service provided has ranged from a course of therapy with ongoing monitoring to answering questions on the telephone. As you will see from the examples that follow, some of the work I did was no different from what many voice trainers would do if they had a spare hour to spend with a student.

One client was referred because she was hoarse by the end of every rehearsal. After one session that focused primarily on alignment and the explanation of healthy voicing principles, her voice stayed strong.

Another young acting student was referred to our clinic for sudden vocal weakness, and was diagnosed with a vocal fold hemorrhage. Many voice pathologists agree that a hemorrhage is the only voice disorder for which total voice rest is likely to resolve the problem. After voice rest, we repeated the videostroboscopy that enabled the ENT to make a medical diagnosis and allowed me to see how the vocal folds were functioning. The hemorrhage was resolving but not completely gone, and we opted for therapy instead of surgery. The hemorrhage resolved with therapy, and she returned for regular check-ups until she moved to another state and was referred elsewhere for continued monitoring.

Singing teachers have often referred young students whom they rightly suspected of having vocal nodules. I have been fortunate enough to collaborate with singing teachers who had an understanding of vocal anatomy and working with an injured voice. This made the transfer of care easy for all involved. The teacher and I discussed our methods, shared progress, and I was gradually faded out of the picture. I've also been lucky enough to talk with some singing teachers who knew they did not feel qualified to work with a student with an injured voice, and referred the student to another singing teacher. Far from abandoning them, these teachers did their students an obvious service and were wise enough to know their limitations.

Recently a resident vocal coach at a local theatre invited me to work with an actor who used a wheelchair. The director wasn't able to hear the actor, and the coach didn't feel confident in her understanding of the vocal and respiratory impact of being in a wheelchair.

I have also been invited to colleagues' classrooms to give workshops about vocal health and maintenance, anatomy and physiology, and voice disorders. I show videotapes of different vocal pathologies, and reinforce whatever the teacher has told the students about vocal hygiene.

Voice vs. speech
The same guidelines apply to speech as they do to voice. If a student has a pathology, he should be seen by a speech pathologist. Speech disorders caused by neurologic disorders, trauma affecting the speech mechanism, or developmental disorders should be referred to a speech pathologist. Mild articulation deviances, however, may be treated by a qualified voice and speech trainer and don't require the expertise of a speech pathologist.

What if you appear to know more than the SLP?
In some unfortunate instances, a highly knowledgeable voice trainer might know more about healthy voice production and vocal hygiene than does a speech pathologist. This is unlikely to be the case if the speech pathologist is specialized in voice, but not all regions are equipped with such a specialist.

To make the best of the situation, collaborate and supplement. It is unlikely that the student will learn absolutely nothing from the speech pathologist, so time is not being wasted. Without telling the student you think you know more that his therapist, you can supplement the information given to him. An ongoing dialogue about the content of his therapy sessions will allow you to fill in any holes you perceive regarding optimal voice production.

Remember, however, that students are not always accurate reporters in describing the content or intention of therapy sessions. If a student can't describe therapy well, or if it sounds as though nothing is happening, that doesn't necessarily mean that the therapy is bad. You will get the best information by talking to the therapist. Asking questions, explaining your work, and asking about what they are doing will provide clarity. Not only will this rapport assist the student, it will build a relationship between you and the therapist that may serve you both in the future.

There are some excellent voice pathologists, often but not always with training in theatre or music, who have a bigger picture in mind. The more time that passes, the greater the number of these professionals. Many people have an outdated view of speech pathology formed before voice was a viable subspecialty in the field. In the past, the person responsible for head and neck cancer, dysphagia, or cleft palate treatment—who incidentally carried the voice caseload as well—saw most voice-disordered patients. The field has grown thanks to some clinical and scientific pioneers, and the science and art are blending well. Both the science behind the treatment and the artistry of those drawn to the field seem to be steadily improving.

What voice/speech pathologists learn that theatre voice trainers might not
Theatre voice training and vocology programs, as defined by speech pathology with an emphasis on professional voice, are diverse in their curricula and methods. Rather than attempting to generalize about what a student might learn in either, I will speak from personal experience as I have been blessed

with what I consider to be excellent training in both theatre voice training and vocology.

I had the privilege of receiving the foundation of my theatre voice training from someone who uses a highly anatomically-based technique and has a keen understanding of vocal physiology. Even so, the depth of my understanding of anatomy and physiology of voice and speech is far greater because of vocology training. This understanding of anatomy and physiology, which was further deepened by providing and analyzing videolaryngoscopies in a professional setting, is the linchpin of my work. Having a sense of vocal mechanics allows one to make an educated guess about the precise manner i n which the vocal folds are vibrating, and therefore how they are hitting one another, upon hearing a person phonate. That knowledge leads to the understanding of how to change the phonatory pattern to a more optimal one. This example relates to voice, but can also be applied to speech production.

I was also fortunate enough to have a vocology mentor who appreciates the artistry of voice and the importance of vocal expression for performers and for life in general. She is a vocal performer herself, with deep respect for theatre voice training techniques. As a result, the clinical work was not separate from the art, but rather merged with it.

While there were many other useful things taught in my vocology program, I will mention two more relevant examples. We learned the myriad of ways in which vocal injuries can arise, and the principles and techniques behind preventing and healing them. We also learned a variety of training techniques and learning theories. These techniques range from methods of breaking a task into component parts with increasing levels of complexity and difficulty, to the use of training modalities that optimize brain function in learning.

Passing the baton (How to work with a student with a voice disorder)
As a voice trainer, the safest path is to know what you are trained to do, know what a speech pathologist is trained to do, and what best serves the interest of the student. If possible, observe a therapy session. Being at a therapy session will give you information about the treatment, and will help you establish rapport with the speech pathologist. It will also assure the student that you are willing and able to participate in her healing process. And, if the therapist is good, the session will be interesting and informative.

If you don't know your local speech pathologist, you might want to introduce yourself by offering an in-service or workshop in your area of expertise for your local clinic or hospital. You may also invite the speech pathologist into your classes to talk about prevention of vocal injury. By cultivating a relationship with voice care professionals in your community, you each learn everyone's strength, and you create a net of care for students.

Finally, if the topic of working with people with voice disorders is of interest to you, you might consider joining the listserv for SID-3, the voice special-interest division of ASHA. Most voice pathologists are members of this listserv, and they are as generous as members of Vastavox with regard to sharing information. As with all subjects, curiosity leads to learning.

The more familiar voice trainers and therapists are with one another, the less complex the concept of cross-referring. Uncertainty about referring a student out of one's care is generally caused by uncertainty about what will happen to her. If the question of whether to refer arises from wondering whether there really is a problem worthy of attention, erring on the side of caution is always safest. Knowledge of the local possibilities for voice care and enhancement assuages much concern. Armed with this knowledge, and holding the best interest of the student at heart, voice trainers can guide their students productively.

Essay by *Robert Bastian, MD*

The Vocal Overdoer Syndrome

Editor's Note: Dr. Robert Bastian has had a long association with VASTA. In the early days of VASTA's history, at our conference in San Diego, he videoscoped the larynx of any of our members who wanted him to, and this prompted me to ask him to present a session at a subsequent conference in Seattle. During this presentation, he showed a videotape of his own larynx both before and after smoking a cigarette. While he is a nationally and internationally known otolaryngologist, he has become known in our circles as one who espouses practical and immediate ways of understanding and dealing with voice problems. In this article (first published in the Choral Journal, *October, 2000, adapted for us, and reprinted with their permission) he presents a scale of measurement to help determine who might be a victim of vocal overuse. We thought this would be especially germane to a discussion of problems inherent in vocal violence, and, since this is a standard available to any voice teacher or trainer's practice, we have included it in this section of our publication rather than under the rubric of Voice and Speech Science.*
— M. Hampton, assoc. ed.

While consulting medically with people who use their voices professionally, a voice clinician gains advantage by knowing via personal experience what a typical rehearsal involves, what is required of performers in leading roles, the demands of performance spaces, the differences between various textual styles, and many other things. Reciprocally, voice trainers, while working with the same individuals to create theatre, can benefit from knowledge imported from the voice clinic. Those of either profession who are armed with knowledge of the other's field may be better equipped to advise the performer/student in vocal trouble. For the trainer/teacher/coach, the list of practical clinical information is long, but the following issue is a good place to start: familiarity with the vocal overdoer syndrome (VOS),[1] as defined below.

Why the VOS? Because the VOS correlates highly with acute and especially chronic injuries of the vocal fold mucosa, e.g. nodules, polyps, epidermoid cysts, vascular abnormalities.[2] That is, actors with these injuries are far more likely than not to be vocal overdoers; by contrast, they *may or may not* have in common allergies, reflux, asthma, or any other apparent cause of vocal problems. In fact, formal review of a large number of patient charts revealed that of self-described overdoers who present with voice symptoms, 80% are found to have a vibratory mucosal injury![3] The VOS is by far the strongest discernable commonality between persons with mucosal injury, and is probably not only *correlated with*, but also a primary *cause of* those injuries.

How does the VOS actually cause mucosal injury? Here's how: The mucosa is the wet, flexible surface tissue covering the vocal folds. It is the main tissue that participates in vibration of the vocal folds and is also the part most commonly injured by that vibration, if it is "overdone" in various ways (amount, loudness, pressed-ness, etc.) Hence, the VOS may often lead to acute or chronic vibratory mucosal injury.

How does one establish a diagnosis of the VOS? The first and most important step is by requesting a self-rating of the individual's *innate degree of talkativeness—or urge to talk*. A simple but useful way to assess this is to ask the subject the following question: "On a 7-point scale of *innate* talkativeness, where

Robert W. Bastian, M.D., professor of Otolaryngology, Head and Neck Surgery, Loyola University of Chicago Medical Center. M.D. from Washington University School of Medicine, St. Louis, where he subsequently completed his ENT residency and served as assistant professor of Otolaryngology. Specializes in laryngeal surgery, evaluation and treatment of a wide variety of voice disorders, dysphagia, and larynx cancer. An accomplished singer; is well versed in phoniatry. Among the first to establish and promote a team approach to persons with voice disorders. Through clinical and academic work, has earned a widespread reputation as an authority on laryngeal surgery, videostroboscopy, and care of the professional voice.

1 represents a taciturn individual, 4 an averagely-talkative person, and 7 an unusually talkative individual, where would you place yourself?"

Most people have a fairly realistic idea of where they are on this scale. Occasionally, however, the answer seems inaccurate based on the questioner's observations. When this occurs, it can be helpful to get permission to ask a friend or family member to answer the question too. Caveats: Some persons need help to distinguish between their *innate* talkativeness and that which is "imposed" by their job. Others need encouragement to answer an honest "7," because they assume this to represent obnoxious talkativeness. If this is suspected, "seven-ness" should be further defined (e.g. as extroverted, friendly, or even "socially brilliant!") to remove any bad connotation from being a "7."

The second determinant of the VOS is the individual's *extrinsic opportunity and need to talk*. An understanding of this arises from basic questions about occupation, family communication style, childcare responsibilities, hobbies, rehearsal and performance schedule, church and community involvement, and so forth. A few minutes of discussion are generally enough to get the picture.

In short, vocally busy 6's and 7's are defined as vocal overdoers; *both the internal urge and the external pull* to use the voice are high. It is logical that both should be high, because "6's" and "7's" tend to self-select into an occupation/life circumstance that invites or requires a lot of voice use. Beyond formal vocal commitments, the high innate urge to talk may find or make informal opportunities to talk or sing any moment of the day. Thus, more detailed questioning will often reveal other ways the "overdoer" uses the voice—singing to themselves, using the phone, or even speaking to strangers in public.

How can voice trainers make use of the VOS concept? The first way is to measure one's self against it. Teachers and coaches can be vocal overdoers too! Self-recognition as a vocal overdoer can be protective in and of itself, by injecting a bit of vocal prudence, even subliminally. It can also help to further the trainer's efforts to be a good vocal role model.

The second is to teach clients/students about the VOS. Given its high correlation with mucosal injury, the VOS could be a featured part of any discussion of vocal health. Performers who thereby recognize the VOS in themselves may also experience an almost subconscious self-adjustment of behavior. Or, when a trainer detects ongoing hoarseness or is approached because of vocal frustrations, questions about the VOS would be an excellent place to start sorting things out.

Questions about the VOS
How do you account for the fact that not all vocal overdoers have a mucosal injury? It is true that one may know a singer, for example, whose brilliant personality makes him or her the life of every party. Yet, he or she continues to sing gloriously to the top of the range, even at *pianissimo*. This is because the genesis of nodules and other vibration-related injuries is of course multifactorial. Physical constitution and manner of voice production are just two additional pieces of the puzzle, not to mention the fact that there are degrees of the VOS.

You've made me worried about my mucosa because I'm a major vocal overdoer by your definition. How do I find out if I have a mucosal injury? Apply singing voice "swelling tests"[4] which detect mucosal injury reliably, albeit with a few false positives. Here's one of the two I use routinely during office evaluations: Ascend by half-steps the first phrase of "happy birthday" sung at very high frequency (e.g. C5-C6 for women) and low intensity. In the context of the VOS, a tendency to huskiness, delayed phonatory onsets, and air escape, all of which increase as one ascends the scale, should lead the performer to pursue a formal medical evaluation to confirm or disconfirm suspicions of a mucosal injury. Beware of subconsciously getting louder, which will often "make" the voice work quite well. The idea is not to "make it work better" but rather to see how the voice works at a predetermined pianissimo dynamic. Detection, not concealment! Therefore, insist on "boy soprano pianissimo" for best sensitivity of the swelling tests.

What if I or one of my "overdoer" student/clients fails the "swelling tests" and is later found to have a chronic mucosal injury? What would be done? Don't despair. The ranks of those in this situation are large indeed, and help is at hand. But first, an exact and comprehensive diagnosis is needed. The primary diagnosis is generally "the vocal overdoer syndrome." But comprehensive evaluation should also specify the secondary diagnoses. What exactly is the mucosal injury? Nodules? An epidermoid cyst? A hemorrhagic polyp? Capillary ectasia? Are there contributing medical issues? From here, an individualized plan may include medical, behavioral, surgical, or some combination of these. In short, the question is not so much whether you can get back full voice capabilities, but exactly *what*, and *how long* it will take to get you there.

Can you be more specific about these medical, behavioral, and surgical treatment options as they relate to mucosal injury? **Medical.** These are of course individualized, and mostly optimizing rather than primary treatment measures. But I think immediately of liberal, regular consumption of fluids; smoking cessation; treatment of acid reflux; and treatment as appropriate of other medical conditions such as allergy and asthma. **Behavioral.** Logically—again since "VOS" is the primary diagnosis—behavioral management, administered by a voice-qualified speech pathologist, is the primary initial approach. Some examples of suggestions you might receive concern spacing, rather than massing voice use. Scheduling breaks into the day. Ongoing training of voice production for both speech and singing so that phonation is efficient and "inexpensive" to the mucosa. Attention to the manner and amount of personal and social voice use. And perhaps, even personal amplification when working in large, acoustically unfriendly rehearsal spaces. And finally, daily self-detection of mucosal status via the "swelling tests." **Surgical.** When the lesion is clearly not amenable to behavioral management alone (e.g. cyst), or when something that often resolves (e.g. nodules), doesn't in spite of high-quality treatment, vocal fold microsurgery is an excellent option.[2,5,6] Though anxiety levels surrounding the subject are generally high due to prevalent misinformation, vocal fold microsurgery is extremely safe and voice-restoring, *when performed by a well-trained, proven surgeon.*

Summary

Formalization of a concept termed "the vocal overdoer syndrome" can help the voice trainers recognize the group most at risk of chronic vocal fold mucosal injuries. It may be useful to teach this concept to student/clients for its preventative value. Daily performance of "swelling test" to detect mucosal swelling is also a valuable habit. Clinical evaluation should be sought by anyone who experiences impairment of tests of mucosal swelling, but particularly by vocal overdoers.

Bibliography

1. Bastian RW, Thurman, L, Klitzke, C. Limitations to vocal ability from use-related injury or atrophy. In Thurman L and Welch G (eds.): *bodymind and voice: foundations of voice education*, Book III, Chapter 1, pp. 329-337.

2. Bastian, RW. Benign vocal fold mucosal disorders. In Cummings CW et al (eds.): *Otolaryngology—Head and Neck Surgery* (3rd Edition), Chapter 111, volume III, pp2096-2129, 1998. Mosby, St. Louis.

3. Bastian RW, Thomas J: The vocal overdoer-underdoer continuum. Presented at the Voice Foundation June 2000, Philadelphia. Submitted to the Journal of Voice

4. Bastian RW, Keidar A, Verdolini-Marston K: Simple vocal tasks for detecting vocal fold swellings. *Journal of Voice* 4:172-183, 1990.

5. Bastian RW. Vocal fold microsurgery in singers. *Journal of Voice* 10:389-404, 1996.

6. Bastian RW, Klitzke C, Thurman L. Vocal fold and laryngeal surgery. In Thurman L & Welch G (Eds.): *bodymind and voice: foundations of voice education*, Book III, Chapter 11, pp. 416-427, 1997

Editorial Column by *Paul Meier*

Pedagogy and Coaching

It has been my pleasure to work with seven fine teachers and coaches in the articles that follow.

Katherine Maes in *Applying Theories of Learning Styles and Modalities to the Teaching of Voice and Speech, Part 2;* and Robert Barton in *Many Right Ways,* both offer us the second of their recurring columns on learning styles we as teachers encounter among our students.

Rena Cook interrogates nearly a dozen leading international coaches in *You've Got to Be a Chameleon,* a quote from her interview with Andrew Wade, Head of Voice at the Royal Shakespeare Company. And Eric Armstrong's interview with Andrew, conducted at Banff, and entitled *Earning the Role* elaborates on that theme. Lyn Darnley, a colleague of Andrew's in the Voice Department, offers us *Rough Eloquence*—in which she touches on themes echoed by Rod Menzies in *Language-Based Voice Training.* Yvette Hardie in *An Outcomes-based Approach for the Optimal Development of the Adolescent Voice,* like Lyn Darnley, addresses questions of voice in working with young people.

Pedagogy and Coaching articles in the next issue will be devoted to the work of coaching for film and television. If you are interested in contributing to that topic, please contact me at pmeier@ukans.edu.

Paul Meier (associate editor). Recent dialect coaching for feature films include Ang Lee's *Ride With The Devil,* while recent theatre productions include *The Glass Menagerie* at the Palace Theatre, London. He has appeared in films such as *Ride With The Devil, Stolen Women,* and *Cross of Fire,* while he has 'appeared' in over one hundred radio dramas for the BBC. Recently published articles include *King of Infinite Space: Tony Richardson's Hamlet,* and *With Utter Clarity: an Interview with Kenneth Branagh.* Paul founded IDEA (International Dialects of English Archive), on the web at http://www.ukans.edu/~idea.

Column by *Kathryn Maes*

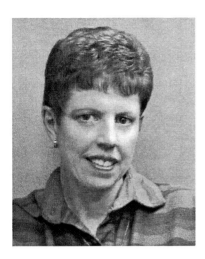

Kathryn Maes (A.D.V.S., Central School of Speech and Drama-London; Ph.D. University of Pittsburgh) Kathy currently serves as Chair in the Department of Theatre, Film and Video Production at the University of Colorado-Denver. Professionally, Kathy has served as dialect coach for four productions for the Royal Shakespeare Company and co-dialect coach with Joan Washington on the Royal National Theatre's Olivier Award-winning production of Arthur Miller's *American Clock*. Kathy has coached such notable actors as Ralph Fiennes and Brenda Blethyn. She served as Head of Voice at the Denver Center Theatre Company for four years prior to coming to the University of Colorado-Denver in 1992.

Applying Theories of Learning Styles and Modalities to the Teaching of Voice and Speech, Part 2

In my last article on Learning Styles, I stated that in order for learning to take place students must first *perceive* the information to be taken in in a sensory-intuitive-experiential way and/or in an analytical-reasoning-logical manner (or some balance of the two, even though there may tend to be a "preferred" way). Once this perception takes place, the students must then *process* the information by actively putting this input to use (often referred to as "active learning") and/or by observing and reflecting (often referred to as "reflective learning"). The combination of how we *perceive* information and how we *process* it ultimately determines how we prefer to learn—how we develop our "learning style".

This, however, is by no means the whole story on learning. This past summer I had the opportunity of attending the Boot Camp for Profs in Leadville, Colorado. This nationally offered program began approximately eight years ago by Professor Ed Nuhfer, a professor in the Geology department and head of our Office of Teaching Effectiveness at the University of Colorado at Denver. The aim of the program is not simply to rectify mediocre or substandard teaching skills, but rather to offer good teachers the opportunity of becoming ever better teachers and, in turn, become first-class mentors and role models for other faculty members.

One of the presenters at the Boot Camp, Professor Robert Leamnson (Professor of Biology and Director of Multidisciplinary Studies at UMass, Dartmouth), offered a further clarification on the issue of how students learn. In his book, *Thinking About Teaching and Learning: Developing Habits of Learning with First Year College and University Students*, he dispels the concept of thinking and learning as ethereal, mystical processes by considering them first and foremost as biological processes. His beliefs reflect the current study on the human brain that has taken place over the past twenty years, and, in educational terms it is often referred to "brain-based learning".

Simply put, the neurons in the brain of the embryo are initially programmed by the genes to continue to reproduce new neurons until there are approximately a hundred billion of them that are arranged in layers and bundles. In order for more advanced brain function to occur and develop, these isolated neurons must connect with other neurons. Neurons make these connections to other neurons by sending out projections (called axons), and once these connections begin to occur, unions or synapses can develop. Since the number of neurons in the brain of the newborn is approximately the same as that of the adult, it is the *number of these spreading neural connections* that is highly significant to the newborn's development and learning. The fact that the adult brain is several times larger than the newborn's brain is a result of the multifold budding of the axons and growth of support cells that occurs after birth. As the human matures and learning becomes more specialized and sophisticated, the human brain continues in its growth and development (Leamnson, p. 12).

There are two points of significance here for teachers. First, it is the multiple connections between neurons that allow perception and thought, and not just the existence or the number of neurons. Second, it is experience and sensory interaction with the environment that promotes and stabilizes neural connections. There is good evidence that neurons bud, or send out new axons, continually. These new axons make connection with other neurons, but the connection, or synapses, are, initially, quite labile, meaning here that they easily regress if not used. New and weak synapses stabilize only if they have produced a useful path. Whether or not a synaptic sequence stabilizes is determined by the frequency with which that path is used. Even potentially useful neural pathways will, then, degenerate if not used. (Leamnson, p.13)

Leamnson, therefore, subscribes to the definition of **learning** as *stabilizing through repeated use, certain appropriate and desirable synapses in the brain* (Leamnson, p. 53.); **teaching** as *any activity that has the conscious intention of, and potential for, facilitating learning in another* (Leamnson. p. 51); and **education** as *learning that has been facilitated by teaching* (Leamnson, p. 54).

While this demystification of thinking and learning offers a multitude of tangible possibilities for teachers, it has specific significance for those of us who teach in the arts. Leamnson theory would seemingly support the *perception* part of learning put forth at the beginning of this article (i.e., we take in the information in a sensory-intuitive-experiential manner and/or an analytical-reasoning-logical way by using the current neural connections present in our brains), but, more significantly, Leamnson's position further explains the *processing* part of thinking and learning proposed in this article (i.e., as "doers" [active learners] and/or "thinkers" [reflective learners] we first use whatever labile networks are available, and by repeated use of these synapses we stabilize the connections which provides us with memory of what is understood). It is truly the "experience and sensory interaction with the environment" (i.e., learning through good teaching, thinking and experimentation) that allows us to "engage and make sense of the world" (Leamnson, pp. 12 and 13).

In the 1950's Dr. Roger Sperry began his research on right and left brain functions. He conducted a series of studies in which the corpus callosum (the thick nerve cable which is composed of nerve fibers that cross-connect the two cerebral hemispheres of the brain) was severed in laboratory animals. The corpus callosum, with its 200 million nerve fibers, provides a rapid conduit for memory and learning between the two hemispheres of the brain. Unexpectedly, there was no significant change in behavior of the animals. Eventually "split-brain" operations were performed on humans with intractable epilepsy, whose seizures were repeatedly spreading through the corpus callosum. Afterwards, a number of tests were conducted by Sperry to discover how the two sides of the brain were functioning post surgery. The major results and findings were: 1) in the split-brain patient, there seem to be two different people up there, each with his/her preferred ways of processing information, each with a different mode of thinking; 2) the two halves of the brain, right and left hemispheres, process information differently, and 3) both hemispheres are equally important (McCarthy, p. 69-72).

The experiments that were performed on split-brained patients reinforce the idea that rather than being a one-brained or half-brained species, humans are a two-brained species, with each half being somewhat specialized. Sperry believes that there appear to be two forms of thinking—the verbal and nonverbal—which function quite separately in the left and right hemispheres of the brain. Sperry further states that he believes our educational system tends to neglect and actively discriminate against the nonverbal form of intellect (McCarthy, p. 71). It is imperative that we educators do all we can to provide activities that require exercise of both hemispheres.

Regarding the processing of information in the two hemispheres of the brain, it appears that the left brain prefers a lineal, sequential type of processing, while the right brain uses a more global process in which information is perceived, absorbed and processed even while it is in the process of changing. Like Sperry, McCarthy believes:

> The left does verbal things.
> The left likes sequence.
> The left sees the trees.
> The left likes structure.
>
> Left brains love school.
>
> The right does visual-spatial things.
> The right likes random patterns.
> The right sees the forest.
> The right is fluid and spontaneous.
>
> Right brains hang around school
> and hope they catch on.
>
> School teaches us
> not to trust our right mode of knowing;
> so our subsequent use of it
> makes us feel guilty,
> less rational,
> less intelligent.
>
> It's not that our right mode
> stops functioning in school;
> it's just that our ability to hear it,
> to respond to it, to believe in it,
> suffers terrible neglect.
>
> The right mode sees relationships.
> It grabs for the whole.
> It draws the big circle.
> It goes after the significant idea,
> the ideas that connect.
>
> While the left mode
> recognizes the relation
> of the new
> to the old,
> the right mode
> explores all the new material.

Together they move toward wholeness.

Knowledge is not fragmented.
Knowledge is coherent and whole.

How well we remember
the things we learn
depends on how well engaged
both hemispheres were
when we first learned it.

People who approach learning
with left-mode processing preference
have beautiful gifts.
They are systematic,
they solve problems by looking at the parts,
they are sequential and are excellent planners.
They are analytic.

People who approach learning
with a right-mode processing preference
have beautiful gifts.
They see patterns,
they solve problems by looking at
the whole picture.
They are random and arrive
at accurate conclusions
in the absence of logical justification.
They are intuitive.

People who access their whole brain
flex and flow.
They have both sets of beautiful gifts.

The goal of education
should be
to help our students
develop the flexible use
of their whole brain. (McCarthy, p. 73-75)

Indeed, both hemispheres are equally important. McCarthy creates a list of activities that she believes favors and will help stimulate and access the right mode. Those listed which are of particular interest to those in the arts include: patterning, metaphors, visualization, imagery, all forms of poetry, all Fine Arts, use of modalities (auditory, visual, and kinesthetic), role-playing, acting, creative dramatics, and movement and dance.

Oftentimes I believe teachers in the arts err by favoring the right mode over the left. By so doing, they neglect the special gifts and balance that the left mode can bring to the arts, such as analysis, memory skills, responsiveness to structure, sensitivity to verbal sounds, writing skills, phonetic discrimination and researching skills, to name a few. Balance in education and training, as in life, remains the key. The point is, we don't have to—nor should we—have one mode without the other. The artist of excellence needs both!

In the next article, I will present a learning cycle based on McCarthy's 4MAT system that will offer teachers in the arts a way of presenting material and helping students develop skills *across* the various learning styles. Rather than teaching to one particular learning style, teachers must try to develop multiple styles of learning, if we are to help students adapt to learning in a variety of ways and, thus, become more open and better learners.

Bibliography

Leamnson, Robert. 1999. *Thinking About Teaching and Learning: Developing Habits of Learning with First Year College and University Students.* (Sterling, VA: Stylus Publishing, LLC).

McCarthy, Bernice. 1987. *The 4MAT System: Teaching to Learning Styles with Right/Left Mode Technique.* (Barrington, IL: Excel, Inc.).

Column by *Robert Barton*

Many "Right" Ways: Honoring diverse teaching and learning modes

In the last issue, this column featured "monologs" from hypothetical directors representing the three basic learning patterns of N.L.P. (Neuro-Linguistic Programming).* A number of you raised questions about actors, pointing out that it is easier to recognize a leader's preferences than a follower's. Actors (until they morph into stars) are accustomed to adjusting to director modes and often wait to be asked what they prefer. So imagine that three different actors have been asked how they like to work.

Visual

(reminders—Visuals are straight-backed, with raised, tense shoulders, a dropped chin, minimal facial expression, few gestures. Speech is rapid, breathy, high pitched, uninflected.)

"I never see any progress until I know what my character looks like, clothes, favorite colors, hair, make-up, and facial expressions. I need to visualize her before I can be her. I love to see the designs so I can get a vision of the whole show, so I love 'Show and Tell' sessions. I look at magazines, paintings, people on the street. I gaze into the mirror and one day I see her! Next, I try to view the world her way. I try to see people and places the way she would. It also helps me to observe a performance by another actor in the role, not that I would *ever* copy someone else, but it is illuminating to be able to picture every moment in the play. The minute I get the script, I highlight my lines—I really enjoy this!—and I often see them when I speak them, what page, where on the page, the page turning, etc. until I replace these images with others. You know, some actors are offended when directors go up onstage and show them what they want in a scene—actually act it out—but I love that! It really helps clarify things for me, especially if there is violent behavior involved. Just show me what you want me to do. If I can see it, I can do it."

Auditory

(reminders—Auditories like to sit, touch their own faces, tap out rhythms, and may turn their ears are toward you when you speak to them. They like to talk, nod often when listening, and may repeat exactly what you've asked before answering. Voices are pleasant and speech is varied.)

"I ask myself, right at the beginning of rehearsal when we are still in the discussion phase, still having those lovely, long talks about text and meaning and the purpose of the show, even *that* early, I ask myself, 'What is my character's sound?' Is her voice strong, weak, deep, light, loud, soft? And I keep trying to hear her, to let her speak to me and through me. When I get that voice, the rest of the character comes very quickly as my body and spirit just seem to follow. It helps me enormously to tape my lines and listen to them in the car. It is also good for me to tape the director's notes. I hate it most when there are distracting background noises in rehearsal. I do not understand how some actors can work under those conditions! I'm totally mystified when other actors get bored or restless during line notes. I *love* to hear about my line delivery and to keep adding nuance, subtlety and shading. And some actors never talk about their characters outside rehearsal! Some don't even want to talk about them *in* rehearsal! Unbelievable!! If I have doubts about the character, I put those doubts into words. I have never found an acting problem that can't be talked out. I'm not real crazy about fight scenes so I especially like to talk those through before actually doing anything that might be risky."

Robert Barton is head of the Acting Program at the University of Oregon and the author of the widely used texts *Acting: Onstage and Off, Style for Actors*, and (with Rocco Dal Vera) *Voice: Onstage and Off* as well as numerous articles. He is the recipient of the ATHE's Best Book Award as well ACTF's Outstanding Acting Coach award. He has acted professionally in most of the plays of Shakespeare and has directed half of them.

*See pp.163-164 of the inaugural *Standard Speech* volume to review this material.

Kinesthetic

(reminders—Kinos need space, gesture big and often, like to be up acting out experiences and feelings, but slump when sitting. Highly expressive and emotionally available, they also may lose the thread of their (or your) main points, so alternate between energized and comatose. Voices are often low pitched, with a speech tendency to lose endings and mumble.

"Okay, the first thing I do is I fall in love with the character I'm playing, hopelessly, helplessly in love! Then I gradually let her seep into my bones and crawl into every pour of my skin until she becomes me and I become her. We share a heartbeat! It feels like giving birth! There's pain and struggle, then release and fulfillment Whew!! Whoa!! The best rehearsals for me are when we are *finally* up on our feet and sometimes it seems to take forever to get to that moment. Once I get props in my hands, rehearsal clothes on my body—oh, the right shoes, the feet have got to feel right!—and I can touch, I mean really connect with, the other actors, it all begins to happen for me. I hate rehearsals that are talk, talk, talk, analyze, analyze, analyze, blah, blah, blah.... Okay, maybe I don't read as much as I might about the character and play's background, whatever, but I will try *anything* in rehearsal! Oh, and I hate actors who always put off everything: 'We'll do the kiss later' or 'Don't really hit me; I'm not ready.' Shit, I'm ready! I also don't like actors who don't seem to feel things, deep in the gut. That, to me, is not acting!"

These monologs reflect actors whose work patterns are formed. Many of our students do not yet recognize their preferences. So study their body language and listen closely for the verbs they choose.

Suggestions:

Let's use this issue's Voice in Violence theme. Imagine that an actor needs to change in order to reduce both vocal and referred tension during a violent encounter and that you have decided what the change should be:

1. **Visuals** need to be shown what they look like when performing with and then without unneeded tension. Encourage them to look at themselves doing it in a mirror or on videotape. The difference will be a strong motivator. Do not be afraid to show them what you see when they do it one way and then another. Let them take the video tape from rehearsal home and review it privately.

Tip: Encourage them to have the script present, to highlight, and notate (in appropriate colors) where they need to make a change during the session.

2. **Auditories** can probably actually hear the difference between excess tension and appropriate use, so are easy to coach (except that sessions always run overtime because they have so much to ask and to say). They may fail to notice certain referred tendencies in the lower torso and appendages because they are so sound-centered. Encourage them to describe doing it the tense way and the right way. Let them wax rhapsodic about the difference. Have them repeat back to you what they accomplished at this session and what they are now assigned to work on for the next.

Tip: Always stress the lines and non-verbal sounds in the fight. Encourage them to discuss the beats and to translate the activity into verbal terms.

3. **Kinos** will instantly recognize and appreciate the less tense approach, but may be concerned that they are not putting out enough, so need reassurance on the effectiveness of the change, on how much more powerful they are without referred tension. If they aren't giving 100% they feel they 're cheating. Make sure they sense that their energy and focus is being re-channeled not reduced. If possible, work in costume, with props, in the real space and with their actual partner present because these elements influence them so strongly.

Tip: Offer constant physical reinforcement (pats on the back, hugs, yes even high fives).

Actors often blend two of the above modalities. Being an Auditory/Kino, for example, is a common phenomenon among actors, even though 80% of the population at large are Visuals. But there is always one mode an actor almost never uses. Recognizing that mode will immediately clarify your communication, particularly if it is the one you most often choose!

(For questions about V.A.K. contact Robert at barton@oregon.uoregon.edu. For a more comprehensive description of V.A.K. and it's place in N.L.P., read Robert's chapter "Voice in a Visual World" in *The Vocal Vision*).

Earning the Role: The Company Voice Coach

Eric Armstrong teaches voice, speech, dialects and Shakespeare text at Roosevelt University in Chicago. He has also taught at Brandeis University in Boston, Canada's National Voice Intensive and at the University of Windsor in Windsor, Ontario. Eric trained with David Smukler at York University's Voice Teacher training program. In VASTA, Eric is well-known as the Director of Internet Services and the Director of Conferences 2001-2002. In 1994, Eric had the good fortune to receive a Professional Theatre Training Program grant from Theatre Ontario to study with the RSC's Andrew Wade in Banff, Alberta and subsequently in Stratford-Upon-Avon.

Andrew Wade joined the Royal Shakespeare Company in 1987 as Assistant Voice Director to Cicely Berry. In 1990 he was appointed Head of Voice. This responsibility involves overseeing the voice work in the RST, The Swan and The Other Place theatres in Stratford-Upon-Avon, the Barbican and The Pit theatres in London. Andrew co-ordinates the relevant voice work during the RSC's residencies and extensive touring programs, working closely with the actors and directors throughout the life of each production. In conjunction with Cicely Berry, he has taken part in the filming of a series of videos on voice and text work for Applause Books, which will be released in 2000.

An Interview with the Royal Shakespeare Company's Andrew Wade.

In 1994 I had the opportunity to assist voice coach Andrew Wade on The Banff Centre's Advanced Actor's Workshop production of The Last Comedy, *a play about rhetoric and persuasion. By coming to Banff I wanted an understanding of the company voice coach's role and how it differed from the role of the voice teacher in a theatre school or workshop setting. As Head of Voice for the Royal Shakespeare Company at Stratford-upon-Avon, Andrew Wade is most qualified to discuss the importance of the voice coach in today's theatre.*

Most days we sat and chatted about what I was observing, usually with my tape recorder running. It soon became apparent that what interested Andrew and me most was how he functioned within the company and not what specific exercises he did. Though voice has fractured into a variety of methods, we both felt that those differences were slight and not worth dwelling on. We found ourselves talking about the role of the voice coach and how it might fit into theatre in a more prominent way.

ea: What do you feel your role is as a voice coach sitting in on rehearsals?

AW: I feel I need to really understand what's going on. My role is to serve the production, to be able to be of assistance to the production, to understand the obsessions of the director. So when I am in rehearsal, I suppose, I am trying to discover what this text demands as a piece of writing, how that is being realized by the director, and how the actors are struggling with that. Is there anything I could do with them away from rehearsals, whether in solo or group calls that is going to enable that journey?

I feel very privileged to be in rehearsal, so I want my presence to be as fly-like as possible. I get equally upset if an actor says, even as a joke, "Oh Andrew's here, I must be conscious of the language or my voice", as I am if I am completely ignored by the director or the process. So I suppose I fluctuate between wanting to be included, and wanting to be as unobtrusive as possible. I feel my energies are always going to how I can help their concentration and their discovery, by my presence, just by my being there. I feel being in rehearsal is hugely draining; it really takes it out of me more than when I am talking.

In rehearsal, I am very, very concerned about encouraging the whole time. I see it as part of my role, and therefore I am completely covering up any area of being judgmental and analytical when I'm in there. If I write a note down, I'm very conscious of how I write that note. If they feel that I am going to give them a note afterwards, I feel I am challenging their vulnerability in that way. I am very concerned about that. I'm being hypersensitive now...

Andrew Wade

ea: But it's very important because actors can be hypersensitive, too.

AW: I'm very concerned that the director is always aware that there is something in me that is smiling with approval. I may have disagreements, but it's not going to help my relationship with that production if I'm not absolutely supporting him or her. I think my role is only about supporting, you know, I mustn't be a director, even if I have contrary opinions to the director. The only time I feel that I have to take a stand is if I actually feel that what is going on is actually disrespectful towards this piece of writing. I have a clout as a voice professional to gently point that out. I think I have a responsibility to get that language, through the voice, heard to the audience.

ea: Is that your primary role?

AW: It falls into two categories. One is, what do I think is in this text that will make this production live? What must the actor honor, connect with, to make this play come alive? Part of the work is letting the language out, or as I would put it, finding *the voice of the language* with the actor. I feel a responsibility towards that. I feel that while I wouldn't say I'm looking for a particular sound, I think there is a "sound" of the language in a text. There is a sound where that text comes alive. I feel our role is to allow the voice of the playwright to be heard in that production.

ea: Serving the voice of the play is more than just about the ideas within the play…

AW: It is about the ideas, but my interest is in the music of the thought, or the way the words are chosen, and increasingly, the inherent cadence that that embodies. It's all part of hearing that piece of theatre.

ea: How does that help an actor?

AW: I don't think I do this in a conscious way with the actors. When you're working with the actors it's about helping them to feel comfortable with that language. The more we can help the actor to feel comfortable, so they aren't ducking the language or manipulating it, then we are more likely to hear the language of the playwright.

I think that when you're taking notes, all the time it comes back to the question "Is that what the language is suggesting you do, or are you just doing something with that language for the sake of it?" It has to become a choice. I feel more and more that my responsibility is to the playwright. I hope the director would say the same.

The second part of my role is the area of the actor as an artist, as a person, and how I can help her to work on herself in order to achieve that. My starting point is the production, and then the actor. My ultimate concern, absolutely, is the actor. However, I get to it not in an objective, judgmental way by analyzing where they are...

I think that the way in is to say, "What does this text demand of the actor and what does this production, in this space demand?" And it is this starting place that determines how one works with the actor. It is different from how one trains an actor, where one might say, "You've got these so-and-so blocks, and you've got to overcome those, otherwise you're limiting your acting." For instance, one of the actors in the company has a tight throat. I would love to help him find an open sound. Since he asked for it last week, I could then do an appropriate exercise the next day. But unless it is annoying him in this show, or messing up the production I won't hit that now and give him a routine on that, because it will make him conscious in the wrong way. But, in the space of a year at the company, it might be appropriate as part of my agenda for that person. That's what I mean by this not being "actor-centered" work.

ea: There is a certain respect that a professional deserves, tied into the fact that those perceived "blocks" may be how this actor has been making her living. What about moments when you feel that the actor is not looking out for his own best interests, for instance, he's doing something that might damage his voice? How do you deal with that? How do you stay positive, when you know that if he continues in that vein he might injure himself?

AW: I would answer in the way that Judith Koltai [the movement coach at Banff] answered in a sense of humor this morning. One of the actors, Val Planche, said "I shouldn't have danced last night," and Judith said, "Why? You probably needed it!" It's an absolute choice, and Val enjoyed dancing last night, even if she hurt her hip or whatever... I mean we have to live; I don't smoke and I don't think smoking is good for people, but actors have to deal with life in their own way. So if they smoke, they have to take responsibility... I think life is about taking responsibility for self, ultimately, and I suppose that anything that I might do is about saying, "that's your choice." Though I do think it is part of my responsibility to note that, in my mind, and to know in the future, on a long run that that is going to cause, ultimately, problems. I would try, depending on the personality of the actor, to find the place to say "If I dare say it to you, I'm a bit worried about that choice, that it might not be the best choice for you. Do you have to do that?" But I would never say you mustn't do it.

ea: Is there a general pattern to what you are "up to" with a session, or is everything geared towards that specific group of people?

AW: There is a basic sequence of work that one feels is appropriate for an actor to go through when they are working. This enables the actor to feel confident that they are able to express that language. The "technical" work is about that: how we handle breath when we speak, how do we perceive thought when we speak, what is our energy, what is verbalizing thought? One is always working on those questions all the time, not so much in ways of How It Should Be Done, but in ways of opening up possibilities. And in doing that, you are building up an actor's resilience and building up their strength, so that they are able to fulfill the demands of a large theatre space, or a long run. That's about muscles in the end, or it's about mental connections to muscles, admittedly.

So yes, there is a routine of repetition that needs to be incorporated. That's a delicate one for us coaches because an actor can perceive that as boring.

Making it interesting for the actor is a challenge, but increasingly I feel that when one is working with serious actors, that isn't an issue. You don't have to entertain them with exercises, because they have more than just curiosity, they know how to use our work, why they need this work, and how it can help them as actors. I think a lot of training is opening actors to the reasons whereby they need this work, whereby it can help them. The stimulation of working with professional actors of some experience is that they take, receive, get from the work reactions way beyond what we can set out as goals for the exercises. Their discoveries make it difficult to say simply what one exercise is for. Clearly, one must know why one is doing them. It's not just about entertaining the actors. There should be some super-objective. But on the other hand, the actors must be given work that doesn't limit them, with the understanding that there is potential beyond your goals. The actors must feel they come into this work on their own terms.

That's why I get very sensitive when people ask, "What exercises are you going to do?" or "What *new* exercises are you going to do?" What interests me more is *when, how* and *which* rather than *what* I do. I think the skill of voice work is in knowing how to choose what is the appropriate thing to do at that moment. To choose a sequence of work, a sequence of text that is going to illuminate something, to further that rehearsal process, or further that journey into the theatre for that production. That is what interests me, and is my challenge. Not "Do I have a new technique for teaching voice?" That is not the value of my role in voice work, and I don't think I am going down that path.

All voice professionals come from their own perspectives, with their own viewpoints and interests. There is no doubt that some voice teachers are more interested in the psychological barriers than others. In the end I think it comes down to our point of entry into the world of the actor. In the end, I do deal with psychological and emotional issues, I just don't think I come at it from that point of view. They are all so inextricably tied up, as we all know, so when they surface, they have to be dealt with. For me it has to be dealt with through the task at hand, and usually that is through the text we are working on. For me, it is not about manipulating an actor, but about respecting what they bring to the work.

Quite often a director might be worried by a particular weak voice; increasingly actors themselves come to me, seeking help, saying, "Andrew, I need to get back in trim." If I noticed a particular actor, and I thought the choices they were making, the way they were using their voice would be a problem, I would try to do a call in the theatre space with them. I think getting stage access is very important. I think directors appreciate the value of it, that it accelerates everything else so it is a good use of time. I have various examples of that sort of thing. Working on a production of *Julius Cæsar*, one of the most useful things was doing a line-run in the theatre with the lights out. Increasingly, at Stratford they will do one in the final week on the previous set or on the bare stage. It is foreboding for young actors to walk on that stage; there is a weight of history on that stage.

ea: I want to go back to the text and its demands. I am aware of at least three things one can look for in the text. Firstly there is Structure, or the use of rhetoric, dialectic, etc., and then Image, the use of words to paint pictures. Finally, and what I'm trying to get at here, there's the specific use of Word Choice, to create a character based on the way they actually speak. How does choice of word specifically help the actor?

AW: In the sense that we are what we say, we are the words we use, it is a reflection of our background, our intelligence, our sensibilities, in every possible way. When it comes to a piece of writing that is about *chosen* words, that's different from everyday life where, in relaxed situations, we're not choosing words that carefully. We're not defining ourselves as a course of action, by the choice of words. It's just about general survival. Whereas, when we meet a character in a play, it is a heightened situation, at a dramatic moment in his or her life, and therefore it is about a charged situation and a charged use of language. It is the meeting of that precision with the word that interests me and is a challenge to actors. We must compare the truth of the articulateness of someone else's shaped thought in a carefully worded line and our own reference point of our truth, and rise to it. I think that choice of word and setting one word off against another is very important in this play. There is a delight in doing that. There is a definition of self when you actually achieve it. Not boasting or a show-off idea, but elation that comes through being precise.

ea: We are coming back to what the playwright we are working with, Michael Mackenzie, said about the physical joy in finding the word that expresses the thought.

> "It's from Wittgenstein…'Sometimes the sound of thought is so soft, that the noise of spoken words can drown it out.' Though a lot of writing today is about the frustration people have with the language they have access to and the fact that they can't express their thoughts in that language, so they're banging up against it. It's actually an interesting theatrical device, which works very well, if you don't overuse it. But people often forget that *the sheer joy of finding the right word which expresses a thought is extraordinary, an emotional rush of an intense kind.*"

AW: Exactly. We want to keep opening those possibilities. It is about hearing the delight in the choice of word, the delight in actually saying it. It's not about a descriptive, external impression, but about the absolute delight of the moment of the word.

ea: That's one of the major reasons for using the poetry in sessions: to play with the words and find that discovery, the need for that word in counterpoint to the other ones.

AW: The big reason for using other texts is the need to let one's ego go and to hear the ego of the text, to see if that choice is another possibility. Rather than impose our own meaning, or our own tune, hearing that the shape of the writing is a tune in itself.

ea: To allow yourself to be shaped by the shape of the text.

AW: And to feel that that is *doing* something as an actor and that it is valuable and satisfying. That's why I want to do lots of things on the difference between a long and short thought. It can be interesting to look at the different lengths of thought, in terms of variety and in terms of that being a reflection of that character. That is opposed to the understandable desire of the actor to feel comfortable and to impose their rhythms of thinking onto the text, which thereby limits the character to their perceptions, truths and rhythms rather than expand themselves to other rhythms, which are somebody else. In prose, certainly, that can be part of humor, the contrast between long and short. It is all part of the writing, of what alerts the ear of the audience, of audibility. Remember that the juxtaposition of long and short is very much what we are doing everyday, but it is heightened in a piece of shaped writing.

ea: As a voice professional, would you say it is important to have a guiding passion? Ultimately, is that passion a political one?

AW: For any of us to carry on working in theatre in our different roles, but certainly as a voice coach, you've got to have a drive that inspires you, motivates you and hopefully, in the end, will produce some fulfillment. That must be a political thing. You have to believe that theatre is going to perform a valuable function in our society today. Certainly in our Western society, with its reliance on the visual, on the acquisition of items, on the value of a human being in terms of the money, it is very important for me to keep in perspective the value of a person being able to define themselves and relate to other people through language. Therefore it also interests me to work with teachers and students on how we relate to language today. Which informs how theatre relates to language and how appropriate that language is. So that theatre does not become a museum piece. Theatre must be about a reflection and reaction, a mirror to what's going on around it. That comes right back to our role in terms of language and working on a classical text today. How do we honor the classical structure of writing and still allow it to ring true to the audience today?

ea: Is there a "mission statement" for the Voice Department that guides your choices?

AW: I think the mission statement of the Voice department is a personification of the work that Cicely Berry has pioneered there in the last twenty years and what I'm trying to do, as part of a larger team, is to expand that and to reflect the demands and challenges of the RSC and theatre today. I see the mission falling into two camps: working on the voice of the language of the play at hand; and working with the actors in the circumstances at the RSC, in the repertoire work, in the two-year cycle, and the demands that that entails. It comes down to rehearsal work on language and voice work for that, and the actors' ongoing work.

ea: It seems that the way you look at our role comes from a broad perspective down to the specific. Could you elaborate on the specifics?

AW: They range from solo calls to group work. In response to what the director wants or what we feel that we could offer that actor in that rehearsal process, at that point in their season, we might work in a solo call. The actors can request those, focussing on areas that they would like to work on, or try out things in the theatre spaces. Group work can reflect the rehearsal process, or address the theatre spaces, or where they've gotten to at that point in the season... it varies a lot as the company grows, and as they get to know each other. Of course it includes warm-ups before shows, but also things like lunchtime sessions on associated poetry. Cicely Berry and I have done modern poetry on the main stage, and Romantic poetry on the Swan stage, where we have tried to find the meeting place between different styles of writing in a theatre space.

I think solo calls are the most difficult area of the work to talk about because they incorporate so many different things for different people. Basically it is practical work for the actor, away from the rehearsal room to work on their voice and on the language, on their terms, for them. To hopefully meet the demands, aspirations, and challenges that the director is putting forward, as well as the production. But as much as one will have an agenda of work that one might want to do, I think it is important for the actor to see it as their time to explore: to meet the challenges of the director with the challenges of the text, balanced by where they're at as people.

ea: Is it important that the actor not feel that the director is sitting in the room with them? That they can explore to a certain extent, with an understanding of the expectations the director has?

AW: Yes, however, I must keep firmly fixed in my mind that my role with them, working with them, is to support what the director wants. That's very important. No matter how much I might have opinions on that, it's not my role. It's not helpful to the actor and that's what is ultimately important. I'm only useful if I'm helping the actor. Within that, a solo call can take many forms. It can take the form of working on a poem away from the play. It can take the form of talking through a run that you have seen, any observations that you may have from your point of view that seem appropriate for the ears of the actor, that the actor wants to hear.

ea: It is very much a question of balancing what you think is appropriate with cues that you get from the actor.

AW: Yes, because I think I'm there to help the actor. One must not sound like one is pussyfooting too much; one has another responsibility to that production and to the play and now and again one can be firm with the work, but not personal.

You've got to be a Chameleon: Interviews with Leading Vocal Coaches

Andrew Wade, Head of Voice at the Royal Shakespeare Company, in an interview conducted on February 16, 2000 said that a vocal coach must be a chameleon. This word, "chameleon," becomes a guiding image in the exploration of the role of vocal coach in the modern theatre. In relation to other roles—actors, directors, and set designers, for example—the vocal coach has a short history. Beginning with the hiring of Cicely Berry by the Royal Shakespeare Company in 1969, the position of vocal coach has slowly worked its way into the ranks of the theatrical production team (Wade 1997: 135). However, the job of the vocal coach tends to be elusive, resisting description or prescription. Consequently the functions of the vocal coach are difficult to codify.

The work of the vocal coach is often done quietly, behind the scenes, where the light of public scrutiny seldom shines. Credit for the voice and text work in a production is seldom directly attributed to the work of the vocal coach. A clear, audible, and fully realized text is more often attributed to the quality of the cast or the excellence of the direction. Finally, vocal coaching serves a support function within the production process, which, by its nature, keeps it from developing the kind of public visibility enjoyed by directors and designers.

Nan Withers-Wilson, in her book *Vocal Direction for the Theatre* begins to define the role of the vocal coach by saying it is the "challenge and responsibility of the vocal director, in collaboration with the entire production team, to assist the play's director and the acting company in making certain that t he language of the play serves its critical function in performance" (Withers-Wilson 1993: 28).

Cicely Berry, in "Shakespeare, Feminism, and Voice: Responses to Sarah Werner," defines her role as opening, through exercises, "the voice itself so that the actor finds his/her true potential...by working on the text—hearing and listening—to give the actor choice, and power over that choice... I want to give the actors that power...to convey the argument, and above all to challenge the listener" (Berry 1997: 48).

Patsy Rodenburg, in her portion of the same article, says, "My job is to release the play, to try to render the text as clearly as I can—giving actors/actresses a spring board to take off from." Rodenburg further adds:

> A good coach offers starting points in the work. All these points can be jettisoned at any stage by actors or directors. If coaches have any power, it is in the teaching of craft, the handing out of tools that can be used by the actor in any way they wish. I also hope I teach a notion of self-discipline in the craft and the right of the artist consciously to make any decision about interpretation that has to include breaking any rule I or anyone else might teach them (Rodenburg 1997: 50).

With the words of these pioneer vocal coaches in mind I set out to determine how current vocal coaches define their role and what their methods and practices are. To this end I interviewed seven vocal coaches in the London theatre. This sample was acquired from responses to an initial letter requesting an interview. Out of fifteen letters sent, positive responses were received from the seven mentioned above.

Rena Cook (associate editor) is on the faculty at University of Oklahoma where she teaches Voice and Acting. She has served as vocal coach for the Illinois Shakespeare Festival on *The Merry Wives of Windsor, Richard III,* and *Wild Oats.* She has directed *Dancing at Lughnasa, The Prime of Miss Jean Brodie* and *Medea.* Rena holds an MA in Voice Studies from the Central School of Speech and Drama. Her theatrical reviews have appeared in *The Journal of Dramatic Theory and Criticism* and *Theatre Journal.*

Cicely Berry has been the Vocal Director for the Royal Shakespeare Company since 1969. She taught at the Central School of Speech and Drama for twenty years and had a private studio in London. She has worked extensively with theatre companies and actors abroad in the United States, Brazil, Korea, Australia, India, China, Poland, Russia, and other European Countries. Berry is the author of *Voice and the Actor, Your Voice and How to Use It,* and *The Actor and the Text.* She organized an international voice conference in January 2000 held at the RSC in Stratford-upon-Avon. She received an Honorary Doctorate of Letters from Birmingham University in 1999.

Mel Churcher has been a voice teacher in London for 18 years. She is vocal coach for the Regent's Park Open Air Shakespeare Company. She also teaches voice at the Central School of Speech and Drama where she also directed plays. Her film coaching credits include *The Fifth Element, Joan of Arc,* and *101 Dalmatians.* Ms. Churcher holds an MA in performance and is currently completing an MA in voice.

William Conacher trained as an actor and worked in the profession before he completed the Voice Course at the Central School of Speech and Drama. He currently teaches dialect and phonetics at the Central School and RADA. He does various freelance vocal coaching including the Chichester Festival in the summer of 1999.

Gregory de Polnay was a professional actor for twenty years before he trained as a voice teacher at the Central School of Speech and Drama. He has an MA from King's College London. He was Head of Voice at the Drama Centre, London and has taught voice, speech and text at Rose Bruford, Central, RADA, and LAMDA. He is also a freelance vocal coach in the theatre, the business world, and film. His most recent film credit is *Mansfield Park.* He is currently Head of Voice at LAMDA and 2nd year classical Acting Director at RADA.

Neil Freeman's groundbreaking work on Shakespeare's quartos and First Folio has led to a second printing of his *Shakespeare's First Texts,* plus his annotated editions of all thirty-six Shakespeare plays, being published by Applause Books, and to lecture/workshops at the SAA, ATHE and VASTA, plus grants/fellowships from the NEA (USA), SSHRC (Canada), and York University in Toronto. Neil has acted and directed professionally in England, Canada and the USA. Based at the University of British Columbia, Canada, he is associated with Shakespeare & Co. (Lenox, Massachusetts); the Will Geer Theatre (Los Angeles); Repercussion Theatre (Montreal); and has worked in several capacities with the Stratford Festival, Canada. He is dramaturge for a Vancouver workshop presentation of all Shakespeare plays/poems over the next two years.

Sally Grace has taught voice in the United States, Australia, Hong Kong, Singapore, France, and Germany (Berliner Ensemble). She is currently Head of Voice for the actors' training program at the Central School of Speech and Drama. She also

In addition to the interviews, questionnaires were sent to a sample of American and Canadian vocal coaches through the list-serv VASTAVOX. Four responses were received, three from the United States, one from Canada.

The vocal coaches interviewed represent a cross-section in respect to number of years in the profession, those that freelance, those connected with an established company, dialect coaches, and voice and text coaches. Cicely Berry and Andrew Wade, interviewed together from the RSC, represent vocal coaches employed full-time by a professional performing company. Freelance vocal coaches include Mel Churcher, William Conacher, and Joanna Weir, all of whom both teach and freelance as voice and dialect coaches. Connected primarily to drama schools are Greg de Polnay, and Sally Grace, both of whom also coach stage and film. Vocal coaches currently working in the US who responded to questionnaires are Jane MacFarlane, Debra Hale, and Tyne Turner. MacFarlane and Hale are affiliated with major university theatre departments and vocal coach in the regional theatre. Turner is currently a freelance vocal coach working with professional theatre companies throughout the US. Responding from Canada is Neil Freeman, an acknowledged expert on Shakespeare's First Folio, a vocal coach and university professor.

A list of questions was devised addressing such topics as the role of the vocal coach, relationship with the director, rehearsals and notes, private sessions, and respect and credit. Each vocal coach was subsequently presented with this series of questions and encouraged to respond openly to any or all of the topics.

All of the coaches expressed their views on the various aspects of their profession with passion and commitment. Similar opinions and common themes run throughout their answers. It is, however, when strong differences of opinion emerge that the personal approaches and individual personalities become clear.

Consequently the job of the vocal coach can be seen as dynamic, constantly changing, flowing, and growing as it is filtered through the various individuals who practice it. As Andrew Wade points out in his interview, "…it is never going to be statutory, nor should it…it is about flexibility and being certain of your ground rules and how you realize them. It is not set in stone…"

Role of the Vocal Coach
Tyne Turner succinctly states that her role as a vocal coach serves a four part support function: "1) to support the actors' clarity of logic, and articulation; 2) to support the actors in achieving healthy vibrant voices; 3) to support the playwright in having their auditory work realized as fully and accurately as possible; and 4) to support the director in auditory story-telling and free them up to focus on visual concerns."

Turner reinforces the service function of the vocal coach by saying that she is only part of the creative team, "by virtue of my power to read the music of the text…I am not there to create, I am there to support, inspire, and enlighten, so those who were hired to create, can do so more fully."

William Conacher's opinion of his role is a straightforward, no-nonsense view. He says, "It is a very ill-defined job. You see, it hasn't been around long enough for people to understand what it is…. The fundamental thing that people don't realize is that it's not a very respected job. You don't have any power in it. You can express your opinion but you are really there to serve everyone—writer, director—you know you are not really in control of it". He adds, "I think you have to offer it up as a service. And they use it or they don't…the designer is in control of the set and the director is in control of the production. A dialect coach is not in control of the dialect sounds. You are not a dialect designer, you are a facilitator and if they don't want you, they don't want you."

Jane MacFarlane also sees the vocal coach as support staff. She views her job as assisting the director and actors in clearly communicating their story to the audience. Though she does not attend production meetings, preferring to work behind the scenes, she feels that her contribution to clear story telling is crucial.

Debra Hale begins her discussion by saying that the vocal coach should play a major role on the creative team. "Ideally she should be exposed to the concept of the play through the director, including set, costume, and lighting concerns as well as discussions of character." She clarifies by saying that the role is dynamic, depending on the needs of the director; therefore it is crucial that the vocal coach should be in close and constant communication with the director throughout the process and be informed of changes in concept or design as the process progresses.

Greg de Polnay simply describes the role of the vocal coach as instilling the love of language, inspiring people to love language. Sally Grace addresses the role of the vocal coach by stating that "too often it is rather marginalized, a side activity where an actor is sent to you and you have to do magic in secret. It's almost furtive really."

Andrew Wade stresses the importance of the role when he asserts that the actors need the resources of the vocal coach more than ever as they [actors] use different vocal skills in each part of their career, moving from stage to film, to radio, to commercials, to industrials. Consequently he views his role as vocal coach at the RSC as helping the actor find the voice of the language. Text is central to the mission of the RSC and finding the voice in the language remains a focus.

In the same interview, Cicely Berry is quick to add that our "perception of language has changed, people's ears have changed totally, method acting, television…. One has had to adjust gradually and get people to feel the language inside them…the actor has to find the language and make it their own." On March 24, 2000 at the taping of a BBC Radio 3 program commemorating the birth of William Shakespeare, Ms. Berry addressed the role of vocal coach when she spoke of a two-fold mission. First, honoring the beauty and richness of Shakespeare's language. Second, helping the actor experience the language in a deeply personal way.

taught at Rose Bruford College, RADA and Juilliard. She is a professional vocal coach in the London theatre and in film, her many credits include *Streetcar Named Desire* directed by Peter Hall and *Jane Eyre* and *Tea With Mussolini* directed by Franco Zefferelli.

Debra Hale is Head of Voice and Speech at Indiana University in Bloomington. She received her MFA in Acting from CalArts, and acted professionally in Los Angeles for several years before becoming a Designated Linklater Voice Teacher. She has taught at University of California at San Diego, LACC Theatre Academy, Shakespeare and Company, and is currently coaching dialect at Indiana Repertory Theatre and teaching in their Professional Conservatory.

Jane MacFarlane is on the voice faculty at Southern Methodist University in Dallas, Texas. She received her BFA in Acting from the University of British Columbia. She then did an MFA in voice with David Smukler at York University. She interned with Bonnie Raphael at the American Repertory Theatre. She was Head of Voice for Shakespeare in Action. For the past two summers, Jane has worked with the Shakespeare Festival of Dallas.

Tyne Turner is a third generation actress and theatre educator, and as a child was surrounded by many great theatre artists of exceptional caliber. She is a graduate of the Professional Actor Training Program now located at the University of Delaware. She received her teacher training from Timothy Monich at Juilliard and Susan Sweeny at the University of Delaware. Ms. Turner has served as a voice/speech teacher for the American Academy of Dramatic Art, the University of Wisconsin - Milwaukee PTTP, and Southern Methodist University's BFA and MFA programs. She now coaches professionally all over the United States.

Andrew Wade is Head of Voice for the Royal Shakespeare Company. He oversees the voice work in the RSC's three Stratford theatres, the Barbican, and the Pit Theatres in London, and the company's touring program. Andrew studied at the Rose Bruford College of Speech and Drama. He taught voice at Rose Bruford, the Arts Education School and was Head of Voice at East 15 Acting School. He has coached productions in Australia, the United States, Canada, France, Belgium, and the Netherlands. In conjunction with Cicely Berry, he has taken part in the filming of a series of videos on voice and text work for Applause Books, to be released in 2000.

Joanna Weir is a Designated Linklater Teacher who was introduced to the work during her acting training in Australia. She taught in Australia on the Acting Program at the Victorian College of the Arts for five years and was Drama Tutor at La Trobe University. After winning a Churchill Fellowship, she continued her voice training with Linklater and Shakespeare and Company in the US. Joanna then completed the voice course at the Central School of Speech and Drama. She currently teaches at Central on the Voice Course. She also works as a professional voice and dialect coach for both stage and film and occasionally directs.

Joanna Weir feels that vocal coaching is about releasing the performance, unlocking what is holding the actor back. "We are not just about the voice…it is about blocks in the acting process that start to manifest themselves in the voice or the breathing. It's not just that they have a voice problem, it's because they have a problem realizing the part, realizing the text."

Mel Churcher, who is the vocal coach at the Regent's Park Open Air theatre, describes her role as vocal coach in functional terms, i.e. services provided. She says she looks to see that the breath is functioning, that resonance is rich, vowels open and consonants strong. "We have a British habit of falling away at the ends of lines and I'm doing Shakespeare and so it is doubly important that you do lots of work with line endings."

Finally, Neil Freeman clarifies the various functions of the vocal coach by stating that his job is to help the actor explore the desired marriage of character and the self as outlined by the director. He further states that the vocal coach deals with the "inevitable and perennial blocks which manifest themselves between rehearsal and transfer to performance." Freeman also feels it is the job of the vocal coach to deal with any problems the play or character presents, i.e. dialect, unusual rhythms, or physical handicaps of character. He adds that the vocal coach is there to assist the cast in dealing with the challenges presented by the theatre space itself. Freeman summarizes by saying it is the role of the vocal coach to the help director achieve the desired overall texture of the production.

Relationship with the Director
From the responses in the interviews and the questionnaires, it is safe to conclude that the relationship between the director and the vocal coach is the crucial first step in allowing the vocal coach to serve effectively as the aforementioned bridge between director, actor, and text. Strategies for developing and sustaining this relationship are ever changing as each director is different and has different levels of comfort in opening his/her process to the assistance of a vocal coach. But the two key points stressed by all vocal coaches dealt with maintaining continuous, open communication, and building a sense of trust.

Debra Hale begins a discussion of the director/vocal coach relationship by saying that it depends on the personalities involved. Some directors depend on and value the coach all through the process; some contact them only for vocal or dialect "emergencies"; and some prefer a more hands-on approach. Hale's strategies for building this relationship are summarized in the following statement:

> I try to let the director know that I am there to serve his/her vision, ask them beforehand what they would like…my involvement to be; if they are comfortable with my doing outside work with actors (this usually comes with trust after working together more than once); offer to show my vocal notes to them before I disperse them to the actors; tell them that I would like to confer with them shortly after a rehearsal before I speak with the actors in case any of my notes may be construed as "acting" concerns rather than "vocal" concerns. I also notify them before I attend rehearsals unless we have worked out a schedule ahead of time; I try to be flexible in terms of schedule, realizing that needs often change during the process.

Andrew Wade states that diplomacy is the only strategy. "I would be a diplomat if I weren't a voice coach. But other than that, it is strange bedfellows." He goes on to clarify how directors may view vocal coaches, "Every director has his or her own concept of what voice work is. So you are dealing with that. They will see audibility solely…others will see you as an integral part of acting language. You have got to be a chameleon, not an arrogant antithesis to what they are not doing, but a support to areas that aren't happening." Wade elaborates this point:

> I have over my desk a quotation from Dorothy Tutin which I see as
> a word of caution for the day, "the problem with voice teachers is that
> they sometimes feel the need to take over your voice." I found that
> quite a salient thing to remind us all really. I must not presume anything,
> because every new rehearsal process is a start, it is a new beginning. That
> chemistry has never happened before with that group of people, with that
> director…don't take it for granted. We voice people shouldn't get
> frustrated by that. That's the job, love, you either get excited by that,
> or in the end it frustrates you, beats you down.

Cicely Berry adds:

> It took a long time to gain respect but we have attained it. It was gaining
> their respect and trust that you weren't just coming in and telling them
> how to do it. You were working with different directors. You had to find
> out how that director worked…It is a totally democratic process.
> Everybody is different. Some directors want to talk about it, some don't.
> It is just about making contact with them. You can't go and ask, "How do
> you want me to work." It's being there, having coffee with them, just
> common sense, how you get to know people.

Joanna Weir explains that in her experience this relationship depends on the director and the show. Sometimes she is brought in to solve a single problem with a dialect. Other times she may function much like an assistant director, being actively involved in many levels of artistic choices on a regular basis:

> The easier task is if the director chooses to speak to me and we talk about
> it. Some are very vocal. Others are feeling so stressed, so pushed… "Oh,
> I am so glad you are here." And then that's it and they expect me to solve
> it. As long as I fix it they are happy. And they often don't care about the
> process. But there are also directors who, if they see me giving a note,
> particularly if they don't know me, will ask, "What did you say?" And
> then I will tell them, they say, "absolutely." They have to feel safe. There
> is a trust.

Weir further states that she speaks to the director as much as she can when it is useful. "You mustn't waste their time," she concludes.

Tyne Turner reinforces the importance of speaking to the director ahead of time to find out how they work and what their auditory needs are. She stresses listening to their needs and then offering some things that might be useful. She has been known to read portions of the script for the director so he/she can hear that she can speak the text herself and has an understanding of the technical demands. She can "pipe up" at rehearsal or remain silent, whichever is more comfortable to the director. She stresses the importance of constant but brief communication with the director. She also advocated typing actor notes and giving a copy of them to the director to approve prior to distribution.

Turner feels it is wise to make the directors and actors "right" as much as possible, and to commit to liking them immediately. "I don't compete with the director, I facilitate their needs. I am completely open and candid and always defer to the director."

At this point, Turner presents a warning to the vocal coach about the dangers of engaging in "that mean director" dialogue with actors. If an actor is having a problem with direction, she tries to find a constructive solution. "Thus actors request to see me more than they are called, because often I can find a solution to their problem inhabiting a direction, through breath or sound."

Jane MacFarlane uses the term *collaborators* when she describes the ideal director/vocal coach relationship. "I try to stay in as close a contact with the director as possible so that he/she doesn't feel as though I am directing behind the scenes.… The artistic director at the Dallas Shakespeare relies on me to do the ground work with text analysis and to make sure the language lives."

Neil Freeman reminds the vocal coach that he is not the director and has not been hired to interfere with or challenge the director's interpretation. In addition he echoes the common theme of regular access to discuss the problems from both the actor and director's viewpoint, and to act as a go-between when necessary.

William Conacher feels that much of his work rests on how willing the director is to release an actor from rehearsal. "They don't see that dialect work is a rehearsal itself. That's what I mean about it being a new job. I never heard of a dialect coach until I went to Central to train as a vocal coach…it is quite a luxury to have somebody coaching you."

In addition Conacher would like to meet with the director prior to the first rehearsal, as well as attend a production meeting. "I think accents have to fit in with the set…those things give you a feel for what the sound is." But he continued by clarifying that this is an "ideal process…this is utopia, it has never happened."

With thirty-five years of experience in the theatre, Greg de Polnay feels that most directors view him with respect. He elaborates by saying:
> A lot of modern directors in the professional theatre never worked in the classics themselves…they don't really know what breathing at the end of a line is about. What iambic pentameter is really like…I work with Peter Hall and that is a very different cup of tea.… You just go in there and help with someone who has got a problem with the voice, due to mismanagement of the voice or the body at the time they are speaking.

De Polnay continues that his job is easier when the director has an appreciation for what it is that the vocal coach does. However, when asked how often he meets with the director prior to the first rehearsal he is quick to respond, "Never, it all depends on his availability and mine. You see the thing…we are so tied up and scheduled."

Mel Churcher explains that a key to the director relationship is to refrain from saying anything in a public rehearsal unless invited to do so. She encourages the "fly on the wall" method during rehearsals. A vocal coach needs to negotiate ahead of time if warm ups are to be conducted, how notes are to be given. She continues:

> You have to build a trust that you are not going to impose directorial things. Although as we all know, and the best directors understand, nothing we do will not influence acting. One way I have found is that you never offer one way, you offer many, many choices…. And if you have talked to the director and know where he is going, then you know you are moving in the same direction as the production.

Churcher also confesses that she is not terribly good at explaining how she works so she tries to build a trust by "making the right noises at the first meeting…then by going in very gently until the director has some trust. I find it very difficult to tell a director how I work…I don't know myself until I meet the people. You look and you listen, it is so instinctive."

Sally Grace explains that she consults with the director and keeps a very open channel between the director and herself in which they talk frequently:

> The delicate line between encouraging and supporting an actor, and directing is a very shady one. A lot of directors think of voice coaches as being would-be directors or dangerous. I think it is important to define the terms you want to work in…. I think cards on the table is the best way and not be pushy at all. "I like to work this way, how do you?"…It very much depends on the director. Sometimes you sense that your way through is to play the low status game. You have to be completely open and honest.

Andrew Wade acknowledges that it is "really building up a relationship with the directors that proves the point…. There is no doubt about it…if the director isn't for the work in the right way, you are battling up the wrong avenue. It is the director's theatre…the director is actually giving authority to voice and language work."

Cicely Berry adds that each director has different ways of using their time, "You have to use common sense." In addition to common sense, which she mentions several times in the interview, Berry summarizes that this feeling of trust between the director and vocal coach is built through time.

It is interesting to note that each person interviewed spent the greatest amount of time and expended the most words exploring ideas about the director/vocal coach relationship. In summary, in both the interviews and in the literature, key ideas that continue to surface are those of on-going communication, trust, common sense and flexibility.

Rehearsals and Notes

Practitioners vary widely as to the number of rehearsals that the vocal coach should attend. However, most of the vocal coaches interviewed agree that attendance at the first read-through is a must. Jane MacFarlane uses that first rehearsal as an opportunity to make notes on what the director says and how he/she envisions the play. "I also try to make notes on what I hear from the actors during the read-through."

Andrew Wade tries to be at the first read-through, "but sometimes we have three read-throughs taking place on the same morning, so you can't always…. Some directors have their own idiosyncratic defenses, 'It's a bit closed at the moment.'" At the read- through he may ask himself such thoughts as, "I am a bit concerned, that is a big journey for that actor and hopefully there is a way out of that." Wade describes these thoughts as human reactions to what he hears. Though he doesn't always confer with the director at this point, he does create an agenda for how the work is to proceed. "And then you start specifically calling the people as you feel the priorities are, the time you are available, their availability as well…You see, you have got to be flexible with that. And you don't get it right all the time, because there are too many things going on."

When asked which he considered to be the key rehearsals, Wade replies, "Certainly if you are working with an actor on a particular speech in a scene it would be great to go into a rehearsal and see how it is happening there…. As you get on to running scenes, it gets important to go in…" Wade continues by specifying that the early rehearsals at the table, when the cast is studying the text in an academic way, are not the most useful for him to attend.

Sally Grace reports that she attends first read-throughs, early rehearsals, and first rehearsals in the space. By dress rehearsals she feels it is too late. Then she adds with a laugh, "For Lion King I was giving notes up to the first night. I was called in very late, at the last minute, at the first of the dress rehearsals. I was giving notes through previews."

When asked how she gives notes to actors, Grace replies that she has given them publicly; but more often than not, she takes actors gently aside if they are not in a scene. Sometimes she asks an actor if it is a good time to give a voice note. At other times she says she may not give a note at all. "You need to know when it is too late, when giving a note is going to make them concentrate on the note rather than what they should be doing. With voice work, as you know, people can get very upset. You can give movement notes and nobody minds; but with the voice…it's different."

On the topic of notes, Joanna Weir explains that she will often give her notes back to the director; she doesn't give them directly to the actor. "I'll talk to the actor directly in a session. I'll say, 'We are going to do exercises. We are not trying to develop a performance, we are trying to unleash the part, give you some new inspiration, connect the voice more.'"

Mel Churcher, when asked how she gives notes, says:
> Asking permission is a very good way rather than barging up. Actors have insecurities whether they are new or been at it for thirty years. I wouldn't go leaping up to one of the leads with notes; I would talk to the director first. The last preview notes are given to the director to feed through as they see fit. Up to that point I just look for the most psychologically opportune moment and if it's a really big problem tell the director I must have an hour with so and so. I don't like to give notes after a public

performance because they are just too vulnerable. Unless they ask for it.

For Greg de Polnay the method for note distribution depends on what the director says. Some directors let you give notes because there is an appropriate level of trust. He continues this thought by saying:

> A director might worry that a vocal coach will say something to contradict him. You have to play that one carefully. Most of my notes will be, "I didn't hear what you said. What was that word? I can't hear you in the back there is too much stage sounds, music and whatever going on. You have got to lift that voice up. When you turn upstage, you have to lift the voice."

Cicely Berry, on the other hand, confirms that she would never say to someone, "I can't hear you." She continued in this vein, "You say to someone, 'when you turn that way it's not coming out.' People's voices are very personal. You can destroy someone by saying, 'I can't hear you.' You have to find a positive way to put it that offers them an option." Berry adds:

> It has to do with total common sense and how you relate to actors. Some can be given publicly, some you wouldn't want to give publicly. You need to take them out, you don't give notes, you have a conversation…. Each director has different ways of using their time. Some trust that you will go around in your time and give notes, some want you to give notes to the cast.

When asked if that was a conversation she might have with a director, she firmly answers, "No, you just get to know them properly, you kind of instinctively know what would be appropriate." Andrew follows up with a quick affirmation, "You're assessing people aren't you? Which is really what we do all the time when we teach. You can't put it down to a statutory or prescriptive thing. It's ad hoc, improvisational."

William Conacher warns that you have to be very political about it. "It is an intensely political job; you are constantly treading on eggshells. You have to make sure you are not treading on someone's toes." He adds that ideally the director will give you time for notes. If not, you just have to "run round to the actors while they are having tea."

Neil Freeman expresses that he rarely gives written notes but prefers to speak to the actors privately. Notes he feels, as Berry also expressed, should lead to discussion. Written notes can be useful for points already discussed, as in agreed-upon pronunciations. Freeman is the only vocal coach who is of the opinion that notes should continue until after the "joyful terror of an audience has been faced," that is up to and even following the opening night performance.

When asked which rehearsals he likes to attend, Freeman states that each new hurdle in the rehearsal process merits a visit from the voice coach: run of a scene, run of an act, run of the play, transfer from rehearsal hall to the theatre space. He also likes to attend rehearsals of problem scenes when the director or actor requests his presence.

Debra Hale states that she likes to attend rehearsals at the beginning, middle and end of the process, more if the director desires it. She elaborates on dialect coaching:

> For dialect, I like to meet with the actors either prior to the first read or after the first read, give them instruction, and then come back in a week's time to see how the dialect is settling in…I like contact with the actor, initially in a private session if possible, at the beginning of the process after I observe/hear the work. After that point, I give written notes (usually on individual cards) to the actors, handing them out before the director gives their notes…Sometimes the director will ask me to speak generally to the whole cast regarding concerns that affect all the actors, like vocal energy at the top of a scene, entrances and exits, difficulties in hearing actors far upstage.

Jane MacFarlane tries to be in rehearsal as much as possible so that she and the director can dialogue about problems as they arise. She is as active in rehearsals as the director invites her to be. Her minimum involvement is two to three rehearsals a week. "If the director is amenable, I will pull actors aside to work or give notes when there is time. I will also let the actors know I have notes and they can find me if they want them."

Tyne Turner attends the first read-through and all table work. When not in private sessions she will "pop in" at rehearsals. She attends all run-throughs and takes notes. She added that, 'I sometimes whisper things to the actors not being talked to by the director in a work session. I am careful about when to talk to actors…I am sensitive about timing'.

From the literature, interviews, and questionnaires, the solution to the question of when and how to give notes depends on the desire of the director and the needs of the cast. The vocal coach should use common sense and remain flexible, adjusting personal preference to the greater need of the production at hand. There also appears to be no hard and fast rule that governs attendance at rehearsals. It is, however, safe to say that it should remain a judgment call based on the needs of the cast and the vocal coach's ability to listen critically and evaluate what she is hearing.

Private Sessions

Entire books have been written about the vocal coach's work with the actor and text, *Freeing Shakespeare's Voice* by Kristin Linklater (1996) and *The Actor and The Text* (1987) by Cicely Berry, to name two. Yet the "nuts and bolts" work that goes into releasing the text remains elusive because it is finally personal, dynamic, and instinctive. It is in the private vocal sessions with the actors that the vocal coach's work takes place, where the vocal coach's deepest impact on the sound of the play takes place. The coaches interviewed were asked how those sessions are set up, who requests them, and what kinds of activities take place within them. It is common across the board that private voice sessions happen in one of three ways: an actor can ask for a session with the vocal coach, the director can request a session, or the vocal coach can ask for time with an actor. What actually happens in these sessions varies widely depending on the needs of the actor and the focus or area of expertise of each voice coach. The interview responses range from highly theoretical to brief and practical. But it is clear that in the private session the vocal coach has an opportunity to work in spontaneous and intuitive ways; the art of vocal coaching begins to emerge.

Cicely Berry speaks of her work with the actors in a historical and philosophical context:

> When I came [to the RSC] there was Trevor Nunn, Terry Hands, John Barton. They were all hammering the form of the language, the rhetoric, the iambic pentameter, antithesis, assonance. All of which have to be honored. It is not like contemporary speech. It just has to be practical otherwise the audience would leave. You have to have a common ground about how the text is spoken…. Actors have to open their ears to classical text…. The whole way of speaking in theatre has changed and one has to find a way for the modern actor to feel truthful in the heightened language and yet honor the extraordinariness of the image…. You have to open people's imagination and to excite them to want to speak. That is my guiding view…

Jane MacFarlane speaks of private sessions with actors in very practical terms stating that she works with rhythm, phrasing, scansion and operative words. She is careful to couch all her work in terms of voice. "I may get at specific moments but I don't use acting terms when I do…. My job is to make the text clear…that said, I do think that voice work is actor work; and that in making the text clear, I am addressing commitment to action, clarity of drive and objective." If there are vocal problems she will address them in private with an actor. Sometimes an actor may come to her looking for help to get through a difficult piece of text. If a director is worried about a vocal health issue, she will bring it up in gentle terms, usually by text analysis or exploring how to get through a particular passage while maintaining openness. Though she stresses that the actual session varies depending on the specific problem to be addressed, she finds herself doing a lot of playing with rhythms, hitting operative words or consonants. In common with many practicing vocal coaches, MacFarlane cites Berry's book *The Actor and the Text* (1987) as a valuable resource tool.

Neil Freeman, whose work with Shakespeare's First Folio has brought him wide acclaim, uses clues given to the actor by Shakespeare himself based on the playwright's original punctuation, spelling, capitalization, line length and line breaks. When asked about his use of First Folio explorations in his coaching, Freeman shares that he uses this work as much as the director will allow. Though he adds that this is always tempered by the ability of an actor to process the information. He also delays First Folio work until the actor is "confident with the rehearsal process, and can function as an active partner with good knowledge of the play and role, so that the whole process becomes discussive and collegial, rather than coach-dominated with information only feeding one way—from coach down."

Tyne Turner describes her private sessions as a flexible process that includes scanning the rhythm, identifying operative words, understanding antique phrases and idioms, parentheticals, weak forms of words, projection levels and clarity. She equates these points with providing a map for the actors. "I don't interpret the map for them, just point out the road signs."

William Conacher approaches the controversial subject of the dangers of giving an actor a line-reading when teaching inflections in dialect work by saying:

> Good question…the pressure not to give line-readings is mainly put on us from other vocal teachers. Most actors find it a great relief to just be told how to say it. Because most of them are clever enough to motivate it. To say that you can't give someone a line-reading is insulting an actor's intelligence. That's what I think anyway. For example I worked with a well-known actor who is naturally a Geordie from Newcastle and I had to coach him in the Birmingham accent. One of the distinctive features of the Birmingham accent is the intonation pattern. It sounds like the inflection pattern is completely relentless. The actor said I don't want the accent to get in the way; I still want to make sense of the text. I said to him, "Are you saying that people in Birmingham don't make sense?" "Well, no." It is a massive issue because inflections are what we all have at our disposal to convey a massive range of stuff. So how can you be sarcastic if the only means you have is "that" (he demonstrates an expressive inflection on the word). I think sometimes you just have to show them how to do it and eventually they just get it.

Respect and Credit

An area that emerged as a hot topic in the interviews was that of respect for vocal coaches from members of the profession and credit awarded to them for their work. Responses to this question tended to be negative as vocal coaches by and large feel that they are not regarded as highly as they would like.

Greg de Polnay expresses the belief that the vocal coach is not perceived highly when he states:

> Most actors believe that their voice training at drama school, unless they need dialect coaching, is adequate…vocal coaches themselves would like to be more relevant. But I don't think, in all honesty, the vocal coach has much relevance. I know at the National Theatre they have vocal coaches, and the RSC, but they have endless battles to get anyone to come to their classes or sessions. Often you're a vocal coach to professional actors who have been doing it much longer than the vocal coach has been alive.

Sally Grace concurs with de Polnay when she says. "A lot of actors don't think they need it…they resent if they are sent for something…the voice coach is regarded as a nuisance. In my experience the better the actor, the more greedy they are for voice work."

Joanna Weir expresses the thought that, "If you're Patsy Rodenburg or Cicely Berry you have a higher standing. I think [with] voice teachers in general…there is a problem that we are viewed as "Mr. Fix It", that it [vocal work] is something aside from the creative process. I think there is a problem there." She went on to relate a story in which she had been highly involved in the coaching of a young actor playing the lead in a television series. Prior to her intervention he was unintelligible and the producers were ready to scrap the project. Following her work, they gave the series the "go-ahead". She was surprised and disappointed to learn that her name was not mentioned in the credits. Weir cites several other examples in which she was inadvertently left off production programs. She concludes this discussion by saying. "I feel the vocal coach shouldn't be forgotten, you shouldn't have to ask for credit."

When asked if he had ever been left off the program, William Conacher replies, "That's happened to me in drama schools, but not in the professional theatre. Sometimes they give you a bio, sometimes not. I personally don't care about that kind of thing." He adds that "some people [vocal coaches] say we must do more. We must form a guild. We must define what we do. But I think that is not possible."

Jane MacFarlane regards the lack of respect and credit afforded the vocal coach as more about ignorance. "I think most people do not know what a vocal coach does…A lot of times I have to make my presence known. Otherwise I am left off rehearsal calls or no one lets me know when a run-through happens, etc. Actors who have had good experiences with vocal coaches and teachers are very open to the work. Others hold me very suspiciously at first."

Debra Hale echoes the thoughts of MacFarlane when she adds, "I think the respect for coaches could be higher. Many theatres don't realize the preparation that goes into a dialect show…not respecting the time you need for…research before coming in….Some directors honestly claim to need the help and respect the coaches work (these I find to be the majority in professional theatre). Others see coaches as a necessary evil."

Tyne Turner provides the appropriate conclusion to the discussion of respect and credit by stating simply that she gets title-page billing and a picture and bio according to her contract. "The rest of the respect I receive, I earn each time. I have never found it to be hard-won, nor is respect an issue I worry about or focus on. I just know if I keep my eye on the project and my ego at home, we'll all have a good time together."

Summary
As can be clearly seen, views concerning the various current methods and practices of the vocal coach in the areas of role, director relationship, preparation, rehearsals and notes, private sessions, and respect and credit are divergent and strongly felt. They bear many similarities in the areas of general functions and responsibilities: open communication, common sense and flexibility; regular attendance at rehearsals particularly at transition periods; communication with the actors at the discretion of the director with awareness of timing; and generating options in vocal terms in private session with actors. It is, however, the individual personalities, instinct, and artistry of each vocal coach that provide the variety that will keep this new field dynamic and exciting.

William Conacher, at the conclusion of his interview, sums up our discussion by saying, "People don't understand what it is. Lot's of time we don't understand…" It is clear that vocal coaches reinvent themselves each time they go into a situation. He continues, "It is perceiving the need, then filling it, and juggling all the pieces."

Indeed, the vocal coach in the contemporary theatre must be a chameleon.

Bibliography
Books
Berry, C. *The Actor and the Text*, New York, Scribner 1987

Linklater, K. *Freeing Shakespeare's Voice*, New York, Theatre Communications Group, 1996

Wade, A. ' "What is Voice For?": Training and the Rise of the Voice Coach', in *The Vocal Vision* (Eds.) Hampton, M. and Acker, B., New York, Applause 1997

Withers-Wilson, N. *Vocal Direction for the Theatre*, New York, Drama Book Publishers 1993

Journals
Berry, C., Linklater, K., Rodenburg, P. 'Shakespeare Feminism and Voice: Responses to Sarah Warner', *National Theatre Quarterly* Vol. XIII, No. 49, February 1997. pp 48-52

Boston, J. 'Voice: The Practitioners, Their Voice, and Their Critics', *National Theatre Quarterly* Vol. XIII, No. 51, August 1997. pp 248-254

Werner, S. 'Performing Shakespeare: Voice Training and the Feminist Actor', *New Theatre Quarterly* Vol. XII, No. 47, August 1996. pp 249-258

Interviews
Berry, C. 16 February 2000, RSC, Stratford-upon-Avon
Churcher, M. 10 November 1999, Arabesque Café, London
Conacher, W. 7 December 1999, at his home, London
de Polnay, G. 14 January 2000, RADA, London
Grace, S. 10 February 2000, CSSD, London
Wade, A. 16 February 2000, RSC, Stratford-upon-Avon
Weir, J. 25 October 1999, Arabesque Café, London

Questionnaires
Freeman, N. Received 6 March 2000, via email
Hale, D. Received 9 February 2000, via email
MacFarlane, J. Received 10 February 2000 via email
Turner, T. Received 9 February 2000 via email

Radio Broadcast Taping
Berry, C. 'Shakespeare's Master Class 1', BBC Radio 3, taped Friday, 24 March 2000, aired Sunday, 23 April 2000

Essay by *Rod Menzies*

In the early years of my career as a voice teacher I experienced repeated disappointment as my students made great connections and produced wonderful sounds in my voice classes, then abandoned everything in acting classes, rehearsals and performances. Some sounded as if they hadn't done a shred of warm-up—dull and disengaged while others carefully intoned "the voice beautiful." Neither choice effectively supported their acting. I was baffled. My quest to resolve this lack of follow-through from voice to acting led me to situate language at the center of my teaching approach. In this article, I expound a rationale for a commitment to oralcy, outline pedagogical principles for language-based voice training, and describe elements of my methodology. By illustrating how language is superior to sound as a medium for developing vocal skill, I advocate wider adoption of language-based voice training.

Rationale

I found my first clue as to the reason for this lack of crossover between voice work and acting early in my investigation. In *The Physiology of Speech and Hearing*, by Daniloff, Sears and Zucker I read that the speech cortex is not functional at birth, and that newborns produce vocal sounds via neural impulses from the brain stem. The ability to speak develops by the eleventh or twelfth month. My volunteer experience in a home for mentally challenged adults gave me deeper insight. There I observed that, while many of these individuals displayed uncontrolled phonation and garbled articulation, they sang much better than they spoke. This suggested to me that not only does basic phonation originate in the brain stem, but singing as well. If so, the "huh" sound is rather more likely to be sounded, or sung, on neural messages originating from the brain stem than uttered from the speech cortex. This calls into question a basic principle in vocal pedagogy that a voice teacher's job is to connect the student with his or her voice first and to the power of words, later.[1] That approach was taken in my own voice training and as a fledgling teacher I held onto the notion that you got the voice going first then went on to language. Alerted to the physiological gap between sounding and speaking, I began to reconsider.

As my focus shifted, I noticed a second factor that encouraged me to approach voice training directly through language, and that is the widespread erosion of oralcy that all voice teachers face. As Patsy Rodenburg notes in *The Need for Words*, we live in a cultural climate where language is systematically debased. A number of factors strip the spoken word of its authentic power. Of particular significance is the strong influence of technology on language in both public and private spheres. Email correspondence and chat rooms frequently replace live conversation and the compression of syntax and grammar that is typical of these electronic exchanges exposes a shrinking capacity for eloquent expression. Film and TV repeatedly demonstrate how visual narrative obviates speech. A particularly banal instance of diminished expression can be seen on Jerry Springer, where guests regularly resort to fisticuffs as their expletive ridden attempts to speak are subsumed by apparently inexpressible fury. Such incoherence barely hints at the true vigor of utterance.

The devaluing of language is furthered by a well-founded wariness of what people say. Language is historically characterized as the realm of deception.

Rod Menzies, coaches voice and acting at his Santa Monica studio. He has taught in professional training programs for twenty years, for the past seven at the University of Southern California. His work on original material best exemplifies his passion for language and he is currently directing and developing three new solo shows. In addition, he has coached two self-written solo shows directed by Larry Moss. *Runt of the Litter*, by Bo Eason premiered at Houston's Stages Repertory in February and the current New York hit *Syringa Tree*, by Pamela Gein, opened its run at Playhouse 91 last September.

1. For example, Patsy Rodenburg in her book, *The Need For Words*, states, "Ultimately my job is to connect you with your voice and then to the power of words as you speak."

It is the coin of the cheat; the currency of hype, flimflam, and double speak. We have adopted vigilance against duplicity thanks to a long line of hucksters from snake-oil peddlers, to used-car dealers, to politicians and their ubiquitous spin-doctors, a legacy of suspicion about what people say endures. The most respected figures in the land, even the President, fudge, mislead, and downright lie. Inevitably, we are reinforced in our suspicion that talk is cheap, that actions speak louder than words. Wariness with regard to eloquence can be traced as far back as the Puritans whose disavowal of hypocrisy and devotion to plain speaking remain powerful undercurrents in American culture. Is it safe to say the religious zealots who founded this country did so because of the importance of being earnest? Perhaps, but the notion that language or the human experience beneath it can be stated in plain or absolute terms is ludicrous. Language proliferates and expands precisely because the essential nature of human consciousness is limitless. To negate this aspect of humanity is repressive. It encroaches upon our freedom and inhibits our instinctual drive to evolve.

Finally, debasement of language may be linked to the debasement of individuals. Dysfunctional families often discourage open expression, and individuals with a background of abuse can also feel silenced in fear and shame. Likewise, women, people of color, gays and recent immigrants may feel a lack of entitlement to be heard. [2]

2. Carol Gilligan documents this very effectively in, *A Different Voice*.

Whatever the general impact of language debasement, young actors often begin in a state of language impoverishment and this issue must be faced. Theatre perpetuates a legacy of language courageously conceived and expressed and we must sustain this vital practice. Its daily application in classes, rehearsals and performances often includes a reclamation of the basic right to be heard. For, whatever the cause, when experience is not animated through language the human spirit dwindles. To train significant artists we must take steadfast action against that. Yet, I suspect voice teachers can and do contribute to the diminishment of language. We may pass on traditional biases unwittingly, as I feel I did. Language may be considered the domain of the acting teacher. Time constraints may reduce the course material to the teaching of a vocal warm-up and the bridge to language may never be built. I have heard voice teachers express reluctance about working with language, but surely every voice teacher must teach speaking as well. Actors cannot build a craft, much less a career, on sound. Routines that enhance breathing, phonation, resonance, range and articulation without connecting to lively utterance do not go the distance. One cannot master the violin by playing nothing but scales and exercises.

I want to look more closely at resistance to language among voice teachers for I observe evidence of bias against language in some pedagogical practices. For instance, language can be perceived as sinister due to being identified with the realm of logic, rationality and judgment. It is therefore suspected of interfering with the spontaneous flow of impulses and relegated to the sidelines. A related bias appears in a fascination with emotional dilation, where released emotions dominate other tributaries to communication without being supported in the container of language. This valuation signals that being washed over by feelings is the ultimate goal of the work, rather than the eloquent expression of feeling through form. Good acting is then in danger of being eclipsed by therapy of questionable merit. Something is amiss when language is abdicated and the journey of story abandoned.

Pedagogical Framework

My primary intention is to enhance the vocal and verbal engagement of the actor in performance. Several key principles and practices descend from adherence to this value. The most obvious commitment, and the theme of this article, is a spirited upholding of utterance as a central element of the training. In addition, I steadfastly abdicate the role of voice mechanic. I don't set out to fix anything and have no compulsion to describe the intricacies of vocal function. Further, because sound is not language, I resist placing undue emphasis on ritualized vocal sequences as an end in themselves and have no interest in training for exercise proficiency unless it obviously connects to acting.

My approach is also fundamentally influenced by the recognition that the voice reflects many different dimensions of experience and that the various tributaries manifest as an integrated whole. By extension, any significant change in vocal habit is a result of adjustments at a number of levels. I am more satisfied with my teaching when these adjustments occur by means of a wholesale shift rather than through a gradual accumulation of piecemeal adaptations and I allow that preference to influence my approach.

I use a Jungian framework as a conceptual platform for this multi-dimensional, integrative process. Jung describes four functions through which we identify and process our experience: *sensation, feeling, thinking,* and *intuition. Sensation* relates to the experience of the physical self, *feeling* to the experience of emotion, *thinking* to the mind and imagination, and *intuition* to the spiritual or creative aspects of the self. Jung suggested most of us are predominant in one or two of these functions and have difficulty accessing others. The undeveloped aspects are the contents of the shadow and call out to be integrated.

Language, because it raises shadowy subjectivity into the light of objective understanding, is a powerful integrative medium. It is a sophisticated technology that illuminates twisting pathways in the labyrinth of human experience by allowing us to name and make distinctions. This can be viewed as both a blessing and a curse. Caliban, in Shakespeare's *The Tempest*, vividly illustrates uneasiness about the power of language. Before the first visitors arrive on the enchanted isle, Caliban dwells in a pure state of nature with no conscious thought of his existence. All that changes when his tyrant and teacher, Prospero, instructs him in language and Caliban decries being taught:

> *how*
> *To name the bigger light, and how the less*
> *That burn by night and day.*

Prospero retorts that he taught him to speak out of kindness, but Caliban argues:

> *You taught me language; and my profit on't*
> *Is, I know how to curse. The red plague rid on you*
> *For learning me your language.*

For Caliban, acquisition of language is loss of innocence and banishment from paradise. He yearns for a return to infantile ignorance and resents how language distinguishes one thing from another. For Prospero, and for those of us who choose to conjure with it, language is a source of power and delight, and a key element of our creativity. Language is open-ended, curious. It invites inquiry. It has infinite capacity to abstract, to conjecture. Language plays. It proliferates. It sparks embellishment, exaggeration, speculation and insinuation. Language is the fertile seed of story and acting. At its root, it is storytelling.

Methodology

I want students to move courageously and optimistically into their work and, because anxiety limits the voice I emphasize proficiency. In the first class I teach a fun, simple group chant. This allows me to comment that everyone's voice is working and I forge an agreement that we not worry about basic vocal function. I characterize our work as an exploration of the voice in the specialized task of acting.

I also initiate individual performance work in the first class by utilizing my favorite language based tool—a word string.[3] I give a prompt word and have them write a free-associated list of response words. We then do a short vocal warm-up and individuals read their word strings to the group. I make it a point not to comment. Once everyone has taken a turn, I have them write brief notes on their experience and take time for a discussion. Their responses typically reveal a variety of responses to the performance activity. For example, individuals may have experienced difficulty in focusing attention, a *thinking* function; a nervousness, or anxiety, a *feeling* function; a shortness of breath, or uncontrollable shaking, *sensation* function; or an unaccountable feeling of elation, an *intuitive* function. I refrain from discussing any of this in the first class, though I make careful observations. I do my best to signal that each person's experience, and their way of expressing it, is valid. My intention is to authenticate their expressive ability.

If an individual falters in her response I invite her to continue. If someone impulsively blurts, "It was, like, you know…I felt, uh, just like, weird." I pass the ball back by asking, "It felt weird, because…?" or, "What does weird feel like?" The follow-up response is usually more detailed. Some choose not to speak in the first discussion, and that is okay. A precedent has been set. Language will be listened to. That is enough for the first class. The cultivation of eloquence has begun. In a year or so they will work on Shakespeare and, if Bill is on the mound, I want them to step up to the plate with reasonable confidence they can get a hit. In the first class we are already taking batting practice. By cultivating a greater connection to their own words, students can see playwrights as allies who give us compelling stories to tell.

With word strings I can evoke elements of nature using prompt words like mountain, seashore, wind or rain, or elicit childhood by suggesting fourth grade or tenth birthday. Such prompts effectively open doorways to creativity and further develop the inner resources of the actor. I find this to be particularly true when I link the prompt words to the imaginative underpinnings of a scene or production by animating its themes and images. If we are working on, say *The Tempest*, I might use prompt words like storm, island, and magic. I use word strings extensively. They can easily be expanded into poems or monologues. In fact, I have developed solo shows as a direct outgrowth of

3. I use word strings as a primary tool in language based voice training. Part of the inspiration for this arose out of my investigations of the intensive journal work of Ira Progoff whose book, *At a Journal Workshop*, is an excellent resource for language based work.

this work and witnessed astonishing growth, not just vocally, but on many levels. I find that voices grow very effectively when linked to that other voice—the inner voice we refer to when we say a writer, or painter, or choreographer has found his voice. Developing individual perspective is essential if one is to make a contribution as an artist. As voices evolve students become more effective interpreters of other writers.

As we continue exploring word strings and short, self-written pieces I target individual vocal issues that can be improved. For example, I may ask someone to work with a more vigorous commitment to the consonants, or feel the resonators more engaged, or register the breath arriving in the body, or notice the heels touching the floor, or other simple targets related to vocal aspects of acting. I gauge each student's ability to improve and keep the adjustment strategy simple. I ask for recognition of difference from the individual first. If she notices a change I then ask for corroboration from her classmates. Once change is obvious to everyone, we can proceed. If actors are made aware too early of a vocal issue that is deeply ingrained in their habit structure it can set up a pattern of relentless investing in the dysfunction. When I hear students make statements such as "I have a tight jaw," I point out how the belief reinforces the condition and does little to promote effective usage. Vocal problem solving through text work is effective because it relates to performance activity, not exercise activity. This promotes effective vocal adaptations in rehearsal and performance. The process of adjustment is a continuous negotiation and not a lengthy journey toward a far off result. With reinforcement small improvements build on one another and eventually become second nature. Gradually a tolerance for more difficult targets develops. Text from master writers is prepared and memorized before class. As the work progresses, new expectations that cross-reference language, voice, and acting are presented. I find it useful to target concerns that are common to several people. For instance, if someone has a shallow breathing pattern I refer to others who share this tendency. A temporary "club" of shallow breathers is formed who go to school on each other on a mutually supported endeavor. This perpetuates conscious witnessing of the pattern, and the expectation of evolving beyond it.

The purpose of technique is to improve performance. As I like to say about vocal exercises, they are tools not rules. Therefore, especially in the early stages, I never ask a student to do something on faith. I willingly put technique on the line and test its worth. If something appears not to work, I agree to let it go. Conversely, if something works, it is right. People learn in different ways, and I endeavor to teach students, not techniques. I also adhere to the premise, "there is no such thing as a voice problem, there are only acting problems," and look to solve vocal problems from an acting perspective.[4] I want actors involved in revealing what happens in the story, not lost in preoccupations with vocal production.

Two favorite strategies I use often provoke a kind of quantum leap in the actor's experience of performing. Both can be used with any text and in almost any situation. In one, I have the speaker say the words while resting the tongue out on the lower lip, making sure that each sound is understandable. The actor must communicate clearly. I then have them speak the words again with the tongue in its normal position. The usual result is more tone

4. This point of view was upheld by Bonnie Raphael at a recent ATHE panel discussion on voice coaching when she said, "there's is no voice note that does not have repercussions in the acting."

in the mouth and clearer articulation. It can also brighten resonance and sharpen acuity of thought, and it often deepens the breath. I find it particularly useful for people with stiff tongue roots or hyper-tense throat walls because it instantaneously awakens the possibility of using the tongue, throat, breath and tone differently.

I call the second, the Duct Tape Game. The premise is that you attempt to communicate your meaning as if your mouth is taped shut. Each syllable of the text is uttered as a hum, and the humming mirrors the natural speaking rhythm of the thoughts. The usual response is an improved connection to resonance and ring. Often there is also a greater awareness of the need to communicate and get one's point across. This one is generally very good for students who are fearful of being strongly connected to open attention, or have issues of entitlement. When I first introduce this game I alert students to the fact that language is aggressive. I like to say that we use language to colonize each other's minds. Both of these tools link to the intentional aspect of language, and because the exploration occurs within a performance context, perfecting the exercise is not rewarded while showing up in the words is.

Specifying and Accomplishing Goals
Early in the work I describe threshold expectations related to the actor's voice. By that I mean the things that directors, producers, casting agents, and other actors expect you to be able to do when you enter a room calling yourself an actor. I expand the list of threshold expectations as the training progresses. Initially I need them to verify that they can be heard throughout the space they are working in. Since they are for the most part able to do that in conversation and we have acknowledged that between us, I can always invoke our initial agreement regarding their innate vocal resources. To frame this expectation I identify two qualities of attention: *dropped* and *open*.[5] Dropped attention is a focused attention on the experience of the self. Open attention focuses on self and included others. Effective performance requires an appropriate balancing of the two qualities and we begin to work on that awareness early in the work. Another threshold expectation is that one must be readily understood. This addresses speech clarity, and opens discussions about regionalisms. In some pedagogic traditions, training progresses methodically through breath, sound, resonance, range and power before articulation is addressed. I identify it as soon as it becomes an issue, and deal with it immediately. Everyone, actors and non-actors alike, is capable of speaking more clearly when talking with an elderly person who is hard of hearing. We also do this with foreign speakers. By referring to simple, everyday adaptations such as these I can usually instigate more focused articulation. When some degree of improvement is quickly achieved it signals that long lasting change is possible with practice.

Language Based Vocal Warm-Ups
During warm-ups I like a noisy room. I encourage uninhibited voicing of complaints. Groans and moans about discomforts are welcome. Muttering and cursing are warmly invited and expressions of joy are given equal opportunity. I find that, given this kind of permission, students are less likely to get caught in "good student" mode or to click on to "auto pilot," by which I mean a mindless repetition of ritual sequences. By welcoming complaints I bypass any requirement to get it right or be good at it and encourage

5. These terms originate with Wendy Palmer in her book *The Intuitive Body*.

candor and spontaneity, qualities I value in acting. I further cultivate verbal expressiveness with a variety of what I call check-in hooks. These are prompts that authorize verbal expression. After rolling up the spine for instance, I might say "More than anything, I feel...." and have them say the phrase back, filling in the blank as each one sees fit. I might then add the rejoinder, "I also notice...." If an individual says, "I also notice I feel distracted," I will add, "because...." This invites them to continue the thought, moving the awareness deeper as new levels of experience are acknowledged and verbalized. I like how these check-in hooks create permission to acknowledge whatever is connecting as experience. There is always a diversity of responses to these check-in hooks and when I implement this device at various points during a single class, surprisingly strong shifts in individual and group response can be noted. This awakens young actors to the notion that change is inevitable. It allows them to embrace process rather than fixate on achieving some unattainable perfect state.

I also find that check-ins can illuminate interesting combinations of response. For example, a student might say, "More than anything, I feel impatient, and I also notice my back feels stiff." When juxtapositions of experience such as this become apparent I can begin to awaken insight into the relationship between the four functions identified by Jung by pointing out that impatience is a connected to *feeling* function and stiffness to *sensation*. Students begin to recognize that while one quality predominates another can be evident beneath it. As each new level is acknowledged and expressed the sense of journeying along a pathway becomes more apparent. Each class is an odyssey that is recounted as it is experienced.

Call and response patterns are also useful. I say something, and have the whole group say it back to me. The subject matter is rarely profound but there can be a sense of narrative progression. Here is an example:

Me	Them
Hey!	*Hey!*
Hey guys, it's me!	*Hey guys, it's me!*
I'm over here!	*I'm over here!*
I thought you'd never notice.	*I thought you'd never notice.*
How you doing?	*How you doing?*
What?	*What?*
No, you go ahead.	*No, you go ahead.*
I'll be okay.	*I'll be okay.*
See ya!	*See ya!*

I also use numbers as a bridge from simple phonation to words. To conclude a warm-up I might sound: hum—muh—muh—muh; then speak: one—two—three–four.

We then use numbers to tell a story, each person having ten numbers to carry the narrative forward. We also activate numbers through specific verbal actions, such as "to scold," or, "to charm," This is followed by individual text work.

Summary

A performance develops in relation to a script with the text serving as a map for the actor's process. The properties of language that an actor needs to engage with are many and various. Language can be a means of induction, instantly conjuring artificial realities. It can charge audiences to give weight and importance to airy nothing. The Chorus in *Henry V*, for example, exhorts us to work, work your thoughts and therein see a siege; inciting us to apprehend what is evoked by words, but not actually there—to entertain the possible, which is one of the most distinctive traits of language. In fact, our innate ability to follow narrative and respond to images is the very base and ground of acting, and storytelling.

The goal of all preparation and training must be to equip actors to skillfully communicate stories through language. Actors must reveal the lively dance of possibility in the words, and voice teachers must train them to do that. Resistance to this view of voice training may arise from a mistaken notion that making sound and speaking words are identical events. A closer look at the language function suggests otherwise. Language is a complex instinctual ability that amplifies and details many more dimensions of human experience than sound does. Voice teachers must therefore become stewards of language by regarding language proficiency as essential to the development of actors, and to the expressive nature of acting and theatre. As oralcy faces greater challenges the fight for eloquent expression must renew its force. It is time for voice coaches to deepen their commitment to the thorny complexity of language with its ability to elaborate, abstract, and infer; to betray, violate and offend.

Peer-reviewed Article by *Lyn Darnley*

Rough Eloquence: Voice and Speech Training for Young People

Voice and Speech in the Curriculum

No matter what area of voice we predominantly work in, most of us come in contact with adolescents at some stage during our professional lives. Working with young people requires us to frame our work so as to answer their specific needs. Why do we teach *voice* and *speech* and what do we want the young people we teach to learn from us? The way in which we answer these questions reflects our approach, our objectives and our choice of texts.

Voice training is traditionally associated with polite, even refined speech. The echoes of elocution have not entirely faded away and the expectation from young people, especially boys, is that by attending a voice or speech and drama class their speech will become *posh* and their street credibility will be a thing of the past. And yet attending a drama class, or an extra-mural voice class is often the only way in which a young person can develop speech skills.

In the United Kingdom, state schools no longer teach *spoken* language but centrate almost wholly on written forms of the language, trusting that speaking skills will be developed along the way. There are clear differences between written and spoken language:

> There are differences of form, differences of function and differences in the manner of presentation. Firstly there are physical differences between the forms of spoken and written language. Spoken language is ephemeral, it occurs in real time and requires the ears for listening. In other words, it is temporary, temporal and uses the aural mode. In contrast, written language is more durable, it is presented in space (rather than time) and requires eyes to read the language. It is thus permanent, spatial and visual.[1]

Reading and writing are obviously essential and form a foundation for the development of vocabulary and written grammatical structures. But it is only some of the private schools, preparing young people for the professions and for university interviews, that still focus seriously on spoken language. Even reading aloud is abandoned beyond the primary school. Drama as a foundation for all other subjects (as advocated by Peter Slade, Brian Way and other developmental-drama teachers in the nineteen sixties and seventies) has been superseded by the ever-increasing demands of the curriculum. Drama at General Certificate level[2] is an optional examination subject, but not a wholly practical one. Increasingly in secondary schools, it is only students who have private classes in Speech and Drama who practise speech, story telling and the skills involved in reading aloud. While spoken English is assessed at sixteen, little if any time, is spent on the teaching of the development of these oral skills. Typically students are merely asked to discuss set works and talk on a subject they feel strongly about.

The Legacy of Elocution

Why should we develop a society in which it is more necessary to be able to communicate through writing than speaking? Why not rather encourage young people to feel the empowerment of language by engaging in it through the body and the ear rather than brain and the eye?

Certainly many parents would wish an *elevation* of their children's speech, to be the outcome of their investment in speech training. If we as teachers are to reach the young in a meaningful and truly developmental way, we have to

Lyn Darnley has been a voice coach with the Royal Shakespeare Company since 1992. Formerly Head of Voice at the Rose Bruford College of Speech and Drama in London, she has an MPhil from the University of Birmingham's Shakespeare Institute. With Stephanie Martin she is co-author of *The Teaching Voice* (Whurr, 1996); and *The Voice Source Book* (Winslow Press, 1992). She has been an external examiner on many courses including the Voice Course MA at Central School of Speech and Drama. Her work has taken her to the USA, the Far East, France and Africa.

1. Alison Garton and Chris Pratt, *Learning to be Literate*, pub Blackwell, UK, 1989, p4.

2. The exams taken in the UK at ages 16 and 18 to qualify for university.

do more than satisfy these outmoded and limited aspirations. As voice teachers we are always refuting the *Elocution* label and asserting our commitment to self-expression, self-confidence and effective communication skills for *today*. Yet by focusing on what is perceived as artistic, embossed language in the first instance, we often disengage the imaginations of young people rather than excite them. Why not rather aspire to encourage young people to use language effectively for argument and debate, so as to use language with skill and dexterity rather than *paint* it. The artistic use of language to express their more lyrical thoughts will grow from a skilful practical use of words to express need. We must return voice work to its earliest roots, so that what is taught is rough eloquence, not accent and affectation.

> It is no longer necessary in Britain to speak with a certain sort of accent to become successful and wealthy, nor does a regional accent of any sort debar people from becoming glamorous and famous. Energy and self confidence are now as important as a knowledge of what is correct. Style is everything. Life is fuller and faster and spoken English gains from the variety this brings.[3]

3. *Roots of English* 2, pub,BBC, p75

Undoubtedly for many parents the reason for sending children to a speech class is still closely linked to a desire to improve the child's prospects in their professional lives. There can be no better way of doing this than to develop their use of language to allow a fuller and clearer expression of their thinking. How many adults say they would rather do almost anything than have to speak in public? 'It frightens me to death' is a commonly heard phrase.

> [In fact,] the fear of speaking in public supersedes the fear of death in this country, as expressed in many statistical surveys. Perhaps this fear relates to the life-and-death importance of speech; or, perhaps, to the fear of loss of self if one is not listened to or really heard. In the latter sense, there is a real death, although not a biological one.[4]

4. Marian Hampton, "The Human Voice: Bridge or Battlefront," *The Vocal Vision*, Ed Marian Hampton and Barbara Acker, pub Applause, New York,1997, p257/258

How can we more effectively give young people the oral skills to participate in the cut and thrust of argument? Apart from the essentials such as parents regularly reading to the young, developing family conversational skills, the most significant way to do this may be through the choice of the texts we present to young people. Before we expect them to be able to connect with the language of the past we must encourage them to explore the language of their own time and their own generation and to understand that language is alive, active, physical and constantly changing. By using the language of other eras and generations, they become aware of the evolution of words and styles.

Where do we start? With the word and what it *embodies*.

Speech Is Action
How often do we hear it said that: speech is movement? Maria Montessori wrote in *The Absorbent Mind*:

> In the development of speech…we see a growing power of understanding go side by side with an extended use of those muscles by which he forms sounds and words.

Movement in speech can be seen, not just in the physical action of the formation of plosive or sustained consonants and the whole word, but in the movement of the phrase, the intonation and in the power of words to provoke action in others and change society. It is therefore important to begin at the level of the *word*. Exploring the infinite small differences between words which otherwise might be lumped together as synonyms is a good starting point. Focusing on the *dynamic aspects*[5] of language allows young people to invest in the power and movement of words, to explore the length of vowels, the impulse of syllables and the physical impact of consonant clusters and combinations. Notice the subtle differences in the qualities of these words

5. Verbal Dynamics is a term coined by Cristabel Burniston, *Into The Life of Things*, Christabel Burniston and Jocelyn Bell, pub, English Speaking Board, 1972, England.

   Plod, prod, teeter, tip-toe, shuffle, saunter, slide, slip.

Only through a physical involvement in these words can their active qualities be really appreciated. Young children naturally use wide range, huge vocal variety and energy in their speech. They do not only employ words but punctuate speech with sound effects, other accents and even other word orders. Often during adolescence the voice loses these impulses and becomes monotonous and disengaged from language. This is often a symptom of a loss of confidence and low self-esteem but re-claiming vocal space and the power of words can do much to restore confidence.

This active and performative nature of language is well documented.
   The unit of linguistic communication is not, as has generally been
   supposed, the symbol or the word or sentence, but rather the production
   or issuance of the symbol, or word or sentence in the performance of
   a speech act.[6]

6. John R. Searle, *Speech Acts: An Essay in the Philosophy of Language*, Cambridge, Cambridge University Press, 1969, p.16.

This shift of language from the page back to speech is what we have to reinforce. Unless we do this successfully, we fail to prepare the young for a world in which their ability to use language effectively, is, by far, their single most useful skill for achieving their goals.

Most people over the age forty grew up in an oral traditional far removed from the visual culture of today. Even if they had no experience of verse or theatre they were accustomed to listening to the radio. Many had been exposed to the Bible in the Authorised Version. Choral verse had been part of the curriculum. The modernisation of fairy tales often diminishes their essential quality: language. Bettelheim says of their value:
   Through the centuries (if not millennia) during which, in their retelling,
   fairy tales became more refined, they came to convey at the same time
   overt and covert meanings – came to speak simultaneously to all levels of
   the human personality, communicating in a manner which reaches the
   uneducated mind of the child as well as that of the sophisticated adult.
   …children […] at all levels of intelligence—find folk fairy tales more
   satisfying than all other children's stories. These tales…start where the
   child really is in his psychological and emotional being. They speak about
   his severe inner pressures in a way that the child unconsciously under
   stands, and—without belittling the most serious inner struggles which
   growing up entails—offer examples of both temporary and permanent
   solutions to pressing difficulties.[7]
The listening culture has given way to the culture of the image, and with our exposure to the Internet and to email even written language is changing. While spoken language is not given significant weighting in schools, the British education system has chosen to introduce Shakespeare earlier than

7. Bruno Bettelheim, *The Uses of Enchantment: The Meaning and Importance of Fairy Tales*, pub. Peregrine Books, 1978, p 5 and 6.

ever before. The stories are now to be found in the primary school syllabus. Schools are now truly multicultural and assumptions that children have had a background in English language and folklore that prepares them for the classics can and should no longer be made. If this is the case, are the classics worth teaching? Yes of course they are. It is not just the folk-lore of the English language that can provide this important background—the folk tales of every culture have similar value. What we should include in schools are the Greek myths and legends as these stories form part of the literary foundation of the classics.

The myths, legends and fairy tales that Bettelheim refers to, ask the same essential questions as the Greek dramas and classical works of the Renaissance. Young people, far from being unable to engage in these stories are very much in touch with the language if given the opportunity and the appropriate approach. This *heightened* language is sometimes referred to as archaic. Pricket says of it:

> ...the language of Shakespeare and the Authorized Version of the Bible is not a dead language in the late twentieth century….It is archaic, but still presents to us as a current linguistic idiom; *in use* every day in churches and theatres, taught and discussed in schools, seminaries, and universities, broadcast in some form every day on radio and television. It is not the language of ordinary colloquial speech, but then, *it never was.*[8]

8 S. Prickett, *Words and 'The Word':Language, Poetics and Biblical Interpretation.* Cambridge University Press, 1986.

Language and Violence

Using archaic language is very liberating for many young people. The psycho-therapists Murray Cox and Alice Theilgaard wrote:

> We can guess, we can infer, but we cannot explain with any certainty why archaic language is so frequently invoked to carry our deepest feelings. Yet it is so. And this phenomenon is independent of formal education and degree of literacy. It may be something to do with the point at which 'everyday language' breaks, because too much is expected of it.[9]

9. *Aoleon Metaphor in Shakespeare*, Murray Cox and Alice Theilgaard, pub.Tavistock Publications Ltd., London, p 142.

Certainly at times the vocabulary used by many young people seems limited and inadequate to express their needs and passions. At such times physical violence can erupt. Any means of expanding their word-power, must be worthwhile if it empowers.

When language cannot be used to negotiate difficulties, frustration is often the result. This can be clearly seen in the behaviour of the toddler. In many this failure to find the words needed to express frustration continues into adolescence, resulting in the frustration breaking out physically.

> Spoken language, too, is used by various groups in society, such as teenagers, to alienate themselves deliberately from other groups (adults and especially teachers).[10]

10. Alison Garton and Chris Pratt, *Learning to be Literate*, Blackwell, Oxford, 1989, p6.

When planning an eloquence project in a young offenders institution, I felt it was important to pitch the text work at the appropriate level and so I asked about reading proficiency. I was told that the reading ages of the inmates were between eleven to fourteen years although the average chronological ages ranged between eighteen and twenty-one.

In our fast, visually rich, and aurally poor culture it is not surprising that young men hit out in anger and frustration rather than formulating the language for debate and argument. After all, in film and television, their preferred form of entertainment over and above reading and even radio, action predominates and language is minimal.

An article in the New York Journal by Adam Gopnik speaks of wonderful work being done in Rikers Island, the largest prison in North America. The work there is about giving young people words so as to increase their chances of staying out of prison once they are released. They are succeeding with decreasing the recidivism rate.[11]

11. Adam Gopnik, "Rikers High," *New York Journal*, February 19 & 26 2001, p142.

It is often during troubled adolescence that the previously communicative child retreats behind a wall of silence. Introducing language that uses metaphor and image speaks profoundly to the young person, without attempting to preach or persuade. It lets them know on a deep level that the pain and anger they experience is common to all.

"We provoke our thoughts by the words we say."[12] This important idea, spoken by leading voice teacher, Cicely Berry, is the best reason I can think of for teaching voice and speech to young people. Speaking at a Forum on Verse Speaking and Classical Text in 1998, she also said:

12. Cicely Berry, while conducting an RSC Company Session, London February 8th, 2001.

> There's a wonderful quote from *Spanish Tragedy*—'*Where words prevaile not, violence prevailes*', and I think that should be the bottom line of all our work. We've got to provoke people into wanting to speak and having delight in speaking. I think young people really want that but the danger is we make Shakespeare too nice in a way. It is violent and we've got to allow that violence to come through.[13]

13. Cicely Berry speaking at The National Theatre Studio, 30 October 1998.

Classical text offers an ideal opportunity to find the violence and subversion in language. It allows the 'darker' thoughts to be expressed, which is important in a world where the pressure is to voice only the positive. This vocal expression in turn, acknowledges that those thoughts and feelings exist not just in ourselves but in others. This makes them safe and their universality helps to give validity to these feelings.

Insults, Oaths and Curses.
In working with adolescents I often use Shakespeare's insults as an ice-breaker.

Examining the difference between the oaths and insults of Shakespeare's time and those of today, illustrates the former, much fuller use of image and metaphor. Language today is generally contracted rather than elaborated. Most importantly for us, Shakespeare's insults are outrageous and enormous fun.

The insults used by young people today are reductive and repetitive and do not involve wit in the same way as Elizabethan insults did. This wit is quickly mastered by young people who may use different conventions but whose linguistic sub-culture has its own system of pun, word-play and irony.

Consider these examples from Shakespeare's texts:
His face is Lucifer's privy-kitchen, where he doth nothing but roast malt-worms (Henry IV, part 2)
What a drunken knave was the sea to cast thee in our way! (Pericles)
Hang! Beg! Starve! Die in the streets! (Romeo and Juliet)
Boys, with women's voices, strive to speak big. (Richard II)

The expletives used today are few in number and used in all situations, to express amazement as well as disgust. The expletives of Shakespeare's plays are far more varied, expressing very specific ideas rather than generalised disdain. Using these insults in voice-workshops allows the students to enjoy the muscularity; experience the differences in build up and release of breath pressure and to explore the word-order, syllabic structures, antithesis and imagery. At the same time the students feel the physical potency and impact of the abuse. Try these examples:
O viper vile; A pox on't; Ancient damnation!; Vengeance, plague, death, confusion!; Peace your tattlings![14]

14. Wayne F. Hill and Cynthia J. Ottchen *Shakespeare's Insults*, pub by Mainsail Press.

While working with a group of twelve and thirteen year olds I presented them with the insults from *Richard* III Not only did they never have to ask, "What does this mean", they enjoyed the wit, handled the word order and delighted in the muscular connection with the sound. They also noticed the alliteration, the potent images, the lists and the contrasts. Suggesting that students create their own insults using alliteration, assonance, dissonance, image and metaphor proved popular. The exercises must be controlled because of the truly provocative and hurtful nature of insults, but as long as the boundaries are clearly drawn the exercises can be enjoyable as well as engaging and educational. Too often we under-estimate the young person's ability with unusual language patterns.

Classic Workshops for Teenagers
I have conducted workshops with Alison Sutcliffe, who as well as being a director, began her career as assistant to John Barton, author of *Playing Shakespeare*.[15] We ran a Summer School at The Other Place in Stratford for teenagers who had worked with the Royal Shakespeare Company. Our objective was to de-mystify the delivery of verse. We considered that what young people need to know was:
The importance of antithesis.
The importance of the last word in the line.
The significance of lists, repetition and alliteration.
The shape of the verse or the prose.
The length of sentences or phrases.

15. John Barton, *Playing Shakespeare*, pub.Methuen, London, 1984.

We felt that young people needed to experience:
The joy (and sometimes pain) of speaking words.
The rhythms of language and what they say.
The preciseness and power of metaphors and similes.
The impulses of thoughts.
The muscularity of words and the energy of consonants.
The space and length of vowels.
The physical vibration of resonance.
The physicality and size or length of ideas.

The way in which character is determined by what is said.
The empowering quality of language.
The persuasive and manipulative power of words.

We began the workshops by placing cards in the centre of the room with
greetings from Shakespeare written on them. The participants would select
a card and then use the language to greet other members of the group. We
did similar exercises with *exit lines*. These were often rhymed couplets and
the group began to feel what part the rhyming played in the conclusion of
the encounter.

After this we explored insults and once the muscularity had been established
we moved on to speeches that involve curses, such as those of Caliban from
The Tempest, or Suffolk in *Henry VI part 2*. We asked the group to divide into
pairs; one of the pair gave a word, the other offered a contrast to it, for exam-
ple: Day/Night; Hot/Cold. We then worked on phrases containing *antithesis*.
After this we moved on to oxymorons and went on to use speeches from
Romeo and Juliet such as Romeo's speech, which begins:
  Here's much to do with hate, but more with love:

The group then considered how the use of the contrast and oxymoron
conveyed Romeo's emotional state. The extreme emotional states are something that young people are able to empathise with. The degree of passion in
the language is expressed in the number of oxymorons that pepper the text
(*feather of lead, bright smoke, cold fire, sick health, still-waking sleep*, to name
a few) which typify the extremes of adolescent emotions. In my experience
young people enjoy the texture of these sounds and the way they are juxtaposed. They can appreciate their dramatic impact and successfully create their
own.

In *King John*, Blanche chooses her words carefully and diplomatically when
agreeing to marry Lewis. Her reason for this and what choices are open to her
provoke debate about free will and verbal tactics with any group of adolescent
girls. Later in the play we understand how torn she is between the warring
factions in her speech:
  Which is the side that I must go withal?
  I am with both; each army hath a hand,
  And in their rage, I having hold of both,
  They whirl asunder and dismember me.[16]

16. William Shakespeare, *King John*, III.1, lines 327-330.

The way the thoughts are framed give a clear sense of her dilemma, of the
way in which she feels her loyalty being pulled, until she feels physically
pulled apart. All young people understand this feeling of being torn apart
by split loyalties. Allowing the group to take both arms of the speaker
and for both opposing sides to physically attempt to pull her over a line,
will *release* this speech and allow the speaker to integrate the words with
the human experience.

Brutus in *Julius Caesar* has some excellent examples of persuasion and Juliet
in *Romeo and Juliet* offers a perfect example when debating whether or not to
swallow the contents of the vial. Personal dilemma can be related to at any
age. Two students can work on one speech, one speaking the lines which offer

one perspective, the other speaking the antithetical ideas.

Cicely Berry developed much of her text work during workshops with young people in difficult schools and in prisons. She has written of the way in which personally experiencing the language can transport the speaker into the heart of the narrative. Looking at the first soliloquy of Leontes in *A Winter's Tale* she writes:

> We first worked on it together in different ways to get them familiar with the taste of the words: I then asked them to move round the room while speaking, changing the direction on the punctuation marks to find the sudden violent turns of thought. We continued to look at this violence by repeating the words that express/contain disgust in some way—e.g., contempt, cuckold, sluiced, bawdy, fished etc.—the list is long: and as they spoke the words I asked them to do something physical like kicking chairs, or banging on the floor, always making sure that the exercise did not get out of control. We did this to open up the hidden agenda of the language and reveal the ambivalence and complexity of the feelings underneath; it also made clear how the words themselves were self-feeding, and lead to action. They began to comprehend/imagine something of the structure of that society through the vocabulary used.[17]

17. Cicely Berry, *The Actor and The Text*, published by Virgin Books,1992, p291

Had these sort of teaching strategies been offered in schools the RSC actor Rex Obano may have had a different story to tell when he spoke of his first experiences of Shakespeare in his inner London school.

> I only studied one Shakespeare text at school, this was *Twelfth Night*. I remember thinking it was only put there to make life more difficult. We were not given any reason for studying the play, no background on Shakespeare, I think they presumed we knew of his significance. It was a very multiracial school so many of us didn't have a British cultural back ground so our first impression was just pointless complex language that had to be made sense of. I realise now that the play has many aspects that are relevant to all young people regardless of culture. I don't know if it is the play I would choose to introduce adolescents to but it opens up many questions about identity, loss, choice, idealistic love and the cruelty of the play certainly has parallels in classroom and playground bullying. *Malvolio's* treatment is appalling…and in a school with a large immigrant population the plight of the outsider should be addressed continuously …with imagination the play could have been used creatively to address aspects of life that worry young people.

For many years it was considered that only the very bright should attempt the classics; that they were too difficult for the average child. In the UK the introduction of the *key stage system* means that young people are now required to study Shakespeare at a younger age than before. The very young are introduced to the stories. These are undoubtedly good stories but we should be encouraging them to begin to speak the words as well as hear the stories. We can do this by introducing the speaking of appropriate verse in the very earliest language classes. The elements that are taught by the speaking of verse are rhythm, structure, image and most of all a love of speaking words. We should also ensure that young people are offered the stories of the classic Greek and Roman periods. With this background the introduction of Shakespeare will be easier. Once young people are introduced to Shakespeare, they should be taken to see the plays. The theatre is the medium they were intended for and because of this they should be spoken—not read silently. Adrian Noble, Artistic Director of the Royal Shakespeare Company asked in a recent interview with the *New York Times*:

> So why is Shakespeare still the foremost poetic playwright of the modern stage? Why does his work endure? Perhaps the stories? Yes, but not just the stories. They are universal, largely filched from the Greeks, the Romans, his Renaissance contemporaries. Shakespeare was a magpie with the knack of the literary alchemist. Shakespeare language, thought and emotion give us the tools to articulate out innermost passions, our outermost public declarations, our interaction with the world around us.'[18]

18. *New York Times*, "Adrian Noble, at Age 43, His Future is Unlimited," April 25, 2000.

It is, surely then, in order to offer young people this ability to better interact with society, that we as voice teachers practice our craft.

Peer-reviewed Article by *Yvette Hardie*

An Outcomes-Based Approach for the Optimal Development of the Adolescent Voice

Yvette Hardie has a Masters (Pretoria Technikon), a B.A. and a Performer's Diploma in Speech and Drama (University of Cape Town). She teaches in the drama departments of the National School of the Arts and the South African School of Film, Television and Dramatic Art. She is an examiner for the subject Speech and Drama and has been involved in curriculum development. Yvette has worked professionally as an actor, director and playwright. She has taught at the Intimate Theatre, the Market Theatre Laboratory and Vocal Impact, and has led numerous workshops, courses and master classes in a variety of contexts.

1. A general survey of these educators was conducted in order to analyse current teaching methods and approaches. Over 30% of the South African educators who participated in the survey do not feel equipped to teach this particular section. (Hardie,1999.)

2. This is a view many South Africans hold...however it is not particular to South Africa. Dudley Knight describes this kind of attitude in his article "Standard Speech", as follows: "training an actor's own speech into a different pattern robs that actor of linguistic heritage and racial or ethnic identity." (Hampton & Acker, 1997:179)

This article is based on research done under the guidance of Marth Munro for a dissertation in partial fulfillment of the requirements for a Magister Technologiae at Pretoria Technikon, South Africa.

Contextualization

In South Africa, as in other parts of the world, there are many drama and/or voice and speech practitioners teaching adolescents the fundamentals of voice and speech work. This teaching occurs both formally and informally in a range of environments, including art schools, government schools, private schools and private drama studios. Learners may take Speech and Drama as an examination subject or they may participate in extra-mural drama activities, including involvement in productions. Due to extensive curriculum changes and the inclusion of 'Arts and Culture' as a compulsory learning area in South African schools, it is to be expected that there will be an ever-increasing number of schools teaching Speech and Drama.

An important component of any drama training is the optimum development of the voice as an instrument for communication and expression. While most South African Speech and Drama educators currently working in the field seem to agree that there is a value in teaching voice and speech work as part of a drama curriculum, many of these educators feel limited in this area and face a variety of challenges.[1] These challenges include the following: considerable time constraints; too large classes (20-40 learners); a multicultural, multilingual environment for which some educators feel ill-prepared; choosing appropriate methods and implementing them in ways which are not potentially damaging for adolescent voices; the lack of knowledge in South Africa regarding vocal function, vocal health and adolescent voice development; the lack of a helpful Speech and Drama syllabus which clearly outlines the intended outcomes for voice and speech work as can be reasonably expected of adolescent learners.

The syllabus for voice and speech work proposed in this article can be motivated on two basic grounds: Pedagogical and Physiological.

A Motivation on Pedagogical Grounds:

The voice is an integral part of the whole being and is used primarily for communication and expression (Lessac, 1997:9; Anderson, 1977:10). It is a complex mechanism, which is generally taken for granted by its user and little understood. While there has always been space within an ideal South African curriculum for training the body (physical education, sports and games), training the voice has seldom been a consideration. In South Africa, the only subject to focus on it at all is Speech and Drama. However, even in this subject, there have been a variety of different attitudes to voice training, many of them negative.

One of these negative attitudes views voice and speech training as politically suspect, because it is seen as attempting to impose a particular kind of sound or accent on learners, which will alienate these speakers from their own culture and try to absorb them into the dominant culture.[2] This is because initially when Speech and Drama was first established as a subject in Natal schools, the aim of speech training was acquiring the 'right' accent, or as Lynn Dalrymple (1987:82) has described it, speech training that involved the mechanical imitation of correct forms of speech for the sake of discriminating a privileged elite.

While accent is an integral part of vocal characterization[3] and can therefore be approached as such within a Speech and Drama programme, it should be remembered that it is first and foremost an expression of personal and cultural identity, and thus should be accepted and respected within the multicultural classroom. Studies in language learning have shown that if training attempts to change the dialect or accent of the speaker, the speaker becomes more hesitant and faltering and may develop problems of personal and cultural identity (Trudgill, 1975:19). This would be in direct contradiction to the expressed aim of most Speech and Drama curricula which is to improve the learner's ability to communicate. Any proposed syllabus within the South African context should aim to formulate a methodology for practical voice work, which is sensitive to the multicultural climate of our classrooms.

Another negative attitude views voice and speech training as placing too much emphasis on the idea of Drama as an art form and the learner as an instrument to be trained for this art form.

This is in part due to the emphasis in schools from the fifties onwards[4] on drama *in* education, as opposed to drama *as* education. This approach, spearheaded by such British practitioners as Peter Slade, Brian Way, Dorothy Heathcote and Gavin Bolton, has had the effect of separating the concepts of drama and theatre. This has resulted in a situation where drama teachers focus almost exclusively on the personal development of the learner, and few of the learning objectives relate in fact to the discipline of drama. While there is much of value to be gained from the work of these practitioners, I believe that their influence has been limiting in certain respects. This view is endorsed by drama educationalists such as David Hornbrook (1991), who calls for a return to the concept of drama as dramatic art and Burgess and Gaudry (1986:51), who say that drama practitioners must recognise the need for objectives which belong specifically to the discipline of drama in order to plan meaningful and significant lessons for their students.

In this article, drama training is viewed as both methodology and content. Drama training involves experiential learning, where doing, sensing, feeling, thinking are manifested in performance through the body and voice (Nyembe, 1998:46). Therefore the voice can be seen not only as an instrument for performance, but also as an instrument for learning.

A Motivation on Physiological Grounds:
Voice training of adolescents presents unique demands, as the onset of puberty sees tremendous changes in the physical structures which produce voice (Andrews, 1991:2).

Some of these changes are:
  the vocal folds double in length;
  the angle of the thyroid cartilage changes significantly in males;
  the epiglottis flattens, grows and elevates;
  the laryngeal mucosa becomes stronger;
  the neck elongates and

3. Dudley Knight (in Hampton & Acker,1997:179) argues that creating an accent is part of the process of "becoming someone else".

4. Drama in education began as a movement in Britain and would reach South Africa only later. In 1972, Robin Malan of Theatre for Youth ran a Teachers' Workshop in Cape Town for some 70 teachers to acquaint them with drama-in-education methodologies. (Malan, 1973: Preface)

the chest enlarges (Sataloff, 1991, Chapter 8).

All of these changes will impact on voice production to some extent and the inability of the laryngeal muscles to adapt quickly enough to these changes may be heard (particularly in young males) as the voice breaking. Robert Sataloff (1991:143-144) claims that it is possible and proper to train young developing voices, but warns that there are certain potential problems, particularly with regard to developing vocal range and increasing projection. This article serves to provide a sound pedagogical framework with which to deal with these problems and challenges.

On the basis of the grounds outlined above, training the voice is thus seen as central to the subject, Speech and Drama (as is training the body). However there are important questions which need to be answered; these include:

What kind of training?
For what purpose?

In order to address these questions, an understanding of the requirements and limitations of the physiologically developing voice needs to be reached by all educators and suitable approaches to training need to be adopted and developed. These training approaches should be effective, adaptable, scientific and stimulating to learning, while having outcomes that can be clearly demonstrated and objectively evaluated. The educator should be clear as to what constitutes a safe, practical, necessary and desirable outcome for any given stage of adolescent development. If outcomes are not defined, or if the outcomes are unsafe, impractical, unnecessary and undesirable, educators could endanger the vocal health of their students, as well as being responsible for a loss of confidence, when unrealistic goals are not achieved.

Much important research has been done in the last decades regarding the physiological changes that occur in adolescence and impact on voice production. I shall not tire the knowledgeable reader with the facts here; however I direct those who are interested to Sataloff, 1991; Andrews & Summers, 1991; Cooksey, 1992, 1997a, 1997b; Gackle, 1997a, 1997b; Thurman & Klitze in *bodymind and voice* (which gives an excellent overview of the maturation process and its effects on vocal development).[5]

This article will outline a proposed syllabus for adolescent voice and speech training, which attempts to meet the challenges outlined above.

A Voice and Speech Syllabus For The Adolescent Learner:
The overall aim for the Drama learner with regard to voice/speech and body work would read as follows:

> Voice and body work should assist learners in achieving efficient, skilful control over vocal and physical characteristics in order to explore and express human experience and in order to communicate meaning to an audience, while preserving and promoting vocal and physical health.[6]

Voice and body work have been combined and are seen as part of a developmental process in which learners work towards achieving efficient,

5. The following are also of interest: Aronson,1985; Brodnitz,1971; Greene & Mathieson,1991; Kahane,1982,1983a,1983b; Stathopoulos,1998; Wilson,1987; Zemlin,1981.

6. This definition is based upon definitions by Hanson (1997:2) and Thurman (*bodymind and voice*, 1997:616), but is not identical to them.

skilful control over vocal and physical characteristics. The skills that are learnt may then be applied to various experiential learning tasks (explore and express human experience) and performance tasks (communicate meaning to an audience).

The proposed definition suggests that learners should aim to achieve efficient, skilful control over vocal (and physical) characteristics.[7] These vocal characteristics need to be clearly defined and the most suitable methodology for training each characteristic needs to be adopted. Within the South African schooling context, where an external school-leaving examination in Speech and Drama is held in Grade 12 (when most learners are ±18 years old), it would be desirable for the outcomes to be practically attainable by this level.

I suggest that the following ten characteristics of voice and speech should be brought under the efficient, skilful control of the learner by Grade 12 (though some may be achieved earlier):

1. *Voice/body Integration*: Posture and body integration play a major role in the optimal functioning of the voice.[8] Learners should develop control over their bodies in order to release unnecessary tension and establish optimal alignment and balance. Kinaesthetic awareness should be developed in order that voices and bodies support one another in performance and in life.

2. *Breathing*: A kinaesthetic awareness of breathing should be developed. Learners should demonstrate an understanding of how the body breathes for speech. They should work towards efficiency in the physical co-ordination of breathing in order to produce just the necessary breath pressure and airflow for effective voice. By Grade 12, learners should have sufficient control of their breathing appropriate to the context of the performance or life situation.

3. *Phonation*: Learners should be able to demonstrate an understanding of healthy vocal fold function. Optimally efficient (flow) phonation should be developed which uses sufficient vocal fold closure to prevent breathiness, but does so without excessive effort or strain. Learners should strive to use their voices in a healthy fashion, particularly when demands are made in terms of volume usage or emotional intensity.

4. *Voice Quality/Resonance*: Learners should be able to demonstrate an understanding of resonance and vocal tract shaping. They should be able to use their optimum vocal tract dimensions in order to create a balanced, pleasant voice quality, which is both unique and appropriate to them (in other words, adolescents should not be expected to sound like adults or to display adult resonance qualities). By Grade 12, learners should be able to use vocal tract shaping safely and without strain in order to create character differences.

7. In this article I shall focus primarily on the vocal characteristics, but outcomes relating to physical characteristics should also be developed.

8. See Book Two: Chapter 4 entitled "The Most Fundamental Voice Skill" In: *bodymind and voice* (1997) for a full discussion of the necessity of balance-alignment and voice/body integration in speaking and singing.

5. *Muscularity/Clarity*: Learners should be able to demonstrate an understanding of how the articulators work to make speech sounds. They should be able to speak distinctly and audibly for clear communication. By Grade 12, learners should be able to explore and utilise the expressive, interpretative and musical aspects of speech sounds and they should be able to adapt their use of these aspects to create differences between characters or express subtleties of meaning.

6. *Use of pitch*: Learners should be able to demonstrate a basic understanding of how the vocal folds function to sustain and change pitch. Learners should make use of a pitch which is well-placed for healthy voice use, and there should be a degree of flexibility depending on meaning, character and emotion.

7. *Use of volume*: Learners should be able to demonstrate a basic understanding of how the generator (breathing apparatus), the vocal folds and the vocal tract contribute to sustaining or changing vocal volume. Learners should be able (within certain limits) to use the appropriate volume for a performance space, without vocal strain. By Grade 12, there should be a degree of control of volume appropriate to meaning, character and emotion.

8. *Use of pace*: Learners should be able to demonstrate an understanding of how rhythmic changes contribute to establishing meaning, character and emotion. Learners should be able to manipulate pace appropriately, while remaining clear.

9. *Vocal expression of meaning*: Learners should have an understanding of how to convey meaning through the use of such elements as phrasing, pause, emphasis, intonation and vocal tone (quality). By Grade 2, they should be able to interpret a text using these elements and communicate the meaning of the text clearly and expressively.

10. *Vocal expression of character*: Learners should be able to demonstrate an understanding of how all the elements of voice work come together to communicate the personality, background, class, age, education and status of the speaker. By Grade 12, they should be able to interpret a text, make appropriate choices for characterisation (within certain reasonable limits) and use these chosen characteristics without vocal strain.

Vocal Health: In addition to understanding and developing efficient, skilful control of the above ten characteristics, learners should be able to demonstrate an understanding of vocal health and should be seen to be following healthy vocal practices in their work at all times. Effective self-expression equals the capability for self-expression, minus any limitations on and interferences with that capability (Thurman et. al, 1997:327). Vocal ability can be limited by unhealthy practices. Some aspects of vocal health which should be examined are: the effects of smoking on the voice[9]; the effects of what we

9. Adolescents are one of the fastest growing groups of smokers. The earlier they start smoking, the greater the potential health problems. Lung growth and the level of maximum lung function are hampered; other health effects are increased likelihood of respiratory illnesses, faster resting heart rates, poor overall health, vocal abuse and vocal fold pathology due to dehydration and irritation of the vocal folds and larynx. (TIPS, 1999; Thurman et. al. 1997:Book 3:Ch. 3).

ingest (hydration, medications, foodstuffs) on the voice; avoiding vocal abuse and misuse (excessive throat-clearing, glottal attacks,[10] coughing, shouting, straining); understanding the importance of a warm-up before strenuous vocal activity and a cool-down afterwards; balancing voice use time with voice recovery time.

The above skills should be developed in order to achieve the two outcomes already highlighted by the overall aim:
> the exploration and expression of human experience
> the communication of meaning to an audience.

In order to achieve these outcomes a range of explorations, materials and performance experiences should be utilised. These could include:
— *Physical explorations and games* (which could include sound)
— *Sound explorations*
— *Verbal dynamic explorations*
— *Chants and Songs*
— *Improvised speech*
— *Poetic forms* (e.g. lyrical, narrative and dramatic poetry, including South African indigenous poetic forms, such as *izibongo* and other forms of praise poetry)
— *Narrative forms* (e.g. individual and group story-telling; sight reading; dramatised prose, including South African indigenous narrative forms, such as the *intsomi* and *izinganekwanexi*[11])
— *Heightened speech* (e.g. oratory, blank verse, propaganda)
— *Dramatic text* (e.g. monologues and group scenes from plays, either scripted or workshopped, with special emphasis on indigenous South African texts which reflect the multicultural nature of our society)

A comprehensive understanding of the needs and limitations of the adolescent voice is crucial to making informed decisions about what kind of training and how much training is required at each stage of adolescent development.

Cooksey (1992, 1997a, 1997b), in several intensive studies, has investigated the changes in adolescent boys and has described five stages of maturation. Gackle (1997a,1997b) has carried out a similar study looking at the changes in the female voice, for which she has defined three stages of maturation. Both researchers describe each stage in detail as showing certain characteristics of range, tessitura, voice quality in speech and singing, register development and fundamental frequencies. Common problem areas encountered with adolescents in this stage of development (for example, increased breathiness or constriction) are also highlighted. The most critical stages of development are the *High Mutation* or *Mutational Climax* stage for males (where the perceived voice quality is huskier and very susceptible to hoarseness and abuse) and the *Pubertal* stage for females (where the perceived voice quality may be hoarse and breathy with unpredictable changes occurring). During these stages, the educator needs to pay particular care to efficient laryngeal co-ordination and easy phonation should be cultivated in the learner.

One of the challenges of working with developing voices is that within a class of 25-40 individuals, learners will be at very different stages of vocal development. Educators need to be sensitive to the possible changes occurring and to

10. It is the experience of this author that adolescent learners are often fond of forms of music (for example, rap and kwaito), which can encourage the use of glottal attack. Learners have been known to develop vocal nodules as a result of excessive practising of these music forms without an understanding of healthy voice use.

11. The *ntsomi* is a traditional Xhosa storytelling form and the *izinganekwane* is a traditional Zulu storytelling form. Gcina Mhlope is a famous South African practitioner of these forms of storytelling.

be aware of potential areas of weakness or vulnerability in the voices with which they are working. Sataloff (1991:143) has said that one of the main goals of voice training with children or adolescents should be to teach the learner how to use his/her voice without strain and how to avoid all forms of vocal abuse. Wilson (1987:324) believes similarly that the emphasis of voice and speech training should be placed on correct, effortless voice use and that all voice abuses and voice fatigue must be avoided.

An Outline Of The Proposed Course:
The proposed syllabus will be discussed in more detail, a grade at a time, and an attempt will be made to outline in a table form what can be reasonably expected as outcomes in each grade. It must be remembered, however, that adolescents' rate of development is sequential, but does not occur at the same time for every child. Educators need to have a sense of the whole process of development (as outlined by Cooksey and Gackle) and they need to consider what is appropriate for the group with which they are working, using developmental age, rather than chronological age as a measure.

Grade 8:
In Grade 8, learners are usually 12-14 years old.[12] Males are thus likely to be in the *Early Mutation* or *High Mutation* stages[13] and females are likely to be in the *Pubertal* or *Post-menarcheal* stage.[14] Thus learners are in a critical stage of development and the following can be expected:

> Males: *either* light voice quality; a breathier tone in the upper speaking register; less flexibility and agility; greater breathiness and constriction; the average fundamental frequency in speaking is 220-247 Hz *or* the voice is noticeably huskier, thicker and sometimes breathier; greater instability of vocal co-ordination; less agility; a tendency towards hyperfunction in attempting the upper pitches; the average fundamental frequency is 196-220 Hz.

> Females: breathiness due to the appearance of mutational chink; a tendency to use excessive constriction to sustain low pitches; hoarseness; a lack of tonal clarity in the tone; upper register is produced with a more breathy, child-like quality; the average fundamental frequency in speaking is 225-275 Hz.

At this point the laryngeal muscles are sensitive to damage due to the extremity of the physiological changes occurring. Brodnitz (1971:61) has pointed out that many voice problems arise during the mutation period and that later voice problems can be traced back to voice change during puberty. The overexertion of the intrinsic muscles of the larynx may cause permanent impairment of the vocal co-ordination necessary for optimal phonation. Sataloff (1991:143) speaks of the difficulty of changing the shape of a muscle once it has been contoured. Thus it would seem that great care needs to be taken to ensure that the voice is used safely during the mutation period.

At this stage of development then, it is crucial that learners understand healthy vocal function. Learners should be introduced to the basic terminology (the ten characteristics) formally (explanations or discussions) or informally (through explorations, in which educators make comments such as, notice

12. The ages of learners in each Grade can range widely, depending on such factors as when learners started school, or whether they have repeated Grades.

13. The descriptions of the stages of voice maturation for boys are from Cooksey, 1992, 1997a and 1997b.

14. The descriptions of the stages of voice maturation for girls are from Gackle, 1997a and 1997b.

what happens when...). Facts about vocal function can be very simply explained (for example, your vocal folds control the note that your voice makes, by lengthening and getting thinner, for faster vibrations so that the note is higher, or by shortening and getting thicker, for slower vibrations so that the note is lower). Learners' auditory awareness should be developed in order to be able to differentiate healthy from unhealthy voice use.

Voice/Body integration is very important at this stage. The growth spurt has either occurred or is occurring for most learners. This results in the acquisition of a new body image and an increased awareness of and sensitivity to the body.[15] Young adolescents tend to be awkward physically. Boys who have experienced a growth spurt resulting in a sudden height increase, tend to stoop; girls tend to hide their developing breasts by stooping, allowing the shoulders to collapse forward. Heavy bags and satchels begin to impact on learners' postures at this time. Slouching is often perceived as cool by learners, who may emulate less than desirable postures as part of the cultivation of an image. These physical changes or choices will impact upon voice production, by creating unnecessary tension and therefore reducing the ability of the body to breathe freely and phonate and resonate optimally. (Munro & Wissing, 1999:1).[16]

Breathing is also an area that should be approached with care. Young adolescents have a smaller vital capacity than adults, limiting the amount of air volume available for speech (Stathopoulos & Sapienza, 1997:596). This vital capacity will also be increasing steadily until 14 -16 years of age, which may introduce problems of muscular control. Children use different combinations of laryngeal and respiratory mechanisms to adults (for example, children tend to use a larger percentage of their capacity than adults). Thus it is to be expected that as children mature, possible problems of motor control or of optimal and efficient usage of the respiratory system may be encountered. It is potentially problematic if adults impose adult-like mechanisms on children whose physicality is obviously different from theirs.

Educators should choose material appropriate to the age group and which is familiar and accessible. In South Africa, we employ African folk tales (*intsomi*), improvised scenes around familiar scenarios and children's rhymes in a variety of languages, etc.

Grade 9:
In Grade 9, learners are usually 14 to 15 years old. Male learners are thus likely to be either in the *Mutational Climax* stage, or in the *Postmutational* stage. Females are likely to be in the *Young Female Adult* stage. The following characteristics can be expected:

Males: See previous section *or* voice quality is firm and clear, but still lacking adult richness; less breathiness and constriction; greater stability and consistency; lacking agility and flexibility; tendency towards hyperfunction; the fundamental frequency in speaking is 131-165 Hz.

Females: voice quality is firm and clear; less breathiness and more consistency; overall pitch and volume range capabilities

15. Ideas based upon those of Andrews & Summers,1991:16-18 and of Greene,1991:101

16. In the article "Teaching Voice in a Multi-lingual Set up: Some Ideas for the Future", Munro & Wissing (1999) stress the need for optimal voice/body integration.

increase; increased vocal agility and ease; the average fundamental frequency in speaking is 210-245 Hz.

Learners' understanding of the ten characteristics and of basic terminology should be extended, though not necessarily formally. Learners should be encouraged to observe healthy vocal usage in themselves and one another. Good habits regarding voice use should be developed and reinforced.

Vocal health awareness should start as early as possible. It is my experience that this is the age group most likely to be experimenting with smoking, and particular stress should be laid on the consequences of these actions.

Educators should choose material appropriate to the age group and which is familiar and accessible. Short scenes or monologues may be written by the learners or taken from South African plays which have been studied in class. Short poems (often self-written or South African in origin) are employed, as well as traditional songs, chants and rhythm games.

Grade 10:
In Grade 10, learners are usually 15 to 16 years old. Males are likely to be in the *Postmutational Development Stage* and females are likely to be in the *Young Female Adult Stage*. Educators must be aware of the possibility that late developers could exist within the group and appropriate care should be taken. The following vocal characteristics can be expected:

Males: vocal stability and consistency continue to improve; pitch range begins to expand; the falsetto register becomes more accessible; for many there will still be a tendency toward excess effort in breathing and voice production; the boy's voice settles at a fundamental frequency of approximately 123 Hz in speaking.

Females: voice quality is firm and clear; less breathiness and more consistency; overall pitch and volume range capabilities increase; increased vocal agility and ease; the average fundamental frequency in speaking is 210-245 Hz.

A deeper practical and theoretical understanding of vocal function can now be developed. Vocal health can also be explored in more detail. Learners should be able to demonstrate an understanding of vocal health and should be seen to be following healthy vocal practices in their work at all times. Specific aspects of vocal health should be examined when relevant. The importance of a warm-up and cool-down for strenuous voice work should be understood.

Educators should choose material appropriate to the age group, which is beginning to extend the learners beyond their own framework of reference. Challenging poetic forms (for example, the sonnet, and the praise poem form known as *izibongo*) or dramatic texts from cultures other than the learner's own may be employed at this point if the educator feels that the learners are ready for these challenges.

Grade 11:

In Grade 11, learners are usually 16 to 17 years old. The same vocal characteristics as Grade 10 apply, although educators are less likely to see late developers in this Grade. Appropriate care should still be taken in choosing explorations and material in order to preserve and strengthen the developing voice. In most schools, Grade 11 learners are likely to be given performance opportunities and therefore using the voice safely in performance should be addressed.

In addition to understanding and developing efficient, skilful control of the ten voice and speech characteristics, learners should be able to demonstrate an understanding of vocal health and should be seen to be following healthy vocal practices in their work at all times.

Educators should choose material appropriate to the age group, which is beginning to extend the learners beyond their own framework of reference. Challenging poetic forms, heightened texts or dramatic texts from cultures other than the learner's own may be employed at this point.

Grade 12:

In Grade 12, learners are usually 17 to 18 years old. Their voices are closer to adult maturity, but the process of development is not complete.[17] Females do have a slight advantage in that adult norms may be matched by about age eighteen.[18]

If the foundations have been laid, Grade 12 learners will be capable of considerably expressive and effective vocal and physical expression by this stage. They are certain to be involved in performance opportunities through their final year of study, even if the only opportunity is their final Grade 12 practical examination. Thus attention must be paid to preparing the voice for performance, preserving it in performance (when the onset of performance anxiety may result in excessive tension) and meeting the challenge of communicating with an audience.

By Grade 12, it is expected that all the outcomes for the course as a whole will be successfully met. This is not to say that these outcomes could not have been achieved earlier in the process of development.[19] The integration of elements such as the voice, the body, the intellect and the emotions within performance should be a conscious aim. A specific outcome for Grade 12 should be to preserve the optimal use of the voice when encountering more emotionally intense texts. It was seen in a Perceptual Assessment of the vocal usage of Grade 12 Speech and Drama learners in their Final Practical examinations that learners demonstrated a general tendency to push and strain voices, particularly in moments of emotional intensity, with voices becoming harsh, shrill and difficult to listen to. Performance nerves seemed to induce greater degrees of constriction and the use of excessive vocal effort.[20]

In terms of suitable material for this grade, the vocal and physical skills acquired should be applied to text as much as possible. The work of Berry (1991), Rodenburg (particularly stages 3 to 7 as outlined in *The Actor Speaks*, 1997), Linklater (1992) and Lessac (particularly the exploration of texts using the vocal and physical NRGies) can all be usefully employed with this

17. An individual's peak vital capacity is reached only in the late teens or early twenties (Greene, 1991:65) and vocal fold maturation is not complete until between 16 and 20 years of age (Stathopoulos & Sapienza, 1997:596). While the adolescent voice tends towards possessing more adult-like qualities, it is not yet physically mature enough to produce the tone qualities and ranges of which the adult voice is capable (Cooksey, 992:63). The first and second average formant locations decrease during this period, "indicating increased size of the vocal tract from physical growth" (Cooksey, 1992:64), but they do not approximate adult norms until the late teens or early twenties. This is the result of the fact that full adult vocal tract sizes are only reached by age 20-21 (Thurman & Klitzke in *bodymind and voice*, 1997:479).

18. Rodenburg (1992:46-47) speaks about the advantage that female voices have in training in that they can be "stretched" (in terms of pitch range) from age eighteen, while male voices should only be stretched from about age twenty-five.

19. See the table of outcomes given below for details.

20. This Perceptual Assessment was carried out as part of research for the author's dissertation. (Hardie, 1999).

age group. Estill's work (1992) can be used to explore different vocal characterisations, provided the educator pays attention to the potential dangers of straining the voice.

Conclusion:

If these outcomes are to be utilised successfully, it is vital that educators develop their sensitivity to the visual, auditory and kinaesthetic signs which will alert them as to whether the outcomes have been met by the learners or not. The constant sharpening of skills of perceptual analysis is important if the educator is to know whether learners have reached the defined targets. It is also a skill that should be developed in learners, so that they can continue to educate themselves and assist one another in the learning process. This can be an important tool in helping the educator deal with large classes.

It is hoped that the proposed syllabus will go some of the way to alerting educators in South Africa and elsewhere to the issues surrounding voice and speech training for adolescents and that the implementation of these principles will ensure expressive, effortless, healthy voice use by these learners. The principles and outcomes outlined in this article should serve as a springboard for further investigation into the education of adolescent learners and may be utilised to develop syllabi for learners at other stages of voice development.

Bibliography:

Anderson, Virgil A. 1977. *Training the Speaking Voice*. New York: Oxford University Press.

Andrews, M.L. & Summers, A.C. 1991. *Voice Therapy for Adolescents*. San Diego: Singular Publishing Group.

Aronson, A.E. 1985. *Clinical Voice Disorders: An interdisciplinary approach*. (2nd edition). New York: Thieme Stratton, Inc.

Berry, Cicely. 1988. *Voice and the Actor*. London: Harrap.

Berry, Cicely. 1991. *The Actor and His Text*. London: W. H. Allen & Co.

Boltezar, I.H., Burger, Z.R. & Zargi, M. 1997. Instability in voice in adolescence: Pathologic condition or normal developmental variation. *Journal of Pediatrics* 130(2).

Brodnitz, F.S. 1971. *Vocal Rehabilitation*. (4th edition) American Academy of Ophthalmology and Otiolaryngology, Rochester, M.N.

Burgess, R. & Gaudry, P. 1985. *Time for Drama*. Milton Keynes: Open University Press.

Cooksey, John M. 1992. *Working with the Adolescent Voice*. St Louis: Concordia Publishing House.

Cooksey, John. M. 1997a. Voice Transformation in Male Adolescents. In: *bodymind and voice: Foundations of Voice Education*. Thurman, Leon & Welch, Graham (Eds.) The VoiceCare Network Press: Book IV, Chapter 4, 495-515.

Cooksey, John. M. 1997b. Male Adolescent Changing Voices: Voice Classification, Voice Skill Development, and Music Literature Selection. In: *bodymind and voice:* Foundations of Voice Education. Thurman, Leon & Welch, Graham (Eds.) The VoiceCare Network Press: Book V, Chapter 8, 589-609.

21. [see following chart] The author is the source of these games, which have been adapted from basic relaxation exercises.

22. [see following chart] Often typical spaces used for drama activities in schools are not conducive to optimal voice work, particularly for adolescent voices. Huge school halls, with poor acoustics, should not be used as a measure for projection capabilities. If learners are in productions that require that a large space be filled, amplification should ideally be utilised to assist the developing voices.

Given below is a table which attempts to outline the specific outcomes which can be expected from a learner through the course of his or her secondary education, based on the aspects already examined. Suggestions are also given as to which voice and speech practitioners may be most usefully employed at each stage of development.

Table of Outcomes for Each Grade

Grade 8	Grade 9	Grade 10	Grade 11	Grade 12
Voice/Body Integration Release of unnecessary tension, alignment and balance of the body. Employ Alexander principles; Bartenieff fundamentals; Feldenkrais awareness exercises; games that are fun and physical, while promoting awareness, e.g. "tension tag", "rag doll" and "puppet on a string". 21	As in Grade 8.	As in Grade 8, but the principles learnt should be utilised in performance to some extent. Educators may want to begin introducing Laban or Lessac-based voice/body explorations into the work.	Develop control over the body in order to release unnecessary tension and establish optimal alignment and balance. Kinaesthetic awareness should be developed in order that voices and bodies support one another in performance and in life.	As in Grade 11. Learners should be able to apply these skills within the performance environment.
Breathing Kinaesthetic awareness and observation of the breathing process. No attempt to teach breathing methods, breath support or any potentially tension-inducing breathing behaviours, unless required to do so by particular circumstances.	As in Grade 8, but there could now be some work on developing effective breathing mechanisms for speech, as efficient use of breath will assist increased vocal agility. Excessive tension-producing behaviours, such as rib-reserve breathing, should be avoided.	Work towards efficiency in the physical coordination of breathing in order to produce just the necessary air pressure and airflow for effective voice.	Demonstrate an understanding of how the body breathes for speech. Develop optimal efficiency in the physical co-ordinations required to produce necessary air pressure and airflow for skilled vocal work.	As in Grade 11. Learners should have sufficient control of their breathing appropriate to the context of the performance or life situation.
Phonation Easy, effortless phonation, within a comfortable pitch range. Learners should be warned against excessive tension in making sound. Learners should be warned against "pushing their voices down" in order to sound more adult. Employ Linklater's sighs of relief.	As in Grade 8.	Optimally efficient (flow) phonation which uses sufficient vocal fold closure to prevent breathiness, but does so without excessive effort or strain.	As in Grade 10. Also demonstrate an understanding of healthy vocal fold function. Ability to extend phonation as a result of better control of breathing and phonatory functions.	As in Grade 11. Learners should strive to use their voices in a healthy fashion, particularly when demands are made in terms of volume usage or emotional intensity.
Quality/Resonance Auditory and kinaesthetic awareness of different resonance qualities can be developed, but no intensive training should occur in this area yet.	As in Grade 8.	Learners use their optimal vocal tract dimensions to create a balanced, pleasant voice quality which is both unique and appropriate to them. Voice strengthening exercises (such as Lessac's y-buzz) which develop both phonation and resonance skills, can be used.	As in Grade 10. Also, demonstrate an understanding of resonance and vocal tract shaping, and use this understanding in their exploration of text and character. Work with projected sound, using calls, chants, singing and other explorations.	As in previous grades. Learners should be able to use vocal tract shaping safely and without strain in order to create character differences and explore texts successfully.
Muscularity/Clarity Visual, auditory and kinaesthetic awareness of how sounds are made, through the exploration of sounds from a variety of language backgrounds, as well as gibberish and non-verbal sounds.	As in Grade 8. While articulation exercises involving rhymes can be fun for this age group, excessive work on articulation, which can be tension-producing, should be avoided.	Learners should be able to speak distinctly and audibly for clear communication. May use Lessac's structural and consonantal NRGies (1997:63-121; 160-199), Berry's Muscularity exercises (1984:43-75) as well as sound explorations drawn from Linklater (1976) and other sources.	As in Grade 10. Also, demonstrate an understanding of how the articulators work to make speech sounds. Explore and utilise the expressive, interpretative and musical aspects of speech sounds and be able to adapt the use of these aspects to create differences between characters or express subtleties of meaning. May use Lessac's structural and consonantal NRGies; Linklater's vowel/consonant explorations (1992:11-29).	As in previous grades. Learners should be able to apply these skills to the performance environment.

Grade 8	Grade 9	Grade 10	Grade 11	Grade 12
Use of Pitch Finding optimal pitch for the learner. While sensitivity to pitch range should be developed, no intensive training of pitch range should occur at this stage.	Finding optimal pitch for the learner. Sensitivity to pitch rage should be developed and an easy use of upper, middle and lower range can be developed with extreme care.	The use of optimal pitch should be endorsed. The pitch range can begin to be exploited with learners beginning to explore their vocal registers. The lower (chest) register and the upper (head) register can be strengthened. Pulse register (glottal fry) and falsetto (flute) register should be avoided at this stage, or approached with extreme care.	Demonstrate a basic understanding of how the vocal folds function to sustain and change pitch. Make use of a pitch that is well-placed for healthy voice use. There should be a degree of flexibility depending on meaning, character and emotion (Linklater's pitch range exercises can be usefully employed here, 1976).	As in previous grades. Learners should be able to apply these skills within a performance environment.
Use of Volume Awareness of when volume is being created through excessive tension and avoidance of these behaviours.	As in Grade 8.	Demonstrate a basic understanding of how the breathing apparatus, the vocal folds and the vocal tract contribute to sustaining or changing vocal volume. Learners should be able to create a certain amount of volume without vocal strain.[22]	As in Grade 10. Also, learners should be able to (within limits) use the appropriate volume for a space, without vocal strain. (If the voice building work has been successfully applied, learners should find that they are capable of better projection without effort.)	As in previous grades. By Grade 12, there should be a degree of control of volume appropriate to meaning, character and emotion within the performance environment.
Use of Pace Awareness of how appropriate pace enhances clarity in communication.	As in Grade 8.	Demonstrate an understanding of how rhythmic changes contribute to establishing meaning, character and emotion. Clarity of communication should be attained.	As in Grade 10. Also, learners should be able to manipulate pace appropriately, while remaining clear.	As in previous grades. Learners should be able to apply these skills within a performance environment.
Expression of Meaning Awareness of how such elements as phrasing, pause, emphasis, intonation and vocal tone contribute to meaning.	As in Grade 8.	Demonstrate an understanding of how to convey meaning through such elements as phrasing, pause, emphasis, intonation and vocal tone.	As in Grade 10. Also, learners should be able to interpret a text using these elements and communicate the meaning of the text clearly and expressively.	As in previous grades. Learners should be able to apply these skills within a performance environment.
Expression of Character Awareness of how character is reflected in the voice.	As in Grade 8.	Awareness of how character is reflected in the voice. Make certain basic choices in order to characterise the voice of a speaker and use these choices, without vocal strain.	Demonstrate an understanding of how all elements of voice work come together to communicate the personality, class background, age, education and status of the speaker. Experiment with character voices to some extent, without vocal strain. Accents and dialects can be explored if desired.	As in previous grades. Learners should be able to apply to interpret a text, make appropriate choices for characterisation (within certain reasonable limits) and use these chosen characteristics without vocal strain within a performance environment.

Dalrymple, Lynne. 1987. *Exploration in Drama, Theatre and Education: A Critique of Theatre Studies in South Africa*. University of Natal: unpublished Doctoral thesis.

Estill, Jo. 1992a. *Basic Figures and Exercise Manual: Level One*. New York: Estill Voice Training Systems.

Estill, Jo. 1992b. *Primer of Compulsory Figures*. New York: Estill Voice Training Systems.

Gackle, Lynne. 1997a. Understanding Voice Transformation in Female Adolescents. In: *bodymind and voice: Foundations of Voice Education*. Thurman, Leon & Welch, Graham (Eds.) The VoiceCare Network Press: Book IV, Chapter 5, 516-521.

Gackle, Lynne. 1997b. Female Adolescent Changing Voices: Voice Classification, Voice Skill Development, and Music Literature Selection. In: *bodymind and voice: Foundations of Voice Education*. Thurman, Leon & Welch, Graham (Eds.) The VoiceCare Network Press: Book V, Chapter 7, 582-588.

Greene, M.C.L. & Mathieson, L. 1991. *The Voice and Its Disorders*. (5th Edition). London and New Jersey: Whurr Publishers.

Hampton, M. & Acker, B. 1997. *The Vocal Vision: Views on Voice*. New York: Applause Books.

Hanson, Anne Marie L. 1997. *An Analysis of the Physiological Assumptions in Vocal Instructional Systems for Actors*. University of Kansas: unpublished Doctoral thesis.

Hardie, Y.E. 1999. *The Emerging Voice and Outcomes-based Education: Voice Building Within Speech and Drama Training in the Further Education and Training Band*. Johannesburg: Unpublished Masters Dissertation.

Hornbrook, D. 1991. *Education and Dramatic Art*. Oxford: Blackwell Education.

Kahane, J.C. 1982. Growth and development of the human prepubertal and pubertal larynx. *Journal of Speech and Hearing Research, 25*, 446-455.

Kahane, J.C. 1983a. Age related changes in the elastic fibres of the adult male vocal ligament. In V. Lawrence (Ed.), *Transcripts of the Eleventh Symposium: Care of the Professional Voice, Part I*. New York: The Voice Foundation:11-20.

Kahane, J.C. 1983b. Postnatal development and aging of the human larynx. *Seminars in Speech and Language*, 4(3), 189-203.

Lessac, A. 1997. *The Use and Training of the Human Voice: A Biodynamical Approach to Vocal Life*. (3rd edition). California: Mayfield Publishing Company.

Linklater, Kristin. 1976. *Freeing the Natural Voice*. New York: Drama Book Publishers.

Linklater, Kristin. 1992. *Freeing Shakespeare's Voice*. New York: Theatre Communications Group.

Munro, M. & Wissing, D. 1999. Teaching Voice in a Multi-lingual Set up: Some Ideas for the Future. In: *Vasta Newsletter*. 13(2) Spring/Summer 1999.

Nyembe, Thulani. 1998. *The Role of Drama Studies in a New Education Policy: A Critical Investigation of Current Curriculum Proposals for Educational Drama*. Johannesburg: unpublished Masters thesis.

Perkins, W.H. & Kent, R.D. 1986. *Functional Anatomy of Speech, Language and Hearing: A Primer*. Allyn and Bacon.

Rodenburg, Patsy. 1995. *The Right To Speak: Working With the Voice*. Great Britain: Methuen Drama.

Rodenburg, Patsy. 1997. *The Actor Speaks*. Great Britain: Methuen Drama.

Sataloff, Robert T. 1991. *Professional Voice: the Science and Art of Clinical Care*. New York: Raven Press.

Stathopoulos, E.T. & Sapienza, C.M. 1997. Developmental Changes in Laryngeal and Respiratory Function With Variations in Sound Pressure Level. *Journal of Speech, Language and Hearing Research*, 40, 595 -614.

Stathopoulos, E. 1998. The Child Voice: Views from Aerodynamic, Anatomic, Respiratory, Kinematic and Acoustic Measures. In: *Transcripts of the 27th Symposium of the Voice Foundation: Care of the Professional Voice*. New York: Voice Foundation.

TIPS (Tobacco Information and Prevention Source). Internet Resource.

Tanner, J.M. 1971. *Sequence, tempo and individual variation in the growth and development of boys and girls aged 12 to 16*. Daedalus, 100: 907 –930.

Thurman, L. & Klitzke, C. 1997. Highlights of Physical Growth and Function of Voices from Pre-birth to Age 21. In: *bodymind and voice: Foundations of Voice Education*. The VoiceCare Network Press.

Thurman, Leon & Welch, Graham (Eds.) 1997. *bodymind and voice: Foundations of Voice Education*. The VoiceCare Network Press.

Trudgill, Peter. 1975. *Accent, Dialect and the School*. London: Edward Arnold Publishers Ltd.

Wilson, D. K. 1987. *Voice Problems for Children* (3rd Edition). Baltimore: Williams & Wilkins.

Zemlin, Willard R. 1981. *Speech and Hearing Science: Anatomy and Physiology*. (2nd edition). Englewood Cliffs N.J.: Prentice-Hall.

Editorial Column by *Louis Colaianni*

Considering our first issue's lively exchange on the subject of "good speech," feedback from the readership has been disappointing. We believe the discussion was well balanced and meticulously peer-reviewed. Ironically, it seems our readers, voice and speech practitioners, have held their collective tongue, rather than continue the discussion. This Department cannot function in a vacuum. To be vital, we must hear from our readers and respond to them. We hope our readers will not remain sideline spectators, but instead, put their perspectives, experiences, observations and practices on the line. Risk confrontation. Perhaps, welcome it.

I, myself, am moved to respond to a question posed to me by Dudley Knight in his paper "Standard Speech: the ongoing debate", reprinted in these pages last year. Citing my book *The Joy of Phonetics and Accents*, Knight wrote:

> To suggest as Louis Colaianni does, that a "limiting, regional accent is merely the by-product of patterns of tension frozen into the vocal tract" is to suggest that all American regional accents would be magically released if only those residual tensions could be released. But released into what? Lurking within this generous pronouncement is the same hierarchical view of speech clarity that reformers like Colaianni would seek to supplant. If a person has grown up speaking a dialect that habitually eliminates a consonant cluster, for example, will freedom of articulation plus intensity of thought actually cause that hitherto unused consonant to magically reappear, without the intervention of any prescriptive model? Is there some strange, shared "deep dialect" hidden within all of us to which we all aspire?"

Released into what? Knight asks. I daresay most teachers of voice production could provide a ready answer. Here is mine: Released into a more resonant, muscularly economical, easily heard version of their own ideolect. Knight would realize if he had quoted me further, that as a teacher, I expect students to retain traces of their regional accents. I celebrate their accents. But, voice freeing exercises, such as, low relaxed breathing, jaw loosening, tongue stretching, and soft palate limbering aid in reducing gutteralness, nasality, breathiness, drawl, or other characteristics which might detract from the intelligibility and carrying power of the voice. The exercises promote muscular economy and in combination with a little ear-training, help students maneuver between native speaking patterns and necessary adjustments, such as stage accents, or perhaps unfamiliar consonant clusters. Yes, voice freeing exercises do, indeed, "release the voice into" a greater stage-worthiness. Furthermore, group voice classes facilitated by a skilled, sensitive teacher; provide a community for ear-training. The influence and study of other student's accents empowers the learner to discern minute pronunciation differences without ever having to buy into the concept of "proper" or "correct" pronunciation. I know of no magical new speech construct to emerge through voice exercises. But my orientation as a voice and speech teacher is more descriptive than prescriptive. The release I guide my students toward is an unselfconscious brand. Knight is way out in left field when describing me as a perpetuator of the prescriptivism I intend to supplant. My only proof of his misguidedness is in the voices of my students, many of whom ply their speech skills in the professional theatre. No two, however, share an ideolect.

Louis Colaianni, associate editor, Pronunciation/ Phonetics/Linguistics/Dialects, is the author of *The Joy of Phonetics and Accents* (Drama Publishers, 1994) and *Shakespeare's Names: A New Pronouncing Dictionary* (Drama Publishers, 2000). He has given workshops and lectures internationally on voice production, speech and phonetics. Colaianni is a tenured, Associate Professor of Theatre at the University of Missouri-Kansas City and a Voice and Speech Coach in the professional theatre. His biography appears in *Who's Who in the World*, (Marquis, 2000).

Our current issue includes a fascinating paper co authored by Kate Foy and Paul Meier on the vocal challenges of open-air theatre. Bob Davis complements this paper with a replication of an early 20th Century study of the carrying power of consonants, to which Dr. Donald Cooper ads a dose of hard data. We are also very pleased to welcome the contribution of Liz Mills from the parallel discipline of performance studies.

As always, we are hopeful that this issue will stimulate discussion and prompt the comments of our readers.

Peer-reviewed Article by *Liz Mills*

The Theatre of Theatre Voice

The methodology of the voice/speech specialist can seem obscure and esoteric to the uninitiated. So too, can seem the language and practices of the Performance Studies scholar. Therefore, we of the voice/speech community should read Liz Mills' article "The Theatre of Theatre Voice" with a spirit of adventure. Our thanks to Professor Jacqueline Martin of Queensland University of Technology, and one of this journal's regular columnists, for providing some useful context in the following introduction. – LC, assoc. ed.

Introduction by Jacqueline Martin
The title of this article is somehow tantalizing. Of course it is the repeat of the word 'theatre' but then used together with the word 'voice' the title becomes charged with instant deductions about what 'theatre voice' might mean. This is naturally intended by the author. We do not know, or have not really ever come to definitive conclusions about what might be meant by 'theatre voice'. Not that other terms, such as 'physical theatre' are as contentious. Why is this? Do we still hold the belief that the voice in the theatre is synonymous with the personality of the actor? According to Liz Mills, this notion should be abandoned.

Liz Mills is a senior lecturer, and currently co-ordinator of the postgraduate programmes, in the Drama Department at the University of Cape Town, South Africa. She teaches voice and acting in the undergraduate Theatre and Performance programme and directing at the postgraduate level. She directs for the Drama Department and also, when the opportunity arises, in the professional theatre.

In a very thorough examination of the role which the voice and emotion/personality has played in the theatre since Antiquity, Mills scrutinizes the voice and its dependence on psychology, the role which it has played in particular on natural and realistic acting practices. This is the thrust of the article, and where Mills' critical view of how little use is made of voice in the contemporary theatre because of its interdependence on the personality/natural voice which realistic acting perpetuates. Mills wants the voice to do more. She even states the …"dialogic possibilities of theatre voice are both present and possible in contemporary theatre voice in that the exploration and extension of the natural voice is the locus of the expressive possibilities of a range of theatrical forms, including, as yet, unknown vocal possibilities."

Reading the article, which is profound in its understanding of the philosophy of linguists such as Barthes and Habermas, is a bit like the gaining of wisdom. It does not come easily, that is, until the conclusion, where quite clearly, the author states that her concern is with the over-articulation of the natural voice in theatre. Many of us would agree with her, and would wish that theatre would return to some form of renewed theatricality, where the voice in all its many paralinguistic forms would come into its own again. —
Jacqueline Martin

The Theatre of Theatre Voice

The impulse for my theatre voice praxis springs from the notion of voice as *central to performance*; a centrality that implies that voice is one of the creative strands of the theatre matrix. When theatre voice engages with the creation of theatre through the voice the *theatre* of theatre voice emerges.

In this paper I will explore the way in which determinants of realism underpin the vocal work in western English speaking theatre; determinants that, in my view, result in a single theatrical vision for voice in the theatre: vocal realism. Stylistically speaking, a realist use of the voice is a theatrical use. But I will argue that a combination of realist acting and the notion of the natural voice, which is a seminal development in contemporary theatre voice practice, result too often in a vocal agency that operates beyond realism as a style and is largely personal. Besides this personalized vocal presence, it is the extent to which a realist use of the voice becomes an assumed vocal presence for the actor that points to a theatre voice practice which is oblivious to its own expressive capability in the medium of theatre and therefore omits a range of theatrical uses of the voice.

The emergence of naturalism[1] marks a separation of a classical theatre voice practice, characterized by vocal artifice, from a modern theatre voice practice characterized by a natural sound. The focus on a natural sound is a logical and creative counterpart to the realist acting methods[2] which have resulted in dramatic character conceived of as personality. In this conception of character the notion of self becomes important for the actor; notions that I will unravel in due course. But again, it is the degree to which the natural voice of contemporary theatre voice practice becomes embodied, for theatre voice, in notions of the *self*, that determines a vocal realism as the prevailing aesthetic of theatre voice. And, where this vocal realism is no more than a reflection of the extended everyday use of the voice, theatre voice, in my view, slips out of the discourse of theatre. This tendency, I have called after Aristotle, a *poetics of the self*.

A focus on self or on the personal identity of the actor is not a modern phenomenon. Martin in discussing the art of rhetoric as the guiding principle for the classical Greek actor notes experimentation with *elocutio*. *Elocutio* refers to the choice of a suitable verbal form and the experimentation manifested in the "use [of] an ornate style in order to reveal personality to the listener".[3] This desire on the part of the performer to be present in performance as *himself* gains strength with an emerging focus on the individual.

After the Renaissance the psychology of the mind changed from the classical and medieval idea of "the mind itself being a reflection of a greater intellect [to] the mind as a bundle or collection of ideas provided by experience and held together by natural and acquired associations".[4] These notions of "experience" and "natural and acquired associations" create a new relationship with craft.

The actor now not only draws on her personality for performance but also needs to consult her own experience of life. As psychology became more and more part of the human frame of reference, the actor's impulse to win the belief of the audience became less centered in the frame of idea and more centered in the expression of feeling and in the recognition of self.

The influence of realist acting methodologies transformed characterization. The contemporary actor's conception of a dramatic character as an individual, as a personality, is a determinant of realist theatre and is reflected through sub-textual layering. It would be impossible for the contemporary actor to return to pre-Freudian concepts of character. Even at the level of the action of the drama, it is realist characterization that influences the actor's impulse. The understanding of action has become an understanding of the psychological motive of character; an understanding which, in turn, inscribes a psychological or personal perspective on the entire content of the play.

1. Styan notes that naturalism and realism were, in effect, two historical movements which differed slightly philosophically. In this paper the terms are used interchangeably to reflect a theatre style representative of real life. This choice accommodates both the works which refer to the acting methodology of Stanislavsky as realist and the voice texts which refer to the natural voice. Styan, J.L., 1995, *Modern drama in theory and practice. Volume 1. Realism and Naturalism.* Cambridge: Cambridge University Press.

2. Contemporary theatre voice notions of releasing and working with an organic sound are consonant with Stanislavsky's exploration of the unconscious, and the intuitive, to inform the craft of acting. Magarshack, David (trans) 1960, *Stanislavsky on the Art of the Stage*, London: Faber and Faber.

3. Foreword by Cicely Berry in Martin, Jacqueline, 1991, *Voice in Modern Theatre*, London:Routledge, p 2.

4. Townsend, Dabney, 1997, *An Introduction to Aesthetics*, UK: Blackwell, p 79.

This is affirmed in the actor's approach to text via the formula of character, situation and motive.[5] This approach to acting has not only served realism well but has also transferred, quite easily, to non-realist pieces of theatre. It is the insertion of person-character into the structure of the actor's agency that has, in my view, inscribed the natural voice with a vocal realism.

Key to the notion of a vocal *poetics of self* is the manner in which the self functions for the actor. The self of the actor becomes both the referential source and the validating means of vocal expression.

The emergence of the director as the new theatrical agent diminished actor agency in the process of creating a piece of theatre. However, parallel to the rise of the director is the emergence of Stanislavsky's methods which empowered actors in an unprecedented way. This empowerment lay in the way that Stanislavsky addressed the classical actor's creative frustration. Stanislavsky recognized that directors always tell actors what *not to do* but cannot tell them *how to do* what is required. His system gave actors autonomy over their own art form in its focus on the *how to* of acting.[6]

The Investment in Self

Realist characterization has become an interpretive puzzle for the actor in a way that the character types of non-realist texts cannot become. The process of creating a realist character offers the depth, the intrigue and excitement of revealing both a human conscious and unconscious intent. The actor's being becomes the source of creativity because the actor needs to rely on parallel personal experience to that of the character, on the observation of humanity and on her own ability to construct that observation into coherent, human patterns of meaning. The actor thus refers to self in a way which is unique; self validates both the art form and the person of the actor.

The experience of appropriate emotional enactment becomes the actor's means of evaluating performance. Actor agency is thus elaborated on two levels through Stanislavsky's system. In the preparation for performance, the actor can abstract her craft, via the Stanislavsky system, and prepare on technical and logical levels as well as on levels of enactment. In performance, expression of character is subjectively-objectively validated: through emotional enactment, the actor can rely on her-self to evaluate performance within the objective frame of the dramatic text.

The verisimilitude suggested by the notion of the natural voice confirms this relationship to self in the creative processes of crafting a performance. Firstly, actor intention relocates from the production intention to the character intention, as shaped by the dramatic text. The dramatic text offers the actor a character that she can *know* via her own experience; something she can voice herself. The dramatic text itself will then reorganize the actor's experience into something independent of the actor's life, giving the illusion of entering another world, the world of the character or author. Context is taken care of by the dramatic text and by the actor's ability to win belief. Finally, the actor wins belief because she sounds like the audience (or like someone they know) and the more real her expression of thought and feeling the more the audience suspends its disbelief.[7]

5. These three elements as summarised by John Barton are the essence of the modern tradition. Wade, Andrew, 1997, ' "What is a Voice For?": Training and the Rise of the Voice Coach' in *The Vocal Vision. Views on Voice by 24 Leading Teachers, Coaches & Directors*. New York: Applause p 136.

6. Magarshack, David (trans), 1960, *Stanislavsky on the Art of the Stage*, London: Faber and Faber, p 11.

7. Berry notes how both actors and audience, influenced by television and film expect a naturalness of speech; "the more 'everyday' it sounds the better". Martin, Jacqueline, 1991, *Voice in Modern Theatre*, London: Routledge, p 17.

Theatrical Conceptualization Eclipsed

There can be no question of the potency of the actor's agency in the realist approach to craft, but it is an agency in which the question of a broader understanding of the theatricality of the voice has been cut loose.

Conceptualization, the development of a theatrical concept or the how to of performance, is the level of abstraction; the level of greater theatrical agency which the actor still needs to consciously engage. The theatrical agency in relation to character is only a part of this greater theatrical agency. For the contemporary actor the two have become conflated. For Stanislavsky, the one clearly served the other.[8]

In the shift of convention from the vocal presentation of the nineteenth century to vocal representation, theatre voice subscribes to a believability paradigm of acting connected to self. Psychological realism has become the meta-narrative for actors. However, the presence of the actor's vocal self becomes a limitation when it determines an actor-personal frame of reference rather than a character-personal frame of reference. The actor-personal frame denies character its interpretive viability as part of the dramatic text viz., that with each successive production, the characters become a function of a new conceptualization: the metaphor for the production in question.

Theatre as a Discursive Rationality

Through the interpretation of the natural voice as everyday speech, the discursive context of theatre voice has become, for actor and audience alike, a socially and personally determined context. Habermas' theory of "communicative rationality" will be used as a way of understanding how the interpretation of the realist acting method, as an appropriation of the everyday voice, has subverted our relationship to language as language in and for theatre.[9] A secondary impact of this tendency is the difficulty of abstracting voice and/or language as *text* when acting is framed by the realist determinants of motive and believability.

Pavis refers to the actor's entire culture which is involved in the preparatory work for performance. He echoes Barba in describing this as the living, theatrical knowledge which actors acquire; a knowledge which, he notes, is not free of codification.[10] Part of the actor's acquired knowledge is an understanding of the natural voice as the everyday voice of the actor. The real life frame, the actor as cultural being, is always present because as Berry states, our voices are our "sound presence"; we are present through language and sound.[11] If we consider language from the notion of self, it becomes clear that our voices do not only declare us to be a member of a particular linguistic community, but that, through language, we declare both a communal and very personal patterning of thought. This patterning of thought can be described, after Habermas, as our individual "reasonableness" which reflects our reliance on a "communicative rationality".[12]

According to Habermas our linguistic practices have a deep, underlying structure of "communicative rationality", a rationality based in a human consensus of truth.

> [Even] our most despotic speech acts betray, despite themselves, the
> frail outlines of a communicative rationality: in making an utterance

8. Stanislavsky speaks of the purpose of performance as "provid[ing] a scenic embodiment of the play-wright's ruling idea'. Magarshack states that "everything in Stanislavsky's 'system' exists for the sake of through-action and the ruling idea". Magarshack, David (trans), 1960, *Stanislavsky on the Art of the Stage*, London: Faber and Faber, pp 70-71.

9. Eagleton, Terry, 1994, 'Ideology and its Vicissitudes in Western Marxism' in Zizek, Slavoj (ed) *Mapping Ideology*, London: Verso p 203.

10. Pavis, Patrice, 1992, *Theatre at the Crossroads of Culture*, London: Routledge, pp 15 - 16.

11. Berry, Cicely, 1987, *The Actor and his Text*, London: Harrap, p 16.

12 Eagleton, Terry, 1994, 'Ideology and its Vicissitudes in Western Marxism' in Zizek, Slavoj (ed) *Mapping Ideology*, London: Verso pp 205-206.

a speaker implicitly claims that what she says is intelligible, true, sincere and appropriate to the discursive situation.[13]

13. Ibid

Habermas states that "a species that depends for its survival on the structures of linguistic communication and cooperative, purposive-rational action must *of necessity* rely on reason".[14] The use of a realist (natural) voice in the theatre has come to reflect too closely the *voice of reason* as described by Habermas.

14. Ibid

This voice of reason informs both silence and language. As Berry points out, the contemporary text is as much about what is not stated as it is about what is stated.[15] That which is not stated is vocally or physically inferred in the enactment and the layering which the actor is able to bring to the text. Sub-textual layering is not only the formula for realist dialogue but, post realism, for classical works as well. Sub-textual layering is also, finally, what Pavis calls a habit of work for actors trained in realist methodologies.

15. Berry, Cicely, 1987, *The Actor and His Text*, London: Harrap, p 47.

Sub-textual layering produces a domestication of text when, within the intent signaled through the action of the dramatic text, the character's motive is vocally patterned through the patterns of the actor's own intent rather than being patterned by the dramatic text with reference to the actor's understanding of her own intent. In the former, the voice of the actor *describes* the interpretation of the character motive.[16]

16. Mairowitz provides a useful reminder of the theatrical intent of naturalism; a frame through which to consider this slippage of theatre intent into life intent: "Oh, what a progressive historical force naturalism once was, and can still be. We have come to associate it with strategies of play-acting or arrangements of furniture, but in its heyday naturalism was a reaction both to social and dramatic artificiality, one which branded the world of bourgeois deceptions as unacceptable. And a major formal characteristic of the more critical naturalist writers was the ability to specify the dominating imagery of social class, to locate a corner of the criticised world in the mouth of the proscenium arch—often just a corner, but a corner in its totality". Mairowitz, David Zane, 1977, 'Peter Stein's Summerfolk' in *Plays and Players*. May: 18-21.

The activities of interpreting and of conceptualizing for theatre are activities essentially for creating communicative structures in and for theatre. The dramatic text, whether written or described through a director's concept for a piece of theatre, becomes in performance, the communicative rationality of theatre relying on the audience/performer consensus of a *theatrical truth*. In the theatre this truth extends to the fictive and the fantastical; all that might be called into play in our willingness to suspend our disbelief. This truth also presupposes the possibility of something we do not yet know. Together the director, designers and cast construct the communicative rationality for the piece of theatre in terms of both text and conceptual ideas. In performance, the discursive rationality will then be redefined by actor and audience. Clearly, the very nature of theatre as not-real is an invitation to theatre to redefine its own discursive rationality, from production to production, even from performance to performance if necessary. This already operates in terms of physical language and pictorial language on stage. It is the operation of developing a concept and an appropriate style for the theatre piece.

The discursive rationality of theatre voice has remained aligned to that of the society in which it operates in spite of other discursive rationalities offered by the avant-garde theatre, in spite of very varied conceptual frameworks for productions and in spite of a modern body of dramatic texts. In the conceptualization process, it seems that the act of talking about the meaning which is being constructed, the fact that language is used to facilitate, drive and create the process of performance becomes of itself the *performance of the human voice* and thereby excludes the notion that the voice can be open to further interpretation. The voice is so present that it becomes invisible as a theatrical force.

17. The term 'intertextuality' is taken from Julia Kristeva's work. Kristeva is a literary critic, psychoanalyst and intellectual of international renown. Abrams, M. H., 1993, *A Glossary of Literary Terms*. 6th edition. Fort Worth: Harcourt Brace College Publishers. Intertextuality is also reflected in the notions of "pluralism" and "double coding". Charles Jencks, whose chief involvement
is in the field of architecture, explores these notions, in terms of art and architecture, in his publication *What is Post-Modernism?* London: Academy editions, 1986.

18. The avant-garde theatre practices referred to here are located in the work of the practitioners included in Innes, Christopher, 1993, *Avant Garde Theatre 1892 - 1992*. London: Routledge.

19. Theatre semiotics, as distinct from a literary semiotics, recognizes two texts: one "produced *in* the theatre and [one] composed *for* the theatre". These are, respectively, the performance text and the dramatic text. Literary text refers to the dramatic text; a text intended for performance. Elam, Keir, 1980, *The Semiotics of Theatre and Drama*. London: Methuen p 3.

20. Barthes, Roland, 1979, 'Barthes on Theatre. Two seminal essays on the semiotic approach to theatre.' trans. Peter W. Mathers in *Theatre Quarterly* IX (33) p 29.

21. Moriarty, Michael, 1991, *Roland Barthes*. Oxford: Polity Press p147.

The Intertextuality of Voice

The use of the voice in theatre can be reconsidered through reference to the notion of intertextuality[17] which challenges a monological view of theatre voice. Crucial to theatre voice and the theatre of theatre voice, is the fact that this construct entertains the unknown; that the performative understanding of theatre voice is expanded.

There are examples of a non-realist use of the voice in contemporary mainstream productions. These offer a use of the voice which indicates a degree of invention, of creation and mediation similar to that which is extended to all aspects of theatre in creating a work. Such a use of voice can be explored, along with the rich vocal practice of the avant-garde theatre,[18] and the innovation of the oral performer, to map a vocal terrain which is theatrical and open to new possibilities.

Dramatic Text versus Vocal Text

To propose the centrality of voice to performance as a paradigm for theatre voice practice appears, at first, to be neither challenging nor contentious. Such a proposal might even be regarded as stating the obvious. Theatre is an art form constructed on language, brought into being in the rehearsal process in an oral tradition (language, speech), participated in publicly (watching, listening, discussing), reviewed in print (text, language), recorded in print (text) or on digitized tape (image, speech, sound) and theorized in books and articles (text, language). Represented in this way, the dominance of the actor's and others' voices, the dominance of voice or sound as part of the theatre matrix is foregrounded. This is a construct of voice as language, and of language as representing text; a construct in which theatre voice simply comes to mean the speaking of the dramatic text. In the mainstream theatre tradition text/language, more often than not, implies a literary text.[19]

Text and language, and therefore voice, are mediums of theatre and, as such, become subtly taken for granted. The result of voice understood as language/literary text/the speaking of the dramatic text, is that the actor's voice is not heard as a theatrical expression of naturalism or of any other style of text. Viewed through the frame of Habermas' communicative rationality, voice as the speaking of text is, in effect, indifferent to changing literary forms and structures. The question of the centrality of voice to performance, is not a question about the *presence of voice* in the theatre but a question which asks: what kinds of presence can the voice have in the theatre?

The notion which conflates theatre voice with language and specifically with speaking the language of the literary text, is a single vision of the centrality of voice to performance. It obscures the multiple possibilities of the theatrical agency of the actor in respect of the voice and it ignores that aspect of theatre which Barthes calls "a genuinely polyphonic system of information, which is theatrical".[20] Borrowing from Barthes and Kristeva, the theatrical use of the voice proposes a view of theatre voice practice as a "polyphonic system" through which theatre voice evidences its own intertextuality. Barthes describes intertextuality as the recognition that all texts are intertexts "for there is no textuality without intertextuality, that is relationships with other texts".[21] Such other texts are present in more or less recognizable forms.

They are the texts of the surrounding cultures. Kristeva's notion of an "intertext" includes "those [texts] which will be written in the future".[22]

In the light of Barthes' argument, the voice can be called a text, one of the entities of theatre's "polyphonic system". An example of the intertextuality of theatre voice, is the recognition of the cultural vocal text of the actor being present in the theatrical vocal text of the character. Filmmaker Gaston Kabore refers to the "internal culture" which distinguishes individual filmmaker's films from each other. His elaboration of "internal culture" as "their sense of space and rhythm" which is both "personal and cultural" could be used to describe the individual vocal text.[23] The theatrical use of the voice which is proposed through the paradigm of the centrality of voice to performance is a use which consciously explores the vocal texts of performance.

This paradigm proposes a view of voice that is plural. If the idea of theatre as the medium remains central, then theatre voice practice becomes engaged in a much broader discourse, the discourse of theatre practice. For example, the postmodern[24] works of Robert Wilson in which "the audience is presented with pure visions and pictures, not with the interpretation of a text or story" excludes current theatre voice practice in its exclusion of text and interpretation.[25] However, if theatre voice is problematised in relation to theatre, then the notions of "pure visions" and "picture" become theatre voice notions and Birringer's description of the performances in Robert Wilson's spectacles as "pictorial lines drawn onto the surface, moved, and then frozen to be redrawn—and presented as positions or numbers within a visual and auditory configuration" points to a sonic choreography with possible vocal outcomes.[26]

It needs to be stated that the above example is not a claim for a new style of sonic representation for all forms of theatre. It is an illustration of the dialogic possibilities of all forms of theatre with theatre voice practice and, more importantly, it states the belief that theatre voice has a discursive place in the creative process of theatre.

Conclusion

In conclusion, at the heart of contemporary theatre voice is a debate about the articulation of the natural voice within theatre, and within the range of contemporary theatre forms. The natural voice interpreted, with reference to realist acting, as reflecting the vocal being of the actor fails to negotiate the basic creative function of the act of theatre which places a range of texts, voice included, in confrontation with each other. The dialogic possibilities of theatre voice are both present and possible in contemporary theatre voice in that the exploration and extension of the natural voice is the locus of the expressive possibilities of a range of theatrical forms, including, as yet, unknown vocal possibilities.

22. Abrams, M. H., 1993, *A Glossary of Literary Terms*. 6th edition. Fort Worth: Harcourt Brace College Publishers p 285.

23. Matshikiza, John, 1999, 'The world of African film' in *Mail & Guardian*, Vol 15, No 35.

24. Jencks, Charles, 1986, *What is Post-Modernism?* London: Academy editions, provides an overall view of postmodernism but for specific reference to theatre and postmodernism refer to Birringer, Johannes, 1993, *Theatre, Theory, Postmodernism*. Bloomington: Indiana University Press, who explores technological landscapes, the manipulation of the body, the re-writing of myth and history and presentations of consumerism as evidence of a postmodern theatre culture.

25. Birringer, Johannes, 1993, *Theatre, Theory, Postmodernism*. Bloomington: Indiana University Press p194.

26. Ibid p 224.

Vocal Clarity in the Outdoor Theatre

Kate Foy (stage name Kate Wilson) has been working in professional theatre for 30 years as actor and director with some of Australia's leading performance organisations, including Queensland Theatre Company, New England Theatre Company and the ABC; in the US with Kennedy Theatre in Honolulu. Ph.D. from University of Hawaii: doctoral dissertation researched developments in contemporary Australian theatre. Since 1987, Head of Department of Theatre and head of voice and speech program at the conservatory actor-training program, University of Southern Queensland, Toowoomba. Continues to work as a voice over artist and has supplied the voice for many corporate and educational videos.

Paul Meier, associate editor: Recent dialect coaching for feature films include Ang Lee's *Ride With The Devil*, while recent theatre productions include *The Glass Menagerie* at the Palace Theatre, London. He has appeared in films such as *Ride With The Devil, Stolen Women,* and *Cross of Fire*, while he has 'appeared' in over one hundred radio dramas for the BBC. Recently published articles include *King of Infinite Space: Tony Richardson's Hamlet,* and *With Utter Clarity: an Interview with Kenneth Branagh*. Paul founded IDEA (International Dialects of English Archive), on the web at http://www.ukans.edu/~idea.

Introduction

In voice coaching *The Lost Colony*, America's oldest and longest-running outdoor historical drama, in its 63rd season in Manteo on the Outer Banks of North Carolina, USA, in the summer of 2000, Paul Meier had the opportunity, in over sixty performances, to study the voice and speech of over fifty different actors, in a variety of atmospheric conditions. This article discusses some of his observations.

Kate Foy has been similarly engaged as actor, coach and scholar. In Toowoomba, southern Queensland, Australia and in a disused quarry, she took part in a production of a masked Greek drama in March 2000 as actor and vocal coach. In the northern summer of the same year, she had the opportunity to observe performance and test the acoustic in the ancient odeon at Paphos in Cyprus. Foy's remarks are based upon these experiences and upon her observation and coaching of previous masked performances indoors and outdoors. Her continuing working relationship with colleague, translator, and director Greg McCart has enabled her to observe, coach and experience first-hand as actor the conditions under which performance in the open air occurs, and the impact this has upon the voice. Both Meier and Foy's experience in the outdoors share some similarities. Mostly however there are differences: from time of year through size and configuration of the amphitheatre in which performances were held.

The cast of *The Lost Colony*, Paul Green's so called "symphonic drama", with over fifty speaking roles, brought seasoned veterans of the English stage together with experienced professionals from the American theatre, and young American college-age theatre majors just beginning their training. The cast of Euripides' *The Bacchae*, in a new translation by Greg McCart, consisted of final year actors-in-training from the University of Southern Queensland's acting conservatory school. Foy (herself an experienced professional actor) was cast as Dionysos.

The Lost Colony, opening in the relatively cool nights of the northern hemisphere's summer (June), with temperatures in the 50s F, and closing in mid-August with actors and audiences sometimes sweltering in the high 90s F, is a huge challenge to performers' voices. *The Bacchae* played a much shorter season—10 days—in the late afternoons in the still-warm southern hemisphere's autumn (March), where average temperatures were in the mid 70s F. Conditions were generally mild although there were to be some extreme weather changes during the season that also impacted upon voice use during performance.

The shows played in very different physical conditions. *The Lost Colony* was in an amphitheatre constructed on the shore of Roanoke Island, North Carolina, on the very site where the unlucky men, women and children of Sir Walter Raleigh's 1587 colony built their short-lived settlement. With the waters of Roanoke Sound at their back, the actors play on a sand-covered stage and a grassed apron to an audience of around 1600 in a steeply raked amphitheatre, prettily lined with ancient water oaks and live oaks, dripping with Spanish Moss. *The Bacchae*, on the other hand, played in the arid space of a disused ovaline basalt quarry on the edge of the Great Dividing Range 2215 feet above sea level. This site has been previously used for a performance of *Oidipous the King* in 1996. The playing space, the *orkestra*, was a 60-foot diameter sand circle enclosed on three sides by the 120 feet high striated cliff 'walls.' There were no trees anywhere in the auditorium.

The Lost Colony Stage Manteo, North Carolina, USA

Audience sat in tiered banks of seats on three sides (from 3-9 o'clock) in the typical configuration of a classical Greek amphitheatre.

For *The Lost Colony*, after nearly sixty seasons without microphones, the last three have seen 'sound reinforcement' introduced. Body mikes in 1998 were found to be impractical in the high humidity. Area mikes strategically placed in the grassy forestage and on the edge of the side stages replaced them in 1999 and 2000, with two speaker clusters placed high above the proscenium walls, one each side of the stage.[1] *The Bacchae* played without any acoustic enhancement.

Although a veteran voice and dialect coach, this was Meier's first coaching of an outdoor drama, and he reports deriving insights, from nightly observation of the show over three months, into voice and speech issues that are not quite so starkly illuminated under the kinder, gentler conditions of indoor drama. The observations that he shares in these pages are offered, not as empirically derived data, but anecdotally, "dear diary" fashion. Foy had worked daily with the company of *The Bacchae* for two years as voice teacher and performance coach. It was to be her first intensive work as a coach and performer in outdoor theatre—and in mask. For her, too, there would be confirmation through observation and personal experience of the demands upon the voice and response in performance to conditions prevailing in an outdoor setting. In most instances, these are much different—hardly surprisingly—to those experienced indoors. What follows are the observations of both coaches on two very different production experiences.

The Theatre Architecture

MEIER: The acoustic design of an outdoor amphitheatre is of paramount importance. From the first season in 1937, attended on August 18th by President Roosevelt himself, celebrating the birthday of Virginia Dare (first child of English parents born in the New World) the cast of *The Lost*

1. Brad Herring, CI Entertainment, Inc., the sound system designer has provided the following technical specifications: "We found that by placing the speakers on the proscenium wall we were able to minimize the number of cabinets needed for good overall coverage. We were also able to cover the entire audience area while minimizing feedback. We used the new X-Array concert speaker produced by Electro-Voice. These speakers were powered by the Electro Voice P2000 amplifiers (Bi-amped). 4 Xi1152 speakers successfully covered the audience area providing more than ample sound pressure for the audience. Ultimately the entire system runs through a DSP (Digital Signal Processor). This DSP controls compression, limiting, delay, and equalization for the entire system.

We utilized 31 band Ashley graphic EQ's to assist in minimizing wind and feedback noises. We were able to successfully eliminate all wind noises up to 15-20 knots. Likewise we were able to EQ many frequencies that gave us feedback from night to night. These EQ's were inserted at the subgroup inserts. This allowed us the flexibility to alter settings on a night by night basis as mandated by ever changing weather.

We found the microflex series from Shure Brothers offered us incredible range in area micing. We used a combination of foam and latex to protect the MX202's from sand and rain (as well as provide some acoustical aide from the wind noises.)

We covered the entire stage with 5 Mx202's placed in the grass along the downstage perimeter of the stage. Complimenting the Mx202's we scattered 5 Crown PZM-30D and 3 Crown PCC-160's along rooflines and stage lines to pick up alternative blocking positions.

Colony has played on a sand-covered stage with a grassy apron. This deprives them of the sound reflectivity that actors on wooden stages or in classical stone amphitheatres have enjoyed. Fortunately the prevailing breezes are favorable, blowing off the Roanoke Sound and carrying the actors' voices into the auditorium. However, when the breeze becomes a wind, the thousands of leaves on the huge old trees that ring the auditorium become so many little percussion instruments providing white noise at just the right pitch to compete successfully with the voiceless plosives and fricatives of the actors' words. There are no natural or constructed surfaces to contain the sound or reflect it back into the house, other than the wall far upstage. Hence, as one seasoned pro who had never played outdoors put it to me, "You speak and nothing comes back!" So actors in this space have very little natural feedback by which to judge their own vocal effectiveness and presence. This was definitely a challenge, resulting in an initial tendency to vocal strain, yet one that most actors in outdoor spaces learn to overcome.

FOY: In *The Bacchae* the cast enjoyed the support provided by the basalt quarry walls, which helped to 'bounce' and enclose voices, providing a natural acoustic bowl. However, the acoustic support provided by the stone features of the landscape was architecturally more typically Roman than Greek. Acoustic enhancement was surprisingly unintrusive—there was little if any discernible delay or echo of speech. There was also no annoying 'white noise' from trees—indeed some small scrubby grasses growing out of clay were the only vegetation in an area strewn with rockfalls. Actors entered the playing space either over a hill of earth and down a ramp that had been bulldozed into the space immediately behind the *orkestra*, or from either side of the *orkestra* itself—upstage 'left' and 'right'—via the traditional *parodos*. The dirt mound provided the support for the *skene* with its collapsible palace gates.[2] As Dionysos, I was required to call offstage i.e., behind the *skene* in the scene when the god, supposedly jailed by the young Pentheus, calls down the wrath of the gods to destroy the palace. I was positioned upstage of the dirt mound *skene*, and faced towards the backing cliffs, where I 'bounced' the lines off the cliff face and back into the auditorium. This required some adjustment to vocal delivery, pitching upwards in stepping, rising inflections and especially in the lengthening of vowels with an extra hard bite down or extension of continuants on consonant formation and release. My final entrance—in full glory as the god— was not (fortunately) *ex-machina* but on foot and at the top of the ramp leading down from the top of the *skene* into the *orkestra*. This position was some 80 feet back from the audience. Again, full breath support and a deliberate focus on firm articulation got me through this most challenging of speeches, about two minutes in length.

2. These were carved from polystyrene and treated to resemble the basalt in the area. Hidden guy-ropes enabled crew positioned behind the *skene* to collapse the structure on cue—as Dionysos creates an earthquake to blast the palace of Pentheus.

The Bacchae in the disused basalt quarry, near Toowoomba, Australia

The blocking of scenes and chorus work on the *orkestra* utilised the centre of the circle as the strong point and most probable site of the first actor in Greek drama.[3] The spokes of an imaginary wheel radiating from this central point proved to be excellent trajectories for other actors as they moved along the radii to and from the first actor at the centre of the axis. Movement and performance around the circumference was also used by actors and chorus.

The *orkestra* itself was created from coarse builder's sand raked each day into a relatively smooth playing surface. However, dust raised during the performance and under a hot afternoon sun, meant that actors needed water to work against the possibility of dehydration and irritation of the vocal tract. "Classical Greek" water bottles were conveniently stashed around the playing space and were available to the company when needed.

Atmospherics and the Voice

MEIER: In *The Lost Colony* when temperature and humidity are low,[4] and with a very light breeze carrying their voices *into* the house instead of *away* from it, with the leaves of the trees quiet, even untrained voices, with a little goodwill, can carry unaided to the 'cheap' seats some thirty or forty rows back. But if the wind (and it can blow mightily in coastal North Carolina) is unhelpful, the white noise from the rustling vegetation provides a most definite challenge, even if the wind direction is favorable. When it crosses the stage, or blows off the land, the wind is even more of a challenge. High humidity poses the biggest challenges though, blanketing the voices and dampening the high frequencies upon which consonant discrimination clearly depended.

The higher the humidity, the harder it is to understand the actors' words. The impression is, interestingly, not one of reduced volume, but rather of loss of distinctness. The sharp crack of [p, t and k], the high frequency voiceless 'noise' of 'f', 'th', 's' and 'sh'—these so necessary auditory signatures were clearly compromised by high humidity (often 90% or higher), while the vowels and the voiced plosives seemed to carry almost as well as in low humidity.

It was clearly confirmed for me on Roanoke Island that consonants rather than vowels carry almost all the burden of intelligibility; so on nights when the voices were indistinct, turning up the volume at the sound board often accomplished little except to amplify what was already compromised. "Louder mush is still mush", I found myself thinking over and over again.

FOY: To a large degree, the amphitheatre of the quarry provides protective space from wind currents and in March afternoons tend to be the stillest. For us, wind direction was from the north, i.e., blowing from stage right to left across the audience and from the land although the often quite strong prevailing winds in this part of the world are southeasterly and are blown inland from the sea. The northerly breeze blowing up from the valley below would make its presence felt from about 5.30pm each day and increase for the next half-hour or so. It was, however, relatively light and, at most, forced audience into jackets. It had little if any effect upon vocal audibility though all actors were aware of the change in air currents around them. One becomes surprisingly sensitive to these things when working outdoors. The season—Autumn, in March—is a time when the rainy season (Summer) is ending and the

3. I can attest to the potency of the 'sweet spot' in the centre of the playing space in the Odeon at Paphos, Cyprus. From this position, it feels and sounds to the speaker as though s/he is wearing headphones and getting immediate feedback. Little conscious effort is required to project and indeed, a conversational level is all that is needed to carry the voice to the back of the auditorium—a tiered sandstone edifice some 40 feet back from the centre. McCart's research into other ancient theatres in Greece supports this contention.

4. Humidity and temperature readings are taken nightly by the stage manager. I was able to correlate observed vocal results with these data.

5. The USA and Australia are quite different in climate, of course. Given the lack of water the further
you go inland and the desert-heart, humidity is
always lower away from the coast in Australia. In
colonial days, the governors had their summer
homes inland away from the coastal humidity of the
capital city and usually (as in Toowoomba) in the
mountain ranges. I think the same held true for India
and other 'hot' imperial spots. Much of America's
interior, east of the Rockies, is notoriously humid in
summer.

Actor in *The Bacchae* wearing a half-mask

6. Of significance in this regard is his contention
that the mask does not and never has supported the
vocal delivery of the actor (Greg McCart, unpublished paper *Explorations in Tragic Mask* 1994-2000
in possession of writer).

average monthly rainfall declines sharply. Toowoomba is also 80 miles from
the coast, and (typically for Australia) the atmosphere is thus relatively dry at
the best of times.[5] In March the afternoon mean humidity is 58%. Despite
this factor actors still needed to focus on timing and the muscularity and
nuance of consonant shaping. Given the fact that the lead actors were working in mask with its natural tendency to muffle the voice, the issue of clarity
of diction was even more critical for intelligibility.

Performances were held in the late afternoon (from 5pm) and were timed to
conclude just after sunset to catch the last of the daylight. The performance
lasted approximately 90 minutes. As the days shortened, we were aware more
than ever of the dying light, the patterns of shadows and the colour of the
setting sun striking the cliffs behind the performance space. Moonrise was an
additional component towards the end of the season, complementing the
cosmic aspects of the play's final moments. On one performance only, precip-
itation in the form of low cloud swirled in with the afternoon wind just after
sunset and during moonrise. Whilst this had the effect of dampening the
voices as noted by Paul above, it provided, along with the flickering light
from the fire-torches a marvelously atmospheric accompaniment to the final
minutes of the play. Such priceless 'effects' (when they happen) have a stun-
ning effect upon everyone involved—audience and actors.

The Mask and Physical 'Size'

FOY: The work in mask spearheaded at USQ by Greg McCart is in no way
intended as a replicative exercise i.e., to reproduce the conditions of ancient
Greek tragedy. Indeed such an exercise would be impossible. The thrust of his
work is to uncover the way classical Greek drama might have worked in performance then by working in similar conditions and for a contemporary
audience today. This experiential research can and does lead practitioners into
surprising discoveries.[6] The use of mask is germane to Greg's approach,
although barefaced work on classical texts (indoors and outdoors) has been
attempted. There is no doubt about the power of the mask in performance.
As a training aid—and it is in this domain that I am particularly interested—
I can attest to its potency in energising the actor.

As voice teachers we are most often concerned with barefaced acting.
Certainly this has been my experience. Until I came to *The Bacchae* I had
never before worked in mask as an actor although I had used the neutral
mask in training and had observed its use in the hands of colleagues.

Working in mask does not come easy to a western actor who is bred in the
modern tradition—itself fuelled by the demands of realistic texts and naturalistic acting styles. Work in mask however can provide the opportunity for
actors to develop vocal technique in a unique and stimulating way. This was
the experience I had as actor and coach on the production of *The Bacchae*.
Almost in spite of themselves, the actors' vocal technique improved through
the use of mask during the exercise, partly because it provides such a strong
'trigger' for the actor's transformative capabilities. With initial work before
a mirror, actors have the known face wiped clean of expression—removed
even. The body and the breath are energised almost, as it were, to make up
the shortfall of the primary signifier—facial expression. McCart's research
charts the response actors have to work in mask and notes the flow-through

effect of such work:

> The mask demands that the actor works at the limit of their vocal and physical energies and this experience is itself liberating. Actors thrust out their chests, open out their shoulders, lift their arms, clench or extend their fingers, place their legs apart and stride purposefully over the ground.

> The outcome is a demonstrative, gestural, athletic performance that removes focus on the actor's face associated with the interpretation of psychologies and forces the spectator to read the entire body and mask in motion, a reading that shifts the attention from psychology to narrative. We can speak of the actor 'dancing the text': a distanced, aesthetic performance where the conceptual, emotional and physical coalesce in gesture, movement and inclination of the mask.[7]

What results is an 'encouraged', physically engaged actor whose vocal expression grows to fill the mask that fills the space.

Full head masks made from paper maché were employed in previous productions of classical Greek drama. For *The Bacchae* half-masks made to a mould of the actors' faces were used. These enlarged the natural features of each actor: the nose, eyes and bone structure of the forehead, cheeks and nose. These half-masks were 'character-rich', i.e., they attempted, unlike the neutral mask, to express the essence of each character. The lower part of the face, including the lips, were painted and enlarged to extend the 'mask' effect whilst retaining mobility of the orofacial area.

This had the advantage not only of fitting snugly and of diminishing the resonance inside the mask cavity (a decided disadvantage of the full 'football-helmet' style head masks), but also of providing movement around the orofacial area and ears, critical to auditory feedback and the demands of full articulatory movement.

In mask, the full use of vocal register proved to be problematical. The light upper register, which is ideal for its ringing, carrying power in the outdoors, seems to be particularly problematical in full-head mask since it is muffled. The false acoustic feedback can be an additional problem especially in masks made from denser materials.[8] In half-mask where the mouth is clear, there is still some additional nasal resonance within the mask's nasal cavity. This also tends to dampen the tone of the upper register. Compensation through firmer diction i.e., care with timing and placement as well as the deliberate use of stepping rising inflections across the arc of long phrases were techniques adopted to overcome this problem. Of course the challenge is to marry this technique to spoken inflections that are believable and in the service of character and situation—not easy for a contemporary actor whatever the pedigree of the text.

Dialect and Intelligibility

MEIER: It was very interesting to work with an international cast, with a broad diversity in the level of training, on a dialect show. *The Lost Colony* story involves the Native Americans encountered by the colonists, the aristocratic leaders of the expedition and the lower social rank men and women

7. McCart, *Explorations in Tragic Mask* 1994-2000.

Oidipous in full mask

8. The half masks were made from strips of kitchen wipe, a light and porous fabric. Layers were bonded with kindergarten glue and finished with non-toxic paint. The earlier full-head masks had been made from a sturdier and denser papier-mache material. This created problems for the actor with loud audio feedback inside the structure. Despite the open-mouth of these masks, the actors had to work hard to project and over-compensate with their articulation of consonants.

who formed the majority of the colony. While the native American roles were originally written in a rather insulting kind of Tonto "me kill white man" pseudo-dialect, Drew Scott Harris, this year's director, was more sensitive to the speech of this group, and although non-Indians played the roles, the lines now included prepositions and conjunctions! The RP for the aristocrats versus the regional British dialects (mostly West Country) for the ordinary folk allowed some insight into factors governing intelligibility and carrying power of various dialects.

Interestingly, both the English actors in the company as well as those American actors assuming RP for their roles tended to be clearer in their speech and I had many nights to puzzle over this. I theorized that RP has a bias toward consonants over vowels and that the higher mean pitch of RP contrasted with GenAm were both factors more conducive to intelligibility under the conditions encountered in this theatre. But more than that, it was observed by both Paul Laprade, the musical director, and myself, that in the speech of some of the American actors, particularly those at the beginning of their training, the ictus seemed to fall just *after* the initiating consonant (or cluster of consonants) of the word, depriving the consonant of power, while in the RP speech the ictus *preceded* the initiating consonant. Thus we documented the tendency for the American actors to say, "p'-ART", while their English colleagues said, "'P-art". The aspiration and the strength of release of the 'p' (for example) are both stronger in the RP version as a result—the listener discriminates between 'part', 'tart' and 'cart', for example, more readily. As you might suppose, the better-trained actors, regardless of nationality, had learned that placing the ictus before the initiating consonant produces the greater clarity needed in the theatre, regardless of dialect used.

Actor in *The Bacchae* wearing full mask

I was able, too, to theorize about the relationship of intonation pattern to intelligibility. It will be readily acknowledged that a rising inflection, say on the items in a list, will mitigate favorably against a too precipitous decay in amplitude. In that speakers are generally perceived as louder when speaking at higher pitches, when a falling inflection is employed (on a list item, or at the end of a parenthetical phrase) there is an inherent danger of losing final consonants with a falling inflection. So in a dialect, like RP versus GenAm, in which rising inflections are favored (at least in my experience), it may be inferred that the outdoor drama may naturally favor some dialects over others for inherent carrying power. During my many hours at the back of the house during the run of the show I formulated one other observation that has its roots in dialect though has a lesson for all actors regardless of dialect. It is a very preliminary theory and one that I hope other scholars will comment on. I observed that the British rhythm of speech calls for delaying strong stresses until *late* in the phrase, in contrast to American rhythm, which strikes me as being typically the reverse. One can observe this phenomenon in single words as well as at the level of the whole phrase. The British say *magaZINE*, *cigaRETTE*, *aluMINium*, *teleVISion*, whereas the Americans say *MAGazine*, *CIGarette*, *alUMinum*, *TELevision*, etc. I have come to think of these rhythmic contrasts between American and British speech as trochaic versus iambic, dactylic versus anapestic, and that they correlate at the macro-rhythmic level as well as the micro. These rhythmic differences have implications for mean pitch, and hence for vocal carrying power. In particular, at the ends of words and phrases, traditionally the actor's problem zone, the tendency of the rising inflection, or the delay of strong stresses until late, may favorably affect clarity of speech in difficult acoustic environments. I look forward to other scholars commenting on these observations. First, have others noticed these intonational and rhythmic differences between American and British speech? For example:

American: "I REALLY DON'T KNOW why you keep saying these things."
English: "I really don't know why you keep SAYING THESE THINGS."

Paul Laprade and I had long conversations nightly at the back of the house about these issues. His choral style demanded very bright vowels from the singers in the knowledge that these vowels carried better and had a more dynamic formant profile. He worked long and hard to achieve 'lonesome' and 'home' using a rounded front vowel in the vicinity of [oe], acoustically brighter than the back vowel [o] of everyday speech. This vowel worked for the singers, and seemed to me to favor the speaking actors too. Professor Laprade puts it like this:

> Brighter vowels, and, specifically, more 'forward' vowels such as 'oo' and 'ee' enhances head resonance in the sustained vocalic art that is song. Such resonances favor high overtones that—in the Lost Colony theatre—were more effective than pure 'bel canto' vowels in projecting choral sound. This use of higher overtones also augmented consonantal intelligibility, but might also have in fact increased the *perceived* volume of vocal sound (called "sones") by placing a greater number of frequencies in physiologically favorable formant ranges. (see Arthur H. Benade, *Fundamentals of Musical Acoustics*. New York: Oxford University Press, 1976, pp. 231-236.)

Mulling all this over, and cross-referencing this with my experience with overtone chanting, both Tuvan and Buddhist, (and in late summer seeing some acoustic analysis of this at the VASTA conference), I came to believe very strongly that we voice and speech teachers would do well to more strongly emphasize vowel shaping which favors the higher formants, regardless of fundamental pitch. This also involves voice placement of course and, for me, confirms the wisdom of invoking the brightness of 'head voice' even while finding the voice impulse (and its breath support) in the solar plexus or the gut. And regardless of where in his or her range the actor's voice is pitched, a good dose of head resonance works wonders.

FOY: In our production no problems would be encountered with variations between standard Australian and 'other' regional dialects. Without getting too involved in the issue of standard speech—itself a contentious political issue in postcolonial, multicultural Australia— all characters in *The Bacchae* utilised what is

The Lost Colony

9. Theatre-standard Australian is not 'cod-RP' i.e., trying to sound English as a measure of status, nor does it contain elements of broad Australian, with its flat and drawled nasal vowels. It's somewhere 'in-between', is indisputably Australian, but with as many minute variations as there are speakers of this 'standard'. As I understand it, it is probably the equivalent of Barton's Theatre Standard American or Skinner's 'Elevated' speech.

called, for want of a better name, 'Australian theatre-standard' speech, a dialect immediately understood in the Australian theatre as representing the widest possible 'standard' of acceptable speech for classical roles.[9] How does a Greek from the 5th C BC sound anyway? Whilst there were undoubtedly character differences between the royal family and the foreigners, no attempt was made to utilise recognisably different regional dialects.

Just as Paul notes the necessity for attention to consonantal and vowel formation in creating clarity, so too I found articulatory precision and vocal placement had to be constantly monitored. Working outdoors and in mask meant that actors needed to be careful even with the normally kind-to-diction vocalised stop plosives and continuants. A general leaning towards slower and more emphatic speech was required. This was not overdone however… an awareness of the necessity for good timing (as Cicely Berry reminds us) was often all that was needed to check the tendency of most actors to fall back on the indoor playing disposition towards a comparatively faster, 'looser' style of delivery—i.e., a style with less emphasis on consonant placement or of letting sounds 'hang in the air' a little longer than normal. The rule of thumb is, of course, the greater the distance to be covered, the slower the base tempo and consequently, the more breath that is needed. This proved easier for the actor in those more solemn sections of the text when a natural gravitas is instinctively manifest in this kind of delivery.

Interestingly, Australian speech also leans towards the British tendency to stress words later in the sentence as opposed to earlier, as noted by Paul above.

Writing Style and Acting Style

MEIER: Paul Green called *The Lost Colony* (his most successful outdoor work), a "symphonic drama", referring not to the use of an orchestra (which the show never had), but, at least in part, to the epic scale of the enterprise. He favored heightened language (some unkindly call it purple) that evokes a rather splendid tone on the part of the actors, often liturgical in its intonation, and nudges them toward the sustained tones of chanting and singing. Those scenes and speeches that are poetic in tone and stimulate the actors' most even amplitude contours are the ones that were the most intelligible. The prayers, the pieces of oratory, the text with the most heightened language—these parts carried well, whether spoken by veteran or neophyte. The less heightened roles, plainer in their words—these parts more easily admitted the weakly attacked and weakly finished phrases of our contemporary speech, and thus required the greater skill and training to avoid the pitfalls. The experienced, well-trained actors in such roles were still effectively and intelligibly 'ordinary' in their style, but the neophytes had some lingering difficulty with this kind of writing. Another way of thinking about this is to contrast those scenes in which the vocal focus is broad (speeches to crowds or to the deity—recipients at a distance) with those with a narrowed focus (speeches to another individual who perhaps is blocked at only arm's length (recipients close by). In the first kind of speech it is entirely natural that a 'calling' voice should be used, instinctively pitched higher, and thus carrying further. It is always more difficult to be both believable and intelligible in the second kind of scene. After all, love scenes rarely call for roaring in your lover's face! And the audience's ears, after hearing the first kind of voice for a spell, longs for the quieter, more body-focused tones of the second. But this is much harder to achieve and calls for considerable skill.

In *The Lost Colony* theatre, as in most larger, outdoor spaces, for the voices to reach the audience, only the most powerful and skilled actors can play for long in profile or facing upstage—too much is lost, unless the show is severely over-amplified. With the lack of any hard surfaces (walls, ceiling, floor) to contain and reflect the sound to the audience's ears, unless the actors' mouths point more or less toward the audience, their voices are lost to the endless sky and out into the woods and fields. Maintaining the necessary sense of intimacy and contact with a single scene partner, while at the same time obeying the physics of the space, requires a clever technique, one which does not come naturally to young actors bred up in the intimacy of contemporary theatre and film. It required the following old saws:

- Face your partner when he or she is speaking, but not necessarily when you are speaking.
- Make eye contact briefly and during pauses, finding natural reasons for turning out toward the audience as much as possible.
- "Find" your thoughts out front and above the audience.
- Don't speak into the sand or grass—it absorbs all your voice.
- Keep the focus high. We understand you better if we can see the light in your eyes.
- Drop the jaw on the open vowels and find as much difference in lip rounding as possible. If we can see you speaking, we hear you better.

If these time-honored but somewhat neglected precepts were followed, then the intimate voice of indoor, two-person scenes could be used effectively, though phrases still required strong beginnings and endings. Consonant clusters were especially important. In phrases like 'dark night', 'foot fall', 'hope not' it became imperative in this theatre to release the final plosive of the first word in such phrases—one could not afford to delete precious auditory cues and force the audience to infer meaning from context alone.

FOY: Paul refers to the 'heightened language' that appears in *The Lost Colony*. Complex syntax is another issue often encountered when dealing with such texts—and you can expect to find this in most classical Greek tragedies. Handling these linguistic challenges can be difficult for actors at the best of times, especially young, contemporary ones. Add mask and the open air to the list, and the breath control needed for those long, often portentous phrases assumes even greater importance than in the indoor theatre. In the productions I have observed, coached and appeared in, emendations during the rehearsal period were possible and indeed were willingly made by the translator to assist the speaking. When a breath-busting, complex compound sentence came up, adjustments were made for speaking comfort without sacrificing meaning. I should add that Greg had, during the actual translation phase of *The Bacchae*, drawn upon experience gained in earlier outdoors performance. He was writing *for the voice and the ear* and not the eye. As a voice teacher and, in the case of *The Bacchae*, an actor, I was extremely grateful for his user-friendly text. As translator-director, he came quickly to note the value-added benefit of longer-vowelled monosyllabic words with their 'natural' carrying power. As translator he was also keen to preserve the original sound of the ancient Greek language in the contemporary English translation; thus a cluster of harsh-sounding plosives in a Greek phrase or word would be replicated in its English translation.

Partly to appeal to contemporary audiences, McCart's translations are often marked by more colloquial or prosaic expression especially in the speech of lower-status characters or during more earth-bound scenes and moments of banter between characters—the 'ordinary' speech referred to by Paul above. Whilst this makes for easier listening on the part of the audience, it can prove surprisingly difficult for actors who are approaching the issue of spoken style in a piece that switches scene by scene—even within a scene such as one finds when working on some Shakespearean text. As we both note, passages of lyric and/or emotional intensity seem to call forth an instinctive size or style of speaking from the actor of all levels of ability. As noted, pitch levels also tend to rise assisting the voice's carrying power and speech clarity. This can and usually does work well in mask and in the outdoors. When switching to a more colloquial tack, actors tended to be caught between two stools— if they speak it with the inflections of naturalistic speech, it won't carry. If they force it into the sounds and demeanour of heightened language, it sounds fake. Some compromise was needed. This most often took the form of an intensification of a 'natural' speech inflection—i.e., the tempo-rhythm was exaggerated somewhat to mimic the size of the original intention.

The 'old saws' Paul refers to above held just as true for the cast of *The Bacchae*. Given they were also masked, actors needed to be particularly aware of their scene partner and their changing physical disposition towards the audience. Peripheral sight is generally lost in mask. Adjustments need to be made e.g., full body turns to indicate a glance towards a scene partner. With facial expression gone and in such a large space, the body and voice needed to engage more fully to accommodate gesture. Most actors looked at their scene partners during the partner's speech but played the 'house' or opened out physically along the 'spokes' from the centre point or with an often-curved trajectory as they moved about the *orkestra*. Such movement and gestural patterns assisted the audience's focus and understanding.

As noted above, the actor's voice and body enlarge to 'fill' the mask. In all masked productions worked on, this enlargement process has involved the development of a series of stylised gestural patterns to complement text and character. The nature of this physical expression fed into and reinforced the spoken interpretation of text. It needs hardly be said that the performance style was energetic and required a great deal of stamina from the actors particularly when moving vigorously across loose sand.

The Sound Engineer and Equalization
MEIER: In an indoor drama, once the sound designer has "EQ'd" the mix, then it is rarely necessary to tamper with the ratios of highs, mid-range and low frequencies which have been set. Not so in theatres subject to fluctuating temperatures and humidity readings. What gives a natural sounding ratio of frequencies one night seems to favor only the lows another, and vice versa. Observing these phenomena night after night, I started advocating a "weather-sensitive" approach from the actors—one in which extra bite and crispness in consonant formation was the rule on humid nights (just the nights when extra energy would be in short supply!)

On some nights with cool temperatures and low humidity, we turned off the amplification entirely and reveled in the unmediated human voice just as the audiences in Kate's production did. But North Carolina's unhelpful weather, the poor acoustic design of the theatre, and the inexperience of many of the younger actors, forced a return to amplification when conditions worsened. And so the sound engineer and the actors "chased" each other all season to a degree noticeable to the engineer and me, but particularly to him. As he raised the volume, so the actors, hearing their own voices more loudly from the speakers, would, perhaps unconsciously, relax their efforts, requiring the engineer to raise the volume that much more, resulting in a more and more amplified sound. When I encouraged the actors to ignore the mikes and play as if they had been turned off, they raised their volume and the engineer could pull back the faders. This merry dance was somewhat true for EQing too, but driven by fluctuating humidity. So the vocal work would go in cycles and never achieved stasis, as is the usual case in indoor spaces where temperature and humidity are regulated. The show was wonderful, however, and as near-capacity houses over its sixty-three seasons attest, has an amazing power to enthrall audiences. But as voice coach I was keenly aware of these cycles.

Disappearing Consonants

MEIER: Among the most challenging parts of the text were those rich in the 'weaker' consonants—the nasals and liquids. If a phrase ended in a nasal, then it became an entirely obligatory practice to finish with a 'shadow vowel': "Christmas cam-uh." "men sang-uh", "must win-uh". Without it, all was silence. Perhaps *shadow vowel* implies too declamatory a result. Phonetically the desired effect merely involves releasing the closure of the final consonants before all phonation has ceased, which succeeds in identifying the consonant and rendering it audible.

What I had long suspected finally became clear—that 'f' and 'th' are an endangered species! They have mutated from fortis fricatives into lenis quasi-plosives in the dialect of today's younger actors, so "three free things" and all similar phrases were liable to be ineffective and indistinct. We worked hard to restore the lost fortis power of those two consonants when they occurred initially in the word. Again, it was apparent to that the young American actor is inclined to place the ictus just before the vowel onset—thus partially robbing the consonant of its ability to distinguish between minimal pairs. (This practice favors the *emotion and feeling* that the vowel carries, so beloved by younger actors, but at what a cost to the *intellectual* content of the phrase!) Young British actors exhibit this far less in my experience and I look forward to learning whether other international coaches will corroborate this.

FOY: As far as weaker terminal nasals and liquids and unvocalised fricatives are concerned, in *The Bacchae* these needed almost the shadow vowel Paul refers to in order to assist in their carrying power (seem-a; rang-a; peril-a). The unvocalised fricatives could also be treated in this way (Pentheus-a; Dionysos-a). Monosyllabic words and long vowel sounds are relatively easy on the actor with their potential carrying power. However, as Paul notes, they do need strong support from firm consonants—the sounds often rushed over or lost with the increased tempo typical of contemporary colloquial speech. We need to remember that emotive carrying power in the vowels with no intellectual shaping also results in what Paul calls 'mush' (with or without acoustic enhancement).

Summary

MEIER: The outdoor amphitheatre is a hugely effective laboratory, where the inherently difficult conditions serve to test vocal technique with unparalled rigour. Just as a metal is 'proved' in a high temperature lab, so the actor's voice and speech are 'proved' when the sky is your ceiling. Those actors who push and yell quickly become sadder but wiser. They learn to *release* instead of *push*, to conserve the energy it takes to produce volume, and to favor consonant clarity and evenness of amplitude contours as more productive and more economical vocal tactics.

FOY: Whilst most actors in *The Bacchae* had little difficulty eventually in 'filling the space' without pushing, all were in the final stages of their training, and none would have attempted to play without the 20-30 min. physical and vocal warm-up that preceded each performance. My observation of this particular company of actors would suggest that they grew as performers in varying and various ways through the project. As a teacher and vocal coach, I am impressed by the residual effect that work in the outdoors and work in mask have upon the actor. In the companies I observed and/or coached, it was clear that vocal technique had improved: voices and bodies were stronger and more flexible, diction was identifiably better and projection on return to the indoor theatre seemed easy by comparison. Of course, as Paul notes, the outdoor experience plays a huge role in this. However I have no doubt that the addition of the mask with its tendency to project the actor into a stronger commitment physically and vocally also played a big role in the vocal development of these actors in training.

The halls of voice and speech research and practices echo with names like
Elsie Fogerty and Daniel Jones. But few may recall the life and work of one
Sir Richard Paget. An Oxford trained chemist who went on to practice law,
Paget had a strong side interest in linguistics. His research on acoustics and
the nature of human speech, studies of synesthesia, or sound symbolism, his
persistent belief that language evolved from gesture and his work with the
education of the deaf, earned him the reputation of being, among other
things, a highly original and imaginative linguist in the early Twentieth
Century. In 1930, Paget published a book titled, *Human Speech*. His aim was
to "give, in simple language, an account of some personal observations and
experiments on the phenomenon of human speech, and some conclusions
and suggestions as to its probable origin and future development." One such
experiment was to measure the carrying power of vowels and consonants,
outside, at varying distances. Enlisting the help of his daughter to test out the
carrying power of vowels and his secretary to test out the carrying power of
consonants, Paget took to the outdoors, pacing out distances in yards, using
his own stride as the approximate measure. He then spoke a series of sounds
at various increments while his assistant made note of intelligibility as she
perceived it. The Paget team was able to make some generalizations about the
carrying power of speech sounds. They found that /f/, for example, was
extremely clear at forty five yards but became unrecognizable at seventy seven
yards.

Paget's only acoustic measuring instrument was the human ear. We know
today that the ear is not the best measuring instrument of sound. But Paget's
curiosity and inventiveness remain compelling. The experiment reprinted
below [modified only to express the sounds in IPA symbols], from Paget's
book *Human Speech*, (Routledge and Keegan Paul, London: 1930 [note: phonetic notation modified for this article. -ed.]) is at once endearing, for its
homespun resourcefulness, and intriguing for its reliance
on the subjective, human experience of sound:

"In fairly good out-of-door conditions, with a moderate breeze and listening
downwind, the following comparative ranges were obtained—the consonants
being articulated by myself and identified by Miss G. M. Barker [Paget's sec-
retary]: —

/f/ maximum range at which identification was certain, about 45 yards;
becoming unrecognizable at 77 yards—not distinguishable from /θ/ (thigh).

/θ/ maximum range for certain identification about 79 yards; becoming
unrecognizable at 96 yards—not distinguishable from /s/.

/s/ maximum for certain identification about 123 yards; becoming unrecognizable at 197 yards.

/ʃ/ (shy) maximum for certain identification 320 yards; becoming uncertain at
326 yards. This is much the most penetrating of unvoiced sounds; it has more
than twice the range of the best-carrying unvoiced [whispered] vowel sound.

/v/ was certain at about 75 yards, uncertain at 153 yards—about twice the range of /f/.

/ð/ was certain at about 220 yards, uncertain at about 400; say four times the range of /θ/.

/z/ was certain at about 500 yards, uncertain at 645 yards—say three times the range of /s/.

/ʒ/ was certain at about 470 yards, uncertain at 700 yards—say twice the range of /ʃ/.

VSR decided to try a similar experiment. Professor Bob Davis of University of Louisiana was good enough to volunteer his MFA students for an informal study using the following steps:

Make the following sounds as vigorously as possible, in an open outdoor space, like a park. It may be easiest to measure distances using your own stride. Pace out 45 yards upwind of your listening partner and then make each sound. Increase distance at twenty-yard increments in order to determine when each consonant becomes ambiguous or inaudible. Use written lists which change the order in which you make the sounds at each new increment. Have the partner make note of the perceived sounds at each increment. Also, have the partner signal when the given sound becomes inaudible. Also make note of any general sound interference or limiting weather conditions. When you are finished change roles with your partner. Have your partner make new sound lists for each increment and repeat the steps above. If you can have your whole class participate in the experiment, so much the better. Return the data to me noting the number of yards at which each sound lost definition and the number of yards at which each sound became inaudible. There may be some sounds which never lose definition, owing to the limitations of the size of the space.

Consonants tested: f, θ, s, ʃ, v, ð, z, ʒ

Here are some of the resulting data Davis sent back:

Five out of six students positively identified /f/ at 45 yards. These same students lost recognition of /f/ at varying points, between 65 and 85 yards. This is in line with Paget's study, in which /f/ became unrecognizable at about 77 yards.

/s/ was identifiable to one student at 125 yards, the other five lost recognition of /s/ at varying points between 45 and 105 yards. Again, similar to Paget's findings. Interestingly, /s/ was mistaken for /z/ by two students at 45 yards, but was recognizable at 65 yards, fading out again at, or after, 105 yards.

/ʃ/ was recognizable to five out of six students at all distances. This supports Paget's characterization of /ʃ/ as the "most penetrating of unvoiced sounds."

Three out of six students recognized /v/ at 45 yards. None of them recognized it at 65 yards or more. Here, Davis's results differ from Paget's, who found /v/ to be twice as powerful as /f/.

Four out of six students recognized /z/ at 105 yards. The two other students

Table 1.   **Professor Davis' Replication of Paget's Experiment**

Consonant spoken	Perception of the sound at specific distances				
	45 yards	**65 yards**	**85 yards**	**105 yards**	**125 yards +**
/f/	f	ʃ	s	couldn't hear	couldn't hear
	f	s	couldn't hear	ʃ	couldn't hear
	f	couldn't hear	couldn't hear	couldn't hear	didn't do
	f	f	couldn't hear	couldn't hear	didn't do
	θ	f	couldn't hear	couldn't hear	didn't do
	f	f	couldn't hear	couldn't hear	didn't do
/θ/	f	s	θ	s	couldn't hear
	s	θ	s	couldn't hear	couldn't hear
	not sure	s	f	f	couldn't hear
	not sure	s	f	couldn't hear	didn't do
	θ	couldn't hear	not sure	not sure	didn't do
	θ	θ	couldn't hear	couldn't hear	didn't do
/s/	s	s	s	s	f
	z	s	s	ʒ	z
	z	s	s	s	couldn't hear
	s.	s	s	s	didn't do
	s	s	s	s	didn't do
	s	s	s	s	didn't do
/ʃ/	ʃ	ʃ	ʃ	ʃ	ʃ
	ʃ	ʃ	ʃ	ʃ	ʃ
	ʃ	ʃ	ʒ	ʒ	ʃ
	ʃ	ʃ	ʃ	ʃ	didn't do
	ʃ	ʃ	ʃ		didn't do
	ʃ	ʃ	ʃ		didn't do
/v/	v	couldn't hear	f	couldn't hear	couldn't hear
	couldn't hear	couldn't hear	couldn't hear	couldn't hear	couldn't hear
	f	couldn't hear	couldn't hear	couldn't hear	couldn't hear
	not sure	couldn't hear	couldn't hear	couldn't hear	didn't do
	v	couldn't hear	couldn't hear	couldn't hear	didn't do
	v	not sure	not sure	couldn't hear	didn't do
/ð/	ð	θ	ð	z	couldn't hear
	not sure	couldn't hear	couldn't hear	couldn't hear	couldn't hear
	θ	θ	f	couldn't hear	couldn't hear
	ð	ð	not sure	couldn't hear	didn't do
	ð	m	θ	couldn't hear	didn't do
	not sure	not sure	couldn't hear	couldn't hear	didn't do
/z/	z	z	z	z	s
	s	z	z	z	couldn't hear
	s	z	z	z	z
	z	z	z	couldn't hear	didn't do
	z	z	z	couldn't hear	didn't do
	z	z	z	couldn't hear	didn't do
/ʒ/	ʒ	ʒ	ʒ	ʒ	couldn't hear
	ʒ	ʒ	not sure	z	couldn't hear
	ʒ	ʒ	not sure	ʒ	z
	ʒ	ʒ	ʒ	ʃ	didn't do
	ʒ	ʒ	ʒ	couldn't hear	didn't do
	ʒ	ʒ	ʒ	ʒ	didn't do

Key
not sure—audible, but ambiguous
couldn't hear—inaudible
didn't do—no data

Donald Cooper holds a doctorate in linguistics (Ph.D. 1971) from Harvard University. Thereafter he studied speech pathology and speech science at the University of Iowa, and worked for several years with Ingo Titze's research group in voice science at the University of Iowa, specializing in voice physiology. In 1984, he moved to Los Angeles to found the Laboratory for Laryngeal Physiology in the Department of Otolaryngology at the medical school of the University of Southern California. From 1997 to 2000 he taught in the Department of Communication Sciences and Disorders and in the Program in Linguistics of the University of South Carolina.

thought they heard /s/, not /z/, at 45 yards. Again, Davis's results differ greatly from Paget, who found /z/ uncertain at 645 yards.

/ʒ/ lost clarity between 65 and 105 yards. Again, at great variance with Paget, who found /ʒ/ uncertain at 700 yards.

After comparing Davis's findings with those of Paget, we consulted Dr. Donald Cooper for a scientific perspective:

Comments on Performers Audibility and Intelligibility by *Donald Cooper*
It is refreshing to look back at the work of Paget (1930) many years after first reading it, and realize that in a number of respects he anticipated modern insights. However, some aspects of his work were quickly passed by the advance of electro-acoustics; e.g. the Paget-Benton vowel theory based on two resonances was soon rendered obsolete by the discovery of Thienhaus (1934) that all vowels possess more than two vowel formants.

Davis's replication of Paget's study on speech perception at a distance raises many intriguing questions. Foy and Meier's discursive treatment suggests analysis of a number of factors, but here it is possible only to note some fundamental factors. A first point concerns the nature of the speech stimulus. We need to be careful in specifying the amplitude scale of the spectrum, and should not forget that many spectral representations boost the apparent amplitude of high frequencies, at which the level of spectral components in speech declines. Even before Paget, Sacia and Beck (1926) had published still useful information on the relative powers of the full range of English speech sounds, which is summarized in the classic treatise on speech and hearing (1929, 1953) of the Bell Labs physicist Harvey Fletcher. Although they could be modernized, these results explain much in the observations of both sets of observers, especially as regards consonant intelligibility [see Table 2, below]. Acoustic characteristics of English speech sounds are well reviewed in the recent texts of J.M. Pickett (1999; emphasizing linguistic and perceptual factors) and J.P. Olive, A. Greenwood, and J. Coleman (1993; emphasizing contextual factors).

Handbooks of electronics describe the complex effects of loudspeakers on sounds, and we must consider the human lips as a loudspeaker, as Fant (1960) does. J. L. Flanagan (1960, 1972) has studied the distribution of sound pressure around the speaker's head in relation to the distance and angle of the listener. The German psychologist Carl Stumpf (1926) exemplified the application of the confusion matrix to specify what speech sounds others were confused with under specific auditory conditions, an approach used in much modern research on speech perception, from Miller and Nicely (1955) to now.

Modern studies on architectural acoustics have contributed to the analysis of the effects of environment on speech transmission. Computer simulations make it possible to specify what would be the sound heard by listeners at any point in a given space. Additional factors are also relevant as noted by Foy and Meier: for instance, at a given temperature and humidity, the acoustic absorption of sound in air does increase with frequency (Wood, 1940; Knudsen and Harris, 1978), probably contributing to the observed deleterious effect on intelligibility. The musically sophisticated Stockholm engineer Sten Ternstrom has analyzed the effects of acoustic environment on the interaction between chorus and director. Both the limited study by Davis and his students, and the more anecdotal treatment by Foy and Meier suggest important and productive perspectives for the understanding of how these different factors interact.

References from Dr. Cooper

Fant, G. 1960. *The Acoustical Theory of Speech Production.* Gravenhage/The Hague: Mouton and Co.

Flanagan, J.L. 1960. Analog measurements of sound radiation from the mouth. *J. Acoust. Soc. Am.* 32:1613-1620.

Flanagan, J.L. 1972. *Speech Analysis Synthesis and Perception.* New York, Berlin, Heidelberg: Springer-Verlag.

Fletcher, H. 1929. *Speech and Hearing.* New York: D. van Nostrand Inc.

Fletcher, H. 1953. *Speech and Hearing in Communication.* Princeton, N.J.: D. van Nostrand Inc.

Knudsen, V.; Harris, C. M. 1978. *Acoustical Designing in Architecture.* Second edition: American Institute of Physics.

Miller, G.A.; Nicely, P.E. 1955. An Analysis of Perceptual Confusion Among Some English Consonants. *J. Acoust. Soc. Am.* 27(2):338-352.

Olive, J.P.; Greenwood, A.; Coleman, J. 1993. *Acoustics of American English Speech.* New York: Springer-Verlag.

Paget, R. 1930. *Human Speech.* London: Routledge and Kegan Paul Ltd.

Pickett, J.M. 1999. *The Acoustics of Speech Communication.* Boston: Allyn and Bacon.

Sacia, C.F.; Beck, C.J. 1926. The power of fundamental speech sounds. *Bell System Technical Journal* 5:393-403.

Stumpf, C. 1926. *Die Sprachlaute.* Berlin: Springer.

Thienhaus, E. 1934. Neuere Versuche zur Klangfarbe und Lautstaerke von Vokalen. *Zeitschrift fuer technische Physik* 15, 637.

Wood, A. 1940. *Acoustics.* London and Glasgow: Blackie and Son Ltd.

ɔ	680
ɑ	600
ʌ	510
æ	490
o	470
ʊ	460
e	370
ɛ	350
u	310
ɪ	260
i	220
r (ɹ)	210
l	100
ʃ	80
ŋ	73
m	52
tʃ	42
n	36
dʒ	23
ʒ	20
z	17
s	16
t	15
g	15
k	13
v	12
ð	11
b	7
d	7
p	6
f	5
θ	1

Table 2: *Average Powers of Speech Sounds, Relative to that of the Weakest.* [Thus, /ɔ/ would be 680 times stronger than /θ/.] For absolute values /θ/ is given as 0.5 microwatts. From Table 7A, Chapter Four, Fletcher, Harvey. *Speech and Hearing in Communication,* Princeton: 1953. Our thanks to Dr. Donald Cooper for referring us to this chart.

Conclusions

Useful information regarding the relative powers of speech sounds, readily available in the Linguistics literature, may seem beyond the purview of the Voice and Speech specialist. But comparing our intuitions and experiential knowledge with the measurements of scientists, may greatly enrich our work. It is one thing to sense that a half-open back rounded vowel has greater carrying power than a voiceless dental fricative and another thing to prove it. With the aid of Harvey Fletcher's chart of the relative powers of speech sounds (Table 2, above) we are able to weigh some of the observations made by Paget, Davis and Meier. The numbers in Fletcher's chart represent the ratio between the weakest sound, /θ/ which ranks 1, and the most powerful sound, /ɔ/, which ranks 680. According to H. L. Barney and H. K. Dunn in, *Manual of Phonetics,* the data in Fletcher's chart "apply to American English

Sources:

Martell, Edward, et al. *Who Was Who Among English And European Authors 1931-1949*. Detroit: Gale Research Company, 1978.

Fletcher, Harvey. *Speech and Hearing in Communication*. Princeton, N.J.: D. van Norstrand, 1953.

Kaiser, Louise. *Manual of Phonetics*. Amsterdam: North-Holland Publishing Company, 1957.

as spoken conversationally by sixteen individuals. The relative powers of the sounds vary widely among speakers, and with different stress for a single speaker. It is probable that different average values would be found in different languages."

Fletcher's objective data, when compared with Meier's (previous article) and Paget's personal observations, offers a caveat to the voice and speech coach. Our ears may deceive us. Furthermore, we may make generalizations about speech sounds based on too little evidence, which, in the long run, won't serve us. To illustrate this point, take Fletcher's ratio averages of the sounds /ʃ/ and /ʒ/ and compare them with Paget's data. Paget found /ʒ/ to be about twice as powerful as /ʃ/. Fletcher, on the other hand, finds /ʃ/ significantly more powerful than /ʒ/.

Similarly, the intuitions and observations expressed by Meier, are at variance with Fletcher's measurements. Meier terms the nasals /m/, /ŋ/ and /n/, and the liquids, /l/ and /r/ "weaker consonants," but, Fletcher ranks them as powerful. Also, Meier's fear that /f/ and /θ/ are "endangered species" is mitigated by Fletcher, who identifies them as the two weakest consonants, innately vulnerable to problems of intelligibility and carrying power.

But, when all is said and done, it is problematic to compare Fletcher's "hard data," gleaned from the conversation of "average speakers," to Meier's anecdotal observations of actors, or, to the sounds which Paget, a speech enthusiast, uttered in his experiments. Hard data is militated against by the ethereal and individual nature of speech, and, in this case, by the fact that most varieties of public speaking require greater articulatory energy than that usually heard in conversation. If the above inquiry is of any use, it is as a rough guideline of the relative strengths and weaknesses of spoken sounds. The applications to voice and speech practice being obvious.
Louis Colaianni

Column by *Jacqueline Martin*

Heightened Text, Verse and Scansion   **Rhetoric Revisited**

Contemporary performance indicators reveal that in discussions about theatricality 'embodiment' is assuming more relevance than 'enactment', and 'showing' is more important than 'telling' as the linguistic or written signs of the text are transformed into the theatrical signs of a performance. The modernist position, where dramatic tension arises from the interplay between mimetic and diegetic space, or between what is shown to an audience and what is mediated by the characters, no longer occupies a secure place in post-modern performances. Rather, the style is one of deploying framing devices or 'layerings' determined by the director/*auteur* and the spectator makes meaning from what s/he can put together out of this polyphony.

A recent conference held by the Federation for International Theatre Research in July 2000 examined the relationship between 'sound space and visual space' in contemporary theatre, as it is generally held that we live in an age where the 'eye has devoured the ear'. This has created a theatre where form predominates over content. However, the balance between form and content in theatre has always been a contentious issue—contributing to experimentation and the emergence of an exciting array of genres in theatre history. A glance at how rhetoric has adapted itself to these changes is educational.

Dr. Jacqueline Martin is Head of Theatre and Teaching Studies at the Academy of the Arts, Queensland University of Technology. She is author of *Voice in Modern Theatre* (1991) and *Understanding Theatre: Performance Analysis in Theory and Practice* (1995). Her professional and academic career includes, Voice teacher at the National Institute of Dramatic Art, Australia and Associate Professor of Theatre Studies, Stockholm University. She has conducted master classes in Voice Pedagogy and Multidisciplinary approaches to Actor Training for the European League of Institutes of the Arts in Amsterdam and Berlin. She is an elected executive member of the Federation for International Theatre Research, where she is co-working on a forthcoming book about the Theatrical Event.

'Spectatorship' was in full swing in the Roman theatre, a practice already started in the Greek theatre, with gods being flown in on *deus ex machina*. The preference was for impressive staging and violent action, gladiatorial shows and sea battles. One could go so far as to posit that the decline of the Roman Empire was synonymous with the style in rhetorical delivery becoming more swollen, ornate and impressive.

Under the Emperor rhetoric was given a secure place in the liberal arts, or requirements of an educated man. Quintillian, the greatest authority on the subject, wrote twelve volumes where every possible rhetorical problem is discussed. In particular, he stressed the importance of training young people in the art of rhetoric, by having them learn long well-structured pieces of text and delivering them for the best effect (a system which all of us have had to endure in our school days) believing that as a consequence of this the student would learn the skills of writing as well.

Here for the first time rhetoric as a written art form was established, and the mark of a well-educated person was acknowledged as one who could speak and write well. These principles have continued through to the present. To this end Quintillian stressed the importance of a speaker gathering and formulating his argument and ideas (*inventio*); arranging them as suitably as possible (*dispositio*); giving a pure spoken delivery (*elocutio*); prior study enabling one to speak from memory or improvise (*memoria*); and finally the actual delivery with suitable declamation, posture and different gestures and facial expression (*actio*). The speaker was never to sound as though he was reading from a written speech, however, because this reduced the effect on the audience, a point which insecure speakers standing before a large ordatoriet for the first time have learned the hard way! On the question of form and content Quintillian was very strict, realising that speech could be dressed up in ornate words and misslead.

In contemporary performances discursive speech and characterisation have given way to multi-art explorations, as the trend towards a more filmic performance style emerges, with frequent use of projections and digital images, or the hypnotic repetitions of movement and rhythms à la Robert Wilson/Heiner Müller. Stories are being told in different ways. In fact the onus is now on the spectator to piece together his/her own story—in other words there are multiple stories depending on the spectator's ability to piece together the elements of sound (spoken and non-spoken), lighting, moving images, and the interplay of body to space, bodies to bodies and bodies to moving images, rather than following a scripted text. There are no longer fictional guidelines for audiences to follow, nor for that matter characters to identify with.

It is obvious that the predominant style in contemporary theatre practice relies on an elaborate, ornate and impressive style through the overuse of visual and aural form, which has rendered our post-modern performances to appear to be lacking in content—just as they were in the Roman Empire— and in a similar manner audiences have become spectators again.

Nevertheless, Roman actor training attempted to accommodate the theatrical conventions of the day, and actors trained in voice, song and dance in order to reach the audiences in the vast theatres and to convey the 'story' of the play they were performing. They even added hand gestures and vocal intonations appropriate to each emotion and type of situation. This does not appear to be happening in contemporary actor training institutions, where the majority are still running programs based on psychological realistic method— hardly suitable for the more epic and expressionistic style which has emerged today.

If theatre is not going to decline again, it is time to revisit rhetoric, revisit voice and movement training, and revisit the role of discursive speech and aural story-boarding in live theatre, before the film medium takes over completely.

Peer-reviewed Article by *Wesley Van Tassel*

Teaching Shakespeare Language Skills

As teachers of voice, speech, and acting Shakespeare, we often find that today's media-oriented student actors love to rely on "natural talent." When it comes to heightened text, relying on technique would be better. Our students are not prepared to accept this idea, because they have spent their lives watching a plethora of actors untrained in voice or language skills being paid large sums of money to work on video and film. By teaching certain language skills, however, we can help our students gain a new appreciation for technique.

The exercises for teaching four introductory skills are presented in this article. These skills are not intended to deal with the depth of Shakespeare's text, but with the acquisition of techniques that instill confidence and will aid the student with the eventual plunge into those depths. Among the fifteen or so speaking and analysis skills most of us teach, the following four can form the foundation for a student's methodology for dealing with Shakespeare and other examples of heightened text.

Because students begin to forget what they have learned in voice, speech, or acting Shakespeare the minute they complete the class and move on, we look for techniques that promote retention. While the approach suggested here is but one among many, it has met with some success. Teachers from high school through college who have used the approach have reported that, when taught first, this basic skill set appears to be the last forgotten.

The four skills suggested here are (1) end of line support, (2) scansion, (3) phrasing, and (4) breathing, practiced in that order. Working with these four skills first is not to suggest that the others will be ignored. We must begin somewhere and this procedure builds confidence; then other skills, like antithesis and imagery, are introduced as needed—which is often quite soon.

Concentration on this skill set provides an added benefit: once learned, these basic skills improve the actor's work (professional or amateur) with all language—heightened text or realism—and all voice work.

The following examples are much abbreviated for space, but each teacher can supplement according to his or her experience, or consult the complete book from which some of the material is excerpted.

Working with the exercises

Each student is asked to select material on which to practice the skills— a ten to twelve line monologue in verse and a sonnet will do. Before introducing the skills, however, each student is asked to read their material aloud without awareness of what is to come. In this way, the group is familiar with the raw beginning point for each monologue and sonnet.

Following the initial reading, the entire skill set is introduced:

    (1) end of line support—stress the final word in the verse line;
    (2) scansion—emphasize the stressed words or syllables;
    (3) phrasing—separate the thoughts;
    (4) breathing—use the punctuation as a guide.

Prior to becoming a university professor, Wesley Van Tassel spent fifteen years as a director in the professional theatre. He served as artistic director of the Westport Playhouse, the Mule Barn Theatre, and the Continental Theatre Company. He has coached acting Shakespeare to several hundred professional and student actors. His book, *Clues to Acting Shakespeare*, from which parts of this article are excerpted, was published by Allworth Press last year. Wes and his wife, actress Dude Hatten, live with their two dogs near Seattle. He is professor of theatre arts at Central Washington University and can be reached at vantass@harbornet.com.

Assure the students that each of these skills will be practiced individually, then all four will be applied to their monologues and sonnets. At that time they may hear a remarkable change from the first reading and may then be ready for more advanced text and analysis study. Explain that "character study," which they are eager to begin, follows, it does not precede this effort. These early sessions offer a good opportunity for the coach to discourage the student from rushing to character choices. The skills required to speak the text must be learned first or the character may sound like the first readings of the monologues and sonnets. They are encouraged to wait and compare.

First Skill—End of Line Support. In the first technique the students are encouraged to stress the final word in the verse line. They can develop this technique by "kicking the box," an exercise explained below. The end of the blank verse line is usually more important than the beginning or middle. When reading Shakespeare aloud, place a slight stress on the end of the line—including both the final phrase and final word—and notice the sudden clarity. This speaking style is dramatically opposed to the modern tendency to allow lines to fade away, like songs without endings.

Here are two examples. The first is Portia speaking to Shylock in the courtroom scene of *The Merchant of Venice*.

Portia: The quality of mercy is not strained, (IV, i)*

Have students read the line aloud and let the second phrase "is not strained" fall away so it is barely heard. When read that way, the line seems to be about something called mercy and something else that we aren't quite sure about. [When clarifying this and all of the following examples, first attempt to solicit these observations from the group, and then reiterate or add clarification.]

Now ask the students to read the line aloud a second time and support the second phrase "is not strained" with equal or more power than they gave the first phrase "The quality of mercy". After hearing some examples, remind them that the final word "strained" needs its own emphasis. Have the line read again. What is the line about? Now it is about a quality called mercy that is not obtained by straining at it. Now the line makes sense and opens the listener's mind to various possibilities.

Romeo has this response to Friar Laurence's counseling.

Romeo: Thou canst not speak of that thou dost not feel. (Rom, III, iii)

Have the students read the line aloud and allow the final word "feel" to drop away. What is the line about? Romeo is telling the Friar he can't speak. Now have them read the line aloud again and support the word "feel." What is the line about? Romeo may be telling the Friar, who is presumed celibate, that he has never known the love of a woman, so how can he counsel? Following this exercise the student may find that the line is now rich with possibilities.

Try the "kick the box" exercise. Ask the students to select a few regular blank verse lines (ten syllables each) from their monologues, then place a cardboard box on the floor in front of them. One at a time, have them read some lines and kick the box on the final syllable of each line. Kick on exactly the final syllable. Working with their monologues, some of the students may be uncertain when to kick. At this point, have everyone take the time to work on the two examples noted above, then return to their monologues. Using Romeo's line, don't kick on "not" and don't kick after "feel." Kick on the "f" of "feel." Have all students practice with the Romeo line then with Portia's line, kicking on the "s" of "strained."

By practicing this skill, the student may discover that supporting the final word through use of the diaphragm—which they can feel "kick in" when they "kick the box"—becomes second nature. They may notice that the other students listen to them. Have them practice this skill on each line of their sonnet and monologue until they support the final words without having to actually "kick the box." "Kicking the box," however, has allowed each student to discover (1) a method of putting physical energy into line readings, (2) a procedure for involving the entire body, and (3) a technique for supporting the end of the verse line.

Second Skill—Scansion. The second skill the acting or voice coach may want to focus on is scansion which includes an explanation of blank verse and the method by which it can be scanned, with feet separated and syllables marked stressed or unstressed. It is our intention to help the student place emphasis on stressed syllables and identify irregular lines. Blank verse—which is a form of writing the English language in ten-syllable lines, not necessarily rhyming—has a specific rhythm which identifies the important words. Each pair of syllables creates one foot. So the regular blank verse line has five feet. Each regular foot has a soft stress and a hard stress. Ask each student to consider his/her own foot; the heel is soft and the ball is hard. Have them walk and call out the rhythm—soft/hard, soft/hard, soft/hard, etc. In blank verse, its dee dum, dee dum, dee dum, dee dum, dee dum—five feet, five soft stresses, five hard stresses, one blank verse line. Have the students walk around and change "soft/hard" to "dee dum, dee dum, dee dum."

Most scholars and stage directors agree that blank verse is the closest written expression of English speech. Illustrate for the students how, without realizing it, we find ourselves speaking blank verse quite spontaneously. For example— "What would you like to do this afternoon? Let's go to town and buy an ice cream cone."—are two lines of blank verse! Ask the students to speak in blank verse for awhile, and to write out a few blank verse lines of their own. After working the following examples, have the students put some of their blank verse lines on the board and check them for scansion problems.

Breaking a blank verse line into feet and marking the stresses is called scanning the line, or scansion. Here is Romeo gazing at Juliet's balcony. Write this line on the board:

Romeo: But soft! What light through yonder window breaks? (Rom, II, ii)

Break the line into five feet, two syllables per foot:

But soft! / What light / through yon / der win / dow breaks?

Now mark the stresses, u for soft, / for hard:

$$\breve{~} \quad \prime \quad \breve{~} \quad \prime \quad \breve{~} \quad \prime \quad \breve{~} \quad \prime \quad \breve{~} \quad \prime$$

But soft! / What light / through yon / der win / dow breaks?

Have the students read the line aloud, stressing the hard syllables "soft", "light", "yon", "win", "breaks." Illustrate how, with the hand, one can beat out these stressed words or syllables on the table or chair while reading the line aloud. Have them do this three or four times. Now ask the students to forget scansion and read the line naturally. After these readings, point out the slight emphasis that was still given to the stressed words, even without the intentional effort. Our goal is to achieve naturalness and honesty while stressing the correct words. By not achieving this goal, we unintentionally disguise the meaning of the line. To prove this point, have the students read the line aloud and emphasize the soft syllables "But", "What", "through", "der", "dow". All should notice the problem.

As Shakespeare's verse is written in this regular dee dum, dee dum rhythm with effects achieved by use of irregular lines, the coach may want the students to identify some irregular lines in either their sonnet or monologue. Encourage them to seek a stressed syllable that is in the unstressed position, which is an example of breaking the rhythm, or an eleventh syllable, a dee without a dum, which is an example of a feminine ending. One might start by putting the following example on the board, then have the students find similar examples in their own material. The rhythm is broken in the opening speech of Romeo and Juliet.

Chorus: Two households, both alike in dignity
         In fair Verona, where we lay our scene,
         From ancient grudge, break to new mutiny,
         Where civil blood makes civil hands unclean.   (Rom, Prologue)

Lines 1, 2, and 4 are regular blank verse lines, but notice line 3. First, separate the line into feet:

From an / cient grudge / break to / new mut / in y,

In the third foot, the verb "break" (in the non-stressed position) is more important than the preposition "to" (in the stressed position). The stress in that foot is inverted—called a trochee—and the actor must read accordingly. Have the students read the line both ways, first emphasizing "to", then emphasizing "break". They may hear the importance of "break". To recognize inverted feet, active verbs are always good clues. Also, irregular stresses often occur in the first or third foot of the verse line. Together with these clues, scansion practice and use of common sense are important.

Hopefully, some students will argue that, in line 1, "Two" is as important as "house". That emphasis is an actor choice, but could be a good one because it clarifies the number of families involved in the fray. Lines often have three or more stresses back to back (it can be argued that some lines have ten stressed syllables), as this line has "Two", "house" and "holds", all of which can be stressed. Note that in the fourth foot of line 3 a student may argue that "new" breaks the rhythm and is as important as "mut". That is a good argument, because it points out that an earlier mutiny is starting over again. Encourage these discoveries, review basic scansion, then have the students find other examples of irregular rhythm.

In their monologue or sonnet, some students will have discovered lines with too many syllables. Writing the most famous line in Shakespeare on the board, we can illustrate how to handle the added syllable—the dee without the dum—as Hamlet contemplates action.

> Hamlet: To be, or not to be—that is the question: (Ham, III, i)

The line scans like this:

$$\breve{}\ \acute{}\quad \breve{}\ \acute{}\quad \breve{}\ \acute{}\quad \breve{}\ \acute{}\quad \breve{}\ \acute{}\quad (\breve{})$$
To be, / or not / to be— / that is / the ques / tion:

This line has eleven syllables and calls for a soft, or feminine ending. The feminine ending, used throughout Shakespeare, allows a line to end without a stressed syllable. Have a student "kick the box" on "ques"—not on "tion." Then have the student "kick the box" on "tion" instead. They should hear the problem. By allowing "tion" to just be there without emphasis, the line is given a soft ending. When scanning a blank verse line, when it doesn't work out to ten syllables and five feet, you're probably, but not necessarily, looking at a feminine ending. Students may ask, what if you're not?

Write the following Hamlet line on the board, or select a similar line suggested by one of the students. Illustrate how one can count eleven or twelve syllables in a blank verse line and then discover that the final syllable must be stressed. In this case, you cannot use the feminine ending. You will need to introduce elision here, but point out that it will have a more detailed study later, as it is one of the other skills but not part of the first set.

In the following eleven-syllable line, Shakespeare has already elided a two-syllable word into one syllable, but the actor must elide another word, as "man" is stressed and would not make a feminine ending.

> Hamlet: Horatio, thou art e'en as just a man. (Ham, III, ii)

The students will note "even" is already elided to "e'en" and pronounced as one syllable. Let them discover that the actor must elide "Horatio" to "Horat'o", pronounced as three syllables. Now the line can be spoken in ten syllables with correct rhythm.

$$\breve{}\ \acute{}\quad \breve{}\ \acute{}\quad \breve{}\ \acute{}\quad \breve{}\ \acute{}\quad \breve{}\ \acute{}$$
Hor a / t'o, thou / art e'en / as just / a man.

Have the students return to their sonnets and monologues to search for regular lines, inverted stresses, feminine endings, and places where elision must be used. Have them clearly mark on their text all of these clues to speaking the verse.

Third Skill—Phrasing. In addition to supporting the end of the line and scanning for emphasis we now add skill number three, phrasing, or separating the thoughts. This is a good time to illustrate that all blank verse lines can be divided into phrases. Each phrase is a thought, and if the students run the thoughts together, the listener will get lost.

Many phrases are separated by punctuation points. When there is no punctuation, separating each phrase with a slight pause is a good identification exercise. This pause is called a caesura (si-zhoor-e), meaning a sense pause (marked //). This is not a breath pause; it is much shorter. It is just a slight pause which allows the ear to place emphasis on the phrase or word you just said or are about to say. Put the following lines on the board and work out the phrasing with the students.

Here, broken into phrases, is Brutus' answer to Cassius who has mentioned that Caesar has grown too powerful. Some phrases are already identified by punctuation, so caesuras are not inserted.

Brutus: What you have said //
                 I will consider; what you have to say //
                 I will with patience hear; and find a time //
                 Both meet to hear and answer // such high things.
                 Till then, my noble friend, chew upon this:
                 Brutus had rather be a villager //
                 Than to repute himself a son of Rome //
                 Under these hard conditions // as this time
                 Is like to lay upon us.   (JC, I, ii.)

Work on the speech by reading it aloud a number of times, separating the thoughts as marked (some actors prefer to circle the phrases), then instruct the students to forget the marks and read the speech naturally. Remind them to support the final words of each line. In this reading, they may discover that, having identified the phrases, individuality is given to each thought, even when they are not trying to do so. (When using this example, take the opportunity to explain that the final line is called a short line, meaning that either a pause sufficient to complete the ten-syllable rhythm is intended, or the line is finished by the next speaker. In this case, Cassius finishes the line with "I am glad" to make ten syllables.)

If you sense that the students are interested in additional phrasing work, introduce antithesis here, although it is itself a skill and will need more time later. Suggest that there is another way to refine the phrasing skill, and that is to locate the antithetical words, phrases, or thoughts in each speech and stress them. Antithesis, the placing of one idea against its opposite, is used frequently in Shakespeare: i.e. "to be" (one thought), "or not to be" (the opposite thought). (Webster's example is "Give me liberty or give me death.")

Refer to the Brutus speech which is on the board and help the students dig out the antithesis. Discover that "I have said" is antithetical to "have to say," "hear" and "answer" are antithetical, also "consider" and "answer." "Villager" and "son of Rome", and "be" and "repute" are antithetical. Also, the thought in the first four lines (I hear what you have to say and will think about it) is antithetical to the thought in the next five lines (I don't want to talk now, but I hate the current conditions). After the antithesis has been marked in the speech, have the students read it again, this time emphasizing all antithetical words, phrases, or thoughts. They might discover how learning and practicing this skill can produce greater clarity.

Have the students identify and mark all antithetical words, phrases or thoughts in their monologues and sonnets, along with all phrases. Emphasize that, if, during rehearsals or early preparation, the caesura is used to separate phrases, later, when the pauses are removed and the actor speaks naturally, each phrase will have been embedded in the mind as an individual thought.

Fourth Skill—Breathing. Adding to the above three skills—end of line support, scanning the line, and phrasing—now introduce the technique of breathing at punctuation points. When reading Shakespeare, random breathing can destroy the sense of the line because the misplaced pause for a breath fractures the thought.

Coaches, directors, and scholars have differing points of view about the technique of breathing when reading verse. One reliable approach to teach your students, although not the only one, is this: Breathe at the punctuation points. Using the Brutus speech, illustrate why the actor does not breathe at the end of a verse line simply because it is the end of the line on paper. In verse, many lines are enjambed—which means the line contains a thought that continues to the next line without separation or punctuation; usually there is no breath at the end of an enjambed line.

In Brutus' speech, only lines 4 and 5 actually end as printed on the paper; line 9 is continued by Cassius. Lines 1, 2, 3, 6, and 7 are enjambed. There is a breath in the middle of line 3, at the ends of lines 4 and 5, and in the middle of line 9. Have the students read the speech and practice breathing only at the appropriate places.

Now write this next example on the board. Here, Macbeth, having killed the king, contemplates killing his friend, Banquo.

Macbeth:　　　　　To be thus is nothing, but to be safely thus—
　　　　　　　　Our fears in Banquo stick deep,
　　　　　　　　And in his royalty of nature reigns that
　　　　　　　　Which would be feared. 'Tis much he dares;
　　　　　　　　And to that dauntless temper of his mind
　　　　　　　　He hath a wisdom that doth guide his valour
　　　　　　　　To act in safety. There is none but he
　　　　　　　　Whose being I do fear; and under him
　　　　　　　　My genius is rebuked, as it is said
　　　　　　　　Mark Antony's was by Caesar.　　　(Mac, III, i.)

This speech contains typical Shakespearean punctuation. The breathing points are the punctuation marks. Have the students circle them, then read the speech aloud and breathe at each mark. They will find that it is quite easy to speak from one breathing point to the next, as the longest stretch is only two and one-half lines. (In the previous Brutus speech, the longest stretch is three and one-half lines.)

Encourage the students not to breathe after "Banquo" in line 2 (the end of a thought) or "that" in line 3 (the end of the enjambed verse line on paper). Have them try it, however, to discover the problem for themselves. Also, have them try breathing after "mind", "valour", "he", "him", and "said". Common sense and a developing ear may tell them that these choices are wrong because the thought in each of these enjambed lines continues to the next line.

Have the students circle the breathing points in their monologues and sonnets. They should understand that they are about ready to read their material with all four new skills applied, and to hear how much the new reading differs from the original reading of a few weeks ago. Remind them to always rehearse aloud. If not, they probably won't be breathing correctly. Encourage them to rehearse in a large area rather than a small bedroom. When working on this material, they need to open up the voice and reach out to a selected focal point—like a distant tree or a back row seat in a theatre. Praise them for correcting themselves and repeating a line or lines whenever they realize they've skipped a skill. Then, after sufficient rehearsal time, have the students read their sonnets and monologues to the class. The group members will probably point out to each other which skills have been successfully applied and which need work.

Once a class begins working with these exercises, the student actors may become student coaches of each other, because each member of the class has learned what skills to listen for. Each student quickly realizes that he or she can speak Shakespeare's language without timidity. This success is a significant confidence builder.

Conclusion
My final suggestion may seem like an entirely new subject and not related to the above four skills at all, but it is actually a companion skill to each of these and all others we teach. By ignoring it, we can destroy the learning process as it is happening. I am speaking about "over-acting." When reading Shakespeare, it's natural for the student to want to "act it out." Actors will often "enhance" the language with sounds, gasps, crying, whispering, pauses for effect, sighs, and ahs. Such enhancements tend to destroy the rhythm. When the rhythm is lost, the thoughts and the audience are also lost.

Overriding blank verse with emotion because "my character would do it this way" simply doesn't work. In this situation, the acting becomes indulgent, because the actor has lost WHAT is being said in favor of HOW it is being said. Generally the student will understand this direction: If you want to cry, cry after the line not during the line. We must hear the words first, then we can experience your sorrow without the irritation caused by a muffled line.

Students trained in subtextual acting methods primarily to handle realism often find it difficult to believe that the emotions needed by Shakespeare's characters are already written into the verse. Have some students demonstrate what happens when emotions overpower this language. Have them try screaming, moaning and crying their lines; then try adding unnecessary subtextual ideas; then have someone apply "painted on" emotions like "be jealous" or "be angry" or "be sarcastic"; and try using a very slow tempo so the actor can "feel it." After watching and hearing these examples, the students may arrive at some very useful conclusions, especially this: If we are listening to the "enhancements," we aren't listening to the words and, as Peter Brook says, "Shakespeare goes on without you."

For teachers interested in more details about the skills presented here and others, plus worksheets for younger students and additional teaching material for all levels, information is available in my book *Clues to Acting Shakespeare* (New York: Allworth, 2000).

Films and Videos: For examples of other actors using the same four skills, and others, check out some of these films. A good list includes *Hamlet* (Kenneth Branagh—some brilliant line readings), *Hamlet* (Mel Gibson), *A Midsummer Night's Dream* (Kevin Kline), *Much Ado About Nothing* (Branagh and Emma Thompson—wonderful duet scenes), Trevor Nunn's *Twelfth Night* (Ben Kingsley, Nigel Hawthorne and others—some nearly perfect readings of text), *Romeo and Juliet* (Leonardo DiCaprio and Claire Danes—some excellent examples of actors forgetting to use the basic skills), *Romeo and Juliet* (Franco Zeffirelli's 1968 film with Olivia Hussey and Leonard Whiting), *Othello* (Branagh and Laurence Fishburne), *Henry V* (Branagh—the St. Crispian speech is a masterpiece worth studying), *Richard III* (Ian McKellen), and the 1955 *Richard III* (Laurence Olivier). Films based on Shakespeare's plays, or life and times, include *Shakespeare in Love* (some very clear examples of the basic skills in beautifully read language), *Rosencrantz and Guildenstern are Dead, Prospero's Books* (John Gielgud), *Ran*, Orson Welles' *Chimes at Midnight* (many excellent speeches read well), Branagh's *Love's Labour's Lost*, and Al Pacino's *Looking for Richard* (a contrast of trained and untrained speaking voices). All of Shakespeare's plays received solid or excellent BBC video productions between 1979 and 1984, and are available in most libraries. Enjoy the Bard!

* All text is taken from the First Folio of Shakespeare with some punctuation supplied by the author.

Ronald C. Scherer, Ph.D., (associate editor) is a Professor in the Department of Communication Disorders at Bowling Green State University, Bowling Green, Ohio. His prior position was Senior Scientist in the Wilbur James Gould Voice Research Center at The Denver Center for the Performing Arts, where he also taught Voice Science in the Theatre Voice Coaches and Trainers Program at the National Theatre Conservatory (DCPA). He is strongly interested in the science and pedagogy of performance voice and speech, as well as in models of voice production.

I would like to share with the readers of this issue a "perspectives" talk I was invited to give at the VASTA annual meeting last year. Due to being indisposed, I asked our *Voice and Speech Review* Editor, Rocco Dal Vera, to read it for me at that meeting, and I am grateful to him for doing so (as well as for giving feedback on an earlier version). The essay below (a slightly edited version of the talk) deals with a number of observations and issues.

VASTA is an organization of people dedicated to furthering the training of voice and speech specialists who help others with their communication needs. This profession does not tell people "how" to think *per se*, but how to express thoughts and emotions. There is profound beauty in this, for it provides the freedom and skill to communicate how one wishes without judging the will of men and women and without promoting biased thought.

VASTA and the profession it represents are of significant importance to society— to train an actor or speaker to effectively recreate the deepest thoughts and emotions of humanity for one's audience is to nurture the awareness by the audience of the best of life, to reveal to them their innate understanding of their own self worth, and to reinforce an understanding of security in their interactive existence. In the public speaking domain, voice and speech trainers empower people to succeed in the world where enhanced communication skills provide the freedom to be creative and to more effectively solve society's problems.

When a child goes to school, the basic tools taught to him or her for the development of broad communication skills are the so-called "three Rs" of reading, writing, and 'rithmetic. Reading prepares the person to take in what others have written, writing prepares the person to be expressive in an external manner with words, and 'rithmetic, a misnomer for reasoning, teaches the person tools in interrelating various concepts. The missing communication tool among these is what might be called "recitation", the skill to speak one's thoughts in a way that is clearly communicated to others and to oneself, with voice and speech that are audible, intelligible, and healthy. This fourth basic tool is critical for the person to feel competent and uninhibited in fully expressing himself or herself through verbal means throughout life. There should be specific courses, equivalent in attention to those in reading, writing, and reasoning (and interrelated with them), to develop this ability to express oneself, for it is this mode of communication that is the most pervasive and most powerful in probably all societies of the world. It is a basic right to be able to learn to read, write, reason, and recite.

VASTA is the proper organization to take on the responsibility of influencing the educational communities in promoting this fourth basic tool development, "recitation". This might be accomplished through strong collaborations at all levels of the educational structure. And this should be justified through research that shows that excellent and healthy speaking skills are highly related to academic success, cooperative citizenship, gainful employment, and professional achievement.

VASTA is an idea with broad humanistic proportions. It is the idea that each person has the right to healthy and effective communication skills. VASTA seeks to find a number of "truths"—the truth of the most efficient and effective voice training, the truth of each stage of voice and speech development, and the truth of character, text, and context related to voice and speech production. Truth is supernormal communication skills of speech, voice, movement, and conveyance of meaning. Truth is constant health, endurance, and forward-seeking attitude related to voice and speech. Above all, truth is human nature, a wide field of potential expressions, each awaiting to be shown to the world, bound in some structure so that we can reflect it as a new touch of emotion, a new moment in a play, a new philosophical thought, a new researchable idea, a new lesson in a story.

The search for these truths and their expression in voice and speech unites those of us in VASTA. It is good to believe that ultimate truths exist, even when we do not see them fully. We strive to reveal the fullest truth of the moment, even as practical constraints of time and resources dictate boundaries. We need to take our students as far as we can on that person's journey to her or his own ultimate truths, seen as competent success, better self management, and more effective empowerment, through enhanced communication skills.

We sometimes know when our pedagogical thoughts are accurate and more truthful—usually when our students react in a predicted manner. This accuracy in a pedagogical moment does not mean we can explain exactly why what happened worked, but we can claim with certainty that it did. If we could bottle the process that showed success and give it to others to also use successfully, we probably would. The bottling process could be a reasoned discussion of what transpired, in terms that suggest faithful replication and probable success. We might publish an essay, for example, or make a training video. We do have numerous training materials that are highly instructive. An additional approach, one that is more evaluative and somewhat foreign to us, is to use science – not just to describe the pedagogical procedures that seem so successful, but to create plans to try them out in such ways that we obtain a stronger opinion about their usefulness and generality.

Not all ideas and methods used in pedagogy are amenable to effective scientific research. However, scientific research is the most secure approach to test concepts of human behavior. Science is a formalization of reason that is accepted across professions as a means to clarify concepts, understand ourselves better, and provide solutions to important problems. A firm foundation of pedagogical theories should become the backbone to pedagogical techniques. Scientific testing of such theories and techniques should be used to verify their conceptual and practical adequacy. Scientific validation of our methods would guarantee respect and cooperation from other professions.

Although uninformed about what VASTA's long range plans may be, permit me to mention eight areas which VASTA might consider.

1.   Let us encourage a cultural need for healthy and clear voice and speech. Let us raise the world's awareness that excellent voice and speech are important for a variety of outcomes: in establishing effective communications throughout the world, in defining highly developed civilizations, and in establishing each individual's potential success. Let VASTA be known for enhancing this awareness, and being a part of the communication excellence

in performance, in business and industry, in education, and in health and welfare organizations. This includes establishing cooperative and equal partnerships with all other professions that deal with speech communication effectiveness and health.

2.   Let us expand voice and speech training to include more course work in voice science, voice disorders, singing, learning theory, efficient skill acquisition training, and other areas, to establish curricula that guarantee thorough general foundations for working with people with communication concerns.

3.   Let us consider official subspecialization in VASTA with an expanded curriculum. These subgroups include, for example, acting, singing, broadcasting, law, education, business, sales, telecommunication, politics, sports, and so forth. Each has specific goals, pressures, requirements, needs, and personnel descriptors that determine our student's necessary knowledge base.

4.   Let us solve the problem of the definitions of responsibility among the various voice and speech professions, especially regarding permissible diagnostic and intervention techniques and ethics.

5.   Let us form a research arm of VASTA to establish the Science of Voice and Speech Performance and Pedagogy. Let us establish the bases for training scientists who study our own important questions. Scientific training should eventually occur within training programs of voice and speech pedagogy, so that VASTA practitioners themselves can perform competent research studies.

6.   Let us consider the promotion of technological feedback in the training arena. Such feedback provides external indications of behavioral changes that are sensed subjectively. Let us follow our sister professions in this pedagogical evolution.

7.   Let us create a strong publication legacy. Let us use the new *Voice and Speech Review* series and its future forms as the written repository of the practical and theoretical functions of the profession. Let us influence the rest f the world through the series with articles that give practical advice, inspirational reasoning, and professional promotion. Let us publish articles that define and expand the highest level of the art and science of the profession. Let us provide in earnest the valid historical record on which future generations will rely.

8.   Let us bring others to this profession as its practical scope expands and its demands increase. Let us bring the awareness of voice and speech training to the lower education levels by working with teachers and students there, and likewise at the high school level. Let us attract the college student who finds joy in helping others and has skill and a deep interest in communication success.

VASTA represents the one voice and speech profession that can apply its mission to all people in order to influence the arts, education, business, religion, and all other areas where better communication skills lead to enhanced qualities of life, creativity, and productivity. VASTA is the potential vehicle to help provide all people the right of healthy and effective communication skills.

It is also the vehicle to find the deepest truths in the pedagogy and production of voice and speech. This follows from the diversity of elements that drive voice and speech pedagogy, from physiology to spirituality. Let us harness this variety into a flexible and accountable structure that defines the profession of Voice and Speech Training and guides its potential expansion of responsibilities.

❦

Dr. Joseph C Stemple received his Ph.D. in Speech Pathology from the University of Cincinnati in 1977. Since that time, he has developed a clinical practice serving a voice disordered population which in 1985, evolved into the Blaine Block Institute for Voice Analysis and Rehabilitation located in Dayton and Cincinnati, Ohio. Dr. Stemple is the author of the texts *Voice Therapy: Clinical Studies* (2nd ed.) and *Clinical Voice Pathology: Theory and Management* (3rd ed.) (Singular Publishing Group, Inc., 2000) as well as research articles and text chapters related to clinical voice disorders. An active speaker and lecturer, Dr. Stemple holds adjunct faculty status with Miami University of Ohio, and the University of Cincinnati. He is a fellow of the American Speech-Language-Hearing Association.

Introduction

In 1978, at the age of 55, my father developed pneumonia. For two weeks, he was unable to smoke and decided that this was the ideal opportunity to stop smoking altogether. As a smoker from the age of thirteen, he had tried to stop many times, without success. Smoking two packages of cigarettes per day, his attempt to stop smoking this time was difficult (on all of us), but he was successful. My father has been blessed with excellent health since then and is an avid golfer to this day. Three years ago, I was in the car with him on the way to play golf. The route that we were taking to the golf course was the same route that he had driven to work every day for thirty plus years prior to his retirement. As he merged on to the interstate, he set the cruise control and then I saw his right hand reach into his shirt pocket and then return to the steering wheel. It was amazing to me that after twenty years of not smoking he subconsciously reached for a cigarette. When I pointed this out to him, he denied awareness that he had reached into his pocket, but admitted that his previous behavior had been merge, set the cruise, and light up. In fact, he stated that he had never lost his desire to smoke.

Background

This true, personal experience reflects the physical and psychological hold that tobacco product addiction has on individuals who smoke, chew, or sniff. Tobacco comes primarily from the plant nicotiana tabacum. It has been used for centuries with the first reports of addiction coming from Spanish soldiers in the New World who said that they could not stop smoking. In 1828, the primary addictive agent in tobacco, nicotine, was isolated and studies were begun to determine its effects on the brain and body. Recent research has shown that the addiction produced by nicotine is extremely powerful and is at least as strong as addictions to other drugs such as heroin and cocaine (Sasek, 2000).

Mechanism of Action

Nicotine readily enters the body. When smoked, it enters the bloodstream through the lungs. When sniffed or chewed, it passes through the mucous membranes of the mouth or nose to enter the bloodstream. Also, as has been demonstrated by patches worn to help people stop smoking, nicotine may also enter the bloodstream directly through the skin. Regardless of its manner of introduction to the bloodstream, it is distributed throughout the body and brain where it activates specific types of receptors known as cholinergic receptors.

Cholinergic receptors are present in many brain structures, as well as in muscles, adrenal glands, the heart, and other body organs. These receptors are normally activated by the neurotransmitter acetycholine, which is produced in the brain, and by neurons in the peripheral nervous system. Acetycholine and its receptors are involved in many activities including respiration, maintenance of heart rate, memory, alertness, and muscle movement. Because the chemical structure of nicotine is similar to that of acetycholine, it is able to activate cholinergic receptors. But, unlike acetycholine, when nicotine activates the receptors, it can disrupt the normal functions of the brain and body (Julien, 1998).

Body Effects

When nicotine enters the body through cigarette smoke, it takes seven seconds to enter the brain and trigger endorphins, the "feel good" chemicals (longer through mucosal absorption). These stimulate pleasurable sensations, prolong good feelings, and cover pain. Nicotine-attracting cells increase, leading to cravings and addiction. Temperament may be affected by nicotine as it blocks the body's ability to absorb caffeine. Perhaps this is the reason that so many smokers also drink unusually large quantities of coffee and caffeinated sodas. Nicotine inhibits natural hunger pangs while raising metabolism causing the body to digest food more quickly. Each time nicotine enters the body, the production of stomach acid is increased often leading to gastroesophageal reflux disease (GERD)(CDC, 1996).

Nicotine also negatively affects the lungs and heart. Lung cells turn red, swell, harden, and die as the lung lining absorbs the nicotine and other chemicals from the smoke. Breathing may become difficult, leading to diseases such as emphysema and cancer. Smoking and its by-products, including carbon monoxide, rob the heart of oxygen and trigger the production of artery-clogging plaque. Nicotine also raises blood pressure (CDC, 1996).

Carbon monoxide in smoke takes the place of oxygen in blood cells. Decreased oxygen in the brain affects alertness, memory, and concentration. Slow blood circulation to the tiny blood vessels in the skin results in wrinkles, crow's feet, and generally poor skin condition. Reduced blood flow from the effects of nicotine has also been implicated in impotence in men and slowed sexual responsiveness in women (CDC, 1996).

Smoking and Voice Production

If the examples given above are not reason enough to quit smoking or to never start, the professional voice user has other career-related reasons to consider the wisdom of this behavior. Cigarette smoking has been proven to be the major cause of cancers of the lungs, larynx and vocal folds, oral cavity, and pharynx—all the speech and voice producing mechanisms. The vocal folds themselves are highly susceptible to the irritations caused by cigarette smoke as they are shelves of tissue that capture the more than 4,000 compounds identified in smoke as it is inhaled (Matsuo, et al., 1983). Sixty of these compounds are carcinogens such as tar, carbon monoxide, hydrogen cyanide, phenols, ammonia, formaldehyde, benzene, nitosamine, and nicotine. Inhalation of these compounds leads to chronic irritation of the mucous membranes of the vocal folds (DHHS, 1988).

Chronic irritation causes the epithelial and mucosal cells to break down, leading to the probability of edema and erythema, polypoid changes, the development of pre-cancerous lesions such as leukoplakia and hyperkeratosis, and cancer. All of these tissue changes will affect voice production by changing the vibratory characteristics of the folds. These changes will lead to modifications of pith, loudness, and voice quality. Greater effort to maintain acceptable quality leads to voice strain and fatigue (Stemple, et al., 2000). The long-term effect is often an unreliable voice. Consistent casting is problematic once the professional voice user gains the reputation of having an unreliable voice.

Secondhand smoke, passive smoke, or environmental tobacco smoke (ETS) is also problematic. Passive smoke not only is in the environment as exhaled by the smoker, but also from the burning end of the cigarette. Indeed, secondhand smoke contains the same compounds and may be more toxic because it is not filtered prior to entering the atmosphere. Clinically, we have observed many non-smoking patients who are exposed to passive smoke who demonstrate more of the characteristics one might expect of a "smoker's larynx" including various laryngeal pathologies (Lee, et al., 1999).

Conclusion

Every day 3,000 children smoke their first cigarettes. The use of tobacco is highly addictive. Most users quickly develop tolerance for nicotine and need greater amounts to produce a desired effect. Smokers become physically and psychologically dependent and will suffer withdrawal symptoms when use is stopped. Physical withdrawal symptoms include changes in body temperature, heart rate, digestion, muscle tone and appetite. Psychological symptoms include irritability, anxiety, sleep disturbances, nervousness, headaches, fatigue, nausea and cravings for tobacco that can last days, weeks, months, years or, as in the case of my father, an entire lifetime (CDC, 1996). The deleterious effects on health in general and vocal health in particular of the professional voice user cannot be overstated.

The world of the professional voice user is highly competitive. Considerable talent and luck contribute to the successful performance career. Every performer has the opportunity to gain an edge on the competition by maintaining health and vitality necessary for this strenuous activity. Your body is your instrument. It represents the "tools of the trade." Not smoking is a strong affirmation of your respect for this invaluable instrument.

References

Center for Disease Control (CDC), Office on Smoking and Health, National Center for Chronic Disease Prevention and Health Promotion (1996) Cigarette smoking among adults—United States. 45(27): 599-590.

Julien R (1998) *A Primer of Drug Interaction*, VIIIth edition. New York: W. H. Freeman and Company.

Lee L, Stemple J, Geiger D, Goldwasser, R (1999) Effects of environmental tobacco smoke on objective measures of voice production. *Laryngoscope*, 109: 1531-1534.

Matuso K, Kamimura M, Hirano, M (1983) Polypoid vocal folds. A 10-year review of 191 patients. *Auris Nasus*, 10(suppl): S37-S45.

Sasek C (2000) Mind Over Matter, Office of Science Policy and Communications, National Institutes of Health. NIH Publication No. 00-3592.

Stemple J, Glaze, L, Klabe, B (2000) *Clinical Voice Pathology: Theory and Management*. San Diego: Singular Publishing Group, Inc.

US Department of Health and Human Services (DHHS) (1988) The health consequences of smoking: Nicotine addiction: A report of the Surgeon General, US DHHS, CDC. Office on Smoking and Health. Publ# (CDC) 88-8406.

Essay by *Robert T. Sataloff*

Vocal Consequences of Pollution

Modified in part from : Sataloff RT. "Pollution and its Effect on the Voice". In: Sataloff RT. Professional Voice: The Science and Art of Clinical Care, 2nd edition. San Diego, CA. Singular Publishing Group. 1997. With Permission.

Introduction

Pollution can be found throughout our environment. We encounter it at home, at work, in the air we breathe, in our food chain, and even in medical offices. Many pollutants are toxic to the voice.[1,2]

Although anecdotal experience is extensive, very little research has been done to determine the vocal effects of various pollutants. Nevertheless, it appears that injury to the vocal tract caused by environmental pollution is not rare. Consequent voice abnormalities may include hoarseness or other changes in voice quality or control, voice fatigue, or other problems. These may result not only in stress, strain, and inconvenience, but also in disability for the many people who depend on good voice quality and endurance professionally. When voice disturbances are considered, several kinds of pollution must be addressed.

Atmospheric Pollution

Vocal tract injury caused by inhaled pollution is most obvious. In extreme cases, the vocal effects of inhaled substances are self-evident. Such problems are usually seen following fires or industrial accidents in which hydrocarbons or other substances are inhaled, and pulmonary and laryngeal dysfunction ensue. More subtle voice dysfunction may result from chronic inhalation of atmospheric pollutants. Some such substances injure the airway topically. Other inhaled pollutants are absorbed into the body and may remain there for prolonged periods of time. In both scenarios, the consequent voice dysfunction may be more severe and prolonged than one would expect, even when there is no secondary gain (such as litigation) that might confuse the clinical presentation. The mechanisms of these problems remain obscure. Certainly, substances that directly injure the mucosal surface of the vocal folds and the respiratory tract can interfere with the mechanics of vibration. When inhaled irritants result in coughing, this physiologic response may also cause substantial vocal fold injury including inflammation, edema, mucosal disruption (vocal fold tears), and vocal fold hemorrhage. It is equally clear that certain pollutants adversely affect pulmonary function and consequently may have adverse effects upon the voice. The lungs act as the power source for phonation. Impairment in power source function can result in compensatory muscular tension dysphonia, voice fatigue, hoarseness and other vocal quality changes, and even structural lesions such as vocal nodules. Such power source alterations may be caused by any agent that produces obstructive or restrictive lung function, or that alters abdominal and thoracic muscle function and coordination. However, clinically it appears that voice dysfunction may also occur following exposure to toxins that do not produce obvious or measurable topical or pulmonary alterations. Allergy is often evoked as an explanation for reaction to pollutants, but the mechanism in many of these cases is not understood. Indeed, it is unclear even whether such conditions result in injury to nerves, control mechanisms, surface integrity, other factors, or combinations of such mechanisms. In order to prevent, diagnose and treat such problems, and predict their long term courses, we need much better

Robert T. Sataloff, M.D., D.M.A.: Professor of Otolaryngology, Jefferson Medical College; Chairman, Department of Otolaryngology-Head and Neck Surgery at Graduate Hospital; on the faculties of Academy of Vocal Arts and Curtis Institute of Music; Conductor of Thomas Jefferson University Choir and Orchestra; Director of the Voice Foundation's Annual Symposium on Care of the Professional Voice; a professional singer and singing teacher; Chairman of the Board of Directors of the Voice Foundation and the American Institute for Voice and Ear Research; Editor-in-Chief of *Journal of Voice*, on the Editorial Board of *Journal of Singing, Medical Problems of Performing Artists, Ear, Nose & Throat Journal,* and numerous other major otolaryngology journals; written over 500 publications, including 22 textbooks.

1. Sataloff RT, The Impact of Pollution on the Voice. *Otolaryngol Head Neck Surg.* 1992;106:701.

2. Sataloff RT. "Pollution and its Effects on the Voice". In: Sataloff, RT. *Professional Voice. The Science and Art of Clinical Care,* 2nd edition. Singular Publishing Group, Inc., San Diego, CA. 1997. pp:387-391.

understanding of the effects of inhaled toxins upon the vocal tract, including not only upper and lower airway structures, but also neurological components.

A general review of environmental pollutants is beyond the scope of this article. However, a few particularly important substances have been identified by the federal Environmental Protection Agency (EPA)[3] and listed in the "Indoor Air Quality Act of 1990." Many of these pollutants have known consequences that strongly suggest concomitant voice effects, although specific voice studies have not been conducted in most instances.

3. Report, EPA/400/1-89/001C, Vol. 2, pg. 2-3

A review of some of the pollutants listed by the EPA provides a useful overview of the problems and potential for adverse vocal consequences. Radon found in soil, well water and some building materials is known to cause lung cancer. However, an association with laryngeal cancer has not been firmly established. Environmental tobacco smoke causes irritation to the mucous membranes, lung damage including emphysema and cancer, all of which can adversely affect the voice. Biological contaminants from humans and animals can cause allergic reactions, infectious diseases and other toxic effects that may involve laryngeal function. Although this subject has not been well studied, it is intuitively obvious, for example, to anyone who is allergic to cats and has tried to speak or sing following acute exposure to feline dander. Volatile organic compounds in paints, adhesives, solvents, office machinery and other substances can also cause irritation, cancer and neurotoxicity. Formaldehyde which is present in plywood, particle board, upholstery and other substances, has also been associated with mucosal irritation, allergy and cancer. Polycyclic aromatic hydrocarbons (PAH) from kerosene heaters and wood stoves are associated not only with irritation and cancer, but also with decreased immune function. Conceivably, this might be associated with more frequent upper respiratory infections and concomitant voice dysfunction. Pesticides may cause neurotoxicity, although specific involvement of the voice pathways has not been studied. Asbestos, present in building materials and other substances, has been causally related to cancer and asbestosis. Asbestosis causes decreased pulmonary function which affects the voice. Carbon monoxide from combustion causes a variety of problems including exacerbation of cardiopulmonary dysfunction in compromised patients. This suggests that chronic carbon monoxide exposure may cause voice dysfunction through power source compromise, especially in elderly voice users. Nitrous dioxide from combustion is known to cause decreased pulmonary function in asthmatics, changes in anatomy and function of the lungs, increased susceptibility to infection in animals, and other compromises of function essential for normal, healthy voice production. It also appears to be synergistic with other pollutants. Similar effects may be seen with exposure to sulfur dioxide from combustion of sulfur containing fuels. Combustion particles (such as soot) when inhaled cause irritation to respiratory tissues and decreased lung function. Various household sprays and aerosols may also cause adverse effects ranging from irritation to cancer.

Clinical experience, and our current understanding of vocal anatomy and physiology, have taught us that the voice is exquisitely sensitive to even subtle changes in health or environment. These changes are particularly obvious in professional singers and actors whose vocal function may be impaired substantially by minor influences such as dust in a theater or decreased humidity on an airplane.[4] Consequently, one is compelled to suspect that pollutants such as those reviewed above can cause voice dysfunction.

Although relatively few studies have been done to investigate the effects of inhaled pollutants upon the voice, review of some of those available in the literature provides helpful insights. In 1968, Klayman reported on the otolaryngological effects of insecticide exposure.[5] He reported on several patients with epidermoid carcinoma of the larynx who had been exposed to insecticides. All of the insecticides were non-arsenicals and highly absorbable through skin, lungs and gastrointestinal tract producing irritation to the eyes, nose and throat.

In 1968, Becker and co-workers reviewed the effects on the health of those involved in the 1966 Eastern Seaboard air pollution episode.[6] They found that there was a definite relationship between air pollution levels and symptoms of irritative phenomena including hoarseness, increased cough, shortness of breath, chest constriction, nausea, vomiting, and irritation of the mucous membranes of the eyes, nasal passages, pharynx and bronchial tree. They also reported that individuals with chronic obstructive pulmonary disease were affected most adversely by increasing air pollution levels

In 1970, Snow investigated the effects of carbon black inhalation on the larynx and trachea.[7] His study utilized golden hamsters exposed for varied periods of time to air containing various quantities of carbon black, a substance used in the manufacture of the majority of black objects including tires, paints, and ink. He found that prolonged inhalation of sufficient quantities of carbon black produced subepithelial changes in the thyroarytenoid fold, including edema, and retention of amorphous eosinophilic material in subglottic and tracheal glands. No tumor formation or pathologic changes in the epithelium were noted. Snow concluded that inhalation of this inert dust "cannot be considered innocuous", and that further study was needed.

Amdur, in 1971, reviewed the toxicology of aerosols formed by the oxidation of sulfur dioxide.[8] She reported that the particulate oxidation product, sulfuric acid, has an increased irritant potency in comparison with sulfur dioxide. Furthermore, particulate size was found to be important in predicting irritant potency and response, suggesting that analysis of mass concentration alone was not sufficient. She observed that the particulate size of greatest importance was at the submicron level. She reported that a sulfuric acid mist promotes laryngeal spasms and spasmodic bronchostenosis which can cause death. It can also produce parenchymal lung damage. She noted that "an equivalent amount of sulfur produces a less irritant response if it is present as sulfur dioxide gas than if it is present as particulate sulfate or sulfuric acid." Laryngeal changes (other than spasm) were not studied specifically, but substantial impairment of pulmonary function was documented. This phenomenon, along with direct irritation, are likely to affect the voice.

In 1972, Baskervill reported on the effects of toxic atmospheric agents on the larynges of children. He attempted to correlate air pollution with dysphonia in children. He quoted previous literature and presented anecdotal observations suggesting that an association exists, but a causal relationship was not established clearly. He also highlighted the importance of respiratory dysfunc-

4.Sataloff, R.T.: *Professional Voice: Science and Art of Clinical Care*, Raven Press, New York, New York, 1991.

5. Klayman, M.B.: "Exposure to Insecticides". Letter to the Editor, *Arch Otolaryng*, Vol 88, July 1968, pages 142-143.

6.Becker, W.H., Schilling, F.J., Verma, M.P.: "The Effect on Health of the 1966 Eastern Seaboard Air Pollution Episode". *Arch Environ Health*. Vol. 16, March 1968, pages 414-419.

7. Snow, J.B.: "Carbon Black Inhalation Into The Larynx and Trachea". *Laryngoscope*; Vol.80:pp 267-287.

8.Amdur, M.O.: "Aerosols Formed by Oxidation of Sulfur Dioxide". *Arch Environ Health*; Vol. 23:pp 459-468.

9. Baskervill, R.D.: "Internal Laryngeal Injury in Children Due to Ingestion of Atmospherical Toxic Agents". *The Journal of School Health*, September 1972, volume XLII No. 7, pages 377-380.

10. Kruysse, A., Feron, V.J., Til, H.P.: "Repeated Exposure to Acetaldehyde Vapor, Studies in Syrian Golden Hamsters". *Arch Environ Health*-Vol 30, Sept. 1975, pages 449-452.

11. Wehner, A.P., Busch, R.H., Olson, R.J., CXraig, D.K.: "Chronic Inhalation of Asbestos and Cigarette Smoke by Hamsters". *Environmental Research* 10, (1975) 368-383.

12. Wehner, A.P., Busch, R.H., Olson, R.J.: "Effects of Diethylnitrosamine and Cigarette Smoke on Hamsters". *Journal of the National Cancer Institute*, Vol. 56, No. 4, April 1976, pages 749-753.

13. The Health Consequences of Smoking: Nicotine Addiction. A Report of the Surgeon General. U.S. Department of Health and Human Services, Rockville, Maryland. 1988

14. Reducing the Health Consequences of Smoking: 25 Years of Progress. A Report of the Surgeon General. U.S. Department of Health and Human Services, Rockville Maryland. 1989

15. The Health Benefits of Smoking Cessation: Executive Summary. A Report of the Surgeon General. U.S. Department of Health and Human Services, Rockville, Maryland. 1990.

16. Matsuo, K., Kamimura, M., and Hirano, M.: "Polypoid Vocal Folds. A 10-Year Review of 191 Patients". *Auris, Nasus*, (Tokyo) 10 (Suppl) 1983. S 37-S 45.

tion and repeated upper respiratory infections upon the voice, asserting that these conditions may be caused by pollution and thereby exert at least secondary effects upon the voice.[9]

In 1975, Kruysse, Feron and Til investigated the consequences of acetaldehyde vapors on Syrian golden hamsters. They noted severe histopathological changes in the respiratory tract including necrosis, inflammatory changes, hyperplasia, and metaplasia; and the upper segments of the respiratory tract were much more severely affected than the lower parts.[10] They examined tissue from various areas including the nose and larynx. Nasal findings included necrotizing rhinitis. Laryngeal studies showed that areas normally lined by respiratory epithelium appeared to be covered with stratified squamous epithelium, often keratinized. The vocal fold edge which is normally lined by stratified squamous epithelium was covered with a thick layer of keratin. Substantial damage to tracheal epithelium was also noted.

Wehner et al. in 1975 studied the effects of chronic inhalation of asbestos and cigarette smoke in hamsters. They found that animals exposed to asbestos developed lung pathology earlier and more severely than controls exposed to sham (placebo "smoke") or smoke. Laryngeal lesions in the asbestos plus smoke-exposed group were essentially the same as those in the asbestos plus sham smoke group. Interestingly, there was a significantly lower incidence of laryngeal lesions and of malignant tumors in the asbestos plus smoke-exposed group than in the smoke-exposed controls. The authors believed that this was due to earlier tissue necrosis from asbestosis.[11] In 1976, Wehner and co- workers at the National Cancer Institute used Syrian hamsters to investigate the effects of diethylnitrosamine (DEN) and cigarette smoke on exposed individuals. They found that DEN caused a significant increase in epithelial lesions of the larynx, including papillomas, and that cigarette smoke inhalation had a significant potentiating effect on the incidence of these lesions.[12]

In 1983, Matsuo, Kamimura and Hirano reviewed 191 patients followed over a ten year period with polypoid vocal folds. They found that long-lasting hoarseness was the most common symptom, that most patients were smokers, and that "vocal abuse, alcohol consumption and air pollution did not prove to be etiologic factor."[13] The study included physical examinations, questionnaires and retrospective review. Exposure to air pollution was recorded as "present" or "absent", and air analysis was not performed. The deleterious effects of tobacco smoke are well-known and have been reported extensively.[13,14,15] The adverse consequences are seen throughout the upper and lower respiratory tract, including the larynx; and both active and passive smoke exposure have been implicated. In addition to pulmonary disease that can impair voice function, and to cancer, cigarette smoke has been associated with a variety of vocal fold lesions including polypoid chorditis (Reinke's edema). Matsuo and co-workers found in 1983, smoking was the most commonly associated factor in 191 patients studied.[16] Interestingly, they noted specifically that air pollution did not appear to be an etiologic factor.

Numerous authors have looked at the association between laryngeal disease and various occupations associated with exposure to environmental pollution. Most such studies have suggested a relationship between occupational exposure to environmental toxins and laryngeal disease, although the causal relationship has not been proven conclusively in most cases. Chovil suggests, for example, that the apparent association of laryngeal cancer with asbestos and possibly other occupational exposures can be accounted for by the hypothesis that chronic vocal abuse peculiar to certain working conditions acts as a promoting factor for active carcinogen found mainly in tobacco smoke.[17] However, this notion is speculative, and extensive further study is needed. In a more recent report, Leonard et al. studied the effect of ambient inhaled ozone on the vocal fold mucosa in Bonnet monkeys.[18] They noted differences in vocal fold mucosa including increased thickness of the epithelial and connective tissues, and inflammatory changes with associated disruptions in glands and blood vessels.

Ozone is a major component of smog, and is a common environmental pollutant in many metropolitan areas. Ozone has also been associated with alterations in pulmonary function including reduced forced expiratory capacity and forced expiratory volume.[19,20] Ozone has also been associated with biochemical changes, cellular injury and structural alterations in the lower respiratory tract[21,22] and in mucosal changes and ciliary damage of the nose.[23] Although these abnormal consequences of ozone exposure throughout the vocal tract might affect the voice in and of themselves, Leonard's investigation appears to be the first to recognize potentially serious voice implications related to ozone exposure. In particular, they noted that after seven days of ozone exposure, epithelium that appeared to be normal clinically was markedly abnormal histologically, suggesting that ozone-induced changes may be difficult to detect using routine clinical methods. The long term effects of chronic ozone exposure remain unknown, but in the lungs, ozone has been shown to produce metaplasia, resulting in replacement of one type of epithelium by another that is more resistant to toxic irritation.[24] The consequences of these and other changes upon vocal fold function and voice quality remain unknown. Clearly, available preliminary evidence dictates a need for additional research into the effects of this especially common environmental pollutant.

Special Considerations for Performing Artists
Singers, actors and other performers are exposed to a great many environmental irritants and pollutants. Some are encountered by almost all performers at some time during their careers. For example, theatrical halls are commonly not cleaned adequately. Hence, actors, singers, dancers and others are exposed to dust and mold in high concentrations during rehearsals and performances. These conditions are aggravated if set construction is carried out coincident with rehearsals. Sawdust (often from wood treated with chemicals), fumes from oil-based paints and other noxious substances are frequently generated only a few feet from performers. These irritants may result in mucosal and respiratory changes that affect performance adversely, and may even aggravate or cause health problems such as acute allergic episodes, asthma, cough and others.

Performers may be exposed to even greater hazardous materials if they work around artificial fogs and smokes, or around pyrotechnic effects. Artificial fogs and smokes may be created using a variety of substances such as glycol-based products, oil-based products, organic chemicals and inorganic chemicals.[25] Often, the situation is aggravated by the addition of dyes or fragrances

17. Chovil, A.: "Laryngeal Cancer: An Explanation for the Apparent Occupational Association". Medical Hypotheses 7: 1981: PP951-956.

18. Leonard, R.J., George, L.C., Faddis, B.: "Effects of Ambient Inhaled Ozone on Vocal Fold Mucosa in Bonnet Monkeys". *Journal of Voice.* 1995; 9(4):443-448.

19. Bedi, J,. Horvath, S and Drechsler-Parks, D.: "Adaptation By Older Individuals Repeatedly Exposed to 045 parts per Million Ozone for Two Hours". *Journal of Air Pollution Control Association* 1989;39:194-199.

20. Horstman, D., McDonnell, W.. Folinsbee, L., Abdul-Salaam, S. and Ives, P.: "Changes in Pulmonary Function and Airway Reactivity due to Prolonged Exposure to Typical Ambient Ozone (O3) Levels" In: *Atmospheric Ozone Research and Its Policy Implications* (Schneider, T., Lee, S., Walters, G. and Grant L., eds.) Science Publishers, Elsevier: Amsterdam, pp493-499; 1989.

21. Folinsbee, L., McDonnell, W., and Horstman, D.: "Pulmonary Function and Symptom Responses After 66-Hour Exposure to 012 ppm Ozone With Moderate Exposure". *JAPCA* 38:28-35.

22. Fujinaka, L., Hyde, D., Plopper, C., Tyler, D., Dungworth, D and Lollini, L.: "Respiratory Bronchiolitis Following Long-Term Ozone Exposure in Bonnet Monkeys: A Morphometric Study". *Exp. Lung Res.* 1985, 8:167-190.

23. Hyde, D., Plopper, C., Harkema, J., St. George, J. and Dungworth, D.: "Ozone Induced Structural Changes in Monkey Respiratory System" In *Atmospheric Ozone Research and Its Policy Implications* (Schneider, T., Lee, S., Walters, G. and Grant, L., eds.) pp 523-532. Science Publishers, Elsevier: Amsterdam, pp523-532;1989.

24. Wilson, D., Plopper, C. and Dungworth, D.: "The Response of the Macaque Tracheobronchial Epithelium to Acute Ozone Injury". *Am. J. Path.* 1984, 116:193-206.

25. Herman HH Jr, Rossol M. Artificial Fogs and Smokes. In: Sataloff RT: *The Professional Voice: The Science and Art of Clinical Care*, 2nd Edition. San Diego, CA. Singular Publishing Group, 1997; pp413-427.

26. Opperman DA. "Pyrotechnics in the Entertainment Industry: An Overview." In: Sataloff RT: *The Professional Voice: The Science and Art of Clinical Care*, 2nd Edition. San Diego, CA. Singular Publishing Group, 1997; pp393-405.

27. Rossol M. "Pyrotechnics: Health Effects". In: Sataloff RT: *The Professional Voice: The Science and Art of Clinical Care*, 2nd Edition San Diego, CA. Singular Publishing Group, 1997; pp407-411.

28. Harkema, J., Plopper, C., Hyde, D., St. George, J., Wilson, D, and Dungworth, D.: "Response of the Macaque Nasal Epithelium to Ambient Levels of Ozone". *Am.J. Path*. 1987, 128:29-44.

29. Barr, B., Hyde, D., Plopper, C, and Dungworth, D.: "Distal Airway Remodeling in Rats Chronically Exposed to Ozone". *Am. Rev. Resp. Dis*. 1988, 137-924-938.

30. Klingholz, F.: "Voice and Noise". Stimme Und Larm Z *Gesamte Hyg*. September 1974, 20(9):571-4.

31. Rontal, E. Rontal, M., Jacob, H.J., Rolnick, M.I.,: "Vocal Cord Dysfunction—An Industrial Health Hazard". *Ann. Otol. Rhinol. Laryngol*. 1979 Nov-Dec;88(Pt 1):818-21.

32. Otto, B., Klajman, S., Koldej, E, Otto-Sternal, W.: "An Analysis of the Relation Between Dysphonia in Shipyard Workers and Working in Noise". *Bull Inst. Marit Trop Med. Gdynia*. 1980;31(3-4):185-92.

33. Krajcovic, I.: "Voice Disorders in Workers in a Noisy Work Environment at the Sverma Ironworks in Podbrezoval". Hlasove Poruchy Zamestnancov Hlucnych Pracovisk Svermovych Zeleziarni Podbrezova. *Cesk Otolaryngol* 1988 Jan;37(1):33-7 (Published in Slovak).

34. Van Dijk, F.J., Souman, A.M., and de Vries, F.F.: "Non-Auditory Effects of Noise in Industry. VI. A Final Field Study in Industry". Int. Arch. *Occup. Enrivon. Health*. 1987, 59(2):133-45.

35. Klingholz, F.: "Effect of Noise on Phonation". Einfluss von Larm auf die Stimmgebung. MMW 1982 Nov. 12;124(45):1005-6.

included for theatrical effect. Guidelines regarding use of artificially created smokes and fogs are not standardized and are controversial. Unfortunately, some of the substances still used commonly contain materials that are toxic and can create substantial health problems. Pyrotechnic special effects may be similarly troublesome.[26,27] The explosives and colorants used to create pyrotechnic effects are potentially hazardous and include substances such as toxic metals (mercury and lead) and known carcinogens (cancer causing agents). Interested readers are encouraged to consult the chapters referenced in this paragraph for additional information.[26,27]

Non-Inhaled Pollutants

In addition to inhaled pollutants, physicians are commonly confronted with ingested substances that may affect voice function adversely through toxicity. Those that cause alteration of neurological function are of particular interest. Such substances include not only widely recognized neurotoxins such as lead, but also more common substances including alcohol, caffeine, and various drugs (prescribed and recreational), and possibly chemicals such as preservatives and insecticides. Optimal vocal health is dependent upon fine motor control. Very little is known about the effects of many commonly ingested chemicals upon the neurological function of the vocal tract. However, the effects of such pollutants need not be neurolaryngologic. They may simply produce mucosal drying, irritation or other topical symptoms. Some pollutants are also capable of provoking respiratory reactivity response that alters voice at least temporarily, especially in people particularly sensitive or allergic to the pollutant. Monosodium glutamate (MSG) may be an example. It is reasonable to speculate that substances which affect neurological control mechanisms or function may affect the voice adversely, and these possibilities warrant further research.

Pollutants need not be ingested or inhaled to affect the voice adversely. For example, noise, intense enough to interfere with auditory feedback and used ordinarily for voice control may be considered a vocal pollutant. The question of causal relationship between noise and dysphonia has been investigated by several authors.[28,29,30,31,32,33,34,35] Most suggested an association between voice dysfunction and high noise levels, attributing vocal fold abnormalities resulting from voice abuse associated with the need to speak over loud noise. However, these studies were primarily anecdotal, and not controlled. Although the hypothesis is intuitively attractive, it is unproven. Interestingly, Van Dijk and co-workers performed a rather extensive evaluation of 539 workers from seven industries, finding no correlation between hoarseness and noise exposure in their study of the non-auditory effects of noise in industry.[34]

Recognizing the substantial body of research on the effects of pollution upon other bodily functions, it is reasonable to wonder why there is so little information about the vocal effects. The paucity of information is due neither to lack of interest, nor to lack of clinical indications that pollution-related voice problems exist. Rather, it is a consequence of technological development. Until very recently, accepted, practical methods for quantifying voice function were not available. Although histologic study of the vocal folds and other components of the vocal tract in animals is possible, the human voice is unique. This is true not only in terms of anatomy (humans are the only species with a vocal ligament), but even more importantly in terms of function. Consequently, assessment of the effects of pollutants on voice quality requires human study. There are still very few clinical voice laboratories equipped for such research. Although reasonable good research is possible today, even now standards for most objective voice measures and for reporting have not been established. As these problems are addressed, and as technology for voice measurement improves, we are likely to see substantial progress toward answering many questions regarding the deleterious vocal effects of pollution. At present, clinical diagnosis and management are guided solely by intuition, imagination and anecdote. Extensive interdisciplinary research is essential.

¶

Peer-reviewed Article by *Jeffrey P. Searl*

Potential Adverse Effects of Herbs and Vitamins on Voice and Speech

Jeffrey P. Searl, Ph.D., currently is an Assistant Professor in the Communication Disorders Department at Bowling Green State University. He received his doctorate from the University of Kansas. Current areas of research interest include the aero-acoustics of speech following total laryngectomy, oral-nasal resonance imbalances, and tongue force physiology of normal speech. He teaches in areas related to these research areas as well as in adult neurogenic communication disorders. Clinically, voice disorders (laryngeal and alaryngeal) remain a primary interest.

Introduction

Two pieces of information have prompted this review of potential herbal and vitamin effects on voice and speech: 1) the number of individuals taking dietary supplements continues to grow, and 2) reports of health risks associated with herb/vitamin supplements continue to appear in the literature. Approximately 20% to 30% of Americans utilize alternative medicines and therapies on a regular basis (Eisenberg, Kessler, Foster, et al., 1993; Eisenberg, Davis, Ettner, et al., 1998; Ness, Sherman, & Pan, 1999). In general, alternative medicines/therapies are defined as those practices that do not conform to the standards of Western mainstream medicine, receive little attention in mainstream medical education (at least in the United States), and are less commonly reimbursed by health insurance plans (Ness et al., 1999). However, it should be noted that some practices that have traditionally been considered alternative therapy do not clearly meet this general definition. Chiropractic therapy, acupuncture, and massage therapies (and possibly others) have all experienced growing popularity in the United States, are covered by an increasing number of health insurance plans, and have at least growing recognition from the mainstream medical community as potential useful therapies. This essay focuses on one type of alternative medicine/therapy—herbal and vitamin supplement usage.

A 47% increase in herbal medicine and megavitamin use from 1990 to 1997 has been reported by Eisenberg and colleagues (1993, 1998). Women are approximately 10% more likely to use herbal preparations than men (Hung, Shih, Chiang, et al., 1997). Differences in herbal usage also may vary among cultural lines. Hung et al. (1997) reported that individuals of Asian descent reported the highest percentage of use (36.8%) followed by African Americans (26.4%), Caucasians (18.2%) and Hispanics (13.9%). In the United States, usage patterns suggest an increase in dietary supplementation across the lifespan (Eisenberg et al., 1993, 1998). Increased use of dietary supplements by individuals in higher socioeconomic classes and in more highly educated people also was reported (Eisenberg et al., 1993, 1998). Finally, the number of dietary supplements on the market continues to grow at a rapid rate. The United States Food and Drug Administration (FDA) estimated that 1,000 new herbal/vitamin products are added annually to the 29,000 different dietary supplements already on the market (Sarubin, 2000).

Surow and Lovetri (2000) provide the sole description of herb and vitamin product usage patterns for vocal performers. Just over 60% of the 142 respondents indicated they used herbal therapies, and approximately 45% used "high-dose" vitamins. Because of the manner in which they presented data and the fact that they also inquired about other forms of alternative therapy, it was not possible to determine how frequently performers used herb and vitamin products. While these data are from individuals in a restricted geographic area (New York and New Jersey), the numbers suggest that a higher percentage of performers are taking herbal and high-dose vitamins than the general population. Broader geographic sampling is needed before generalizing these results to the voice profession in total. As Harvey, David, and Miller (1997a & 1997b) have argued, professional singers need to pay close attention to their nutrition, both in order to avoid illness/fatigue and to potentially optimize their voice. The percentage of users reported by Surow and Lovetri (2000) may simply be a reflection of performers recognizing the need for good nutrition and using herbs and vitamin supplements as a means of obtaining that goal. Gravitating toward use of dietary supplements is not wholly unexpected for performers given that many dietary supplements are marketed as enhancers of health, energy, physical prowess, and mental well-being.

Ancillary support for the notion that individuals concerned about their voice might have a high interest in herbal/vitamin products stems from survey results by D'Antoni, Harvey, and Fried (1995). They reported that 41% of patients at their voice center had inquired about alternative medical practices to help manage their voice disorder (data taken from a 3-month survey of patient inquiries). This information was not specific to voice professionals or to the use of dietary supplements.

A review of the literature to identify dietary supplements with potential voice and speech impacts is prudent given the growing body of literature on adverse side effects from various herbal and vitamin products in general. Despite growing popularity and some confirmed reports of benefits, there are compelling reasons for professional voice users to learn more about herbal preparations and vitamin regimens that are currently popular. The fact that herbal preparations are not subject to the same United States FDA approval process as prescription drugs and food additives has not deterred many nutritionists, pharmacists, and physicians from agreeing that herbs can act as drugs or can interact with prescription drugs (Stein, 2000).

Dietary supplements may have both intended and unintended effects that can influence the voice professional. An intended effect might be a substance marketed to improve circulation by thinning the blood. The product may do just that. However, because of the elevated risk of vocal fold hemorrhaging, a voice professional may opt not to take such a product. Similarly, conventional pharmaceuticals can create certain problems for the professional voice user (e.g., aspirin products, antihistamines, diuretics, etc.). Effects of prescription drugs and over-the-counter drugs regulated by the FDA are not included in this review. A number of reviews on this topic are available for the interested reader (e.g., Harris, 1992; Lawrence, 1987; Martin, 1988; Sataloff, 1992).

Self-dosing of herbal products at high quantities presents additional concerns because the health effects may be unpredictable and go beyond that intended by the dietary supplement manufacturer. Herbal preparations cannot be marketed for the prevention, diagnosis, or treatment of diseases or conditions. However, the purported influence on body structures and functions, as well as general well-being, can appear on the label according to the Dietary Supplement Health and Education Act of 1994 (Public Law No. 103-417, 1994). Unfortunately, consumers may mistake these claims as an indication that the product has undergone studies of clinical efficacy and safety. This, in conjunction with the public's general belief that herbs are natural, and natural implies safe, may lead to excessive intake of dietary supplements (Cupp, 1999; Stein, 2000). As the review below indicates, at higher quantities of intake, herbal effects may be toxic, health may be affected negatively, or allergic reactions may be elicited. Additionally, effects of impurities in herbal products, or variability in the potency of the herb within a given batch may be amplified when an herbal preparation is taken at a high dose.
Better guidelines exist regarding the intake of vitamins. The Committee

on Dietary Allowances (1980) has developed the Recommended Dietary Allowances (RDA) as a referent for measuring vitamin needs. The RDA is based on the vitamin needs of an "average" person free from disease or errors in metabolism. However, differences in individual needs for essential nutrients are unknown. Therefore, the RDA levels were set to exceed the requirements for most individuals to ensure that the needs of a large percentage of individuals are met. Since 1994, FDA regulations require nutrition labels to use the terms "daily value" (DV) to guide consumers in their understanding of the product's nutrient content, rather than RDA levels.

Vitamin supplements providing nutrient doses approximating or slightly exceeding the RDA are readily available. This review is not intended to discourage multivitamin intake. In fact, the literature is quite clear that vitamin supplementation is appropriate for some individuals who have inadequate vitamin intake, absorption or utilization, or who have increased vitamin excretion, destruction, or requirements (Herbert, 1980). However, the benefits of megadose vitamin intake by healthy individuals are less clear. A megadose has been defined as ingestion of at least 10 times greater than the RDA (Herbert, 1980; Hodges, 1980). Formulations providing 10 to 250 times the RDA in a single tablet are readily available without a prescription. When vitamin intake exceeds the body's needs, pharmacological effects are possible (Blair, 1984). Like herbs, self-dosing with high quantities of vitamins may be perceived as innocuous by some, and as potentially healthy/beneficial by others (Podell, 1985).

This review is intended to raise awareness of the possible adverse effects of herbs and vitamins on the professional voice user. The word "possible" must be emphasized because the database is not large and at times is not clear on the issue. The review is not intended as a general condemnation of the use of herbs and megavitamins. In fact, a number of clinical trials suggest that certain herbs can offer benefits exceeding a placebo and certain diseases are effectively treated with megavitamin therapy (e.g., Linde, Ramirez, Mulrow, et al., 1996; Loescher & Sauer, 1984; Rogers & Friedhoff, 1996).

The following limits were imposed by the author to keep the review manageable.
1. Potential benefits of herbs/vitamins are not discussed. A review of dietary supplement efficacy is beyond the scope of this article. The interested reader is referred to meta-analytic and controlled clinical trials addressing herbal preparation efficacy and other homeopathic practices (e.g., Kleijnen, Knipschild, & ter Riet, 1991; Linde, Clausius, Ramirez, et al. 1997; Linde, Scholz, Ramirez, et al., 1999; Vallance, 1998; Vandenbroucke, 1997; Walach, 1993). Ultimately, consideration of both benefits and risks will be important.
2. Supplement use by healthy adults is the focus. Risks (and benefits) may vary markedly for those who are ill or for children and the elderly.
3. Herbs/vitamins that are currently in popular use are reviewed to the exclusion of thousands of others. Current popularity was inferred from a MEDLINE search of the literature on the topic.
4. Effects directly related to professional use of voice/speech are covered. Dietary supplements may have other effects less directly related to the issues of a professional voice user.

5. For herbs, the effects described may be an intended outcome of the product (but one that is adverse for the professional voice user), a negative side effect of the product, or a description of interaction with a commonly prescribed medication. The effects described for vitamins are those that occur at mega-dosage.

Ideally, an indication of the toxic range for each of the herbs/vitamins would be offered. This is not possible for the herbal products which are not required by current FDA regulations to include data on product labels specifying maximum safe dosages and the published literature is lacking in this regard. Toxic ranges for vitamins are reported in some instances although the ranges tend to be quite large. The interested reader is referred to Blair (1986) or Omaye (1984) for further detail on vitamin dosing.

Review
Potential Blood Coagulation Effects
A list of vitamins and herbs with possible impact on blood coagulation is given in Table 1. In most cases, the effect is toward anticoagulation, either on its own or as a potentiator of warfarin (a blood thinning prescription drug). Products that predispose toward anticoagulation pose a potential threat to performers because of the concern regarding vocal fold hemorrhaging. Sataloff (1991) cautioned against the use of aspirin and aspirin products because of its tendency to promote bleeding. Agents such as ginkgo biloba, ginger, ginseng, feverfew, and vitamin E may have a similar effect. Of particular interest to the laryngologist considering vocal fold surgery for a professional singer/actor is the possibility of prolonged post-operative bleeding for patients taking garlic supplements. Vocal fold hemorrhages are not the only concern. At least four reports of spontaneous hemorrhage in either the eye or brain have been associated with ginkgo biloba products. Vitamin C is the exception in this list as it may interfere with the anticoagulant properties of warfarin (Loescher & Sauer, 1984). This interference appears to be dose-related, although the clinical significance has not been fully defined (Alhadeff, 1984).

Potential Cardiac and Blood Pressure Elevation Effects
Given the anxiety that professional voice users may experience prior to and during performances and rehearsals, along with the physical demands that may accompany performing, an elevation in heart rate and blood pressure may be anticipated. In most instances then, it seems prudent to not further elevate blood pressure. Three of the four substances listed in Table 2 have the potential to cause

Herb/Vitamin	Comments	References
vitamin C	can interfere with anticoagulation	Alhadeff, et al (1986), Blair (1986), Loescher & Sauer (1984) properties of warfarin
vitamin E	potentiates the effects of warfarin (i.e., anti-coagulation effect)	Blair (1986), Loescher & Sauer (1984)
ginko biloba	anticoagulation effect	Heck et al (2000), Johns (1999) Matthews (1998), Rowin & Lewis (1996), Smolinske (1999)
ginger	anticoagulation effect	Heck et al (2000), Miller (1998) Ness et al (1999)
garlic	increased risk of prolonged post-operative bleeding, additive effect with anticoagulant substances	Heck et al (2000), Ness et al (1999), Petry (1995), Stein (2000)
ginseng	possible interaction with warfarin	Heck et al (2000), Janetzky & Morreale (1997), Stein (2000)
feverfew	possible anti-coagulation effect	Heck et al (2000)

Table 1
Herbs and Vitamins with Possible Blood Coagulation Effects

hypertension. Both ephedra (ma-huang) and ginseng may be attractive to performers because they are marketed as substances that increase energy, improve circulation, and enhance athletic performance. Although no studies with performers have been reported, it seems possible that these products in conjunction with the naturally occurring body stress responses could unduly elevate blood pressure. At a minimum, flushed skin, dizziness, and headache might result. Cardiac arrhythmia has been reported with niacin (Committee on Dietary Allowances, 1980; Alhadeff, 1984) and ephedra (Cupp, 1999). Of great concern regarding ephedra products is that serious cardiovascular effects have occurred at a high rate in relatively young adults. Ephedra-related deaths secondary to cardiovascular events have been reported (Powell, Hsu, Turk & Hruska, 1998).

Herb/Vitamin	Comments	References
niacin	arrythmia	Blair (1986), Committee on Dietary Allowances (1980), Halpen (1983)
ephedra	hypertension arrythmia & myo--cardial infarction	Cupp (1999), Powel et al. (1998), Stein 2000, Theoharides (1997)
ginseng	hypertension	Cupp (1999), Heck et al. (2000), Janetzky & Morreale (1997), Smolinske (1999
liquorice	hypertension	Stormer et al. (2000), Miller (1998)

Table 2
Herbs and Vitamins with Possible Blood Pressure and Cardiac Effects

Potential Gastro-Intestinal Effects
Conditions that interfere with abdominal function may pose a serious problem for professional voice users because breath support for speech can be negatively affected (Sataloff, 1991). A number of vitamins taken at high doses can cause diarrhea and abdominal cramps as indicated in Table 3. Others may cause nausea. If vomiting is induced, an additional concern is possible tissue changes in the esophagus, larynx, and pharynx. Changes in tooth enamel are also possible if the vomiting is chronic (Morrison & Morris, 1990). Finally, peppermint can promote relaxation of smooth muscle, contributing to gastroesophageal reflux (Balch & Balch, 1997).

Potential Neurological Effects
Singers and actors clearly require optimal neuromuscular and sensory functioning throughout the body. At times, performers need to be able to speak/sing simultaneous with physical activity involving all or part of the body. Any compromise to the neurological system would be detrimental to a professional singing/acting career. Table 4 lists some vitamins and herbs that may have neurological consequences. Cases of severe sensory neuropathy have been associated with megadoses of vitamin B_6 (pyridoxine). The neuropathy included tingling sensations in the extremities, difficulty handling small objects and trouble walking (Davidson, 1984; Schaumberg, Kaplan, Windebank, et al., 1983). Fortunately, these patients showed substantial recovery after stopping the B_6 intake, but recovery was not complete in all cases. The sensory neuropathy associated with St. John's wort occurred in a 35-year old female who experienced pain on sun-exposed areas of her skin after self-medicating with the herb for four weeks. Symptoms resolved over two months following cessation of the herb. Motor symptoms have varied from induction of extrapyramidal symptoms (tremor, oral/lingual dyskinesia, etc.) to general muscle weakness.

Potential Allergy, Asthma, and Respiratory Effects

Allergic reactions manifested as changes in respiration could negatively effect voicing by altering breath support for speech. Dermatological allergic reactions also are of concern to the professional singer/actor because physical appearance and/or comfort may be compromised. Some of the more commonly taken herbs and vitamins that have had reported allergic responses are offered in Table 5. Skin rash is the most common symptom. If the rash appears on skin that is covered by make-up or on skin that will be exposed to bright lights for extended periods, further exacerbation of the rash might be anticipated. In some reports, rashes have shown up with a combination of herb ingestion plus sun exposure (kava and St. John's wort). The suggestion has been that the dietary supplement may induce some degree of photosensitivity in certain individuals. Echinacea could induce an allergic response on its own; however, exacerbation of sunflower allergy is the more common report (Mullins, 1998). For individuals who are already asthmatic, excess amounts of niacin can aggravate the condition because this substance may be involved in the release of histamine in the body (Blair, 1986).

Potential Headache and Fatigue Effects

Long hours at rehearsal, demanding physical activity, a reduction in the amount of sleep or unusual sleep patterns, and altered eating habits are all potential contributors to fatigue that voice professionals may experience, particularly around major performances. Singers and actors should be aware that certain vitamins taken in large quantities reportedly can induce fatigue (Table 6). Avoidance of those products (or at least large doses of those products) may be prudent.

While a headache might be considered a fairly minor inconvenience during the workday for many individuals,

Herb/Vitamin	Comments	References
vitamin A	nausea vomiting	Blair (1986), Caldwell & Hausen (1983), Davidson (1984), Snodgrass (1992)
vitamin C	diarrhea, abdominal cramps, flatulence	Blair (1986), Goodhart & Shils (1980), Hodges (1982)
vitamin D	nausea, vomiting	Blair (1986), Holmes & Krummerow (1983)
folic acid	nonspecific gastro-intestinal irritation	Alhadeff et al. (1984), Blair (1986), Omaye (1984)
pantothenic acid	diarrhea	Alhadeff et al. (1984), Young (1983)
St, John's wort	nausea & constipation	Cupp (1999), Ness et al. (1999)
ginko biloba	nonspecific gastro-intestinal complaints	Cupp (1999), Ness et al. (1999) Stein (2000)
peppermint	may relax smooth muscle, contributing to gastroesophageal reflux	Balch & Balch (1997)

Table 3
Herbs and Vitamins with Possible Gastro-Intestinal Effects

Herb/Vitamin	Comments	References
vitamin B	sensory neuropathy	Blair (1986), Davidson (1984), Podell (1985), Schaumberg (1983) Snodgrass (1992)
vitamin D	general muscle weakness	Alhadeff et al. (1986), Holmes & Krummerow (1983), Omaye (1984)
folic acid	can interfere with Dilantin elevating risk of seizures	Alhadeff et al. (1986), Berg et al. (1983), Hodges (1982)
ephedra	tremor, seizures -	Cupp (1999), Federal Register (1997)
kava	oral/lingual dyskinesia & torticollis	Schelosky et al. (1995)
sage	tonic-clonic convulsions	Miller et al. (1981)
St. John's wort	can result in tremor, hypertonicity and/or myoclonus, also sensory neuropathy post sun exposure	

Table 4
Herbs and Vitamins with Possible Neurological Effects

Herb/Vitamin	Comments	References
vitamin A	skin rash	Hoffman et al. (1978), Korner & Vollum (1975)
niacin	exacerbation of asthma	Alhadeff et al. (1984), Committee on Dietary Allowances (1980)
ginko biloba	skin rash	Ness et al. (1999), Stein (2000)
echinacea	anaphylaxis in cross-reactivity with sun-flower allergies	Mullins et al. (1999), Stein (2000)
kava	rash (face, chest, back) with or without sun exposure	Armedia & Grimsley (1996)
St, John's wort	rash following sun exposure	Golsch et al. (1997), Ness et al. (1999)
feverfew	skin rash	Hausen (1996), Hausen & Osmundsen (1983)

Table 5
Herbs and Vitamins with Possible Allergy Asthma & Respiratory Effects

Herb/Vitamin	Comments	References
vitamin A	headache, fatigue, general irritability	Caldwell & Hansen (1983) Loescher & Sauer 1984)
vitamin D	headache, joint pain	Alhadeff et al. (1984), Holmes & Kummerow (1983), Omaye (1984)
folic acid	disturbed sleep, malaise	Alhadeff et al. (1984), Omaye (1984)
St. John's wort	fatigue and dizziness	Ness et al. (1999), Woelk et al. (1994)
ginko biloba	headache	Ness et al. (1999), Stein (2000)
kava	lethargy/confusion when in conjunction with CNS depressants	Almedia & Grumsley (1996)

Table 6
Herbs and Vitamins with Possible Effects of Headache & Fatigue

a headache may significantly interfere with a singer or actors ability to perform at a high level because of possible changes in concentration and mental focus. Megadoses of vitamins A and D as well as ingestion of some products containing ginkgo biloba have reportedly been associated with headaches.

Other Potential Effects of Interest

Table 7 lists herbs/vitamins with possible side effects of interest to the professional voice user that do not fall clearly into any of the previous six categories. Lawrence (1987) reported that individuals on high doses of vitamin C might experience drying of the vocal tract mucosa. Reports of dry mouth associated with St. John's wort also have been made (Ness et al., 1999). Changes in the lubrication of the vocal folds can result in less than ideal function for voice production. Voice professionals may experience dryness or thickening of secretions as part of the body's natural autonomic nervous system response to stress/anxiety. Products that might exacerbate tissue dryness should be avoided when possible.

Pantothenic acid and licorice have water retention as a potential side effect. If this results in edema within the vocal folds (i.e., in Reinke's space), phonatory effects may result. It is unclear whether the sore throat and tongue tingling that can accompany intake of Echinacea are part of an allergic response in some people. These symptoms may represent local tissue irritation rather than a true allergic response. Lastly, halitosis may result from intake of garlic. Even some of the "odor-controlled" tablets do not fully eliminate the problem. Bad breath may be a minor side effect for some individuals. However, to the professional singer or actor, bad breath can seriously affect their ability to work because intimate contact with others is often required.

Comments

Herbs and vitamins that have *possible* adverse affects on voice and speech were identified. The focus was on side effects of particular concern to professional voice users. Because these individuals are highly dependent on speech and voice, a decision was made to include dietary supplements that might pose even a small and/or rare risk. As such, individual case studies of adverse affects were included. This was not done to disparage a particular product or the dietary supplement industry in general. However, at this initial stage when safety data on many dietary supplements are limited, a conservative review mandated inclusion of all possible negative effects no matter how infrequently reported. Ultimately, stronger evidence regarding the benefits and the risks of dietary supplements are needed to help consumers and health professionals make informed decisions about their use.

Most of the supplements in Tables 1-7 were included because of possible *unintended* effects. Exceptions to this include some of the substances in Table 1 that have anticoagulant effects and some substances in Table 2 that are marketed as energy enhancers (e.g., ephedra, ginseng). Whether these products actually do improve circulation and energy level and how they do it may be open to debate. However, if they have this *intended* effect and it happens by the most likely mechanism (i.e., anticoagulation and/or an increase in blood pressure), the risk for hemorrhaging or prolonged bleeding would be present. This risk (or just a suspicion of the risk) may be sufficient cause for individuals dependent on their voice to avoid these products, at least until further evidence is available. Some might view this stance as overly cautious. However, a conservative decision might be bolstered by the fact that the effectiveness of many dietary supplements remains to be demonstrated. In essence, the thinking may be, "Why place my vocal folds/body at risk of hemorrhaging by taking a product whose positive effects may not have been demonstrated, particularly if the positive effects I am seeking are possible through other means without the same risk (e.g., better diet, exercise, meditation, yoga, etc.)?"

Herb/Vitamin	Comments	References
vitamin C	dry mouth, throat	Lawrence (1987)
St. John's wort	dry mouth	Medical Letter (1997), Ness et al.(1999)
pantothenic acid	water retention	Alhadeff et al. (1984), Young (1983)
liquorice	water retention	-Stormer et al. (1993)
echinacea	sore throat, tongue tingling	Ness et al. (1999)
garlic	halitosis	Ness et al. (1999)

Table 7
Herbs and Vitamins with Other Possible Effects of Interest

The issue of *unintended* effects (i.e., side effects) of dietary supplement is a difficult topic to cover considering the type of evidence currently available. In the review, any report of a side effect that might negatively impact the voice professional was included. Ideally, controlled laboratory studies and strong clinical trials would be available to guide decisions regarding dietary supplement safety and side effects. While a number of adverse effects related to herbal and vitamin products have been reported in the literature, much of the "evidence" has been in the form of single case reports. This is particularly true for the herbal preparations. Single case reports can be quite helpful, particularly as a means of alerting health care professionals and consumers about potentially hazardous products. However, more scientifically rigorous laboratory and clinical trials are needed to adequately pursue the suspicions raised in the single case studies.

Unfortunately, the single case or small series reports have not always spurred on large-scale controlled clinical trials. For some health care providers and voice professionals the single case reports may be sufficient to prompt a conservative reaction – i.e., avoiding dietary supplements (or avoiding large quantities) until more information is available. Again, a cautious approach is defensible on several fronts.

1. **Current FDA regulations regarding the evidence needed to demonstrate a product's safety allow manufacturers to decide when an ingredient can be introduced on the market.** In the United States, side effects from dietary supplements often are not known until a product has been on the market for some time because these products are not under the full regulatory controls of the FDA (Johns, 1999). According to the FDA's "Guide to Dietary Supplements" (1999), federal law requires that supplement manufacturers

ensure that the products they put on the market are safe, but companies do not have to provide the FDA with information before marketing a product, and the FDA does not analyze supplement contents before they are marketed. Typically, adverse reactions are discovered post-marketing when physicians see reactions in their patients.

An oversight and review document prepared by the U.S. General Accounting Office (2000) of the United States Government regarding the FDA's regulation of the dietary supplement industry states: "...FDA has not defined in regulations nor provided other guidance to companies on the evidence needed to document the safety of new dietary ingredients...." (p.13). In essence, the supplement manufacturers, in the absence of clearer FDA regulations, are left to decide when a product is safe. Obviously, dietary supplement companies are not in the market to harm individuals. While some companies may evaluate product safety in detail, others may not, either because of fiscal pressures (i.e., to save money with less safety testing and to make money sooner by getting a product on the market), or simply because the FDA regulations are permissive enough to allow products to market with an unspecified amount/type of safety research.

2. **Quality control for purity and potency may be an issue.** The FDA "Guide to Dietary Supplements" (1999) stated: "Poor manufacturing practices are not unique to dietary supplements, but the growing market for supplements in a less restrictive regulatory environment creates the potential for supplements to be prone to quality control problems" (p. 7). Allergens, pollen, spores, heavy metal, toxic plant residue and other undefined substances have been found in some dietary supplements (e.g., Moore & Adler, 2000; Stein, 2000). Even though an herb may ultimately prove to have beneficial health effects, impurities in the product may be present which might impact the user. If an impure product is consumed in large quantities, the harm from the impurity may be magnified. A lack of production quality control for some supplements makes it difficult to attribute adverse effects to a particular herb (e.g., the side effect could be the result of the impurity that is present, not the primary herb in the product). Regardless, the limited federal regulatory controls over product purity introduce the possibility of health risks to consumers. Likewise, batch-to-batch differences in product potency are possible without stricter regulations. Consumers (and possibly manufacturers) may be unaware of a product's potency, and thus may be unaware of the risks they are assuming.

The Dietary Supplement and Health Education Act of 1994 gave authority to the FDA to establish good manufacturing practices (GMPs) to govern the production, packaging, and storage of supplements. To date the FDA has not done so, although it lists the establishment of dietary supplement GMPs as part of its recently created 10-year plan (to be completed by 2010). In the absence of FDA imposed GMPs specific to dietary supplements, some companies have initiated their own internal standards. Some trade organizations, such as the National Nutritional Foods Association (NNFA), have established GMP programs through which association members can be certified as meeting GMP standards. While industry self-regulation is a potentially good start, it is not mandated. According to the NNFA Newsletter (September 2000),

13 of its 1000 members have requested and been granted a GMP seal by the association in the first year of the program (another 60 or so have requested inspections toward obtaining the seal).

3. **Lenient labeling standards create additional concerns regarding consumer awareness of product safety and effects.** Consumers bear some responsibility for carefully reading the product labels of the supplements they take. The question is whether the labels contain enough information for consumers to make an informed decision regarding a products content, safety, and benefits. According to FDA documents (FDA Guide to Dietary Supplements, 1999), manufacturers are required to list the ingredients in their product under the ingredient label. A separate nutrition label must appear on the product that lists the dietary ingredients that are present in "significant amounts." The definition of "significant amount" is left to the discretion of the manufacturer. Consumers must be careful to read not just the nutrition label (which usually appears in larger print), but also the ingredient label (usually appearing in smaller print). It is possible that some supplements are manufactured to contain various products that might be allergens to some people (e.g., sunflower, various flower pollens), but these may show up just in the ingredient list in some cases.

Of greater concern to consumers is that the FDA has provided little if any regulation regarding the type of safety information that should be placed on the labels of dietary supplements. According to the U.S. GAO, "FDA has not prescribed by regulation or clarified in guidance what information is 'material' or provided guidance on when or if certain safety-related information should be included on labels…" (2000, p. 16). The GAO report criticized the FDA regulations for not requiring dietary supplement manufacturers to include information on maximum safe dosages, potential interactions with other drugs, or the need for specific groups to avoid the supplement. Presumably, the FDA has not required supplement manufacturers to include such information on the product labels because the FDA also has not determined what the evidentiary standard for product safety should be to get a product on the market in the first place.
The lack of safety information required on labels becomes potentially more problematic in light of the types of effectiveness claims that are allowed which attract consumers to the product. Supplements can include "health claims" that describe the connection between the supplement (or some of its ingredients) and a disease or health condition. "Health claims" are defined by the FDA and a product can carry that label only if the content of the product meets the FDA guidelines (FDA, 1999).

More often, however, supplement manufacturers include "structure/function" claims rather than "health claims." Manufacturers can describe how a part of the body (a structure claim) or a system in the body (function claim) will be affected by consuming the product. Structure/function claims also can include claims regarding a person's general well-being. The FDA regulation states that these "claims must be true and not misleading" (FDA, 1999). However, by FDA regulations, manufacturers can make claims based on the company's own internal review and interpretation of the data. Manufacturers must be able to substantiate the claims, but companies do not have to share the substantiation data with the FDA or the public. According to the July 2000 report from the GAO, the FDA has never asked a company marketing a supplement with structure/function claims to provide the agency with evidence supporting the company's claim. This is somewhat surprising considering that some products appear to make rather significant claims (e.g., improving circulation, strengthening the immune system, etc.).

Without the FDA providing more explicit rules for defining the type and quantity of evidence necessary for a claim to be made, consumers must simply trust that the manufacturer has appropriately investigated and labeled the product. The FDA has at least recognized this regulatory deficit at this time. One of their priorities is to establish more stringent regulations on the dietary supplement industry by the year 2010 (as indicated on the website for the U.S. Food and Drug Administration, Center for Food Safety and Applied Nutrition, VM.CFSAN.FDA.GOV, January 2001).

4. Individual characteristics that may predispose a person to have negative side effects are not known. A dietary supplement may be benign to all but the smallest percentage of the population. However, without more careful delineation of who comprise this small segment, consumers may be assuming more risk than they want. Many of the products listed in Tables 1-7 have had negative reactions reported for only one or a few individuals. Even though rare in occurrence, the negative effects are quite severe in some cases (e.g., seizures, sensory neuropathies, etc.).

There will always be some portion of the population that negatively reacts to a product. This certainly happens with prescription drugs and foods that go through rigorous FDA procedures. With conventional pharmaceuticals and food additives, however, an attempt has been made through clinical trials to inform physicians/consumers about who the drug is and is not appropriate and what the anticipated side effects might be. Such attempts are not mandated for dietary supplements. Additionally, some consumers may assume that herbal and vitamin supplements are safe because they are "natural" and can be obtained without a medical prescription. However, many health care providers (physicians, dieticians, etc.) stress that herbs can act as drugs in the more traditional sense (e.g., Barrett, Kiefer, & Rabago, 1999; Omaye, 1984; Stein, 2000). As Surow and Lovetri (200) summarized, individuals are susceptible to the intended and unintended effects of what they ingest "whether the product is herbal, natural, or made by human beings" (p. 404).

At present, it is difficult to determine the number of adverse effects occurring related to dietary supplements. From 1993 to 1999, just under 2,800 reports of negative side effects were reported to the FDA. This number includes 105 deaths thought to be associated with dietary supplement intake. Given the large numbers of individuals taking supplements during this time frame, the number of adverse effects appears small. Certainly in comparison to the number of deaths and ill-effects that occur from prescription medications and from conventional foods, dietary supplements appear rather safe. However, a 1999 consumer survey conducted outside of the FDA auspices presents a less positive picture. In this nation-wide survey, approximately 12% of all respondents using herbal supplements indicated that they had an adverse reaction attributed to a supplement (as cited on p. 16 of the oversight report of the GAO, 2000). One could dispute the strength of survey data from individuals who are self-reporting adverse effects. Similarly, though, the reporting mechanism through the FDA is a voluntary system that has underestimated the number of health problems in the past (see U.S. GAO, 1999).

When dietary supplement health concerns are raised, current FDA resources significantly limit the ability to investigate the reports (U.S. GAO, 2000). The FDA has indicated that the current computer system used to monitor health reports associated with supplement intake is "severely" limited in terms of tracking and analyzing the adverse risk reports. Additionally, there were three part-time FDA employees available to investigate health reports related to dietary supplements, limiting the reviews to less than 40% of the total reported health complaints.

5. **Herbs and vitamins may interact or interfere with prescription drugs**. Further research is clearly needed in this regard. The issue has become of enough concern in the past few years that review articles of alternative medicine practices appearing in more conventional Western medical journals often list those herbs/vitamins with suspected or documented interaction with prescription drugs (e.g., Cupp, 1999; Smolinske, 1999; Stein, 2000). A survey by Eisenberg et al. (1993) found that 25% of individuals used unconventional therapies, although only 70% of them informed their physician. A more recent survey reported that 18% of adults were using prescription drugs concurrently with herbal or vitamin products (Smolinske, 1999).

Until consumers are better informed of potential dietary supplement-drug interactions, it seems prudent for physicians to seek information from patients regarding the dietary products they may be taking on their own. Likewise, performers should take the responsibility for telling their doctors what dietary supplements they are taking if the physician does not actively seek this information. The study by Surow and Lovetri (2000) indicated that performers often do not discuss what types of alternative treatments they utilize when consulting with their physician. This reluctance must be overcome in the interest of the performers own health.

6. **Toxic levels have not been determined for most herbs on the market**. Likewise, the lowest human neurotoxic dose of most vitamins has not been clearly defined (Snodgrass, 1992). Not until controlled laboratory and clinical trials are completed will this data be known. Large differences in individual susceptibility to specific vitamin and herb toxicities may be present. In fact, the individual case reports that make up the bulk of articles reviewed may be a reflection of individual susceptibility. Without information to explicitly define safe and unsafe levels of dietary supplement ingestion, self-dosing at high levels will be a concern, particularly if the mindset is that herbal products are "natural" and natural equates to safe. Self-dosing at high levels may be encouraged by the lack of regulatory control and lenient labeling standards resulting in absent, unclear, or scientifically unfounded dosing instructions on dietary supplements.

Conclusion

Dietary supplement usage patterns within the community of professional voice users remains to be investigated in further detail. Clearly, more information is needed to define the role of herbal and vitamin supplements in the diets of healthy individuals. There are uncertainties regarding what side effects may be associated with a product, who is at risk, and at what ingestion level adverse effects are likely to be manifested. At present, relatively lenient FDA regulations, contradictory reports of benefits/risks, case reports of possible adverse effects, and the voice professionals strong need to avoid damaging the speech/voice mechanism may be enough to instill caution regarding these products, if not full avoidance. Even though the negative effects may be reversible or occur infrequently, the risk may be either unnecessary or too high for professional voice users to take. This may be a difficult decision for singers/actors given the competitive nature of the profession, especially with products on the market that claim to enhance health, strength, energy, etc. Some products ultimately may live up to these claims. However, further investigation to define dietary supplement benefits and risks is needed in most cases.

References

Alhadeff, L. Gualtieri, C.T. & Lipton, M. (1984). Toxic effects of water soluble vitamins. *Nutrition Reviews*, 42, 33-40.

Balch, J.F. & Balch, P.A. (1997). Prescription for Natural Healing. 2nd ed. Garden City Park, NJ: Avery Publishing Co.

Blair, K.A. (1986). Vitamin supplementation and megadoses. *Nurse Practitioner*, 11, 19-36.

Committee on Dietary Allowances. (1980). *Recommended Dietary Allowances*, Washington, DC: National Academy of Sciences.

Cupp, M.J. (1999). Herbal remedies: Adverse effects and drug interactions. *American Family Physician*, 59, 1239-1244.

D'Antonio, M.L., Harvey, P.L. & Fried, M.P. (1995). Alternative medicine: does it play a role in the management of voice disorders? *Journal of Voice*, 9, 308-311.

Davidson, P.A. (1984). Complications of megavitamin therapy. *Southern Medical Journal*, 77, 200-203. Dietary Supplement Health Education Act, 1994, Public Law No. 103-417.

Eisenberg, D.M., Davis, R.B., Ettner, S.L., Appel, S., Wilkey, S., Van Rompay, M. & Kessler, R.C. (1998). Trends in alternative medicine use in the United States, 1990-1997. *JAMA*, 280, 1269-1575.

Eisenberg, D.M., Kessler, R.C., Foster, C., Norlock, F.E., Calkins, D.R. & Delbanco, T.L. (1993). Unconventional medicine in the United States: Prevalence, costs, and patterns of use. *New England Journal of Medicine*, 328, 246-252.

Harris, D. (1992). The pharmacologic treatment of voice disorders. *Folia Phoniatrica Logopedia*, 44, 143-154.

Harvey, P.L., David, D.E., & Miller, S.H. (1997a). Nutrition and the singing voice. *Journal of Singing*, 54 (1), 41-48.

Harvey, P.L., David, D.E., & Miller, S.H. (1997b). Nutrition and the singing voice: Part Two. *Journal of Singing*, 54 (2), 43-49.

Herbert, V. (1980). *Nutrition Cultism*. Philadelphia: George F. Stickley Co.

Hodges, R. (1980). Food, Fads and Megavitamins. In R. Hodges (ed.), *Nutrition in Medical Practice*, Philadelphia: WB Saunders, pp. 288-322.

Hung, O.L., Shih, R.D., Chiang, W.K., Nelson, L.S., Hoffman, R.S. & Goldfrank, L.R. (1997). Herbal preparation use among urban emergency department patients. *Academic Emergency Medicine*, 4, 209-213.

Kleijen, J., Knipschild, P. & ter Riet, G. (1991). Clinical trials of homoeopathy. *British Medical Journal*, 302, 316-323.

Lawrence, V.L. (1987). Common medications with laryngeal effects. *Ear, Nose & Throat Journal*, 66, 23-28.

Linde, K., Clausius, N., Ramirez, G., Melchant, D., Eitel, F., Hedges, L.V. & Jonas, W.B. (1997). Are the clinical effects of homeopathy placebo effects? A meta-analysis of placebo controlled trials. *Lancet*, 350, 834-843.

Linde, K., Ramirez, G., Mulrow, C.D., Pauls, A., Weidenhammer, W. & Melchant, D. (1996). St. John's wort for depression – an overview and meta-analysis of randomized clinical trials. *British Medical Journal*, 313, 253-258.

Linde, K., Scholz, M. Ramirez, G., Clausius, N., Dieter, M. & Jones, W.B. (1999). Impact of study quality on outcome in placebo-controlled trials of homeopathy. *Journal of Clinical Epidemiology*, 52, 631-636.

Loescher, L. & Sauer, K. (1984). Vitamin therapy for advanced cancer. *Oncology Nursing Forum*, 11, 38-45.

Martin, F. (1988). Drugs and vocal function. *Journal of Voice*, 2, 338-344.

Mullins, R.J. (1998). Echinacea-associated anaphylaxis. *Medical Journal of Australia*, 168, 170-171.

Ness, J., Fredrick, S. & Pan, C. (1999). Alternative medicine: What the data say about common herbal therapies. *Geriatrics*, 54, 33-43.

Olson, N.R. (1986). The problem of gastroesophageal reflux. *Otolaryngology Clinics of North America*, 19, 119-134.

Podell, R.N. (1985). Nutritional supplementation with megadoses of vitamin B6. Effective treatment, placebo, or potentiator of neuropathy? *Postgraduate Medicine*, 77, 113-116.
Rogers, S.L. & Friedhoff. L.T. (1996). The efficacy and safety of donepezil in patients with Alzheimer's disease: results of a United States multicentre, randomized, double-blind, placebo-controlled trial. The Donepezil Study Group. *Dementia*, 7, 293-303.

Sarubin, A. (2000). The Health Professionals Guide to Popular Dietary Supplements. Chicago, IL: The American Dietetic Association.

Sataloff, R.T. (1991). Reflux and other gastroenterologic conditions that may affect the voice. In R.T. Sataloff (ed), *Professional Voice: The Science and Art of Clinical Care*, New York: Raven Press, pp. 179-183.

Sataloff, R.T. (1991). Drugs for vocal dysfunction. In R.T. Sataloff, *Professional Voice: The Science and Art of Clinical Care*. New York: Raven Press, 252-257.

Sataloff, R.T. (1992). Drugs and Voice. In R.T. Sataloff (ed.), *Care of the Professional Voice*, New York: Raven Press, pp. 253-257.

Schaumberg, H., Kaplan, J., Windeback, A., Vick, N., Rasmus, S., Pleasure, D. & Brown, M.J. (1983). Sensory neuropathy from pyridoxine abuse: a new megavitamin syndrome. *New England Journal of Medicine*, 309, 445-448.

Stein, K. (2000). Herbal supplements and prescription drugs: A risky combination? *Journal of the American Dietetic Association, 100, 412.*

Surow, J. B. & Lovetri, J. (2000). "Alternative medicine therapy" use among singers: Prevalence and implications for the medical care of the singer. *Journal of Voice,* 14, 398-409.

Theoharides, T.C. (1997). Sudden death of a healthy college student related to ephedrine toxicity from a ma-huang-containing drink. *Journal of Clinical Psychopharmacology,* 17, 437-439.

U.S. Food and Drug Administration. (1999a). An FDA Guide to Dietary Supplements. *FDA Consumer* (originally published Sept.-Oct. 1998, revised January 1999).

U.S. Food and Drug Administration. (1999b). Overview of Dietary Supplements. *http://vm.cfsan.fda.gov/~dms/ds-oview.html,* viewed January 2001.

U.S. General Accounting Office. (1999). *Dietary Supplements: Uncertainties in analysis underlying FDA's proposed rule on ephedrine alkaloids.* (GAO/HEHS/GGD-99-90). Washington D.C.: U.S. Government Printing Office.

U.S. General Accounting Office. (2000). *Food Safety: Improvements needed in overseeing the safety of dietary supplements and "functional foods."* (GAO/RCED-00-156). Washington, D.C.: U.S. Government Printing Office.

Vallance, A.K. (1998). Can biological activity be maintained at ultra-high dilution? An overview of homoeopathy, evidence and Bayesian philosophy. *Journal of Alternative and Complimentary Medicine,* 4, 49-76.

Vandenbrouke, J.P. (1997). Homoeopathy trials: going nowhere. *Lancet,* 350, 824.

Wilson, J.A., White, A., von Haacke, K.P., Maran, A.G., Heading, R.C., Pryde, A. & Piris, J. (1989). Gastroesophageal reflux and posterior laryngitis. *Annals of Otology, Rhinology, and Laryngology,* 98, 405-410.

Walach, H. (1993). Does a highly diluted homeopathic drug act as a placebo in healthy volunteers? Experimental study of Belladonna 30C in double-blind crossover design – A pilot study. *Journal of Psychosomatic Research,* 37, 851-860.

Outside the Ivy Walls: A Meaningful Past that Looks Toward the Future

The late TV personality and educator Sam Levenson once opinioned that each person born into this world brings a unique message for the world... a message held tightly in the fist. As I recall, Levenson felt that it was the mission of loving teachers, parents, and others to help unclasp the fingers one-by-one to set that message free. I love this idea! I also think it really rings true as to what our real mission might be! What do you think? We facilitate the birth of a message, a message that humankind needs desperately. Isn't this true?

If Levenson is right, I can't help but think how tragic it is when for some reason the waiting world must go without the message! How tragic! How sad when that young person grows old without the world ever hearing that special message. This is true poverty isn't it? It is sad for the world and sad for the messenger too.

Certainly, VASTA private teachers and nurturing professionals play a special role in this free-the-message drama. As a matter of fact, I believe teachers and healers whether they are institutional or private share the same awesome task of helping the student to realize his or her divine potential.

Think of magical performances where everyone on stage and in the audience *knows* that something otherworldly has just taken place. Some of the tearful, thankful, and proud applause comes from members of that audience who have spent countless hours in the studio or classroom providing the building blocks (or pathways) and encouragement for actors and singers. Isn't this what we do? It is truly profound. We realize with Carl Gustav Jung that "what is essential in a work of art is that it should rise far above the realm of personal life and speak from the spirit and heart of the poet as man to the spirit and heart of mankind." I believe this is the magic that springs forth as artists and teachers commune in their various ways with the audience.

As difficult as it can be for teachers and healers to function in places that sometimes seem just flat out hostile to creativity, I think we must not despair of doing our best. I think we must "free the message" wherever and whenever possible. I want to pay special attention to this "wherever" aspect in a moment.

Going back to a "magical" performance, the actor and singer know that seated out beyond the footlights there may well be that special arts-loving speech pathologist or otolaryngologist. Perhaps that specialist has helped the artist overcome an untimely illness or avoid unhealthy vocal habits that could ruin a robust career—and/or stunt "the message." The wise artist pays tribute to a whole group of voice professionals. (Thank God, some of the teachers and healers are beginning to learn to work together as a team!)

One of the joys of this work is to get a letter from some thankful soul for the work that has been done in their behalf. Yet, as we continue to overcome the tragic with joy and creativity, there is a larger venue out their waiting for us. I believe we would be wise to venture out on to the stage that Shakespeare speaks of: "the world." There is a need for a VASTA-like team of voice professionals out there on that wonderful and terrible "stage."

Entrepreneur and founder of Presenter's Studio, Jack Horton (associate editor) teaches cultural voice/presentation development for Business, Media, and the Arts. Upon graduation (WVU Creative Arts Center), Jack traveled and recorded with the Robert Shaw Chorale, and toured with Goldovsky Opera, NY Sextet, and Men of Song Concert Quartet. His leading opera roles were with Lake George, Miami, Eastman Opera Theatre, The New School; as tenor soloist: Capitol Hill Society, NY Choral Society, West Point, C.W. Post, WNYC, NYU, WVU, Shreveport Symphony, St. Patrick's Cathedral and Garden City Cathedral. After 23 years of private study, teaching, performing in NYC, Horton now lives in Louisville, KY.

There are folks out there who need us and don't yet know it. George Bernard Shaw word-crafted a vision for us in this regard and he seems to have had some fun presenting it. I refer to Shaw's remarks in his preface to *Pygmalion*: "I wish to boast that *Pygmalion* has been an extremely successful play, both on stage and screen, all over Europe and North America as well as at home. It is so intensely and deliberately didactic, and its subject is esteemed so dry, that I delight in throwing it at the heads of the wiseacres who repeat the parrot cry that art should never be didactic. It goes to prove my contention that art can never be anything else."

So yes, there are acres of "wiseacres" out there. Yet, as I said in my last article, we can overcome their house-of-cards attitude with some user-friendly changes in the way we do business. We can change the way we dialogue with this new and larger media and business group located out beyond the ivy walls and beyond the theatre we all love so very very much.

The articles that follow will inspire you to take new steps toward the expansion of your teaching and healing business. I consider Lorraine Merritt and John Lohrey to be real pioneers in taking the arts and the teachings of the arts to the medical profession and beyond. Their peer-reviewed article opens our eyes to a sea of possibility for us to "free the message" beyond the theatre. They and others are living proof that it can be done.

Ginny Kopf told us in her last article that she planned to expand on ways to market our teaching/practice. Well, she surely made good on her promise to do just that! There is no way you could read her new article and not find something to use in your own business. She virtually sparkles with can-do ideas.

Lissa Tyler Renaud reaches into the depths of dozens of artistic endeavors and puts polish on a somewhat hidden concept called "The Focus Point." When you try this concept on for size, you (if you are like me) find yourself going farther and farther into the picture she is painting for us. It is a mystery, a wonderful mystery that calls us to be more creative!

So friends, are we going to move forward and "free the message"? Think about it as you go through the following articles. I say let's get busy and do it. We and our world will be richer and wiser for our artistic labors. Let the creative spirit abound!

Cheers, Jack

Essay by *Lissa Tyler Renaud*

On the Focus Point: The Next Generation

My boy, who is six, spent last summer in a rigorous children's opera program. Of course I was eager to see how the director, Sanford Jones, would run rehearsals for his original, full-length work, *The Awakened One*. His cast ranged in age from five to about twelve, and it was a pretty unruly gang that greeted him on the first day. I wondered what he would do to bring focus to the group. Then, to my pleasant surprise, I saw the three large Xs taped just above eye level on the back wall, and felt great confidence in him.

These Xs marked the three "focus points" of the theatre—house center, house left and house right. They were an absolutely integral part of my growing up in the theatre, in both my training and performing—especially The Focus Point, the point at the center. Over the years, I have seen the Focus Point gradually lose vitality as a training concept here in America, and in turn, virtually fall out of use here in performance. In my own teaching, however, I promote its use with tremendous conviction; I have found nothing comparable to it for helping students calm their breathing, gather themselves physically and collect their thoughts—all of which are aspects of my teaching responsibilities at the Voice Training Project.

My private voice studio, in Oakland, CA, is called the Voice Training Project. There, I provide instruction and consultation to individuals whose professions require them to have an especially excellent speaking voice. This includes those who give speeches and talks, stage and film actors, television and radio anchors, and singers, as well as other professionals who are committed to superior vocal delivery and persuasive communication.

For over twenty-five years, my voice work—with actors, as well as with high-profile figures in public service, business and the media—has been stimulated by the beauty and authority of the speaking voice. Vocal training today takes advantage, of course, of the work of well-known teachers such as Cicely Berry and Kristin Linklater. At the same time, my practice also benefits incalculably from the work of many other brilliant contributors to the voice field, many of whom are not yet well-known or have already been forgotten. In my experience, a student's affinity for a particular vocal "method" is best nurtured after comprehensive training is completed, so that the period of actual training serves to broaden rather than narrow a student's focus. I have been loyal to this belief in all of my teaching work over the years.

The needs of my students typically fall into two categories: 1. The mechanics of vocal production, or issues related to breathing, placement, resonance, range, diction, reduction of accents and regionalisms; and 2. The principles of oral interpretation, including information about basic oratorical notions such as structuring, intonation patterns, dynamics, phrasing, style, tone and gesture.

There are two things that are most characteristic of my approach to these needs. First, I am convinced that vocal instruction itself is made most fruitful by simultaneous training in physical alignment. After twenty years of conventional dance training, my interest in movement took a decisive turn when I met dancer/choreographer John McConville in 1984. His inquiry into physical alignment and the performer's voice represented a profound synthesis of his own *bel canto* studies and professional bodywork practice with the

Lissa Tyler Renaud: award-winning actress, accomplished director, respected teacher of acting and voice, recognized scholar. 40 years performing (Eliza, Hedda, Rosalind, Beatrice, Alcestis) and directing (Strindberg, Yeats, Picasso, Gertrude Stein, Brecht). M.A. 1984; Ph.D. Theatre History/Directing, UC Berkeley 1987. Studied speech from 1963 on; studied *bel canto* for six years with soprano Christine Sanders (now on UNM faculty). Founder/Program Director: Voice Training Project, 1975 to the present; Actors' Training Project, 1985 to the present. Popular on-line columnist: "Commentary and Collaborations from the Actors' Training Project." Founding Member: Network of Cooperating Studios, 1999. Scholarly specializations: Wassily Kandinsky, Bauhaus, 20th century avant-garde.

disciplines of Mabel Todd, Joseph Pilates, Moshe Feldenkrais, ballet, modern dance, Eastern dance and yoga.

Thus began our studying, performing, collaborating and teaching together. With his guidance, I have gone on to sustained Pilates study, and received additional instruction in Ideokinesis, Feldenkrais, Somatics, Eutony, and many other physical re-education approaches relevant to the care of the performer's body. Breath and body being inextricably linked, I have made a deep professional commitment to learn skills for training breath and body simultaneously. Most often, what actually brings them together is the Focus Point.

The first thing, then, that is characteristic of my teaching is my emphasis on physical alignment. The second thing characteristic is my attention to related fields. My method of working is inspired by principles gleaned from related fields that can inform the voice work, drawing parallels between disciplines which can enrich the inquiry into effective use of the voice. For example, I teach text analysis using musical principles, acting using painting principles, and stage movement using choreographic principles.

Sometimes, however, this approach ends up highlighting the differences between disciplines rather than their relatedness. For example, "jaw tension" doesn't always mean the same thing to the dentist and to the singer; "inhale" doesn't always mean the same thing for the *bel canto* singer and the yoga practitioner. But one principle that I have found common to public speaking, singing, dancing and acting—and therefore emphasize in my teaching—is the Focus Point.

At my students' request, I wrote the following notes in February of 1999:

The Focus Point
This is the point at the center of the farthest surface from you (e.g., the back wall of an auditorium), about two to three inches above eye level.

On this point, we "see" a "screen" on which we let the mind's eye see what we are talking about.

This is the same point on which dancer Dame Margot Fonteyn, singer Feodor Chaliapin and actor Sir John Gielgud focused when they worked. It serves many a purpose:

1. It gives you a way of "taking stock of" or acknowledging all of the space you will need to fill with your performance, i.e., a way of adjusting the size of what you will do (shouters and whisperers are performers with no Focus Point).

2. It gives you the specific place you need to send your breath when you are speaking. When used expressively and efficiently, the breath moves out through the frontal sinus cavity with great concentration and travels in an arc to the Focus Point (imagine the trajectory of the water when you have your thumb over a garden hose, or the path of a ball thrown overhand). If you have no place to send the breath (voice), it loses focus and wanders around over the audience's heads looking for a destination—and they actually

hear the sound as lifeless, wooden, flat, without energy, etc. An archer organizes his efforts while concentrating to the utmost *on the bull's eye*. The actor's "bull's eye" is the Focus Point.

3. It simplifies your performance so that it can be seen—i.e., your eyes are not wandering around, you aren't spending your energy trying to figure out what to look at, or trying to focus in a vague "middle distance"—your face is fully visible so that we can enjoy your artistry optimally.

4. It keeps you from looking at the ground. Remember that "the eyes are the window to the soul"— so that if I cannot see your eyes, I don't know what's happening in your soul.

5. Remember that the audience will look at whatever you look at—they rely on you to tell them where to focus their attention. Stage floors are generally not dressed. Generally, the most astonishing and luxurious of sets will end at the stage floor, which will be bare or otherwise neutral. We do not, therefore, do anything to draw the audience's attention to the floor.

6. Ever had the feeling that a lecturer was directing his/her comments directly to you? Paradoxically, this was a speaker with a Focus Point.

Note that in the matter of looking or not looking at the audience, there is a wide range of opinions available to a student to choose from, all expressed by talented professionals. At one end of the spectrum, you can find teachers who recommend looking directly into the audience, even singling out individuals to address directly. At the other end of the spectrum, you can find teachers who suggest that you not address anyone in particular. For my part, in the context of dramatic material for theatrical production or audition, I am entirely at the latter end of the spectrum. In my experience, when you look out into the audience and single people out to address, everyone else feels left out (and embarrassed); when you look at a Focus Point, everyone feels included (and relaxed).

7. When you are on stage and everyone you're talking to is on the Focus Point (including dead bodies), the audience feels that they are in the action, it's happening all around them. When you put all of the action on stage with you, the audience members are observers rather than participants. Remember that stage space is *illusory* space and *not literal* space—and what you see on your Focus Point is as far away or as close as your mind's eye finds it to be. You can be talking to someone at the other end of a ship in a storm, or whispering to someone so close you can feel the heat on his or her face. The audience is the middle of whatever, which is exciting.

Some Practical Notes
1. Some performers experience this as an area of the back wall rather than a "point"—and have a "sense" of a "presence" there rather than a visual experience. The important thing is to experiment until you find what gives you a consistent sense that there is a receiver or partner there.

2. Make the distinction between "looking" and "seeing." Looking means your eyes are set on a point and glazing over (the "deer-in-the-headlights"

look, or the "phoning-in" look). This usually happens when you are holding your breath; one's mantra in this case should always be *exhale, exhale, exhale.* Seeing means that your eyes are registering stimuli from without. Never let your mouth say what your mind's eye has not seen first—then you'll never glaze over.

3. In a full play, playing a scene with a partner or partners, maintain a "split focus": feel or otherwise stay connected to, aware of, your Focus Point, *and* focus on your partner. Also, some plays require you to help create the illusion that there is a "fourth wall" between you and the audience; in such cases you will need to stay aware of both Focus Point *and* fourth wall. Sometimes you will create the illusion that there is a fourth wall by turning your back to the audience. When you do this, you stay connected to the audience if you stay aware of the Focus Point *and* whatever you are looking at on stage.

4. In film, the camera lens is the Focus Point. So: in the theatre, the Focus Point is stationary, just as the audience's eye is stationary in relation to the action. It is the actor who moves: upstage is the stage's "long shot," and downstage is the stage's "close-up." This is why understanding the principles of stage space is so critical for the theatre actor. In film, the actor may be still while the camera lens (standing in for the audience's eye) is moving—out for the long shot, in for the close up.

It is said that an auditioning director can see the quality of an actor's work in the first few lines. Actually, what the actor does with his or her Focus Point before he or she opens his or her mouth is also a good indicator of what will come. There are the actors who prepare on stage to begin the audition monologue by looking intently into the floor, or who start to speak without a sense of where the sound is headed out in the house. Since the voice will sound wherever you put your breath, I know that this actor's voice, when he starts to speak, will sound in a puddle around his feet or in a fog over the stage lip. It *cannot* be otherwise. An actor who hits center-center—or even better, up-center (if there's light, of course), takes a moment to find his Focus Point, then to connect his breath to it, is an actor who has the technical skills that inspire trust and respect from the viewers.

Then let the audience see all the study and love that have gone into your preparation! Break that leg!

As for the children's opera, I saw all of these practical ideas at work last summer. It was inspiring to see skills from my own early training making such a contribution forty years later. Sure enough, Sanford Jones used the large taped Xs on the back wall in every aspect of what happened over the next weeks. At the opening of each rehearsal, the Xs were an important part of the warm-up: the noisy children were led through a sequence of prompts, simply to look first at one X, then at another and another. "See what you know is there," he urged them. They fell quiet, engaged by looking and imagining. In singing rehearsal, Jones would remind them, "The key to the singer's success is the focus of his eyes." And during performance, this turned out to be the case. When a young performer faltered, Jones would gesture gently towards the big center X from the piano where he conducted, and instantly the performance would teeter back on track.

During the same period that the children's opera was in preparation at the theatre, I taught a lovely young woman how to use the Focus Point in my studio. A violin prodigy at five, she can trace her musical lineage to Heifetz; at age 11, she debuted with the New Orleans Philharmonic. Nevertheless, her breathing and alignment have posed problems for her as her career has developed. She was very unsure of herself when we began experimenting with the Focus Point. Once she found it, however, her whole body released, her breathing lowered and slowed, her face opened and lit up. "That feels perfect," she said. And that experience was deeply expressed in her playing. Connecting the feeling she had with the expressivity I heard is, of course, the focus—the point—of the Focus Point.

Peer-reviewed Article by *Lorraine Merritt & John Lohrey*

The Communication Needs of Medical Practitioners:
The Application of Voice Training to a Non-Theatre Based Context

Lorraine Merritt has long been associated with the voice, the body, and the way in which they work together. Originally qualifying at the National Institute of Dramatic Art, Sydney, in Voice Studies, Lorraine pursued further studies through the National Voice Centre at the University of Sydney. Diversifying into areas such as the corporate world, the medical field and the Arts environment, Lorraine has given the benefit of her vast experience to many hundreds of people from all walks of life. She is recognised by those in her field as the leading voice trainer to the corporate sector in Australia.

John Lohrey, Associate Professor, Head of the Theatre program, School of Visual and Performing Arts, University of Tasmania. Formerly, Head of the University's Centre for Performing Arts. Extensive experience as teacher and examiner of speech and drama; for the past 15 years Chief Examiner for Tasmanian Secondary Assessment Board. Associate of the Drama Board of the United Kingdom, frequent adjudicator at eisteddfods and drama festivals. In addition to application of theatre voice training to other professional contexts, research interests encompass consideration of variables affecting the processes of examinations in drama and theatre and the political economy of the performing arts in Australia over the past two decades.

Preface from *Lorraine Merritt*

As the voice teacher in the School of Visual and Performing Arts at the University of Tasmania in Australia, I have always been a theatre practitioner and as such have been very much at home in that role and with its vision. However, part of the role of being an academic in Australian universities today is to be active in the field of research. This role does not sit so comfortably with many of us in performing arts departments, as there is a limited history of research in our field in Australia. By decree rather than by design, I found myself challenged to seek out research opportunities.

A few years ago, I conducted a presentation skills workshop in Tasmania. One of the participants was the Tasmanian Health Commissioner. He is a great visionary and immediately after the workshop bounded up to me with brimming enthusiasm to ask if he could discuss with me further the application of what he had experienced in the workshop to the medical profession. In an instant, I had found an interesting and exciting research opportunity.

What followed was a series of meetings with the Commissioner, often done informally over lunch and with good wine. We fuelled each other's passion for our respective fields of work as we threaded together the appropriateness of voice work in addressing the communication needs of medical practitioners.

The Commissioner then arranged further meetings with key figures in medical practise (for example the spokesperson for general practitioners and the head of the Medical Council). These meetings allowed me to listen to the perceived communication needs of medical practitioners. At the same time, no doubt, the medical representatives were determining the appropriateness of what I could offer for their colleagues.

The greatest challenge for me at this stage was to address their fear that coming from a theatre base, the work that I would offer would be far too "airy" for their profession. This is where my own passion and belief in the value of voice work allowed me to develop a concrete language with them that ultimately convinced them of just how important skilled communication in their profession is.

From such discussions, I charted what I believed would best assist the communication practice of doctors. What was becoming evident was that medical practitioners are very skilled readers of their patients, yet at times are not as skilled at reading their own communication behaviour. Their awareness is very much "other" focussed rather than "self" focussed. In setting the goals of the program and developing the work-shop structure, I was constantly assisted by the Commissioner and members of his staff who had extensive experience with health professionals. They were very clear that there were real issues to be addressed in the vocal and nonverbal behaviours of many medical practitioners.

Having open access to their experience and knowledge allowed me to make very specific choices in the material I would introduce to the participants in the project. I am sure I would have been off target at times if I had not had such professional access.

The constant dialogue I conducted with the Commissioner's staff also allowed me to refine my language and thinking. I became confident in being able to think and talk from the perspective of the medical practitioner's world rather than the theatre practitioner's world. This was invaluable. I also learnt to trust how valuable the theatre practitioner's knowledge is when challenging other communication cultures.

A few years ago, I could never have imagined myself encouraging a neurosurgeon and an anaesthetist "to breathe" or "to find the appropriate vocal energy for the message." Now that I have, I feel like an explorer constantly excited by the challenges that the "outside" world offers us in translating our practise into their language.

Introduction: the importance of communication

The knowledge and practice of communication should include the understanding of the importance of the congruent transmittal of messages (ie. what we say, how we say it and what we look like when we say it are all giving off the same message) and the physical components of nonverbal communication, knowledge of the differences between nonverbal communication as an idiom and nonverbal behaviour as a skill, awareness of appropriate and inappropriate physical communication, and the ability to use the voice to enhance communication effectiveness.

These skills are essential for professional proficiency. Professional competence involves the development of cognitive, technical and communication skills (Hargie, 1986). Yet the training of many professionals places emphasis on the first two at the expense of the third (Field, 1990; Hargie, 1993; Karpin, 1994; Marginson, 1993).

Lack of appropriate training in communication leads to disappointing standards of communication in the workplace. As the following writers have observed:

> Attention...has been directed to deficiencies in the basic training received by, for example, pharmacists (Hargie and Morrow, 1987), nurses (Davies, 1976) and doctors (Pendleton, 1984). The interpersonal dimension has all too frequently been ignored, underestimated or misunderstood (Hargie, 1993, p6).

However, contemporary Australian workplace policy literature identifies communication skills as vital tools for success in the workplace. Currently in Australia these skills are identified as generic competencies (Karpin, 1994) in many workplaces and vocations. This paper will expand on this imperative in the specific professional context of medical practice and describe the application of voice work to the communication needs of medical practitioners.

Background

A common factor appearing in the analysis of patient complaints, as conducted by the Offices of the Health Commissioners in Australia has been the percentage of these complaints that are related to communication issues. In his 1995-6 report, the Queensland Health Rights Commissioner, Ian Siggins, made the following statement:

> Health complaints agencies in every jurisdiction, here and overseas, are unanimous that the most common cause of complaints is some form of communication failure...it is the experience of the commission and a growing body of research literature on adverse outcomes, that failures in communication by providers...have the most serious impacts on clinical outcome (P21).

Data gathered in 1996 from several states and territories in Australia illustrates the extent of this problem. In three states, issues related to communication were in the order of 17.7%, 19.6%, and 36.3% of complaints received. In 1998 complaint bodies in Australia reported that over 60% of all complaints received had as their primary cause a communication issue (The Health Complaints Commissioner, Tasmania, 1998-9).

This issue of communication in the health complaints area led to an investigation in the state of Tasmania by the Tasmanian Health Complaints Commissioner as to what actually were the causes of the communication complaints. A statewide consultation with the community showed that the communication complaints stemmed from a perceived lack of congruence in the communication by medical practitioners. It was noted that health professionals in general are very good at observing the congruence of the patient/client communication but it was discovered that they sometimes forget that patients are also listening and observing, as they seek clues to reinforce the message of what is being said. So, when there is a lack of congruence in the practitioner's spoken communication, which may be totally unintentional, mixed messages are received that may distract from the central issues and can leave the patient confused and vulnerable.

The importance of congruence in spoken communication is well documented in the literature. There is recognition of the verbal components of messages being the least significant indicator of the message (Drummond, 1993, p25). It is widely accepted that there is more to communication than a written transcript of the words. It is through the paralinguistic (pitch, tone, volume, accent, pause), extra linguistic (habitual, long-term biases that the individual speaker imposes on the vocal performance of linguistic and paralinguistic elements) and nonlinguistic (proxemics, kinesics) mediums that the subtle cues of communication are delivered. It is the nonverbal aspect of communication that is the vital expression of an individual's subjective experience and is understood by way of intuitive interpretation (Newham, 1993, p. 34).

From the analysis of complaints against medical practitioners, it appears increasingly important that they not only understand these nonverbal components of communication, but also integrate them into practical and continuous use. Within the professional medical literature (Nisselle, 1998), there is constant encouragement for medical practitioners to analyze their idiosyncratic behaviours and adjust, for example, their vocal use so as to create an environment of positive communication. The literature (e.g., Hargie, 1993) notes the principles of good communication practice. However, the author's research indicates that there appears to be a gap between the intellectual analysis of the knowledge and the transference of it into practical use. The "what" is established, but the detail of the "how" is often not recognized. It is within the field of theatre arts that the answer to the "how" of this practice exists. The domain of theatre training is an important and unique repository of significant resources and strategies that could be applied to assist medical practitioners to be more effective communicators.

The Tasmanian Health Commissioner was intent upon the application of the communication training. He saw its application as a positive contribution of the Commission to a problem that extends far beyond Tasmania.

Voice work for medical practitioners

The Tasmanian Health Commissioner, in understanding the pivotal role that communication plays in the delivery of health care services, approached the then Centre for Performing Arts at the University of Tasmania, Australia, to introduce practical voice work to general practitioners and specialist medical practitioners. Three sessions of three hours duration were conducted with three groups of ten participants. The sessions were conducted in the training room at the Division of General Practice, an environment that was familiar to all participants. There were 26 males and 4 females.

The intention in conducting these sessions was not to develop any sort of "performance trickery," but rather the participants were challenged to take responsibility for themselves as communicators in the same way as they would hope their patients would in turn take responsibility for their own health.

The design of the voice training program was influenced by references in the literature that vocal and physical factors feature prominently amongst the negative consequences of poor communication use (Bunch, 1999), as well as the author's professional practice in teaching theatre and voice skills. The vocal program goals and methodologies of Linklater, Berry, and Rodenburg, and the principles of the Alexander and Feldenkrais techniques also informed the development of this training program. The voice training program for the medical practitioners, therefore, was designed to develop skilled behaviour in vocal and physical use, specifically in physical centering, vocal variety, speech clarity, and pace of delivery.

In session one, the medical practitioners were asked to describe what is required of them in their interaction with patients. They responded that they are required: to concentrate their energy totally on an individual for a period of time; to listen; to empathize; to observe; to examine; to filter what might be relevant or irrelevant; to analyze; to establish trust; to problem solve; to sort through often complex issues and needs; to respond in terms that the particular person could digest, understand and be receptive to; to have the patient feel they were listened to and understood and treated with respect and dignity; to explain clearly the structure and functions of that most efficient yet complex machine ever designed, the human body; to create an environment where patients feel comfortable about the discussion of their special needs; to provide reasons for recommendations of treatment or procedures; to be relatively assured that the steps suggested will be followed; and then be able to start the process all over again with the same, energy, focus, skill, and empathy many times a day. In identifying that this is what their profession requires of them in an interactive sense, the medical practitioners also noted that in doing this, clear communication is essential to obviate any confusion on the part of the patient. In Australia the greatest cause of stress in this profession is fear of litigation (Crawford, 1997).

Following a discussion of these physical, mental and emotional demands, the issue of awareness of the participants' vocal and physical behaviours was raised. The greater number of the participants agreed that due to the multiple demands upon them, they believed they had become desensitized to just how they were using their voice and had little awareness of what messages were being sent by way of their physical cues. They noted however that they understood the importance of good vocal and physical use. Yet, they were open in their comments as to how little awareness they had in their ability to "read" themselves in this area. Another strong response was that as their focus was placed so completely on the patient, this gave them even less of a sense of themselves.

The participants were then videotaped in a simulated clinical situation. The briefing for this activity was that each participant was required to consult with a "patient" (another participant) on a health issue that the "patient" was anxious about. The videotaped material was not played back to the group at this point but was kept for the session that followed the practical voice activities.

At this stage, the participants were introduced to the principles of correct postural use. Through the experience of exercises for the spine, shoulders and neck, they were encouraged to investigate how the quality of communication can change markedly through honouring the architecture of the body as opposed to using idiosyncratic physical behaviour. They were given the opportunity to demonstrate what they considered to be the inappropriate features of their postural use and to gauge the impact this had on the quality of the communication. The participants noted that simply slumping in a chair through sheer fatigue might be read by a patient as lack of interest or boredom. They were surprised to note how the visible presence of tension in different parts of the body may communicate a lack of availability to the patient or send the message of preoccupation.

In session two and three, the use of the voice was investigated. By imposing distracting features into their vocal use, participants experienced the impact such features have on communication. They experimented with the impact that the following had on clear communication: an irritating quality like nasality or throatiness; de-energized speech; monotonic speech; failure to signpost key words, by the subtle shifts in intonation and inflection; the inappropriate use of pace; the lack of commitment to be physically engaged in the message.

The participants found that when the voice is restricted with habitual patterns, a variety of inappropriate messages are transmitted. For example, an irritating quality such as nasality can lead to the mere communication of a sound rather than meaning. The monotonic voice can be so lacklustre, that the potency of the message is limited. Speaking with no sense of engaging the body in speech can lead to a conspiratorial sound. De-energized speech due to lack of freedom in the jaw and lips can convey that what is being said is for oneself and not for the patient. The quality of giving in the communication can be easily lost. Limited signposting of key words can lead to the words all sounding the same. The listener can find it too difficult to sift out what is important. An excessively quick pace can lead to the alienation of the patient as he/she struggles with the medical practitioner's instinctive use of language, a use that may reflect only his/her own intellect and education. The participants experienced simple exercises to shift the vocal habits they considered inappropriate for their communication needs.

In the final half of the third session, the videotaped material from session one was played back to the group. This allowed the participants to see and hear themselves as their patients would. As they had already had the experience of the practical voice exercises and their awareness at this stage had been well raised, they were then able to be very specific in their feedback when encouraged to discuss what they had seen and heard during the patient consultation.

Conclusions

The application of theatre voice skills to another very specialized professional context proved a very valuable and challenging experience. The merits of this voice communication program were recognized by the medical profession. Following the period with the three trial groups, the program was accredited by the Royal Australian College of General Practitioners and there has been considerable interest nationwide in this work. Papers have been presented at Health Care Complaints Conferences and talks have been delivered to medical groups throughout Australia.

The voice program directly addressed the most basic of skills that would ensure ease and competency in vocal delivery and hence communication effectiveness for medical practitioners. The success of the program has important implications for voice teachers in private practice. It provides valuable information that can inform the development of similar programs in other medical professional contexts and in communication programs for undergraduate medical students. In the long-term, the implementation of such voice training has the potential to improve the communication skills of future doctors.

Most importantly, discussion of this project will reinforce the power that theatre skills and communication arts skills, specifically voice skills, have in addressing the communication needs of specific professions. It raises the challenge of how the rich storehouse of resources held within theatre practice can be most effectively transferred into non-theatre based professions. There is opportunity for constant challenge of other communication cultures.

References

Barlow, W. (1977). *The Alexander Principle*. Knopf: New York.

Berry, C. (1987). *The Actor and His Text*. Harrap: London.

Berry, C. (1973). *Voice and the Actor*. Harrap: London.

Bunch, M. (1999). *Creating Confidence*. Kogan Page, London.

Crawford, P. (1997). How GP's try to Deal with Workplace Stress, *Australian Doctor, 11 July, pp. 26-28.*

Drummond, M. (1993). *Fearless and Flawless Public Speaking*. San Diego: Pfeiffer.

Feldenkrais, M. (1977). *Awareness through Movement*. Hammondsworth, Middlesex: Penguin.

Field, L. (1990). *Skilling Australia*. Melbourne: Longman Cheshire.

Hargie, O. (Ed.) (1986). *A Handbook of Communication Skills*. London: Croom Helm.

Hargie, O. (Ed.) (1993). *Communication Skills Training for Health Professionals*. London: Chapman & Hall.

Karpin, D. (1994). World Class Leaders: Australia's Business Challenge, *Business Council Bulletin*, July, pp. 36-40.

Linklater, K. (1992). *Freeing Shakespeare's Voice*. Theatre Communications Group: New York.

Linklater, K. (1976). *Freeing the Natural Voice*. Drama Book Specialists: New York.

Marginson, S. (1993). *Arts, Science and Work*. Canberra: Australian Government Publishing Service.

Newham, P. (1993). *The Singing Cure*. London: Rider.

Nisselle, P. (1998). Good Expression is an Essential GP Skill, *Australian Doctor*, 9 October, pp. 50-51.

Queensland Health Rights Commission, (1995-6) *Annual Report*. Government Printers, Brisbane.

Rodenburg, P. (1997). *The Actor Speaks*. Methuen Drama: Great Britain.

Rodenburg, P. (1993). *The Need for Words*. Methuen Drama: Great Britain.

Rodenburg, P. (1992). *The Right to Speak*. Methuen Drama: Great Britain.

The Health Complaints Commissioner Tasmania, (1998-99). *Third Annual Report*. Hobart: Government Printers.

Column by *Ginny Kopf*

Have you been working solely with actors or singers and are now thinking of expanding your private student clientele to include businesspersons? I have been training private students in theatre voice and speech for twenty years. I expanded my teaching to include the business world about twelve years ago. I learned a lot, sometimes the hard way (the embarrassing way) during those twelve years. So let me share some great ideas for breaking into that business market that are based on my own experience. In my next article, I'll share more of what to do with business-oriented people once you're into that market. This is important because these people have a little different way of looking at things than theatre people.

Some Basic Marketing Tips
People are definitely looking for services such as yours, if they only know you're out there. You need exposure so they can find you. You need to get people talking about you. Pass out your business cards like candy. If you get exposure, even by volunteering for speaking engagements that don't pay, someone attending who is impressed by your presentation will tell other people. If you're good at what you do, people will talk about you. They'll pass on your name to their family, friends, coworkers, and fellow club members. Word of mouth is absolutely your most vital marketing tool. Anyone who has a successful private training or consulting business will tell you that word of mouth is what sells them.

Constant networking is the key. A commercial acting teacher I know advises his actors: "It's not who you know, it's who knows you." All of these avenues for marketing that I'm mentioning here are what will keep your name out there. But you absolutely must do follow-up. This is always where we as artists seem to fall short. As any sales and marketing expert will tell you, you must not just send out your promo and make calls, but follow up. The experts call within ten days to see if their material was received. Then, they follow up ten days later and a month after that, and so on. Sales people admit they don't even expect much of a response from a first call or first mailing. Bulk mailings of fliers, for example, usually only yield a one to two percent return. So they send out a second and then a third mailing before they expect a positive response.

Keep in mind that the average busy executive can simply overlook a piece of mail or a message the first time around. If something else is on their priority list, like family issues or a vital business deal, they might have to put off returning your call. To get into this business market, you'll need to be persistent and expect refusals…not unlike refusals in the world of acting or singing. One must be, as I like to call it, *pleasantly tenacious.*

Expect the process of establishing yourself in this new realm to take about three to five years. I worked very hard at it for three years (ads, mailings, calls, free workshops, making my rounds). After that, I had to advertise less and less. After ten years, I began pulling all my ads. I was getting so many referrals. It really was a wonderful feeling to finally get to the place where I didn't have to advertise as much…and the phone still rings!

Campaign Strategies
Here are some ideas for waging your marketing campaign, from placing ads

Ginny Kopf, author of *The Dialect Handbook* and *Accent Reduction Workshop for Professional American Speech* (3-CD set), is well known throughout Florida as a Voice, Speech and Dialect trainer for public speakers, broadcasters, and actors. She coaches privately and has given hundreds of workshops locally and nationally. She has done extensive speech coaching for Disney World, and Universal Studios. Corporate clients, include United Telephone, AT&T, Florida Power, The Golf Channel, and numerous television shows. She teaches vocal courses for the University of Central Florida's theatre program, and courses in voice-over and accent modification at several studios. Ms. Kopf holds an MA in Theatre and also an MFA in Voice and Speech Science.

for a cost to advertising for free. (Go ahead and skip to the "Free Advertising" section if you need some encouragement!)

Placing Ads

You can put ads in local business magazines, trade papers, and business newsletters of all kinds. Place ads in theatre programs, art shows, grand openings—shows the general public attends. Simply pick up one of these publications and contact their advertising editor. A business card ad is probably the smallest you should go. Make sure the artwork and logo are quite eye-catching. Advertising costs are pretty high ($100, $200, $500 or more, with better deals if you buy ads for a number of issues). But there are many very inexpensive and free ways to advertise. To be honest, I have personally found that my free advertising paid off, and my expensive advertising usually yielded little or nothing. That has been quite disheartening for me the half dozen times I've budgeted money for such ads after an editor of a magazine or newsletter spent considerable time convincing me that their publication "has a circulation of 50,000 people, so your ad, Ms. Kopf, will be seen by thousands a month."

When someone calls for my services, I make sure to inquire about where that person saw my name. So far, no one has ever mentioned seeing my ad in one of those large circulation publications. Perhaps I'm a cynic, but I think of how the average person looks through a magazine or even a trade paper; and I wonder how many readers really look at the ads. Perhaps if one were looking for a product in particular, an ad for that product would draw attention. Or if the ad really jumped off the page, it would demand attention. Your logo or font would have to be really eye-catching for use in this type of publication. I tend to think there are better and more cost-effective ways to advertise, however.

Newspaper ads may work for you, but they are expensive. You might need to place your ad in several sections. An acting and image studio here in Orlando admits they get a great response to their ads when they place the ad in the Business Section, Local, Arts and Entertainment, and even the Sports Section.

You might want to consider placing your ad in the Yellow Pages. But again, that would be costly and you'd need to figure out what section to be listed under. Cross-referencing is always best (as for advertising on a web page). Will business people look up under "Speech," "Speaking," "Public Speaking," "Voice," "Diction," "Schools," "Speech Therapy," "Image"? This is important: The average person does not really know how to find you. They're not sure where to look. Many, many of my clients tell me they asked around for a year or more, not really knowing where to look for help. A huge part of your marketing will be in educating them about what you do, where you train, and how you can help them.

Advertising On Your Own Web Page

There are countless companies that will help you set up a web page, at varying costs. I don't have one. I'm probably the last holdout. So I cannot speak for it's effectiveness, but business people definitely "shop" via the Internet probably more so than busy theatre people. If you do decide to advertise on a web site, I believe that clever cross-referencing is a must.

Additional Suggestions

How about an ad in your Homeowner's Association Newsletter. Or, is there an advertising newsletter for your city or community? A discount coupon book that advertises local businesses? Brainstorm. Be creative about all the places you could advertise inexpensively.

Become a member of your city's Chamber of Commerce or your Visitors and Convention Bureau (it's a yearly fee) and see what they offer in terms of promoting your business and providing networking opportunities. They have networking "mixers" every month, plus many activities where you can meet business people. At these mixers, be prepared to be barraged by everyone else in the room passing out their own cards, hoping you become a client of theirs. This may turn you on or turn you off. I joined once, years ago, but I personally had trouble schmoozing with a huge room of strangers who were all talking business. It seemed a very different world than the theatre receptions I was used to.

Organizations like The Chamber of Commerce and Visitors and Convention Bureau offer deals for advertising in the Yellow Pages and in their members book, but negotiate with them about what category your service should be listed under. Otherwise, as I mentioned before, your ad will simply get lost in their huge publication.

Join your region's Speaker's Bureau. It may be listed in the phone book under "American Speakers Association," or "National Speaker's Association," or "(your state's name) Speakers Association." These organizations serve as an agent to get you speaking jobs in corporate venues. The pay would be significant, simply because you would be playing with the big boys.

I was approached by a speakers' bureau years ago, after the president had heard me speak at a seminar. I was asked to write and rewrite my promo material in order to meet their standards. I was asked to fit all of my promo information neatly on an 8 1/2" x 11" piece of paper. He explained that the one-page flier is how corporate people prefer to do business. He said it was very important that it was in a form that was faxable or could be E-mailed. That page has to include a photo (I had to redo my headshot to have something very corporate looking), my bio, the seminar description with engaging attention grabbers, and four or five quotes from clients.

Needless to say, it is difficult to fit all this on one page. But if you developed such a flier, then it could be a wonderful addition to your promo packet. Or you could post these fliers or use them to do a mass mailing if everything about you is on just this one sheet.

Additionally, the bureau asked me for a professionally produced half-hour video of me teaching a seminar, because that was the only way they could sell me to corporate clients. I didn't have one, so their interest dropped. My book and articles and two accent reduction CDs were in that year's marketing plan, so the video they wanted needs to be my next project.

Doing a competitive "demo tape" of this kind takes a chunk of money and careful planning. If you should choose to go this route, I suggest you hire a professional videographer to videotape one of your seminars.

If your workshop were interactive, you'd have to get the class's permission in writing to be videotaped, stating that they will receive no fee, and that the tape would be used solely for your personal promo. You could even control the workshop situation a bit more by setting up a free class of very willing participants that you've hand-picked, in a professionally lighted space made to look like a classroom.

Free and Low-cost Advertising

Now for the good news...the myriad of creative, classy ways to advertise for free or at low cost! I mentioned that very few clients come directly from the ads I've put in papers. They come through word of mouth from someone who's worked with me or heard me speak.

So give a few of your business cards to loyal students. You can't lose. I'm constantly amazed at how often someone will hang on to a business card that was passed to them. That person will call me to say they got my card from an associate or friend six months or a year before. That's just the way it is—they will call you when they are ready to train.

Think about having a business card designed with the executive in mind, saving your snappier actor-oriented card for your theatre/film/television marketing. Give it careful thought. If you don't know a designer who could help you, ask the manager of a reputable printing shop if they could refer one to you. I recommend you get professional help when it comes to putting together your best promo packet. You could hire a networking and marketing consultant. The consultant would look over your promo material and help you class it up for the business world. Ask if that person would agree to trade a speech lesson for an hour of their advice.

When you get your new cards, simply ask if you could put some up at local businesses. Often they have those little racks for business cards. Target places where people come for self improvement—gyms, health food stores, massage clinics, dance studios, photography studios, etc. Places like MAILBOXES ETC and PostalAnnex also have bulletin boards for you to tack up five or ten of your cards. No, I don't think it's tacky to advertise this way, if your card isn't tacky! Remember that people need help in finding you.

Make a list of every place you visit, and make sure to revisit these establishments every month or so to replenish the supply. Keep a notebook of all your contacts. Include a date, name of contact person, what you dropped off, any notes that may help you to remember the business, i.e., "They just hired a new head of training who was used to the rapid pace of Manhattan," or "The boss' secretary just had a baby boy, Eric," "The Vice President goes golfing with his clients, makes all of the financial decisions." Taking notes and following up is tedious, but this is what will help you get results.

The very best way to advertise for free is to write a short article. This article should give hot tips about speech and image improvement, something practical that the reader would feel they could implement. It could be as simple as five or ten bullet points. Get this article into newsletters of businesses in your area, such as the phone company, power company, various business firms, doctor's offices, health food stores, massage therapists, etc. You might need to have a contact who could introduce you to the editor and push your article through for you. Usually these newsletter editors love to have a pithy article to print. If you have the skill to write and sell a longer article for a general interest or business magazine, it certainly would be the best way to build your credibility, and your income. Check books in the library for more information on how to get your magazine articles published. I will admit though, it is more complicated than you might think.

Another way to advertise for free is to do seminars that reach the general public. Even twenty years into my private practice, I continue to teach free or low-paying seminars in order to promote myself, and simply because I enjoy them so much. Though they take up time, they never fail to get me at least one client.

Is there an adult education or noncredit school in your area? I've taught a "Professional Voice Image" seminar and an "Accent Reduction and Diction" course at one of these schools in my area for the past five to seven years. It's low pay, but I always get private students following the completion of these courses; and I am able to sell dozens of my diction tapes. The best part is that the school actually advertises for me! Their course description book is sent out to every household. Stacks of them are sitting around in lobbies of businesses, schools, bookstores and libraries. Not a week goes by that someone doesn't say they saw my photo and class description in that booklet. Yes, your photo or a snappy logo does get more attention in such a booklet. So whether they end up taking the class or just telling a friend about it, it promotes your name.

Volunteering to give workshops will always pay off in the end. Volunteer to speak (twenty minutes, one hour, two hours) to Toastmasters groups. There are probably several chapters of these in your city and they look for guest speakers with your skills. The people who attend are incredibly open to improvement, so it is very likely you'll get clients from such a group...if not directly, then through word of mouth.

Volunteer to give a workshop at a trade show. Your city probably has many throughout the year, with names such as "Southern Women's Show," "Consumer's Trade Show," "Senior Living," or anything geared towards the white-collar professional or hopeful entrepreneur. Plan well ahead though. When you go to one of these shows, get the name of the trade show planner to see if they are taking proposals for guest speakers for next year's show.

Consider giving a workshop at business networking groups in your area. There are probably groups like this listed in the business section of your newspaper. Ask your business friends if they belong to such a club. Go down to your Chamber of Commerce to see if you can volunteer to do a workshop or at least to put business cards up on their wall. They usually have a special area for them. Also check to see who at the Chamber is in charge of bringing in special speakers.

Docents, tour guides or lecturers who volunteer their expertise at a museum, would probably welcome some speaking tips at one of their monthly meetings. My next door neighbor is a retired teacher, now a docent, and asked me over the back fence if I would be willing to do a free seminar. I've gotten paid and unpaid work from a number of my neighbors merely by chatting with them in the front yard about what I do. Your own block is a potential market, just by letting them know what you do for a living. You won't alienate people, because what you do is a service; you're not trying to persuade them to buy encyclopedias.

Distribute your promotional materials to schools, both the Speech and Theatre Departments. Include the Speech Pathology Department if it is separate from the public speaking classes, and also the Music Department's vocal section. If you do accent modification, then contact the English as a Second Language Department. Begin with community colleges and universities, and then add high school contacts to your list.

The department secretary is the one who receives incoming calls from community people. You'd be surprised how many calls a week secretaries get from people asking for a referral. These callers are often not sure whom to ask for, so you would need to educate and remind the secretary that such a person as you exists. You will want the secretary to be on your side, and have your card handy in his or her Rolodex. Stop in and see him or her about every two to three months with more cards. Also contact the instructors in all those departments. If you don't have time to call them, simply put a flier in their mailbox with some of your business cards. They most likely would love to have someone they could refer for private lessons, as many of them have schedules that don't allow time for private teaching.

It might even be worth it for you to invite that secretary or fellow teacher to one of your seminars (free). This way, he or she could refer people to you as a result of their firsthand exposure to your work. At any of these workshops, free or not, make sure the attendees have something to take with them—several of your business cards or a flier. At any of these workshops, ask if you can pass around a pad so you can put their names on your mailing list. Then stay in touch with them every few months (phone call, postcard, or a quick E-mail blurb). They may not really need your services that month, but the next month, a big presentation may come up, or a job change, and they'll think of you. But they'll only think of you if they have recently heard from you.

You can send out or place fliers in all kinds of locals. Just ask friends or current clients who run businesses if you can put up a flier on their bulletin board, in the window, or in their lobby.

You can offer a workshop for a fee (unless your state has limitations). Put up fliers and do a mass mailing and see what happens. If you have one person or a hundred, you still win. My state limits the assembly of a paying group to fewer than five, if the class is held in my home. But if you ask around, maybe someone will donate a space for your workshop. Don't underestimate the power of doing some trade-outs of services. Offer free lessons to the person or their kids, in return for advertising favors. If you need to rent a space, check with your local "Jazzercise" gym or a church. On off-hours, some groups or organizations rent space cheaply.

With regard to trading your services for some business service or other, don't do it if you feel you are really not in need of their service. Many businesspersons are accustomed to exchanging favors (especially "negotiators," like lawyers and stockbrokers). In my experience, lessons are kept more on a professional note when you do not barter your teaching services.

If you have a book or audio tape or video tape that you can show at all your workshops, it profoundly raises your credibility in the business world. At the very least, you can self-publish a workbook or drill packet or warm-up tape. Bring these materials with you for purchase when you do a seminar (with the hosting client's permission, of course). The money you make can go back into your marketing fund. I recommend you bring an assistant with you, to sell your product after your seminar. It looks more professional and keeps you free to answer questions of attendees who come up to you afterwards. In your promotional packet, be sure to include a blurb about each piece you have published (including magazine or newsletter articles), perhaps on the bottom of your bio sheet.

Get a local news reporter to interview you. This is fantastic exposure— especially if you're working on an interesting project at the time. The reporter may jump at the chance to write about you. Get to know some DJs, and get an on-air interview.

Approaching large corporations without first having an internal contact is tough, but not impossible if your promo material is excellent. You can find out the name of the head of "Training" or "Human Resources." Unfortunately, nowadays, many companies are paring down and letting their Human Resources person go. Even with a contact in the company that knows your work, the person in charge of the budget may not see the need for speech training as keenly as your original contact did. It's the person who handles the purse in the company that has the power. I've lost many a deal with a corporation because, although everyone else was excited about getting speech training, the proposal made it to the head of finance and was dropped. This is disturbing since we are used to working with artistic directors and heads of theatre departments whom we can speak to directly about what we do. I'll say more about the corporate mind in my next article.

Your Promo Packet
You will need a classy, professional-looking promo packet to send out to big corporations. Yours material should be in a folder, and include business card(s), cover letter, full resume or bio, sample proposals, fee schedule, quotes from clients, and some fliers. You could have embossed folders made for you, but all you really need is a nice folder from an office supply store that has a slot inside for your (classy, professional-looking) business card. I also glue my business card on the front cover so it can sit on a desk and still gain some attention.

Your promo pack should include a succinct cover letter with a carefully worded description of what you can do for a particular company. Speak to their needs rather than all about you. It can be professional and positive, but should not be emotional. They, frankly, do not care if you "would love to" or "would be delighted to" or "have always had a dream to work with this wonderful company." They are interested in quick results, cause and effect.

In the cover letter, tell your client that you can design a training program to meet their individual needs, their schedule, and their budget. Prove your point by informing them that you've included several proposals you have designed for other companies, how you implemented the training, and if possible, the company's response to the training. Then tell them that you've included in their pack a sample proposal for their company that you would be glad to discuss with them. List the contents of your promo packet in the cover letter. End by telling them exactly when you will call to set up a meeting (about two weeks away). Avoid saying, "Call me to discuss this proposal." Call them.

Your first call may only confirm that they received the promo, but have not had a chance to look at it. So tell them you will call again the following week. Your training proposal should have their company name on it and demonstrate that you are keeping their distinctive needs in mind. From talking to the client on the phone, or better yet, by arranging a meeting with them, find out what is important to them, and problems they've had in the past with their employees' speech or image. Listen carefully to the lingo and wording they use and then use those buzz words in your proposal. For example, for my Walt Disney World proposals, I always include the words "team" and "cast members" and "onstage presence" and even "safety." For another corporation, the president used phrases like "corporate image" and "putting a smile in your voice" and "intonation," so I wove these words in. I have written and rewritten my proposals countless times over the years. It is the most agonizing part of the work. Every proposal will be slightly different. After you've written a few, you'll find you can steal phrases for the next one.

For the sake of time and ease, many businesses will prefer that you fax or E-mail your promo, so ask what they prefer. It's certainly not as impressive-looking, of course. But when you have your first meeting with them, you will then want to give them the full promo packet. Bring two extras (one for you, one for them), even if you've mailed it to them, just in case it got buried somewhere in their office. All of the material in your promo packet should be faxable, even E-mailable. Be sure your logo, font, and artwork will still look sharp and clean on a black and white fax.

After my resume, I include a paragraph bio. They can use this summary about you in a newsletter, program, or seminar packet. In fact, I have a long version (10-15 lines) and a short version (no more than 4 lines), so they can choose the one they have room for in their material. The bio also helps them formulate a spoken introduction of you. Before I did this, people's introductions of me were either slightly inaccurate, or they struggled to read things off of my resume and ended up saying things that really were not the most important points. Your clients will really appreciate your short bio. If you have books or tapes you've published, you can include a brief description and publisher's information on the bottom of the bio page.

Even if your material is theatre oriented, it is still a published work, and lifts your credibility. Your promo packet should definitely include one page of client testimonials. Quotes from clients are extremely important in the business world. Choose very short excerpts, never long letters on the client's letterhead. Obviously, the most influential clients' quotes bear the most weight. If all you have is actors' quotes at this point, start with these until you can include more and more businesspersons' quotes. You just need the person's name and their occupation or company. You can label it "Client Recommendations." I put "This is what her clients are saying about her" on mine. It's easy to get quotes of praise.

Keep in mind, however, that if you ask busy clients to write you a blurb, and even include self-addressed, stamped envelopes, you'll probably never get any back. The best way is to call them (or ask when they come in for a lesson). Tell them you are collecting short quotes of recommendation for use in your promo material, and ask them if they could say a line or two about you right then, for you to write down. They'll be glad to do it. Read it back to them, so they won't fear they'll be misquoted. If you indeed use their quote, send them the page you type up of all the recommendations. If the person seems hesitant about what to say, simply show them some of the short quotes you've collected from other clients.

Another even easier way to get quotes is to note when any of your clients says something complimentary in a lesson session. Ask if they'd mind if you quoted them, as you're collecting recommendations for your promo. You can also get some good statements by asking for a short class critique right after teaching a seminar or course.

One more thing that your promo packet can contain is copies of any newspaper or magazine articles that have been written about you and your work. It's tempting to overload your promo packet. Over the years, I've worked on paring mine down. If it comes across as succinct and efficient, I believe it will have a better chance of being considered.

Press On!
Don't expect that you will get direct results from your direct marketing. Anyone in the marketing field, selling any product or service, will tell you this. I find it odd, but I seldom get the jobs I've sent promo materials to. It can be frustrating. I second guess myself and wonder what I did wrong, or worry that my material wasn't professional enough. But I just keep sending out promotional material, doing my networking, teaching workshops, and never let up on my marketing, and somehow my name gets around. Toss the seeds out there and they'll sprout—probably in places you've never anticipated.

Make a definite marketing plan and stick to it. Then keep track of all your steps. When someone calls me, I always ask where he or she got my name, and I write the referring party in a column next to the prospective client's name. If you do this, you'll be able to check where your marketing is paying off—you'll know which ads to keep and which to scrap. You'll also know who your greatest supporters are and can nurture those relationships; and you'll know just where to focus your attention for the next month in terms of marketing.

Be tenacious—pleasantly tenacious!

Dorothy Runk Mennen, (associate editor) Professor Emerita of Theatre/Visual and Performing Arts, Purdue University, developed the original voice curriculum for their MFA; vocal director of musicals, contralto soloist, actress. Prior to university teaching, taught vocal music, theatre-speech, English in public schools in Ohio and Indiana. In 1985 was given a national award for Leadership and Performance by University and College Theatre Association, American Theatre Association. She does consulting, teaches privately; a member of NATS (served on Board of the Indiana chapter), The Voice Foundation, Founding President of VASTA. On Editorial Board, and contributor for *The Vocal Vision,* author of *The Speaking-Singing Voice, a Vocal Synthesis.*

What is singing? What is good singing?

In our first Journal, we said we would explore Singing wherever we found an interest. In our second journal we are asking those simple questions. (Did I dare say "simple"?)

"When I was young and twenty…" At least, when I was younger, I was certain I knew what good singing was, or should be. Each year I am less positive, less sure. I find myself listening differently from in my youth.

Paul Thomason has an editorial in *Opera News*, October 2000, "Second Hearing." He was asked by a friend for some tapes of great singing. Enthusiastically he began his search; completing his labor of love he began his letter; he was amazed to find that his answers of twenty-five years ago were quite different from his answers today. I am tempted to quote from his comments, but I prefer you read the piece and think about how your response may differ from his.

In my own search for what may be the unanswerable, I can be much clearer with a student who is studying with me than I can with others. I tell the student that I don't know what their voices will be like, I only know what we need to work towards. I assure them that working on singing, as in acting, is a constant discovery. I keep refining my definitions, but I am aware that many have the same conflict that I have had. Can I really love musical theatre and immerse myself in Bach for weeks at a time? Can I work with a student on *Caro Mio Ben* and then work on her singing and characterization of *Wouldn't It Be Loverly?* Why not? Understanding the differences is paramount. (I find I can do that and admit there is a lot of the singing literature I don't know, and much that I don't like, past or present.)

In considering our posed questions, we accept that we are constantly bombarded with choices in music. Theatre music is experimenting at both the classical and popular level, as well as at the folk and religious level. What do we sing? Do we make standards for ourselves or let someone else establish the standards? The definitions?

As a member of the National Association of Teachers of Singing (NATS) for more than twenty-five years, I am very mindful that the members reflect changes in attitudes and standards. *The Journal of Singing*, the official journal of NATS, to me is a far superior journal to the one I read early in my membership. It is more comprehensive, more inclusive, more exciting in these later years. The featured columns on vocal technique and health, especially those of Ingo Titze and Dr. Robert Sataloff, who are scientists as well as accomplished singers, speak to a variety of concerns for vocalists and teachers. The scope of interest has broadened beyond the classical, art songs and repertoire. Early evidence of change was demonstrated some years ago in an experience of the Indiana Chapter of NATS. One of our singing teachers spoke eloquently of the diversity of his students, the demand for their talents in high school musicals or civic productions and often church music. He asked for the organization to open auditions to Musical Theatre as a category for auditions. The change was made. Most were happy about it. Many of our teachers are not teaching prospective opera singers. They have as their objective to teach all of their students to sing well, and in their own language.

Belting, a familiar term to many of us for years, was frowned upon by most of the classically trained. Surely that can't be good singing, said many. The consensus was that it would damage the voice. In these past few years one of the most popular columns in the *Journal of Singing* is "The Bach to Rock Connection," by Robert Edwin. NATS has been offering workshops in Belting! At the 2000 National Conference in Philadelphia a featured presentation was Elizabeth Howard's "Born To Sing," a demonstration of many styles of singing.

Are we any nearer to answering the questions? Or are we more confused? If, at one time we might have considered belting as vocal abuse, what about the singing of other cultures? Do we include them in our definitions? There is no end . I just saw part of Ken Burns' documentary on Jazz on PBS. One statement was that Louis Armstrong changed the way every singer would sing. Did I hear correctly? What does this mean to our historical study of singing?

VASTA's International Voice Conference 2000 held at George Mason University outside of Washington, D.C., in August, was VASTA's effort to go beyond our own borders in a greater way than we have done in our fourteen-year history. We presented singing from different cultural viewpoints. It was exciting and revealing. We felt a little more comfortable and freer with our Gospel singer, Tonya Barnett, and sang along with her. We were astounded by the sounds of Tran Quang Hai, his demonstration and teaching of Overtone Singing. Some of those in attendance were excited about their own ability to follow his instructions in learning the technique. The traditional vocal styles of Bali demonstrated by Desak Made Suarti Laksmi, with her partner I Nyoman Catra, Bali's most renowned artist of traditional dance, voice and theatre, left us with delight and awe.

The oriental culture has a different concept of good singing from ours. Hearing and seeing their performances may open our minds not only to accepting another way of singing, but to ask many questions of them and of ourselves. The subject of vocal violence is presented in this issue of the Journal. How does this fit into our attitudes toward strongly different techniques? We find a real dilemma in how we reach out and how we embrace different techniques. This journal will stretch our minds and bodies further by learning in our section of *P'ansori*, Korean traditional singing.

The richness of our membership in VASTA is the variety of persons working with voice and speech. We have members (as was our original group) who were for the most part, working with theatre voice. In some instances we have individuals trained in more than one aspect of vocal training. Our assistant editor for this column shares with us expertise and experience in several areas of voice. How did this happen? Read her fascinating story of a journey that brought a gifted singer to unusual career choices with a romantic element that is intriguing.

Does all this help to answer our original questions? What is singing? What is good singing? The path to discovery is open. Let us hear from you.

Editorial Column by *Linda Carroll*

From Here to There: Becoming a Voice Specialist

Linda Carroll: (assistant editor) Director of Undergraduate Studies at NYU, known for her work in care and assessment of the professional voice. Has published widely in journals and contributed chapters to major textbooks on voice care. A regular presenter at The Voice Foundation Symposia and other international congresses; a guest on NPR and PBS. Currently completing her Ph.D. at Columbia University, holds advanced degrees (MPhil, MS) from Columbia University, and undergraduate degrees (BM, BS) from The University of Maine. Clinical experience with Dr. Robert Sataloff and Dr. Peak Woo. Private practice includes singers on Broadway, the Metropolitan Opera, lawyers and comediennes.

Growing up in Maine ensured a deep appreciation of "Downeast humor." Often dry and quite witty, the jokes often reminded "Mainers" of our limitations, and ability to dream. One classic joke goes something like this:

> A foreigner (non-Mainer) finds himself lost along a country road in central Maine. Seeing a farmer, he stops to ask for help. "Which way to East Vasselboro?" asks the foreigner. The downeast farmer replies "Well, let me see. You go down the road a piece, turn left and …..no. You go down the road a piece, turn right, then left and then…no. Well, you can turn around, go back about a mile and then…no. Come to think of it, Mister, you can't get there from here."

Music and singing, in particular, was always a part of my upbringing. Weekly junior, youth and senior choir rehearsals mixed with weekly piano lessons, voice lessons, play rehearsals, band practice and school chorus rehearsals were the norm for our family. It was not unusual, therefore, for this little girl near the coast of Maine to declare from an early age that she wanted to be a singer and "other things involving voice." My parents were avocational musicians and prided themselves in their brood of young singers and musicians. As far back as elementary school, the teachers were concerned that I was so analytical, and yet so involved in music and singing. Teachers at school thought I should receive formal psychological counseling.

Following high school, I was accepted as a scholarship student at The University of Maine as a Voice Performance major (Bachelor of Music). My undergraduate mentor and voice teacher, Ludlow Hallman, found that my ability to be a "quick-study" caused significant problems in vocal development. During my first semester in college, I learned 22 new songs/arias and had them prepared for memory and performance. In an effort to slow down my voracious appetite, he created an assignment for each new song/aria. I was to fully research and explore the composition: music theory analysis, word-for-word translation, orchestration, timeline of the composition from the composer's other works, singer for the premiere of the composition, other roles during that same time frame for the premiere singer, other musical works that may have influenced the composer, world events at the time of composition, and any trivia I could exhume from Fogler Library (the main library at The University of Maine). As hoped, the research allowed my voice to grow into each new song/aria. The research also heightened my love of analysis and the joys of research. Any fears of the ivy walls of a library were dispelled.

As I explored each composition, I questioned the limitations of my own performance degree. Students majoring in Music Education were required to take valuable courses on the process of learning. As a Voice Performance major, I was not allowed to enroll in those courses unless my major was changed to Music Education. For nearly 3 years, I regularly changed majors each semester to allow enrollment in those courses, and completed both degrees the same semester. Throughout my undergraduate years, I maintained any course that could enrich overall skills should be taken.

After completing my undergraduate degrees, my career path led me to Philadelphia, where, for a short time, I worked as a clerical assistant in the Department of Internal Medicine at Thomas Jefferson University. Earlier intimidations of medical terms were abolished. Months later, Dr. Robert Sataloff, a leading otolaryngologist, hired me as administrative assistant and voice trainer for his medical practice. This began my intensive training in the world of voice research and rehabilitation.

Dr. Sataloff's medical practice often received tertiary referrals, and patients needed (and deserved) a solution for their impairments. Working in team management with a speech pathologist (at that time, only in the medical practice one day every 2 weeks), it was my responsibility to assess vocal function from a technical and performance standpoint. Shortly thereafter, Dr. Sataloff requested that I establish a voice laboratory in the medical practice to perform acoustic and aerodynamic measures on injured and normal voices. Attending The Voice Foundation Annual Symposium: Care of the Professional Voice alerted me to these factors: (1) Although I had good instincts, I lacked adequate knowledge on neuroanatomy and neurophysiology that could affect laryngeal function; (2) a Masters degree in Speech-Language Pathology would be the best avenue to increase my knowledge base (and to become a voice therapist legally); (3) a Ph.D. would likely be needed if I really wanted to "play the big boy's game," and (4) even the most respected researchers remained open to sincere questions by aspiring researchers. So, with a wing and a prayer, I began my experience as a junior researcher before completing my Masters in Speech-Language Pathology.

Beginning my Masters at Temple University was ill-fated. After completing the necessary pre-requisites (essentially the requirements for a Bachelors in Speech-Language Pathology and Audiology), nearly all graduate courses and over 200 clinical hours as a speech pathologist in training, the faculty requested that I cease all professional singing obligations and discontinue working in a medical practice. They felt working in a medical practice was a conflict of interest (their views have since changed). I left the program and vowed that I would continue my path at a later time when the Ph.D. seemed "right." Three years later, I woke up and realized it was time to do the Ph.D. in laryngeal biomechanics and complete the dogged Masters. Teacher College, Columbia University eagerly accepted my application. By that time, I had published in peer-review journals, written textbook chapters, presented internationally on normal and disordered voices, and had amassed a large collection of "who's who in the world of voice" as trusted friends and colleagues.

Ron Baken, brilliant researcher and author of the voice laboratory "Bible" (Clinical Measurement of Speech and Voice), agreed to mentor me and direct my Ph.D. research at Columbia University. Nearly ten years have passed and the Ph.D. ("Airflow characteristics in loud singing during register transition among highly skilled classical singers") is now in the final oral defense, slated for "hooding" in Spring 2001.

Over the past seven years, I have joined academe with appointments at Columbia University (Department of Speech and Language Pathology), The University of Iowa (Department of Speech Pathology and Audiology), Pace University (NYC) (Department of Communication Studies), The New School University (The Actors Studio MFA School of Dramatic Arts), The University of Maine (Department of Music), and now New York University (Department of Speech-Language Pathology and Audiology). This whirlwind of activity was all accomplished through the most untraditional route.

My personal life has been marked with a whirlwind collaboration (also known as marriage) with another well-known voice trainer, William Riley (his clients include Celine Dion, Ben Vereen, Gretha Boston, former President Bill Clinton, Deborah Voigt, Marquita Lister, John MacMaster, and dozens of other Metropolitan opera and Broadway singers/actors). Our 2-year old daughter has proven to be equally atypical in her path of knowledge. Matching rhythms to vocal exercises at 13 days of age, pitch and rhythm at 9 weeks, first song at 4 months, and now sings Caro Mio Ben at age 26 months, Jennifer Lassie Riley is a delight and treasure (and highly verbal). Bill and Jennifer are proof that there are no real limits.

The typical route for becoming a voice expert is a background of the Bachelors, Masters and (if necessary) a Doctorate, and then embark on clinical, academic and/or research loves. There are many avenues however to the non-conformist with perseverance. For those who want to "play with the big boys" but don't mind being confined to an associate position within the voice care team, there are courses and programs (such as the Summer Vocology Program at the Denver Center for the Performing Arts) that help train the interested and curious.

If you have a desire to make a significant impact on voice training, care or research and feel that your background does not match the "typical," remember that there is no real typical person in voice care. The only requirements are perseverance, dedication, and enthusiasm. You can get there from here. There are many roads (in many countries) that can lead you to a world not thought possible without the desire. So, if the first farmer says, "You can't get there from here," find another farmer.

Peer-reviewed Article by *Tara McAllister-Viel*

A Cross-Cultural Examination of Breath and Sound Production in Pansori

Written in cooperation with Han, Myung-Hee, Pansori-Actor/Translator and Park, Mi-Kyong, M.A. Simultaneous Translation, Hankuk University of Foreign Studies

In *American Theatre* magazine's January 2001 issue, Kristin Linklater and Anne Bogart debate the effectiveness of American actors-in-training practicing actor-training techniques from non-Western cultures. The questions and opinions found in this article paralleled a discussion in which I participated when I delivered a version of this paper at a voice symposium held at the Korean National University of the Arts in Seoul, Korea, December 1, 2000. Several Korean theatre professionals at the symposium wondered, as Linklater had a year ago in the "Far Horizons" article that sparked this debate, "Actors-in-training are often submitted to a kind of transcultural grafting that dilutes their art (30)."

To Korean artists who have struggled with the onslaught of Westernization after establishing a democratic government in the late 1980s, the process of discovering and nurturing a Korean voice, both literally and philosophically, lead to passionate debates. When the traditions of non-Western and Western theatre are practiced simultaneously, must one training discipline be compromised by another or can two unique traditions strengthen and inspire each other? More specifically, can Linklater's vocal method be strengthened and inspired by non-Western actor training techniques? Or, for Korean artists the question is reversed, can Korean actor training techniques be strengthened and inspired by a non-Korean vocal methodology, such as Linklater's?

Korean actors, like their US counterparts, also come from a tradition that is "densely *verbal* (ibid, 32)," as evidenced in the vocal traditions of Korean *pansori*. And based on the discussion at the KNUA voice symposium, Linklater's opinion could have been uttered by several of the Korean theatre professional in attendance. "I think if you get your roots deep enough into this tradition you have earned the right to meet other, international ones. The depth and discipline of those traditions are extraordinary. If we come to them as if we're going to the street fair—to see what we can pick up to decorate our living rooms—then we're in trouble (American Theatre, 32-33)." I think both American and Korean theatre professionals would agree that 'grafting' and 'decorating' their artistic traditions with another cultures' training techniques would not be useful. However, a serious study, comparing and contrasting both traditions might prove very useful within the context of practical application. KNUA's own theatre voice training program provides the unique opportunity to explore the philosophical questions debated by theatre professionals on both sides of the Pacific.

Undergraduate and graduate KNUA actors-in-training must study Kristin Linklater and Cicely Berry techniques while simultaneously studying the vocal training techniques of a traditional Korean vocal training method, Pansori. This comparison between pansori and Linklater/Berry techniques may not only help Western vocal practitioners familiar with these vocal techniques for the stage understand pansori better, but may also encourage possible intercultural study between the two methodologies similar to the acting training program at the Korean National University of Arts. In case one is totally unfamiliar with pansori, a brief introduction to form, content and history may be useful.

Tara McAllister-Viel is Visiting Professor of Voice, School of Drama, The Korean National University of Arts, in Seoul, Korea and pansori trainee under Han, Nongson. She earned a Master's of Fine Arts in Acting from the University of Wisconsin-Madison and Bachelor of Arts degrees in Music (violin studies), Comparative Literature, and Theatre Arts. She has workshopped with Cicely Berry, voice director for the Royal Shakespeare Company, as well as voice and movement artists from the Moscow Art Theatre and GITA schools in Moscow, Russia. She has been a professional actor in the Chicago area and with numerous regional repertory companies around the U.S. for the past 10 years.

Most academics generally agree the word *pansori* (sometimes spelled in English as *p'an-sori* or *p'ansori*) is derived from *pan* meaning "performance area" and *sori* meaning "sound." Alan Heyman in his article, "Pansori," *The Traditional Music and Dance of Korea* defined pansori as "a narrative-epic-dramatic folk vocal art form (209)." The National Theatre of Korea publicity designed for English-speaking Westerners in its fall Program Guide 2000, advertises, "pansori is a universally renowned Korean epic music performance by one singer (www.ntok.go.kr)." Many English-speaking Westerners commonly refer to it as "traditional Korean opera (Don Kirk, International Herald Tribune)" though pansori differs from a Western cultural understanding of 'opera' in both form/content and vocal training technique. "The vocal techniques of Pansori are different from Western opera or other types of classical vocal music in terms of breathing and use of classical vocal chords (*www.agrakr.co.kr/9804/50.htm+pansori&hl=en*, author unknown)." Marshall Phil notes, "Some writers have used the expression 'one-man opera' to explain the term [pansori]. The oddity of the expression aside, it does succeed in conveying the four essential characteristics of p'ansori: it is a solo oral technique, it is dramatic, it is musical, and it is in verse (3)."

In trying to understand and appreciate pansori, it may be more useful for Western vocal practitioners to resist definitions for a moment and instead examine pansori's basic components of breath and sound production by contrasting them with familiar Western vocal production techniques for the stage. Instead of equating pansori with Western opera techniques this article will compare it with the breath and sound production techniques for the Western theatrical stage. Kristin Linklater and Cicely Berry techniques have been chosen because their training methodologies are taught along side pansori methodologies at The Korean National University of Arts, School of Drama department that will be examined later in this paper. This comparison between pansori and Linklater/Berry techniques may not only help Western vocal practitioners familiar with vocal techniques for the stage understand pansori better, but may also encourage possible intercultural study between the two methodologies similar to the acting training program at the Korean National University of Arts. In case one is totally unfamiliar with pansori, a brief introduction to form, content and history may be useful.

Form
The performance form of today's pansori can either be *recital* or fully staged productions (*chang-geuk* style). In the more traditional *recital* format, a single vocalist is accompanied by one drummer playing a barrel drum, (*puk*). The vocalist usually stands as the drummer sits cross-legged on a straw mat (*sori-pan*) which is situated on the apron of a contemporary proscenium stage. Traditionally, pansori artists wouldn't have performed on a proscenium stage but would have performed amidst the loud hurried crowds of the marketplace. The singular pansori vocalist wears traditional Korean dress and holds a fan and/or handkerchief as *props* with which to gesture (*pallim*), while performing traditional folktales. The form of the folktales themselves is divided into singing (*chang*) passages and speaking (*aniri*) passages.

Chang-geuk, fully-staged versions of these same folktales, owes it's origins to pansori but has grown into it's own distinct form. "For the last one hundred years, Chang-geuk has been developed as a stage form of Pansori, a type of traditional Korean singing. In the early phase, it was simply an expanded form of Pansori: songs originally sung by one singer and accompanied by one drummer were performed by several singers on stage. In later phases, theatrical elements were added in scripting, characterization and make-up. It has since developed into a multi-dimensional performing arts (Program Notes, National Theatre of Korea joint production, China, Japan and Korea *Choonhyang-Jun*)." Chang-geuk dramas include large casts, imaginative costumes and sets, and a full pit orchestra of traditional Korean instruments. These performances can last up to 6 hours, including a 30-minute dinner break. For some experts, Chang-geuk is a popularized version of pansori. "The theatrical trappings such as the scenery, lighting, special costumes, and make-up used in changguk performance have nothing to do with a real pansori performance. Although the changguk is much easier for general audiences to appreciate than the pansori, the changguk's artistic value is much less. Changguk has, therefore, never replaced pansori, but rather the two musical traditions have co-existed (Po-hyong Yi, 245)."

In both formats the performer/spectator relationship at times dispenses with what Western theatre practitioners would recognize as the "fourth wall." Robert Barton defines *fourth wall* as, "imaginary partition through which the audience watches (159)." The pansori artist can break through this 'imaginary partition' that separates performer and spectator and directly address the audience. For example, while the singular pansori artist performs, audiences follow the drummer's example and shout traditional phrases of encouragement to inspire the vocalist (*chuimsae*). At times during the performance, the pansori artist will step out of role as character or out of role as performer/narrator and speak directly to the drummer or the audience, thanking them for their encouragement. These shifts of direct address can be physical, the performer faces the audience and makes eye contact, as well as vocal, the performer changes her tone of voice. "When in the character of narrator, her tone is peremptory and pompous, but when she exits the narrator, the tone of her voice instantaneously changes to that of a polite hostess sensitive to the feelings of the audience. Here, the performer is completely on her own, and like a stand-up comedian, enjoys a direct rapport with the audience outside the narrative (Park, 151)."

Content
The content of the 6-7 hour performance for the singular pansori artist begins with a vocal warm-up in front of the audience, usually a short epic story (*tanga*). Then s/he begins the one pansori story that will be performed that afternoon and into the evening. Historically, these performed folktales developed from Shaman rituals through oral traditions. They were narrowed to a cannon of 12 songs during King Sunjo's reign (1801-1834), and finally edited into a cannon of 5 songs by Shin Jae-hyo (1812-1884). These remaining 5 pansori songs or traditional folktales are known contemporarily as "The Five Great Pansori (Hayman, 214)," or more simply translated, 'five pansori narratives' (*pansori oh patang*). These five are based on the "5 Cardinal Relationships" of Confucianism: king to subject, father to son, husband to wife, brother to brother, friend to friend (Po-hyong Yi, 245). Each story contains multiple characters and a wide emotional range. In recital format, one singer is responsible for vocalizing the same number of characters it takes an entire cast to impersonate in Chang-geuk. Even with the addition of the

female voice joining the ranks of male pansori performers in the mid-1800's many aspects of the *sori* or sound of the pansori voice haven't changed; both genders are expected to cover the same vocal range, embody multiple character voices, fulfill the broad emotional range required in the texts using only the voice, and project the sound throughout a large performing hall.

Pansori Voice Training Methodology
In order to perform these requirements of form and content, the pansori voice, or *sori*, must be trained using unique methods. These methods have been used for generations and although the vocal product may differ slightly from one performer to the next, based on artistic license or the performer's school of training, the basic principles of breath and sound production are transferred from master to trainee using mimetic training techniques. Pansori practitioner and researcher, Chan E. Park, writes in her Ph.D thesis, *P'ansori Performed: From Strawmat to Proscenium and Back*, "As a rule, a trainee under a master does not deviate from what he receives to be the rhythmic, and melodic paths in the learning of narrative. Yet, after years of training, every singer has his own melodic, rhythmic idiosyncrasies noticeable by discerning ears, a delicate deviation from the acquired heritage but not from its tradition (263)."

In today's classroom, most pansori students bring a tape recorder to their lessons in order to imitate their teacher's voice exactly. Students may have a copy of the story/song text but generally do not have written music to help them adhere to a traditional vocal performance. Students observed in An, Sook Sun's class at the Korean National University of Arts trained with tape recorders and only the written pansori script. They depended upon their master teacher, who was awarded National Living Treasure status in 1997 and is the current Artistic Director of the National Chan-geuk Company, to teach them the rhythmic and melodic paths. Occasionally they made notations above or below a word or phrase that helped them remember whether the tonal inflection rose or fell or the rhythm broke into *staccato*, though terms like *staccato* were not used during class. Professor An explains, "We have a written script. We have 5 notes to a scale and Western music has 7 notes to a scale so later people wrote the music in Western scale but I don't think it's very good. Pansori is a kind of theatre sound; to show the situation vividly we don't use the written music. We just teach the scene; how to express the scene vividly to the audience (Personal Interview, April, 2000)."

So, students relay heavily on their teacher spending the majority of the lesson vocally repeating after the master to learn the rhythmic and melodic traditions. Students spend very little time during the lesson discussing vocal training techniques or questioning their teacher about ways to produce breath and sound. This necessitates that the students train their eyes and ears to the nuances of breath and sound production based on what they see and hear their teacher producing. As a result, most successful pansori students have taught themselves to become keenly aware of breath and sound production. But, this does not necessarily mean that the student has developed a vocal vocabulary by which s/he can articulate traditional training techniques in conversation. And, the pansori student would not necessarily approach a conversation about breath and sound production with the same vocabulary or questions as would a Western vocal student.

Western Voice Training Methodology

Today's Western student's vocabulary and questions are influenced by a vocal training tradition that changed drastically after the mid-1800's when "naturalism" entered the classroom. "This has eliminated any attempt at using mimesis, or imitation, which is the foundation upon which the actor creates a character. In its place, he attempts 'to be' the character (Martin, 29)." Contemporary Western vocal training has also been heavily influence by science. "Modern voice training has been based upon the finding of voice science which maintain that the act of voice production consists of an interplay between the following four areas: breathing, phonation, resonance and articulation. These four areas have formed the basis of most textbooks written on voice training in the twentieth century (Martin, 37)." Western students questions about vocal training technique are influenced by the training's scientific, anatomic understanding of breath and sound production. In a personal interview (September, 2000) Berry stated that the vocal techniques she teaches "cannot fail because they are designed for your anatomy" and states in her first book, *Voice and the Actor* that she believes "those [exercises] appearing in this book are foolproof (Berry, 17)."

Western students of vocal technique trained in the tradition of Kristen Linklater may begin their understanding of breath and sound production based also on the science of Psychology. In her second chapter, Linklater discusses the emotional blocks that prevent the voice from responding with spontaneity. "Most mental and emotional habits...are formed unconsciously and by people other than oneself, in childhood. There is no choice attached to such conditioning. Behavior that is suggested or demanded from outside develops the ability to respond to secondary impulses rather than primary ones...'Big boys don't cry.' 'Nice little girls don't shout' (Linklater, 11)."

If Westerners wish to understand and appreciate pansori they must first understand that Western and pansori vocalists speak different vocal vocabularies and ask different questions of their training techniques. But, once vocabularies are *translated* (meaning more than simply language translation, i.e. Korean to English) each tradition has the potential to inspire the other. The intercultural vocal training work at the Korean National University of Arts, School of Drama can be examined as a potential site for *translating* vocal traditions between pansori and Western techniques.

The Korean National University of the Arts

The fact that today's pansori artists can still perform and train as generations before them have is due in large part to the way in which the Korean government has responded to preserving Korean traditional arts. "After 1956, the traditions of both ch'ang'guk and p'an-sori were revived with the government's decision to designate outstanding p'an-sori singers as 'Human Cultural Treasures' and the 'Five Great P'an-sori' as 'Important Intangible Cultural Properties' to be protected and preserved for futre (sic) generations to enjoy and appreciate (Heyman, 220)." Park adds, "The present government's support finds a 19th century counterpart in the royal patronage for p'ansori singers that included the bestowing of court titles. The difference is that while the royal patronage of the past century was aimed at refined perpetuation, the present government's goal is preservation from extinction. Other than the honored treasureship, the designated singers are awarded a small monthly subsidy as well as two official students who are designated to learn the art in a stipulated period (76)."

The government has also supported institutions designed to encourage pansori study. In the late 80's and early 1990's, the newly established Korean democratic government turned the former Korean CIA building, a symbol of torture and repression to many student activists during the 1970's and early 80's, into a university whose mission was to preserve and rebuild Korea's rich artistic culture, though this was not the only university with departments specializing in traditional Korean arts. The Korean National University of Arts in Seoul also provides pansori vocal training through its School of Traditional Arts while cultivating Western vocal training techniques in its School of Drama.

But the university's pansori training is not limited to the School of Traditional Arts. The acting students in the Theatre Arts undergraduate and graduate programs are required to learn pansori vocal technique to add to their Western dramatic voice training for the stage, based on the vocal training techniques of Kristin Linklater and Cecily Berry. These acting students are not expected to become pansori artists; they would have had to begin their pansori training at an early age, spending years cultivating the unique vocal techniques of pansori and would be students of the Traditional Arts program, not the Theatre Arts program. The School of Drama's vocal training explores, interculturally, both traditional Korean and Western techniques. One challenge, however, in combining these methodologies is Western dramatic vocal vocabulary; Western theatre vocal terminology such as *vocal violence* and *vocal abuse* must be redefined in order to understand how the pansori *sori* is developed within the context of its cultural beauty aesthetic.

"Vocal Violence" in Pansori Voice Training
What Westerners might call *vocal violence* of the pansori voice is necessary in producing the sounds that comprise the beauty of pansori. For a contemporary Western definition of *vocal violence* one might refer to an article published in *The Journal of Voice*, Official Journal of the Voice Foundation entitled "Vocal Violence in Actors: An Investigation into Its Acoustic Consequences and the Effects of Hygienic Laryngeal Release Training." "Actors, in rehearsal and performance, frequently engage in emotionally charged behaviors, often producing voice accompanied by extreme physical exertions (as in a staged fight), or sudden emotional outbursts, such as screaming, shouting, grunting, groaning, and sobbing. These vocally violent behaviors appear to involve extremes in pitch and loudness, increases of muscular tension in the circumlaryngeal area, and explosions of air across partially closed vocal folds. Such behaviors are generally accepted to be vocally abusive, and may contribute to vocal fold mucosal injury and voice mutation (Bless/Nelson/Ryker, 215)."

Pansori vocalists do not scream or sob on stage as a Western actor might because they don't embody character using the conventions of *naturalism*. But the pansori artist, like the Western actor, must engage in "emotionally charged behaviors." Both types of performers must represent characters on stage in heightened emotional states. When representing characters in a heightened emotional state the pansori artist, like the Western actor, engages in "vocally violent behaviors" which involve "extremes in pitch and loudness, increases of muscular tension in the circumlaryngeal area, (possibly) explosions of air across partially closed vocal folds." And like the Western actor, the pansori artist's vocally violent behavior may "contribute to vocal fold mucosal injury and voice mutation," especially since the pansori vocalist engages in these behaviors more frequently and for longer performance periods than most Western actors. For example, according to Po-hyong Yi in *The Annotated Pansori* , translated by Bangsong Song, "The vocal technique of pansori generally resembles bel canto in terms of breathing from the stomach with pressure exerted on the diaphragm. It contrasts, however, there is [sic] the bel canto technique in which one constricts the throat in order to obtain a hoarse or husky vocal timbre. It is not surprising that many pansori singers develop a husky quality even in their normal speaking voices due to the tremendous demands made upon their voices (252)."

The Journal of Voice article continues, "Although the professional voice literature is replete with references to vocal 'abuse and misuse,' there is little objective information defining what constitutes 'abusive' sounds, how they are made and what frequency, intensity, and duration of abuse produces perceptible changes in voice or laryngeal tissue (ibid.)." Therefore, it is not the purpose of this article's subtopic to objectively assert that either Western actors or pansori artists vocally abuse their voices but instead to examine similar vocal training and breath/sound production techniques that are employed to represent the sounds of "vocal violence."

Mountain Training (*Sankongbu*) as a foundation for performing "vocally violent behaviors" in character
In a personal interview (March, 2000) Mr. Chung, Hoi Suk, who teaches at the Korean National University of Arts, School of Traditional Arts, asserted that the unique sound of pansori, begins with the training.

> Basically it is…the training…to have a louder voice because in older times we didn't have microphones. We performed pansori in the marketplace so we needed to have a big voice. That's why we train our voices this way. Still, one out of ten succeeded in training their voices. Nine others fail training their voice. Those who fail the training play instruments or do other things. Now when I go to a doctor, the doctor says I have wrinkles on my vocal folds…um…nodes. It is a very unique training method but it is not scientifically proved…"this is good or not good." It is true that we have to train our throat…or our "voices" to express a very dramatic voice. Also we can make a very pretty sound but we still need to express a very extreme sound. It is also good for pansori singers to train in nature. That's why they train themselves down by the waterfall. You have to penetrate the sound of the waterfall.

According to Mrs. Han, Nongson, who in 1981 achieved the position to inherit "Living National Treasure" status from the Korean government, pansori artists traditionally visit one of the many mountain retreats found all over Korea to study individually or in small groups for "100 days study." Today, many pansori trainees usually study in the mountains for a month during their school summer vacation break. The majority of the training time for today's pansori trainees is not spent training in the mountains but in their pansori master's studio. The tradition, however, is to strengthen the voice using natural obstacles, such as a waterfall, a grove of pine trees, or a canyon. For Western theatre practitioners "penetrating the sound" is not the same as "release the call" which Kristin Linklater describes in chapter 9 of her book *Freeing the Natural Voice*. "Set up a simple scenario in your mind's eye…. You see your friend. What you see fills you with the need to call to him or her. You release the call. You relax, breathe, and wait for the reaction. Throughout the scene your body is acted on: first by the outside stimulus, then by the desire to communicate. There should therefore be no need to push or strain in order to call (92)." Instead, the intention in mountain training seems to be to lose one's voice by extended use at extreme volumes in an effort to compete with the natural obstacle. Traditionally, losing and regaining the voice (Westerners might view this as "vocal abuse," or damaging the vocal folds) will create what Korean artists describe as "big" or "thick" voices. Indeed, this process could leave the vocal folds "thicker" literally since the elasticity of the folds may be effected and thus would have difficulty physically elongating, become "thinner" so to speak, when producing certain upper-range pitches.

In Marshall Pihl's book *The Korean Singer of Tales* he writes, "Chong No-sik's biographical sketches frequently tell of learners who not only sang themselves hoarse, but who vocalized in the wilderness or challenged the sound of a waterfall to produce voices of great power, often pushing themselves to the point of spitting up blood in the process (105)." Pak Hon-bong in his work *Changak taegang* details the process, "'First, for many days and months, scale the voice vertically from low to high, at the same time expand it horizontally. In time the voice turns hoarse and gets lost, until it becomes hardly audible even to a person standing next to you. Keep scaling your voice for years, even through occasional bleeding from the vocal cords, until at last, the voice returns, reinforced and expressive and will endure singing for many hours at a time…the voice has entered the realm of mystery at last' (Park,70)."

Outdoor Vocal Use in Western Voice Training
Traditional mountain training, *sankongbu*, may contradict contemporary Western vocal training, but has some similarities to historical Western vocal training which also practiced periods of extreme vocal use outdoors. Jacqueline Martin, in her book *Voice in Modern Theatre* writes, "Great emphasis was placed on having a strong voice in the huge Greek and Roman amphitheatres and later in the nineteenth century, when it became necessary to speak to large crowds outdoors or in large auditoria. Even Quintilian's warnings against the ill-effects of vocal strain did not deter force and vigorous action of the voice from becoming popular well into the first two decades of the twentieth century…." Diverse factors have contributed to the change in this practice today, as teachers have become aware of the abuse which unnecessary strain can cause and have begun to develop carrying power by other means, "by breath control, openness of the throat and laryngeal areas, effective vowel formation and clear articulation" according to Anderson [V.S. Anderson, *Training the Speaking Voice* (66)], (40)."

Influence of *Sankongbu* in Pitch Range
One of the reasons contemporary Western vocal artists avoid straining the vocal folds with resulting conditions of laryngitis, nodes or polyps during voice training is because they believe these conditions limit the performer's vocal range. Of course pansori artists must also have a considerable vocal

range since a single vocalist is responsible for multiple character voices. To understand the effects of *sankongbu* on the voice's producible range, one must first keep in mind that the concept of pitch range is different to a pansori vocalist. Pansori has a moveable pitch range because there is no fixed tonal center. Therefore, pitches and pitch ranges are not categorized by such Western concepts as octaves or by such vocal categories as bass, tenor, alto and soprano. A study done by Yonsei University Voice Research Center with pansori performer Cho Sanghyon determined that the moveable pitch range of pansori, could be converted to reflect three and a half Western octaves. The pansori performer Song Uhyang's voice could cover over three and a half octaves (Park, 246). In a personal interview with Professor An, Sook-Sun (April, 2000) she asserts that her own pansori vocal range is 7 or, she roughly estimates, a pitch range of 4 to 5 Western octaves. (This range conversion may include the pansori "falsetto projection," discussed later in this article, which is usually not included in measuring a Western vocalist's pitch range).

In her doctoral thesis, Chan E. Park categorizes the pansori voice as having seven vocal ranges: quadruple high (*choesangsong*), double high (*chungsang-song*), high (*sangsong*), middle (*p'yongsong*), low (*hasong*), double low (*chungsangsong*), and quadruple low (*ch'oehasong*), (246)." In an interview (May, 2000) Mrs. Nongson Han, who performs an "Eastern-style" of pansori, (*dongpyunchae*), stated that one pansori singer is expected to cover a range of pitches that would in Western music be divided into multiple categories of bass, tenor, alto, and soprano and executed by various artists. The same pitch range is expected of male as well as female artists. Only the singer's tonal center or "starting pitch" for a song will vary from artist to artist. This "starting pitch" seems to be determined by one's natural vocal pitch as well as where the student is developmentally in his/her vocal training. Other than the moveable tonal center, the Western concept of melodic progression measured in "half-steps" and "whole steps" is similar in pansori although those specific terms are not used. Once a song has begun at the performer's preferred "starting pitch" the melodic progression of the song simply adjusts to the "key" set by the tonal center. Please note, however, that pansori does not recognize a "key signature" as does Western music.

Similar to the pansori concept of "starting pitch", today's Western vocal training recognizes that an actor's natural pitch level should be the foundation of his/her pitch range. "Scientists have determined that an individual's natural pitch level, which is often referred to as 'optimum,' lies somewhere near the third or fourth tone above the lowest which can be produced clearly. Many teachers now realize that locating this 'natural' pitch level constitutes a basic step towards improving voice and a number of methods are easily available for its determination (Martin, 39)." Note that Martin credits science with helping Western teachers incorporate this realization into Western vocal methodology. In contrast, Mrs. Nongson Han credits generations of traditional mimetic practice for her knowledge of "starting pitch." So, this similar concept is incorporated into each methodology by very different means based on what is "valued" in a culture. In this example, Western culture values scientific discoveries and adds them to its training whereas pansori values traditions and bases its training on generations of performance practice. This is not to suggest that pansori artists do not value science or that Western vocal artists do not value tradition. This example simply illustrates how a similar concept is used in both pansori and Western vocal training but was arrived at as a result of different cultural influences on vocal training methodologies.

Western practitioners might ask this question based on their Western understanding of vocal training: if pansori artists must embody multiple character voices in a single pansori performance, and reach from "bass" to "soprano" while creating the emotional intensity of the pansori drama wouldn't *sankongbu*, which could "damage" the vocal folds, possibly limiting vocal range, be antithetical to the demands of a pansori performance in which a wide pitch range would be advantageous? Park explains the seeming contradiction, "For a singer to be equipped with a wide scale of pitch is clearly advantageous, for her voice has wider range of expression. But according to Chong Kwonjin, a singer must not insist on high pitch, but try to stay with middle and the low pitch. Sometimes motivated by erroneous notion that high pitch is always better-sounding, or driven by a desire to be showy, singers do pursue high pitch. But in so doing, they tend to lose the strong basic sound of the middle and the low pitch and sound rather flighty and flashy (250)." Even if a pansori artist has access to his/her extreme upper register, the cultural beauty aesthetic of the performance shapes the vocal training by valuing middle and lower pitches over an upper pitch range.

In Western practice pitch range is usually viewed as a vertical process, from lower pitches to higher pitches and back down again. Linklater and Berry have several exercises in their books that utilize "glide" to increase the student's pitch range. The "glide" exercises focus on expanding pitch range without straining the vocal folds in contrast to the "glide" technique detailed by Pak Honbong in *sankongbu*. In a voice workshop held in Seoul, Korea (September, 2000), Cicely Berry suggested using vocal "glide" exercises for actors concerned with "pitch break" problems. But pansori artists often employ "pitch break," that area between the chest and head voice, to create sorrowful, melancholy sounds during emotional passages. "Pitch break" doesn't seem to be perceived as a problem resolved with training exercises but is instead cultivated as a means of vocal expression.

Also in pansori, pitch range is viewed not only as a vertical process but as a horizontal process. Park quotes Pak Hon-bong's work *Changak taegang* when she writes, "the aspiring singer works for months on end on strengthening her voice, by 'scaling up vertically from low to high as well as horizontally from narrow to wide' (249)." In interview, Mr. Chung of the School of Traditional Arts asserts," Of course, we believe a big pitch range is important but we also in fact believe the wideness of the sound is important." When asked what he meant by "wideness of sound" he demonstrated his meaning. It appeared from his demonstration that a "widened" pitch is similar to Linklater's "placement of the sound" which can change the tonal quality of the sound by placing this sound in different resonating chambers. Mr. Chung demonstrated a "wide" sound by placing the sound towards the center or back of the chamber of the mouth and dropping his jaw. Placed there the sound appeared to resonate within the chambers of the mouth, throat and chest. In contrast, he demonstrated a sound that was not "wide" by placing the sound towards the front of the mouth allowing it to resonate in the mask of the face.

In Western voice training placing the sound in various resonating chambers not only changes the quality of the tone but also is used to alleviate "pitch break" problems. "In an effort to acquire the resonance needed for the voice to carry through a large hall, even at a low intensity, and at the same time minimize effort and avoid 'break' in the voice, a number of factors come into play which are dependent upon lack of tension (Martin, 38)." Please note that Martin asserts resonation depends upon "lack of tension" but in Mr. Chung's demonstration tension was used to help create the resonating chamber of the throat. Martin continues, "A condition of 'spontaneous relaxation' of the spine, as well as the larynx, mouth and tongue is now considered to be of prime importance in the production of a good vocal quality (38)."

The Role of Breath (Inhalation/Exhalation) in Sound Production
Aurally, in Mr. Chung's demonstration it seemed he was broadening the sound through placement and resonation. Visually, when he demonstrated a "widened" sound, his neck became very tense, the veins in his neck were straining, and his neck increased in width during the exhalation. There seemed to be no visual tension on the inhalation, nor was there an audible tension/sound of sucking the air into his lungs. In fact, his muscles appeared very released, allowing the air to simply fill his body. This process of inhalation is similar to Berry's breath capacity exercise (*Voice and the Actor*, 23-30) in which she encourages the vocalist to wait for the need to breathe after the exhale and simply allow the air to fill the body, releasing any tension that might inhibit this process. Both contemporary Western and pansori breath inhalation techniques appear to share a similar way of releasing tension in order to access breath.

But during the exhalation, the breath appeared to be held in the throat, visually expanding the neck. Indeed, the neck physically "widened" (the width of the neck increased) so perhaps this is one reason why Mr. Chung described the sound in English translation as having a "widened" pitch? Park identifies this sound production as "laryngeal projection." In many Western voice classes one would probably identify this exhalation with sound as "pressing," a term describing excess tension used in the throat muscles creating an environment that encourages vocal fold damage. Mr. Chung's interview continues:

Q: So when you're seeking to produce this sound, it's not a sound that comes out of the front part of the mouth but actually a sound that is coming up from the neck and placed more towards the back of the throat?

A: (he nods)

Q: Is that, for the most part, where you want to always place the sound or are there instances in which you would want a more frontal placement?

A: We do have the frontal sound too. But basically from the *danjeon* (center) we generate the sound.

Here too, pansori and Western vocal training share an extremely similar breathing technique. Linklater and Berry devote considerable time in their training books teaching students how to breath from their "center," the area just below one's navel. Mr. Chung also locates the beginning of the inhalation at the *danjeon* or one's "center."

Q: You produce the breath from the center? (I point to the area above my navel at my diaphragm) Or here? (I point to the area below my navel).

A: (He places my entire hand over my navel and nods. He demonstrates part of a song I observed him teaching earlier during class using *danjeon* breathing).

If pansori and Western breath production share similar inhalation techniques, their techniques begin to deviate during the exhalation, in part because of the way in which breath is turned into sound using noticeable amounts of tension. The start of the exhalation is recognizable as a combination of "punch" and "press" techniques pushing the air past the vocal folds quickly and forcefully using the strength of the abdominal muscles. Park identifies this technique as "tubular projection." She explains, "Tubular projection (*tongsong*), projected straight from the abdomen without interruption, has been revered for its beauty and strength…without the sturdy abdominal muscle developed over a long period of voice training, tongsong can rarely be projected (252-253)." Exhalation differences continue to increase, however, when sound is shaped into a variety of tonal qualities using, again, sound placement to resonant in different chambers.

The Role of Cultural Aesthetic in Sound Production
The way in which pansori vocalists shape the sound into tonal qualities depends heavily on their cultural beauty aesthetic. Mr. Chung explains:
> Basically, we think in Yin and Yang. It's important. It is like this in shape [draws the yin/yang on the floor with his finger] and is like…female and male…so we try to express the Yin and Yang in our sound. Yin sound is like…um…suppressed, muffled sound. Yang sound is very bright. *Woo-Jo* sound is bright [note to reader: think of the brightness of tones in a major key] and *kye-myun-jo* is the other [note to reader: think of the tones in a minor key].

Heyman adds that the tension used to create the unique sounds of pansori is part of the cultural aesthetic of yin-yang. "Known as the concept of yin-yang (*eum-yang* in Korean), the dual forces that govern the universe, this cosmology underlies the basic melody and rhythm in both contrast and tension-release structure…. Distinction is made between a 'continuing' voice and a 'closing' or 'blocked' voice; between a 'spreading out' voice and a 'restrained voice' and between a high-pitched 'lifting' voice and a low-pitched 'descending' voice (217)."

A more complete understanding of pitch, tonal quality, and sound placement and their relationship to yin/yang can be understood through Park's work when she translates Pak Honbong's 12 different tonal qualities into 5 distinct vocal aesthetics.

First, the 12 different tonal qualities in pansori are categorized:

Tongsong—tubular projection
Cholsong—metallic voice
Surisong—husky voice
Sesong—falsetto projection
Hangsong—laryngeal projection
Pisong—nasal projection
Pasong—cracky voice
Palbalsong—tremolo projection
Chongusong—clear spring voice
Hwasong—harmonious projection
Kwigoksong—grieving ghost tone
Agwisong—molar tone

Park adds, "The desirability of pansori voice is directly related to pansori aesthetics, which requires the presence of both sides of cosmic gender, yin and yang. Insofar as the vocal narration of pansori is the portrayal of life's picture within, its artistic process must start with the selection and training of the kind of voice inherent with such qualities as capable of portraying different aspects of life: different moods, emotional changes, and multiple characterization (250)." Park's categorization of Pak's 12 tonal qualities are divided:

Inherently ideal voice = *metallic voice, husky voice,* and a *clear, spring voice.*
Inherently undesirable voice = *cracky voice.*
Overall harmonious projection = *hwasong* or *harmonious projection* (refers to the voice capable of clear and correct differentiation of high, middle, and low pitches)
Undesirable projection = *nasal projection* and *tremolo projection* (similar to the Western understanding of a tight vibrato).
Projection for dramatization = *tubular projection, falsetto projection, laryngeal projection, grieving ghost tone,* and *molar tone.*

Some of these aesthetics have Western counterparts (i.e. *tubular projection* = combination "punch/press") while others are described so metaphorically (*grieving ghost tone*) that a demonstration proves more descriptive. For aural demonstration of these aesthetic techniques one might listen to recordings of such great pansori artists as Song Mangap (1865-1939) or Im Pangul (1904-1961).

The Role of Resonance in Sound Production
Resonance plays an important part in shaping the tonal quality of the pansori sound. The sources of resonance for a pansori artist, according to Park, are "nape" for a high relative pitch, "thoracic cavity" for a middle relative pitch, "solar plexus" for a lower middle relative pitch, "center of abdominal region" for a low relative pitch, "spinal column" for the highest relative pitch, and "occipital region" for a high falsetto relative pitch (265). Linklater too explores resonating areas in some similar regions of the body (i.e. solar plexus) but expands the areas in her resonating "pyramid" (*Freeing Shakespeare's Voice*, 25). Certain resonating areas such as "nasal" or "sinus" resonation are avoided in pansori because of the "undesirable projection" in it's beauty aesthetic. The main difference between the two methodologies seems to be not only which resonating areas are used but also the amount of tension used in accessing these resonating areas.

For example, the amount of tension the pansori vocalist uses in the resonating area of the throat not only changes the throats space for resonation but also the potential for the breath/sound to pass through the throat and fill resonating spaces above the throat into the head resonators. "The vocalization of pansori utilizes the increased pressure on larynx resulting from not lowering it, thus confining the resonating area. Due to the pharyngeal tension, it is mostly larynx that does the amplification as well as resonation. It creates pharyngeal tension that in turn characterizes pansori's 'songum' as being hard pressed and husky, rather than elevated and smooth (Park, 268)." The pansori vocalist uses what Park calls "increased pressure" or what may visually look like neck muscle tension, which prevents the larynx from lowering. This laryngeal positioning contrasts with Western practice. "More recently, research has indicated that optimum resonance is achieved by being able to lower the larynx during voice production (Martin, 38)." Laryngeal positioning due to "increased pressure" or throat tension may also be one reason why Western listeners interpret the demonstrated pansori upper pitch range as strained and forced.

Summary

In summary, both pansori and Western vocal stage techniques seem to practice similar breath production, "tubular projection" from the *danjeon* compared to "centering" of the breath in Western training (Linklater and Berry techniques). They also appear to share similar inhalation techniques but not exhalation techniques. When converting the exhaled breath into sound, the difference between pansori and Western vocal techniques seems to depend on the use of tension, resonating chambers, desirable pitch range and the beauty aesthetic of each culture. This aesthetic in pansori, influencing both vocal training (*sankongbu*) and vocal performance (laryngeal projection), produces the desirable "thick voice" of the *sori*. During the process of producing the *sori*, the cultivated vocal break is used to create heart-breaking, sorrowful harmonics by playing with the space between chest and head voice. To a pansori artist any "vocal abuse" done during training is viewed as vocal strengthening that helps, not hinders, characterization and emotional vocal range. For pansori, the beauty of the sound comes from the tension but for Western theatre vocalists tension "murders" the vibrations necessary to create a rich, resonating sound (Linklater,41). As Park notes, "Pansori as a vocal art is not unique in the sense that its vocal techniques strive to interpret faithfully its distinct aesthetic, just as the Western classical singing strive to reveal its own aesthetics (266)."

By "translating" pansori training techniques in the areas of breath production and sound production (pitch, tonal quality, placement and resonation) into familiar Western voice training "counterparts", Western vocal practitioners may be able to better understand and appreciate this traditional Korean art form. And both Korean and Western actors may benefit from an intercultural approach to exploring vocal production, which strives to represent the idea of mutual influence of and exchange between cultures. When "translating" vocal vocabulary, Western vocal practitioners for the stage must take care in using terms like "vocal abuse" which need to "translate" into terminology that doesn't devalue a vocal training technique valued in another culture. The efforts at the Korean National University of Arts, which explores an intercultural approach to breath and sound production, may be a blueprint for other voice training programs that strive to incorporate the methodologies of both East and West.

Acknowledgements
I would like to gratefully acknowledge those who gave of their time and talents to make this article possible. First, the master teachers who graciously welcomed me into their classrooms and gave me the gift of their knowledge in interviews: An, Sook-Son, Han, Nong-Son, Chong, Hoi Suk, and Cicely Berry.
Also, a special debt of gratitude must be extended to my colleagues at The Korean National University of Arts, especially Professors Kim, Soogi, whose insightful criticism and support were invaluable, and chair of the School of Drama, Suk, Choong-Sik, who encouraged me to share my work in symposium, *Where the Voice Begins*, December, 2000, Seoul, Korea.

My tremendous appreciation to Lee, Yu-Kyung, translator, and the staff and assistants of the School of Drama and School of Traditional Arts at the Korean National University of Arts who demonstrated great patience while helping research and translate pansori materials.

I am particularly grateful to Han, Myung-Hee for introducing me to pansori and my pansori teacher, Han, Nong-Son. Without her participation this article would never have been written. I am also equally indebted to the talented Park, My-Kyung who translated interviews, pansori materials, and this article for Korean publication.

A special thanks to Professor Karen Ryker, University of Wisconsin-Madison, for assisting me with research on "vocal violence," critiquing several drafts, and nurturing my work in both the US and Korea. Also, I would like to thank VASTA, Voice and Speech Teacher's Association, and the Voice and Speech Review: Rocco Dal Vera, editor-in-chief, for encouraging me to write this article and Dorothy Mennen, associate editor, and Linda Carroll, assistant editor, for contributing their valuable time reading and critiquing this paper for US publication.

Finally, I am grateful for the work of Chan E. Park, whose pioneering Ph.D thesis at the University of Hawaii *P'ansori Performed: From Strawmat to Proscenium and Back* inspired my own work in intercultural methodological research.

Works Cited
An, Sook-Sun. Personal Interview. April, 2000. Seoul, Korea.

Anonymous. "Pansori." www.agrakr.co.kr/9804/50.htm+pansori&hl=en.

Berry, Cecily. *The Actor and the Text*. New York: Applause, 1987.

———. *Voice and the Actor*. New York: Macmillan Publishing Co., 1973.

———. Personal Interview. September, 2000. Seoul, Korea.

Chung, Hoi Suk. Personal Interview. March 2000. Seoul, Korea.

Heyman, Alan, ed. "Pansori," *The Traditional Music and Dance of Korea*. National Center for Korean Traditional Performing Arts: 1993.

Han, Nong-Son. Personal Interview. May, 2000. Seoul, Korea.

Kirk, Don. "A Korean Film Lifts the Veil on Ages Past." *International Herald Tribune*, www.iht.com/I.../dk020300.html+pansori&hl=e.

Linklater, Kristin. *Freeing the Natural Voice*. New York: Drama Book Publishers, 1976.

———. *Freeing Shakespeare's Voice*. New York: Theatre Communications Group, 1992.

Martin, Jacqueline. *Voice in Modern Theatre*. London: Routledge, 1991.

National Theatre of Korea. *Program Guide, 2000*, 9.10.11.12 Seoul: http://www.ntok.go.kr., 2000.

National Theatre of Korea. *Choonhyang-Jun Program- A Joint Production by China (Zhejiang Xiaobaihua Yue Opera Troupe), Japan (Shochiku Co.,Ltd..), and Korea (National Chang-geuk Company)*. October 19-22, 2000. Seoul, Korea.

Pak, Hon-bong. *Changak Taegang*. Publisher Unknown, 1966.

Park, Chan E. *P'ansori Performed: From Strawmat to Proscenium and Back*. University of Hawai'i. 1995.

Phil, R. Marshall. *Korean Singer of Tales*. Cambridge: Harvard University Press, 1994.

Yi, Po-hyung. "What is Pansori?" tr. Bang-Song Song. *Annotated Pansori*. Seoul: Korea Britannica Corporation, 1982.

Essay by *Joan Melton*

Sing Better, Work More: Integrating Singing Technique into Theatre Voice Training

Joan Melton is Associate Professor and Head of the Voice/Movement Program in the Department of Theatre and Dance at California State University Fullerton. She has taught at leading drama and music centers in the United States, Britain and Ireland, including the Manhattan School of Music in New York, the Central School of Speech and Drama in London, and the Drama Summer School in Dublin. She is a published author and composer, a specialist in 20th Century vocal music, and a Master Teacher of Fitzmaurice *Voicework*.

In January, 1999, an astute young actress said to me, "Sing better, work more." What she meant was that if her singing were at the same level as the rest of her acting skills, she'd be cast more frequently and in a wider range of material.

During the fall semester, 1999, I changed the syllabus for second year graduate actors at California State University Fullerton, to include a unit on music reading and on singing, specifically for the purpose of auditioning. Twelve "non-singers" emerged singing really well, and the rest of the faculty were amazed at the transformation. Auditions for the spring season were dynamite, confidence levels were way up from fall, and performances were "so together." Twelve actors had learned a lot more than how to sing; they'd learned to deal successfully with a different kind of material and that had stimulated their overall growth as actors.

Basic skills regularly taught in theatre voice classes include techniques for speaking, laughing, crying, screaming, wailing, fight sounds, and accents and dialects. Singing may be included in a peripheral manner, but actual singing technique is seldom an integral part of the theatre voice curriculum.

Singing is often considered an outsider, an elite outsider. For many actors, it is a fascinating, but strange and frightening vocal activity. "I can't sing," "I don't know anything about singing," "When I have to sing in an audition I am terrified." These are the kinds of comments I hear almost daily from students and professional actors alike.

When singing is included in the acting program, it is often taught from the perspective of a coach, who does not deal with vocal technique, or from the perspective of the classical singing teacher, who may be unaware of the rest of the vocal life of the actor. Typical results for the student, are confusion, apparent contradiction between the singing class and the acting studio, and a strong conviction that there are two voices, one that speaks and one that sings.

It is possible to view singing as yet another use of the voice and to make the technical connections in the context of theatre voice work. When this is done, the actor tends to emerge "whole." The work on singing enhances the understanding of breathing, diction and vocal range, while skills developed in the acting studio transform songs into powerful monologues that happen to be sung.

Integrating singing technique into theatre voice work is not an easy task, and may involve teamwork on the part of two or more instructors. It requires:
1. Individual, as well as group instruction;
2. The teaching of music reading and sight singing–these skills go a long way toward raising the actor's level of confidence;
3. Training in the singing of harmony parts as well as a main melody;
4. Guidance in the preparation of audition material, including such practical matters as:
   a. How to make a 16 bar cut;
   b. How to prepare and present the written music to an accompanist;
   c. How to interact successfully with the accompanist (a person who can

make or break your audition);

    d. How to work the song as a spoken, then sung, monologue, with the same word and syllable stress as if the words had never been set to music, and with all of the acting elements in place;

5. A block of time to focus previous training in alignment, breathing, range, resonance, articulation, and dialects, on material that is to be sung.

Ideally, the actor sings as easily as s/he speaks, and with essentially the same technique. There are specific differences, of course, in breath use and other physicality for certain vocal activities, e.g., laughing, crying, screaming, and wailing, so the actor is trained to make appropriate adjustments skillfully. Singing and speaking require little or no discernible adjustment and should flow easily from one to the other in a trained voice.

When the actor studies singing from a non-acting perspective, it is *breathing* that tends to confuse and complicate matters. Breathing techniques are the great divide among singing teachers and between singing and theatre voice trainers. Breathing is the passionate ground, where there are as many methods as singer/actors and where each of several different methods may be touted as "the only right way to sing."

Specific requirements of the acting profession can provide useful guidelines for the actor who must choose among a variety of valid approaches to vocal technique. In western theatre, and in the United States specifically, the actor should:

1. Be able to produce vocal sounds in any physical position, moving or still;
2. Be willing to have multiple voices, or to "discover" the character's voice in the process of research and physicalization;
3. Be able to speak and sing without changing technical gears or dialects;
4. Be able to sing with or without a microphone in a variety of spaces;
5. Be prepared with appropriate types of audition material, mostly from musical theatre, and know how to interact appropriately with an accompanist;
6. Be able to sing brief or extended solos, confidently and accurately, over a vocal range of at least two octaves;
7. Be able to sing a harmony part accurately;
8. Be able to read the musical portion of a script and learn it without the guidance of a CD, tape or accompanist;
9. Be skilled at giving the song a history that allows the character to move into singing out of a need to express;
10. Be able to sing in the appropriate style for the material, e.g., belt, legit.

In addition, the actor who specializes in musical theatre must have an extensive vocal repertoire and be an excellent dancer.

Guidelines at a deeper, more technical level, may be useful in assessing effective singing training, regardless of the approach. Here are some of the things I look for in a trained singer:

1. Silent inhalation;
2. Absence of harsh glottal attacks;
3. Clear sound throughout the voice;

4. Ability to navigate the whole voice without obvious "breaks" and unintentional changes of voice color and strength;
5. Wide range of pitch, tempo and volume easily executed;
6. Articulation that is specific and integral to the material;
7. Freedom of response to impulse, imagination and a wide range of physical/vocal demands;
8. Physicality that is appropriate and specific to the material;
9. Ability to engage in dialogue with a partner through the song;
10. Ability to communicate the play/song to the audience.

In the spring semester, 2000, I initiated an undergraduate unit on singing, in the context of the Voice/Movement classes at Cal State Fullerton. Outcomes were similar to the graduate response, but the sheer number of undergraduates per class (25-30) made the work more difficult. Student suggestions in the form of written comments, along with my own sense of what was needed in the curriculum, led to the development of a full-semester course entitled "Singing for the Actor," which will be offered for the first time in the spring of 2001, with a limited enrollment of 12-14 students.

Each of us works in our own world to make it better, drawing on our particular perspective and strengths to enrich the profession as a whole. There are categories within the specialization of theatre voice that have developed from strong interests and expertise, e.g., in accents and dialects, voice science, speech, vocal production, and voice/movement integration. Singing calls attention to itself by not being a category. The rationale and history of its alienation is material for another article, but the need to "put it in its place" is becoming obvious.

Actors should feel that they have the technical skills to meet the vocal demands of their career, and those demands realistically include singing. Actors will sing better and work more when singing technique is part of their training, and theatre voice training will be enriched and strengthened by the inclusion of an essential category.

Editorial Column by *Mandy Rees*

Mandy Rees (associate editor) teaches acting, voice and movement at California State University, Bakersfield and regularly directs in their theatre season. She earned her BA at Pomona College and her MFA at the University of California, Davis. She has worked with Cornerstone Theater Company in Los Angeles, CSU Summer Arts, Madison Repertory Theatre, and the Los Angeles Actors Theatre. Mandy is a board member of VASTA, and is also active in the Association of Theatre Movement Educators and has served as editor of their Movement Bibliography.

Bookstores are one of my favorite places to linger. As a college student, I went directly to the theatre section, loading my arms with plays and acting books. The more I studied, the more I wanted to expand my knowledge. I started to buy books on costuming, directing, and theatre theorists. In graduate school, my interests grew to voice and movement, enormous subjects in their own right. My bookshelves were suffering under the burden of excessive weight, wayward books crammed above those lucky enough to be placed upright, and my wallet was suffering from all the money it had sacrificed to fund its owner's spending sprees. Despite the explosion of materials available on the internet, I still prefer the tactile pleasure of holding a book.

Now serving as the associate editor of Reviews and Sources, I find myself in a dangerous position. I have to keep my eye open to new publications, I scan the titles at the Samuel French bookstore in Hollywood, and I work with reviewers to evaluate new books and videos. Hiding from temptation is hard to do under these circumstances! I fear my shelves will soon have more books piled on top of them. I have enjoyed working with the six reviewers in this issue and am intrigued and interested in the works they have evaluated. From the weighty tome of *bodymind and voice*, to the thin pamphlet of the Denver Center's *Voice Handbook*, you will get to read about some of the latest works in the voice and speech field. A couple of books guide actors through speech challenges (*Shakespeare's Names: A New Pronouncing Dictionary* and *Accents: A Manual for Actors*). Two reviewers approached me anxious to share resources they had found useful; Ruth Rootberg had studied with Carl Stough and thought other voice teachers would find his videos valuable, and Judylee Vivier wanted to spread the word about the text, *Make Your Voice Heard*. I hope you will read these reviews and find yourself tempted, as I am, to make a purchase or two.

Included in this section are two reviews of plays. One, an experimental production of *Twelfth Night* set in the Rave culture, is considered by Joan Melton, and the other, Wendy Wasserstein's latest work, *Old Money*, is reviewed by Lynn Watson. Lynn had the opportunity to interview Mark Harelik, a leading actor in *Old Money*, and you will get to read excerpts from this fascinating discussion which covered thoughts on language and rhythm to issues of miking in the theatre.

You will find other standard features in this department. Supporting the main focus of this issue, Marlene Johnson has scanned the materials available on the topic of Voice in Violence and has provided a list of the best resources. We continue to publish abstracts of recent theses in the field of voice and speech, highlighting the work of students around the world.

bodymind & voice: foundations of voice education
Leon Thurman, Ed.D. and Graham Welch Ph.D., co-editors

Pamela Prather received her MFA in Acting from UCLA. She began her teaching career at UCLA before moving to New York City, where she has taught Voice and Speech for Actors at The Academy of Music and Dramatic Arts, The School for Film and Television and Marymount Manhattan College, and currently teaches at New York University in the Playwright's Horizons BFA program. She has a private coaching practice in Valhalla, New York, and enjoys acting and voice-over work. She is particularly interested in applying cross-cultural techniques, having spent several years in Japan. Her "whole-body" approach to voice-training draws from psychological, physical and spiritual influences.

Thurman and Welch have pulled together 17 authors with more than 150 illustrations (44 in color) in this comprehensive 650 page publication. It is comprised of three volumes containing 54 chapters and organized into five sections called "books." Although the number of pages may seem daunting, the authors have presented the material in a logical and friendly manner. The editors suggest that readers skip around and investigate whatever topics interest them; if a previous chapter includes necessary background information, readers are referred back to it.

Book I, "Bodyminds, Learning and Self-Expression" is a fascinating scientific exploration of the "bodymind" which Thurman and Welch define as the "neuropsychobiology of perception, memory, learning, behavior and health". The authors explore the various systems of the "bodymind" such as the nervous, endocrine and immune systems, and conclude, "self-expression with our voices is connected to the deepest, most profound sense of who we are."

The second book is entitled "How Voices are Made and How they are "Played" in Skilled Speaking and Singing". This book is packed with useful information, illustrations and "do this" activities, which would be useful teaching tools when covering resonance, pitch and volume. This book also looks at vowel and consonant sounds as they relate to speaking and singing vocal qualities.

I found one of the most useful books to be Book III, " Health and Voice Protection." It looks at how vocal abilities can be affected by different diseases and disorders, related injury or atrophy, body injuries and neuropsychobiological interference. All of the medical terms are clearly explained for the layperson. Book IV follows with an exploration into "Lifespan Voice Development." Of particular interest are the chapters on male and female adolescent vocal transformation. Book V looks at "Practical Voice Education Methods" and devotes several chapters to singing as well as a brief introduction to the Alexander Technique.

This publication could be compared to the *Physicians' Desk Reference* book for voice and speech. The level of detail, including extensive bibliographies, makes it a valuable educational resource and teaching tool.

Book Review by *Patty Raun*

**Accents: A Manual for Actors
by Robert Blumenfeld**

What actor doesn't like to do dialects? A dialect contributes so much to the unique impression of a character, and it's as much fun to change dialects as it is to try on different hats. The challenge for actors and theatre voice coaches has been the dearth of accurate, appropriately complex, interesting, and accessible resources. At long last, a thorough, modern, and extremely useful dialect manual (with accompanying CD-ROM!) has been created by Robert Blumenfeld. As might be assumed from the title, *Accents: A Manual for Actors*, the book is written with the actor in mind, but it will be a tool for coaches, directors, and anyone else who enjoys experimenting with the voice.

Blumenfeld carefully initiates the reader when he writes, "This book is a work of fiction…because accents are fictions, in that they are descriptions of models of the way groups of people speak, and in reality everyone speaks in an individual way." Throughout the book, Blumenfeld helps the practitioner understand the general principles of each dialect covered (from Albanian to Zulu) while presenting options for individual variation. The important, as well as less emblematic, changes made for each dialect are clearly and concisely detailed.

Patty Raun is a professional actor who has been fascinated by dialects since she was a child. She is an Associate Professor in the Theatre Arts Department at Virginia Tech in Blacksburg, Virginia, where she teaches voice and acting.

The book covers nine accent groups (British Isles and Commonwealth, North America, Romance Language, Germanic Language, Slavic Language, Miscellaneous European, Middle Eastern, African, and Asian). Each group is divided into chapters (e.g. "Yiddish and Its Dialects," "Greek," "Chinese Accents: Mandarin and Cantonese"). All chapters begin with useful information about social, political, and historical aspects of the country in which the accents are rooted, along with a general description of the accent. Each chapter also contains suggestions of roles that require the accent, and lists of examples of films in which a variation of the dialect is spoken.

One drawback of the book may be the phonetic symbols used to illustrate the sounds. The book lists and uses a simple and logical denotation of sound, but for those who are used to the IPA there will be some translating required. Another shortcoming, this time in the CD, is the brevity of some of the examples. Vietnamese, for instance, consists of one three-word phrase of approximately 5 seconds. In the author's defense, it must be noted that no claim is made that this is the definitive or only source required for perfection of a particular dialect.

These two caveats aside, this original and helpful book is a strong starting place in the creation of dialects for stage and film. If its sales match its value, it will soon be in use by most actors and voice coaches. It is much more reasonably priced than many of its dialect predecessors, which makes it even more attractive as a first source.

Make Your Voice Heard:
An Actor's Guide to Increased Dramatic Range Through Vocal Training by Chuck Jones

Judylee Vivier is an Assistant Professor in the Theatre Department at Brooklyn College City University of New York where she directs the MFA program in acting and teaches acting and vocal production. She is also an actress and director. Vivier has an MFA in Acting from the Tisch School of Arts at New York University, and an MA from the University of Natal in Durban, South Africa, her country of origin, where she worked collaboratively with Athol Fugard. Her approach to voice for the actor has been influenced by the training practices of Chuck Jones, Cecily Berry and Patsy Rodenburg.

This small book, only 141 pages in length, offers a most refreshing, lively and accessible guide to practical voice training. It is written for actors and voice students who strive for honest performances and desire a voice that responds naturally to their inner selves. Chuck Jones, a remarkable teacher, has pioneered his voice training practices through many years of acting and teaching experience, guiding innumerable voice students and performing arts professionals to integrate fully expressive voices into their work.

Jones' approach to vocal training is unique since he clearly and very convincingly focuses on the relationship between vocal training and acting, thereby supporting American actor training in which actors are encouraged to draw on their own emotional lives and resources. Jones explains that "…voice training does more than solve vocal problems: Voice training allows actors to extend their range, develop power, and create that mysterious quality known as presence…helps put actors in touch with their deepest emotional states and allows them to connect to their roles in a profound way…helps actors to develop the capacity to reveal the full range of their inner lives."

In the first half of the book Jones examines fundamental acting issues that relate specifically to the vocal instrument such as being heard, character choices, and vocal power. In the second half of the book, Jones introduces a very specific, logical sequence of exercises as part of a daily vocal workout that releases, stretches, strengthens, increases the expressive range, resonance and flexibility of the vocal anatomy and physical instrument, leading to a heightened physical and emotional awareness.

Jones brings the book to a close by defining how to connect the voice to the emotional life, how to use breathing as part of acting, and finally, how to adjust to the new sound resulting from his vocal training practices. Thus Jones addresses integrating the expressive voice into the emotional, physiological and physical aspects of acting, helping to eliminate the "mystery" from voice training.

Book Review by *Krista Scott*

Louis Colaianni's [one of this journal's associate editors] *Shakespeare's Names: A New Pronouncing Dictionary* is a long-awaited updating of pronouncing guidelines for the most prevailing dramatic texts of the western world. It is an essential resource text for the most seasoned veteran to the greenest amateur director or actor who has any inkling of producing or acting in a Shakespeare play, not to mention every American university professor of theatre or dramatic literature. It's a definite must for any vocal coach practicing in this country, whether they advocate a "General American" sound in classical texts or the more homogenous tradition of "Theatre Standard" or "Good Speech."

The previously published pronouncing dictionaries of Theodora Irvine (*A Pronouncing Dictionary of Shakespearean Proper Names*, 1919; revised 1945) and Helge Kokeritz (*Shakespeare's Names: A Pronouncing Dictionary*, 1959), while often providing a scholarly reference to sources of pronunciation and insightful definitions, use antiquated methods of IPA transcription or dictionary diacritics which do not make the transition to current IPA usage or a layman's phonic understanding. Their transcriptions confuse those who have a working knowledge of IPA by not distinguishing vowel symbols (/i/ is used for both 'sit' and 'seat', the higher vowel distinguished only with a colon /:/ usually meant for an elongated vowel; the same is true for the 'u' sounds in 'wood' and 'pool' and the two lower back vowels in 'law' and 'caught'). This constantly sends those who don't have formal phonetic training flipping through the introductory pages to figure out what symbol is which sound.

Colaianni aptly sums up the advantages of this volume over past publications: "User-friendly transcriptions; the capability for a quick overview of name-pronunciations in each individual work; and, above all, pronunciations which are in step with current usage."

In his descriptive manner of giving both a General American and British RP pronunciation, Colaianni sidesteps prescribing which is "more correct" and provides instead a comparative pronunciation in each dialect with both the current International Phonetic Alphabet (sans diacritical markings) and "Simplified Phonics." This gives the reader a quick recognition of pronunciation, a choice of which sample best suits his/her linguistic sensibilities, and at the same time offers the novice in phonetic transcription an education in IPA. Rather than listing all terms in one long alphabetical list, Colaianni gives a complete list of all the names on a play/poem basis, subsequently omitting line citations, tedious discussions of differing pronunciations in various texts, theories of what the pronunciation was likely to be in Shakespeare's time, explanations of whether the spelling came from a Folio or Quarto source—inclusions which bog down the citations in the Irvine and Kokeritz publications. This updated source also includes approximately one hundred names overlooked in the previous dictionaries, providing a more comprehensive list for each work.

The organization of the text not only makes it a handy pronouncing reference, but a useful learning tool as well. In the Preface, Colaianni outlines the evolution of classical acting practices in this country up to the current trends and the need for updated resources and pedagogy. His statements are backed with quotes from contemporary voice and speech experts and dialecticians such

Krista Scott is a certified Associate Instructor of Fitzmaurice Voicework, and holds an M.F.A. in Acting from the University of Minnesota. She is an Assistant Professor at the University of Mississippi, where she teaches voice, speech, dialect and acting classes. She previously taught at the American University in Cairo, Egypt, Saint Cloud State University and Concordia College. Krista has acted professionally throughout the Midwest, and was co-founder and associate director of The New Tradition Theatre Company in St. Cloud MN. Her current research includes acquisition (as Associate Editor for Mississippi) of authentic dialect samples for IDEA (International Dialects of English Archive).

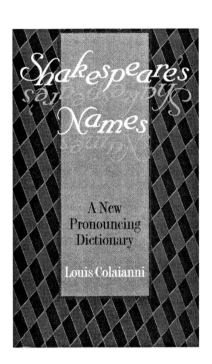

as Kristin Linklater, Dan Mufson, Dudley Knight, Gillian Lane-Plescia and Fausto Cercignani. The Introduction gives a refreshingly brief and concise explanation of the transcription styles used. Beginning with *All's Well That Ends Well* and proceeding alphabetically by titles of texts, three simple columns run down each page of the Dictionary Proper. The first provides an alphabetical list of names as they appear in the text. The shaded middle column provides the IPA transcription of the General American pronunciation(s), below which appear the British RP pronunciation(s). As a further distinction, the RP pronunciations are marked by a diamond. A "Simplified Phonics" transcription in the third column coincides with the IPA transcriptions, except in RP variances which are "too subtle for transcription in Simplified Phonics Alphabet transcription and the user is referred to the IPA transcription of that entry." In addition, the first page of each work's list includes a box at the bottom with the pronunciation keys of both transcription methods. This graphic layout makes for quick reference as well as a visually uncluttered and immediate comparison of linguistic choices.

Perhaps the best feature of the text is the "Detailed explanation of the Symbols" which follows the dictionary listings. This provides a detailed beginner's guide to the International Phonetic Alphabet, with an explanation of each vowel and diphthong and its General American and RP usage, a key of General American phonemes and the subsequent additions for British RP pronunciation, and finally an explanation of the Simplified Phonics Symbols. Colaianni very cleverly keeps all word references for symbols in the context of Shakespearean proper names. Even the mnemonic devices become tools for delving deeper into the Bard's work.

Some teachers of IPA in actor training may disagree with one or two of Colaianni's assumptions of the "General American" sound. Following the pronouncing tables of J.C. Wells' *Longman Pronouncing Dictionary*, the lowest back vowel, /ɒ/, is excluded from any American pronunciations, leaving it a defining RP variant; those who align themselves with the Skinner IPA tradition will surely notice the complete omission of the "ask list" /a/ (Colaianni explains and corroborates his reasons for this omission in a footnote). Also omitted (ala Wells) is the distinction of the unstressed terminal /i/ from /i/, as in /nɔrmandi/ (Normandy). If one discriminates between /ə/ and /ʌ/, this distinction would only seem to follow suit. However, if the objective of the dictionary is simplicity and accessibility, the fewer symbols needed to reach the intended pronunciation, the better.

Louis Colaianni fully acknowledges that the same evolutionary quality of spoken English that makes *Shakespeare's Names* an essential acting resource today will most likely render it obsolete in decades to come. "This dictionary is a plea that Shakespeare's plays not become museum curiosities, but remain a vital part of our living language…These pronunciations, witnesses to contemporary speech, remain, forevermore open to revision." Let's hope that the next compilation will continue the spirit of providing informative options to performers rather than empirical prescriptions of the "definitive" sound of Shakespeare.

Book Review by *Deena Burke*

Voice Handbook: Materials from the Voice Workshops
Presented at the Denver Center for the Performing Arts, Florence B. Blager, editor

This slim book of 48 pages is compiled from voice workshops given at The Denver Center For The Performing Arts. The Voice Handbook offers a small but nice selection of exercises for the beginning voice practitioner as well as the more experienced performer or teacher. It is divided into six categories: "Care of the Voice," "The Speaking Voice," "The Singing Voice," "Breath and Movement and the Voice," "Selected Readings," and "Biographies of the Contributors." The categories provide basic information about the voice as well as practical and experiential exercises for speaking and singing. There is an opportunity for crossover application of some of the singing material to the speaking voice and vise versa.

Some of the material may be too clinical/technical for a beginning voice person but much of the material can be useful to people at all levels. This is not an in-depth exploration of any one methodology nor of a single type of exercise. Instead, it offers a few brief, simple exercises that address a variety of vocal issues. The exercises are easy to follow, so anybody can use them, even those without much experience. I particularly liked the exercise for increasing breath capacity and for nasal resonance. The weakest area is that of "Breath, Movement and the Voice." However, if one can pull even one new idea or one new exercise from the collection it is worth the extremely reasonable purchase price.

Deena Burke is an Associate Professor at Cornish College of the Arts in Seattle, WA where she heads the voice and speech component of the BFA Professional Actor Training Program. As an actress, Deena has worked in many regional theatres including The Old Globe, Oregon Shakespeare Festival and A Contemporary Theatre in Seattle. Deena also coaches voice and dialects for film and in most of the Seattle area theatres. Deena is a graduate of the Juilliard School and a board member for VASTA.

Breathing: The Source of Life
Produced by the Stough Institute

Ruth Rootberg is a designated Linklater teacher and Certified Laban Movement Analyst. A professional actress and singer, Ms. Rootberg holds Masters Degrees from the New England Conservatory of Music, Columbia College and Loyola University of Chicago. She has taught at Northern University of Illinois, The Theater School of De Paul, Shakespeare and Company and most recently, The Yale School of Drama. In the fall of 1999, Ms. Rootberg led a workshop, Moving Towards Vocal Centre, at the first SAP-VAME conference in South Africa. While studying to be an Alexander Teacher, Ms. Rootberg lives and takes private students in Amherst, Massachusetts.

The Stough Institute of Breathing Coordination, founded as a non-profit organization in 1965 to research and educate in the field of Respiratory Science, produced two videos in the 1990s. As the later one, *Breathing: The Source of Life*, © 1996, is more introductory in nature, it will be discussed first.

In this 60 minute video, one learns briefly how Carl Stough, graduate of Westminster Choir College (1949), moved from a successful choral conducting career in New York to experimental work with emphysema patients, then on to train the 1968 Olympic Athletes for the high altitude competitions in Mexico City. The voice-over narrative tells us that Stough's ability to visualize, his ear for sound, and his heightened sense of touch led him to the discoveries which later became known as "The Stough Method of Breathing Coordination."

The video also demonstrates movement of the diaphragm through animation and film. These views of healthy and diseased diaphragm motion are worth the price of the video alone. (A brief excerpt of the animation is located at their Web site).

Intermittently, Mr. Stough speaks about his technique on-camera. It is based on using the least amount of tension while increasing the length of the exhale (reducing residual volume) to trigger a reflexive inhale. Credibility is lent by Dr. Robert Nims, a pulmonary physician, who states that although it was formerly thought that the diaphragm could not be developed, Stough's clinical results have indicated otherwise.

The video is replete with success stories and testimonials from Stough's students who are people with various diseases and/or respiratory problems. Among those of particular interest to the VASTA population would be a number of performing artists and Alexander teachers. From these testimonials, one infers that the technique helps restore an easy process of breathing which relieves tension, allows the performer to concentrate on expression, and, as one singer states, enables her to move from tragedy to humor and joy.

Even though Mr. Stough was not trained in medicine or a complimentary medical therapy, he was allowed to help patients with symptoms caused by their pathologies. When he was developing his techniques in the late 1950s, the regulations and litigation ever-present in today's world were not in force. The narrator suggests that Stough, not a healer but a musician, was able to treat respiratory problems in a new way because he didn't have the same frame of reference as the medical community. If Mr. Stough were conducting his research today, he most likely would not have the same opportunities to work with pathology. Doctors usually refer breathing and related voice problems to certified specialists such as Respiratory Therapists and Speech Language Pathologists.

Although it seems his "layman's" approach is what made his discoveries possible, once he established his methods there is no indication that Stough took advantage of any research from the Voice Science field more recent than his own which might corroborate and/or refine his work.

Disappointing are the generalities near the end when Mr. Stough discusses what a person can do for himself. For instance, the suggestion to have children watch less television, although a good one in this reviewer's opinion, is not specific to the purpose of the video.

The earlier video, *An Introduction to Respiratory Science*, © 1991, runs 110 minutes. Mr. Stough works with three people: a tenor, oboist, and soprano. Although the viewer is advised not to use the video as a training tape, one sees the technique in action. In each instance, the student performs before a live audience. Mr. Stough then has the student lie in a semi-supine position. The student speaks a variety of counting and alphabet exercises while "Dr. Breath," as he has been nicknamed, works primarily on the student's thorax. Some work is done with the student sitting, legs dangling off the table.

At the end, each student performs again. Not only can one hear notable improvements in resonance, but each performer shows surprise and delight at the ease with which he or she can produce the improved sound.

Although one wonders whether counting exercises are merely a drier form of such chestnuts as "This is the House that Jack Built," it appears that the hands-on technique coupled with the voiced exhalations lead to ease and improvement of the breathing.

Together the two videos are quite informative and worthy of investigation. Unfortunately, *Breathing: The Source of Life* has the tone of an infomercial. Despite the inclusion of well-known performers such as Paul Winter and Lauren Flanigan, this tone detracts from the credibility of the material. The other video, however, gains from its setting at the Aspen Music Festival.

The videos can be purchased through the Stough Institute by calling 212/308-7138, or on-line at http://www.carlstough.org.

Besides the above-reviewed videos, Mr. Stough co-authored with his wife, Reece Stough, a heartfelt autobiographical account of his life's work. The book, *Dr. Breath: the story of breathing coordination* was first published in 1970 by William Morrow. The 1981 copyright is held by The Stough Institute. Although popular on-line booksellers list the title, availability appears to be faster, more dependable, and less expensive by ordering directly through the Stough Institute at the phone number or Web site listed above.

Carl Stough, born in 1926, died October 2, 2000. While preparing to publish an announcement of his retirement, his health deteriorated so rapidly that he was unable to sign the letter. When it was released with a posthumous date, included was his encouragement to those who knew his work to disseminate their knowledge. As of this writing, a self-help instructional audio tape will go into production in March, 2001. A video training tape will follow, pending success of the audio tape and sufficient financial resources.

His fees were high, but a new student had to wait an average of six months to get the first set of five lessons. Although he never organized a formal training, there are "several dozen teachers who have experienced their own development to the degree that they are including the Principles of Breathing Coordination within their teaching." (The Stough Institute Review, Fall 2000.)

Twelfth Night by William Shakespeare
Produced by the Shakespeare Festival LA, the New Experimental Lab Series

Joan Melton is Associate Professor and Head of the Voice/Movement Program in the Department of Theatre and Dance at California State University Fullerton. She has taught at leading drama and music centers in the United States, Britain and Ireland, including the Manhattan School of Music in New York, the Central School of Speech and Drama in London, and the Drama Summer School in Dublin. She is a published author and composer, a specialist in 20th Century vocal music, and a Master Teacher of Fitzmaurice *Voicework*.

Shakespeare Festival LA mounted an excellent production that might have been subtitled "*Twelfth Night* meets *Hair*!" It was set in the Rave culture, used actual Ravers for interludes between scenes and had an unbeatable ensemble feel to it. The house was packed, mostly with young people from the Los Angeles area. The price of admission was a toy for a child not blessed with the material goods that most of us enjoy. I saw the last performance, and it was easily the clearest, most accessible, most delightful Shakespeare I have ever experienced. A voice coach could have made it an even better professional production with corrected pronunciations and individual voice work, but the actors communicated the play to the audience and thoroughly captivated us throughout the fastest two and a half-hour show on record. They left us wanting more and lifted our spirits to the level of their own joyous enthusiasm.

So what is the Rave culture, and why would Shakespeare Festival LA set its production of *Twelfth Night* in that milieu? You've heard of all night dance parties in secret locations that require a map to find. People who frequent them are called Ravers, and the parties themselves are called Raves. The Rave culture seems to be a humanizing force in what is perceived as an inhuman and mechanistic world—the information age. It bears some resemblance to the hippie culture of the 1960s, minus the political agendas. It has been called 'The Cult of the DJ' and 'Dancing With a Wand of Energy Dust.' "The touch taboo of our society is broken–strangers are embraced and words are usually not necessary." (program notes, *Twelfth Night, Shakespeare* Festival LA).

The vision of the Artistic Director of the company, Ben Donenberg, and his wife, dramaturge, Dani Bedau, has always been to bring Shakespeare to the masses, and especially to the underprivileged youth of Los Angeles. Ben is a Juilliard graduate who was inspired by New York's Shakespeare in the Park to develop a similar kind of program in LA. Shakespeare Festival LA is a year-round operation with a touring company that performs in a variety of venues, including the backs of trucks, botanical gardens and warehouses. Its outreach program, Will Power to Youth, trains and employs at risk youth. The price of admission to most SF/LA productions is a can of food for the homeless. The first toy drive was initiated with the New Experimental Lab Series, and paid admission is charged during the last two weeks of the summer season.

All members of the cast of *Twelfth Night* were either working professional actors, recently graduated students of American theatre programs, or currently enrolled students. Three young actors had studied in England, at the University of London, the Royal National Theatre, and the Oxford School of Drama, respectively. Three of the more experienced actors served as official mentors throughout the rehearsal and performance period.

Music for the show was composed by Gabe Lopez, who is on the staff of SF/LA and the composer for Will Power to Youth. The space was an un-renovated warehouse.

In this production, Olivia's brother has died of an overdose of drugs, so she is shunning the Rave scene. Orsino is still an active participant. Ravers begin the show with lights, dancing and squeals of pleasure. Orsino steps out of the crowd to say, "If music be the food of love, play on..." It worked. We bought it.

The casting was interesting in terms of gender. Feste was played by a mature actress (Sharon Madden) with a low, husky voice. Toby Belch (Jennifer Lankford) became *Lady Toby*, and although her voice was tight and unsupported, her skills as a drummer were excellent and well used during the revels scene with *Andrea* Aguecheek. The character of Andrea (Gloria Calderon) was one of the weakest in the show, in that her relationships were unclear, especially to Viola and Olivia. The crafty Maria (Joe Keane) became a boyish *Mario*, and was more convincing as a confidant to Olivia than he was as a lust object to Toby.

The warehouse setting was acoustically problematical and presented a real challenge to most of the actors. The building will be renovated eventually and is now owned by the Shakespeare Festival. Viola (Katie Tyszkiewicz), whose voice and speech work were lovely overall, had a particularly difficult time filling the space. Even Olivia (Marika Becz), who was by far the most skilled actor vocally, tended to avoid the lower notes of her voice and worked primarily in a medium range. Orsino (Brandon Williams) had a rich baritone sound but was often swallowed up by the room, music or other competing sounds. A couple of hours with a voice coach could have improved the balance of sounds in the show and provided invaluable feedback for all of the actors involved.

Twelfth Night, Sharon Madden as Feste and Joe Keane as Mario, photo: Maureen McVeish

Speech work for the show was a mish-mash, in that there was little consistency from one actor to another. The use of a General American for most characters was quite effective, but without the aid of a voice director, regionalisms frequently marred the effect. For example, Feste substituted the alveolar nasal for the velar in all *ing* /ɪŋ/ endings, which became *een* /in/, and Orsino used the West Coast "*ah*" /ɑ/ in words like all and fall. Contractions were frequently ignored or misunderstood.

Another view would say that the play was set in LA, so West Coast sounds were absolutely appropriate. But then Olivia and Viola were speaking a relaxed Standard American, Malvolio was General American, and most of the rest of the cast seemed to be going for a General American. As a voice coach, I'm saying, "Make a decision," but there is yet another view. If the play is in LA, a random selection of accents and dialects may be representative of the population! So, perhaps mish-mash is the decision. Ignored contractions though I'll not excuse.

Music provided a kind of glue that connected scenes and supported the Rave theme. Accompaniments were live and lively. The final ensemble setting for the song "Once I was and a little tiny boy" had the audience clapping to the rhythm and thoroughly involved in the event. Then Feste *spoke* the last lines of the song and the curtain call began, accompanied by music and dance, as in the opening of the show.

Sincere thanks to Marika Becz (Olivia), who kindly spent an hour or so with me several days before I saw the show. Marika and I discussed the background of Shakespeare Festival LA, the concept for the show, and the fascinating rehearsal process in which the company explored and experimented freely with the text. What evolved was clarity. The actors really knew what they were saying and so did the audience. There was no mystery, no strange language and no fear. In spite of technical weaknesses, the show did what Ben Donenberg envisioned. It brought Shakespeare to the masses, and especially to the youth of Los Angeles.

Play Review by *Lynn Watson*

Old Money by Wendy Wasserstein
Produced by Lincoln Center Theater at the Mitzi E. Newhouse

Directed by Mark Brokaw
Dialect/Vocal Coach—Deborah Hecht
December 17, 2000

"Artists are cheap," claims a robber baron in *Old Money*, "all you have to give them is a little recognition." His self-assured statement reflects one of the central themes of Wendy Wasserstein's *Old Money*: the uneasy symbiosis between Money and Art. The play suggests that the two are more inextricably bound and mutually dependent than partisans of either camp would care to admit, and brings to mind something Jerzy Grotowski once stated, that "poor theatre always costs a *lot* of money."* Expense is relative, and through the course of the play we see art—in this case, architecture and visual arts— being commissioned, saved, restored and protected by the very wealthy. But the reasons for this munificence are portrayed as less than altruistic. Art is shown as a means by which new money, which causes in its new possessor some degree of guilt or unease, can achieve legitimacy and be transformed into solid, staid, respectable, comfortable, old money. And as the first quote indicates, Grotowski notwithstanding, it is by and large an extremely cost-effective method of transformation.

Lynn Watson is an Assistant Professor of Theatre at the University of Maryland, Baltimore County where she teaches voice and acting. She was the voice and dialect coach for Arena Stage's 50th anniversary production of *The Great White Hope*. With South Coast Repertory, her coaching included the world premieres of Howard Korder's *The Hollow Lands* and Richard Greenberg's *Hurrah At Last*, and the West Coast premiere of *Amy's View*. Other credits include *A Streetcar Named Desire* at the American Conservatory Theatre and David Hare's *Skylight* at the Mark Taper Forum. She has acted Off Broadway, and in leading classical and Shakespearean roles regionally.

The play is set in "the conservatory of the only remaining Beaux Arts mansion in Manhattan that is currently used as a private residence." Time is unstable and shifts fluidly between the years 1917 and 2000. The figure that serves as the primary link between the time periods is Tobias Vivian Pfeiffer III (played by John Cullum), grandson of the self-made coal mining baron who built the mansion. Each actor plays two characters, one in each time period, but the correlations between each of the two characters are often more metaphoric than direct. The characters shift back and forth between time periods during the course of the play, and voice and speech are important factors in helping the actors quickly make their character/time shifts.

The most obvious vocal challenge in the production was switching convincingly between 1917 and the present day. The actors' vocal shifts were mostly successful. Mark Harelik's (see interview) speech and tone of delivery for his newly moneyed character [*Jeffrey Bernstein*] was one of studied affability. His, "I'm just one of the folks" style fit well with Bernstein's ambivalence about his vanished youthful idealism. Jodi Long [*Penny Nercessian/Betina Brevoort*] made an impressive vocal transition from yuppie-come-lately to grand dame at the top of the social register. Her contemporary character moved in short, choppy bursts of energy, which were paralleled in a vocal delivery that was chirpy, preternaturally upbeat and slightly breathless. As the social maven, Long's body and voice became grounded. Her speech was pitched lower with a smooth and measured vocal dynamic, fittingly reflecting the character's imperiousness. She also made a seamless transition to a more Mid-Atlantic style of pronunciation.

* Robert Cohen, "Putting a Tree in a Box," address, Grotowski at Irvine and Beyond: A Symposium and Performance Event, U. of California, Irvine, February 16, 2000.

Dan Butler played coal baron Tobias Pfeiffer in 1917, and Sid Nercessian, the aptly named, self-absorbed Hollywood mogul in the year 2000. Both characters use the arts to help them gain legitimacy—Pfeiffer by endowing the creation of a major art museum and Nercessian, to great comic effect, by producing blatantly commercial Hollywood movies ostensibly based on literary masterpieces. Butler captured the noisy bravado of the modern mogul,

but made little change—except perhaps lessening volume—in shifting to the earlier period. Since Butler's characters had the most direct correlation, the choice to make little vocal differentiation may have been intentional. However, Pfeiffer rose out of the West Virginia coal mines, so it might have been interesting to see that factor more specifically dealt with: still a trace of West Virginia dialect perhaps, or maybe a shifting back and forth between the vaguely British speech of Mid-Atlantic to echoes of West Virginia in times of heightened emotions.

From the standpoint of the artist, the modern character played by Mary Beth Hurt [*Saulina Webb*] has watched her artistic stock plummet because of her dependence on the whims and changing tastes of the people who bought her sculptures. Although a Midwestern native, Hurt beautifully captured the Mid-Atlantic pronunciations of "old money" that linger to the present day. Her modern character's delivery had a constricted, throaty quality, conveying someone overwhelmed by circumstances beyond her control, whose art no longer sells because it is no longer "fashionable." Her voice conveyed the burden of struggle against defeat as she poignantly expressed the angst shared by artists: "I'm just so sick of being criticized." The contrast to her 1917 counterpart [*Sally Webster*] was striking—that character was one whose very life was a joyous work of art. She filled the space she inhabited with raucous, open sounds, in her speech and in her infectious laughter.

Charlie Hofheimer and Mark Harelik in Wendy Wasserstein's *Old Money*. Photo: Joan Marcus

Old Money was an excellent example of how aspects of voice and speech work to vividly illuminate character, shifts of time and place, and themes in a dramatic production. It was satisfying from a vocal perspective in that it demonstrated how specific and conscious considerations of voice and speech deepen and expand levels of communication the theatre.

An Interview with Mark Harelik
by Lynn Watson

Mark Harelik sat for an interview immediately after performing in Wendy Wasserstein's new play, Old Money. *[Additional comments by actress, Monique Morgan.] Also a playwright, Harelik wrote* The Immigrant—*which has proven very successful for regional theatres around the country,* Lost Highway-The Legacy of Hank Williams *and* The Legacy.

lw: Since you're a playwright and an actor, do you feel more, or less respectful of another writer's work, or does it depend on the writer?

MH: No, completely respectful because a playwright doesn't just say, "Oh, I think I'll have them say this." Most writers very carefully craft every single word. A good writer, if they are there working on the play, will make adjustments from actor to actor. Wendy's work presents a challenge because she is, I think, as much an essayist as she is a dramatist. She enjoys the written word and she writes in almost a nineteenth century style. She writes very long sentences with a lot of digressions and parenthetical thoughts that she will pick up at the end of the sentence and restate, and you can't take a breath.

lw: So she is interested in the argument.

MH: Yes, and she is interested in the complexity of an argument. How a single argument can branch off in two directions, and then bring those back in, which is very literary and very appropriate to the essay style, but on stage it can be difficult to say because you don't know where to breathe. Or you have to remember to take a huge gulp of air while you're being fed your cue.

lw: Would you talk about how you dealt with that?

MH: Well, it's only a technical problem. One of the signs that it's a technical problem is that it's very difficult to memorize, and when something is difficult to memorize it's because it's not organic. It's not being absorbed by the brain. Shakespeare is a snap to memorize, as complex as it is, because there is something about it that just soaks right in.

lw: The rhythms—

MH: The rhythms help…and just the sounds of the words…sometimes just rhymes, or even sort of a mnemonic quality to Shakespeare's writing. This play was difficult to memorize, not throughout, but the tough places. Her phraseology is circuitous, so sometimes you just have to practice saying the lines over and over. So that's a technical solution. Another technical solution—as in working on a song—is to identify those sections that are not written with human breathing and just be ready when they come. In the first scene, my son is talking about how much he admires this city historian and the books he's written, and my line to him is: "Ovid, don't become the kind of dilettante intellectual who wastes their life dwelling on the past. It's great that you read, but read for a purpose." There's a lot to hang onto in that and you have to trust that the audience is following it. Because if you break it up, especially if you break it up with breath, the audience is going to lose the sense, but you have to kind of sing it so the audience has the key word.

lw: You have a great rhetorical sense in the most positive meaning of the word, which is that rhetoric is intended not only to convey ideas, but also to evoke emotions in the listener.

MH: Shaw—that's what Shavian thought is.

lw: Passion and—

MH: Passion and intellect.

lw: Is this something you're aware of on any level as you work, or is it unconscious?

MH: No. It's a very practical acting tool, because when you're talking to someone, you're working on them somehow. You know, Acting 101 stuff. You're trying to get them to do something; you're trying to get them to understand something. You're working on them with words as though the words are physical actions. But if every word comes out in the same way, it's not very useful. In most sentences, there's usually one word that's the "bullet." Everything else delivers the bullet.

lw: Spoken like a vocal coach.

MH: There's one word that is the *coup de grâce*, and you can *feel* it. An audience will get all that prefatory stuff, and all you need is one word that achieves your point. The audience knows what you're talking about, and whoever you're onstage with gets something marvelous to set them off. So rhetoric is just common sense. If you just listen to what you're saying and you know what you mean, it's very easy to tell when you're obfuscating with lots of noise in the spoken word—lots of extraneous white noise.

lw: Or slowing down too much. Taking too much time to get to that "bullet word" that you were talking about.

MH: You have to assume that the audience is smart. If they don't seem to be, sometimes the tendency is to ram it down their throats. I've observed actors who break up their sentences a lot. They lose comic impact by doing that. They confuse the sentences. I think it's a mistrust of the audience— that they're not going to understand. Or even that the actor you're working with is not going to understand. One of the greatest sins is being over-explicit. It's ironic—there's no quicker way to confuse somebody than being overly explicit.

Monique Morgan: There's that theatre phenomenon—I'm sure you've seen it—when you think you can hear someone, but it's all volume with no sense.

MH: That's right. It's easy to fall asleep in front of a noisy air conditioner. It'll just lull you right to sleep.

lw: Were there any particular voice or speech challenges for you in *Old Money*?

MH: It's a small theatre—it's amphitheatre style, and the stage is at the lowest point so most of the audience is above your projection plane, so you have to remember to play up in the house. You have to do things like—THINK up. When a thought comes to you, look for it up in the ceiling and not in the floor. Also because it's a three-quarter round, you have to scan a lot of stuff. You start the line stage left and as you're talking, turn to stage right. It feels like a very small and intimate room, but if you talk at just conversational, across-the-table level, you can't be heard, so it has to be lifted a little bit. The other interesting thing to work with was that everyone has two characters—one in the present, one in the past. The vernacular speech was pronounced slightly differently, especially in the upper classes, because "good breeding" tended more towards Mid-Atlantic. We all attempted to make a bit of an adjustment that way, and character adjustments as well so there would be two different voices. For my character it wasn't so extreme.

lw: On another subject, what do you think about miking? Are you disappointed when you go to see a play and it's miked?

MH: No, I'm grateful.

lw: For non-musical plays?

MH: Yeah, because our theatres are too big and the naturalistic trend continues in the way characters relate to each other onstage. When I go as an audience member, I like to hear it. I don't mind the artificiality of it at all.

lw: Even in a house that's acoustically good?

MH: One production…I had a hell of a time hearing them. And I guess it's a smallish theatre. The set had a lot of hard, reflective surfaces on it. But I was sitting in balcony right, and I wished that I'd gotten the assisted hearing system, because I could just barely lean in and hear what they were saying and it drove me crazy and screwed up my experience. I think for a lot of people in the theatre the answer to that question is: "No, I hate miking in the theatres," and it's a matter of principle.

lw: Well, it is for a lot of vocal people, I can tell you.

MH: I suppose you can go back to the source of people's training and get them going with a strong…get their voices developed. You know, David Mamet in his *True & False* says the only requirements for an actor are to have your words memorized and have a strong vocal instrument—that's all you need. You don't need to know what the play is about. You don't need to know any back-story on your character. Just get out there and talk and the play will do everything else. And be understood and heard. He's a troublemaker, but there is some truth in that. He's like Shaw in that respect, in that he's just being a troublemaker and there's a lot of truth to it, but there's also a sly wink to it. I mean obviously if the actor's not feeling anything, they're not responding to anything internally, they're not going to fulfill the requirements of a piece. I think that miking is necessary a lot of the time, especially in larger theatres. But the Mitzi Newhouse is not a commercial theatre. You could not run a play commercially in that theatre. It doesn't have enough seats, but it's small enough that they don't have to mike anything. And also, orchestras are louder so in musicals if you're not miked, forget it.

lw: How and where did you start out? A.C.T.?

MH: That's where I first got my Equity card and worked in rep…and worked with really wonderful professionals on the stage in this huge house, unmiked. There was a company acting style that was designed to play to the top balcony and fill the theatre. Actors who were able to fill this theatre with this sun-hot aura of truth that would come out of them and fill the theatre with light and sound. That kind of theatre can only be executed by a mad genius and an infuriating autocrat. Mild people can't create something like that.

lw: Isn't that similar to a line in *Old Money* that refers to your character: "To be successful, you have to be a little prickly."?

MH: It has to be the energy of mastery, in the sense of overpowering everyone around you. And if they don't rise to it, they're obliterated; they're not seen onstage. It's that irresistible force that comes off the stage.

Selected Thesis Abstracts from *Mandy Rees, associate editor*

Editor's Note:
The following abstracts are provided as a service to help researchers and interested readers stay abreast of current thesis and dissertation work in the field of voice and speech. The papers themselves have not been read or vetted by the Journal editors. Material submitted to this department may be edited for space and style.

Title: Balancing Theory and Practice in Voice Training
Author: Helen Lie
Type: MA in Speech and Communications
Year: August 2000
Institution: San Francisco State University, Department of Speech and Communications
Faculty Advisor(s): Carolyn Chaney and Mercilee Jenkins.

This creative master's project is in the form of a teaching curriculum that integrates voice science theories with psycho-physical vocal exercises in order to develop a method of vocal instruction balancing theory and practice. It includes a brief discussion on the history of speech training at American colleges which traces contemporary theory-based training methodology and the psycho-physical approach to the elocution and the expressionist movements of the mid-19th century. These two movements, influenced by the emergence of voice science during this period, resulted in a divide in voice training. One side emphasized the anatomy and physiology of voice production and the other emphasized sensations and imagery to produce an expressive voice. A review of some contemporary texts that use the theory-based and psycho-physical approach is provided, followed by a rationale for integrating the two approaches, the methodology, and an overview of the teaching units. The ten teaching units cover such topics as effective breathing for speech, relaxation and the voice, vocal quality, loudness and projection, reducing tension in voice production, articulation, and proper care of the voice. The lessons include accompanying exercises, activities, charts and diagrams that may be useful in a classroom setting.

Title: An Interdisciplinary Approach to Character Study in *Macbeth* combining Voicework, Movement and Visualisation where textual manifestation is the ultimate aim
Author: Kevin Crawford
Type: MA Thesis in Voice Studies
Year: 2000
Institution: Central School of Speech and Drama
Supervisor: David Carey

This thesis suggests that a valid case can be made for approaching character-study in *Macbeth* from a non-textual point of view, where the student can investigate character through the medium of Voicework, Movement and Imagination. Based on practical research with second-year students at The School of Drama, Trinity College, Dublin, the thesis traces a series of workshops, describes their contents and reports on interviews with students and the non-participant observer. The relevance of a strategy that is weighted towards a physical, vocal and emotional exploration of themes, images and relationships is assessed and a full discussion is made of its contribution to the final performance of scenes from *Macbeth*.

The author prefaces the description of the practical aspects of research by summarising the 'tradition' that he is issued from (as a founding member of the Roy Hart Theatre) and placing it into the wider perspective of practitioners who influence Voicework for Shakespeare (Barton, Berry, Linklater and Rodenburg).

The thesis is completed by an appendix which describes in detail some of the class strategies and key exercises. Extensive extracts from interviews and journals are also included.

Title: The Necessitative Value of a Consistent Sound Transcription System Within the Contemporary American Theatrical Context
Author: Matthew L. Harding
Type: M.A. Thesis
Year: May, 2000
Institution: Northwestern University
Faculty Advisors: Linda Gates and Leslie A. Hinderyckx

There is a need for performers to address sounds and pronunciation in a uniform manner. However, not every voice trainer uses the same sound transcription system, and even when two individuals do, there are frequent inconsistencies. These inconsistencies include incongruity in form, practice and the alphabet/notation systems themselves.

In order to explore this problem, questions regarding the importance of transcription systems and their functions, transcription systems in use today, and the possibility of codifying all systems into one universal form are posed. These questions are explored through discussions of scientific pursuits in artistic forms, analyzes of the histories and idiosyncrasies of the most common transcription systems currently in use (Respelling, Lessac, Skinner and the IPA), observations of different educational focuses of current transcription systems, comparisons of current transcription systems and, finally, an endorsement for an "optimal sound transcription system."

This debate is as sticky as it is old, and this thesis comes to a particular conclusion sure to be debated by others. In the end, it provides useful charts for the reader to compare transcription systems without bias of the author's opinion by juxtaposing ten common or representative forms in an easily accessible format. The document also contains a fairly comprehensive annotated timeline of the development of modern sound transcription systems.

Look for more information regarding this thesis at:
http://www.stagerage.com/mlh

Title: Stanislavski and the Actor's Voice
Author: Robert Anglin
Type: MA Thesis
Year: 2000
Institution: Northwestern University
Faculty Advisors: Linda Gates and Leslie A. Hinderyckx

This thesis is based on the belief that the Stanislavski System is made up of two parts. The inner, or psychological, portion of the technique is addressed primarily in *An Actor Prepares*, while the outer, or physical, portion of the technique is addressed in *Building a Character*.

The inner technique deals mainly with the impetus of creative work. In regard to the training related to the inner technique, Stanislavski wrote: "All this preparation trains your 'inner creative state,' it helps you to find your 'super-objective' and 'through line of action,' it creates a conscious psycho-technique, and in the end it leads you to the 'region of the subconscious.' The study of this important region is a fundamental part of our system. The fundamental objective of our psycho-technique is to put us in a creative state in which our subconscious will function naturally." It is this inner technique which the majority of modern actor training upholds as its foundation.

However, Stanislavski also knew that once this inner creative state was achieved, it must manifest itself in physical form or it would be lost to the audience. In *Building a Character*, he wrote: "Without an external form neither your inner characterization nor the spirit of your image will reach the public. The external characterization explains and illustrates and thereby conveys to your spectators the inner pattern of your part. "

In order to give the "inner characterization" its "external form" Stanislavski devised an outer technique as described in *Building a Character*. It is in the conveyance of the actor's internal state that voice training is important.

Marlene Johnson teaches voice and speech at Florida State University and serves on the VASTA Board of Directors. She has taught at Virginia Commonwealth University, Muhlenberg College, Lafayette College, and Miami University. She recently appeared with James Earl Jones at the Union League in Philadelphia in a reading of *John Brown's Body*. Shakespearean text and psycho-physical re-education techniques are her primary interests/passions.

Girard, Dale. "The Sounds of Violence." *Actors on Guard.* New York: Routledge, 1997.
In this section of his book, Girard reminds the combatant to release the voice and breath without suppression during a fight—a habit many need to break. Quotes Bonnie Raphael that it is the "held and released breath…the voluntary and involuntary vocal sounds" that "carry the ring of truth." Discusses need for centering, grounding, warming up the head, neck and shoulders during the physical warm-up to prepare for proper vocal release, voluntary and involuntary sounds. Briefly defines the reactive physical vocal range with the voice rising in pitch the further a hit is received from "center." Cautions to seek out a vocal coach for specialized vocal techniques like screaming.

Lessac, Arthur. *The Use and Training of the Human Voice: A Bio-Dynamic Approach to Vocal Life.* CA: Mayfield Publishing Company, 1996.
Sections on what Lessac refers to as "Tonal Action"—both "Y-buzz" and "Call"—may provide useful insight to persons learning to scream in a healthy manner. If you do not know how to do these techniques, reading the book without a teacher trained in the method is not recommended, but may provide a theoretical basis for the technique. Although Lessac does not deal with screaming or heightened vocal use per se, many voice teachers who teach screaming use some of these principles for placing the scream on the mask or facial resonators, rather than on the back of a tense throat where damage is more likely to occur.

Rodenburg, Patsy. "Vocalizing Heightened Emotions." *The Right to Speak.* London: Methuen Drama, 1992.
Helpful, specific exercises to aid in performing crying, shouting, screaming, and laughing. Most sobering is someone of Rodenburg's stature as a voice professional cautioning about doing this work, freely admitting that she is a "coward" in approaching it. She trains only individuals who are at a highly advanced stage of training in these techniques, but claims many of these still do not have sufficiently open throats or supported voices. She refuses to teach these methods in short workshops (under three weeks) and never where she is unable to fully assess one's vocal capacity. Never undertake this work lightly.

Barton, Robert and Rocco Dal Vera. "Healing Your Voice." *Voice: Onstage and Off.* New York: Harcourt, Brace and Company, 1995.
Helpful overview of different vocal problems and strategies for coping with them. These include lists of what to do and what not to do. Some of these strategies are housed under headings of "voice doc" and "voice shrink" with useful diagnostic questions. These suggestions are offered to help in self-diagnosis, but are not intended to replace insights from professional healers. Particularly useful are the sections on shouting/yelling, failure to warm up before extended vocal use, dehydration, coughing/throat clearing, and excess tension of tongue, jaw and neck muscles.

Martinez, J.D. *Combat Mime: A Non-Violent Approach to Stage Violence.* Chicago: Nelson-Hall Publishers, 1982.
This text covers numerous combat techniques, all of which are clearly illustrated and explained. Although only brief references are made to using the voice during combat, voice trainers may find this book useful for

understanding movement sequences and body positioning, helpful information as they approach issues of breath and physical tension.

Roy, Nelson, Karen S. Ryker and Diane M. Bless. "Vocal Violence in Actors: An Investigation into Its Acoustic Consequences and the Effects of Hygienic Laryngeal Release Training." *Journal of Voice*, Vol. 14, No. 2 (June 2000), pp. 215-230.

This article describes a study designed and conducted by two Speech/Language Pathologist professors: Nelson Roy, Department of Communication Disorders and Otolaryngology - Head and Neck Surgery, The University of Utah, Salt Lake City, Utah; and Diane Bless, Departments of Communicative Disorders and Otolaryngology-Head and Neck Surgery,University of Wisconsin-Madison with Voice and Speech Trainer professor Karen Ryker, Department of Theatre and Drama, University of Wisconsin-Madison.

The study investigated the effects of voice training on the actor's production of vocally violent sounds. Twenty-seven actors ranging in age from 17-48 years were recorded producing four vocally violent behaviors: grunting, groaning, sobbing, and shouting. They were then trained by author Ryker in techniques generally recognized by theatrical voice and speech trainers as effective for producing vocally violent sounds for stage. After training, the actors were recorded a second time, repeating the same experimental protocol as in first recording session. The experimental protocol consisted of 1) warm-up, 2) pretest audio recording of actor producing vowels at three pitch levels, 3) flexible laryngovideostroboscopy recording of actor producing four vocally violent behaviors, 4) warm-down, 5) post-test audio recording of actor producing vowels at three pitch levels. In the first phase (the subject of this article) the audio recordings made before and after training were measured and compared to determine differences.

After vocal violence, no consistent acoustic changes were detected for voice generated at modal and low pitch; however significant increases in pitch range were observed. After training, several measures including those attributable to pitch range and voice quality indicated improvement. The results indicated that vocal training does defend the actor's voice from undesirable changes that might surface at the extremes of an actor's pitch range after producing vocally violent sounds. Because the training techniques used in this investigation were multimodal, interesting questions are raised regarding which aspect of training is primarily responsible for the observed effects. Further study is required to identify such factors.

This study represents the first phase of the larger investigation in which audio signals, visual signals, stroboscopic measures will be analyzed. The second phase of analysis, Vocal Violence in Actors: A Study of Physiological Correlates, Marina Papangelou, Nelson Roy, Karen Ryker, Diane Bless, is in progress. The physiological results are being analyzed and compared to the acoustic results reported in the first phase of study. Findings will be presented at the 2002 International Voice Symposium in Philadelphia, then submitted to the *Journal of Voice* for publication.